A COLLECTION OF THOUGHTS

THE PHILOSOPHIES & IDEAS OF A HUMAN PERFORMANCE COACH

JOE STAUB

ISBN: 9781686360237

Cover Design by Randee Willett (Randee.Willett@gmail.com)

CONTENTS

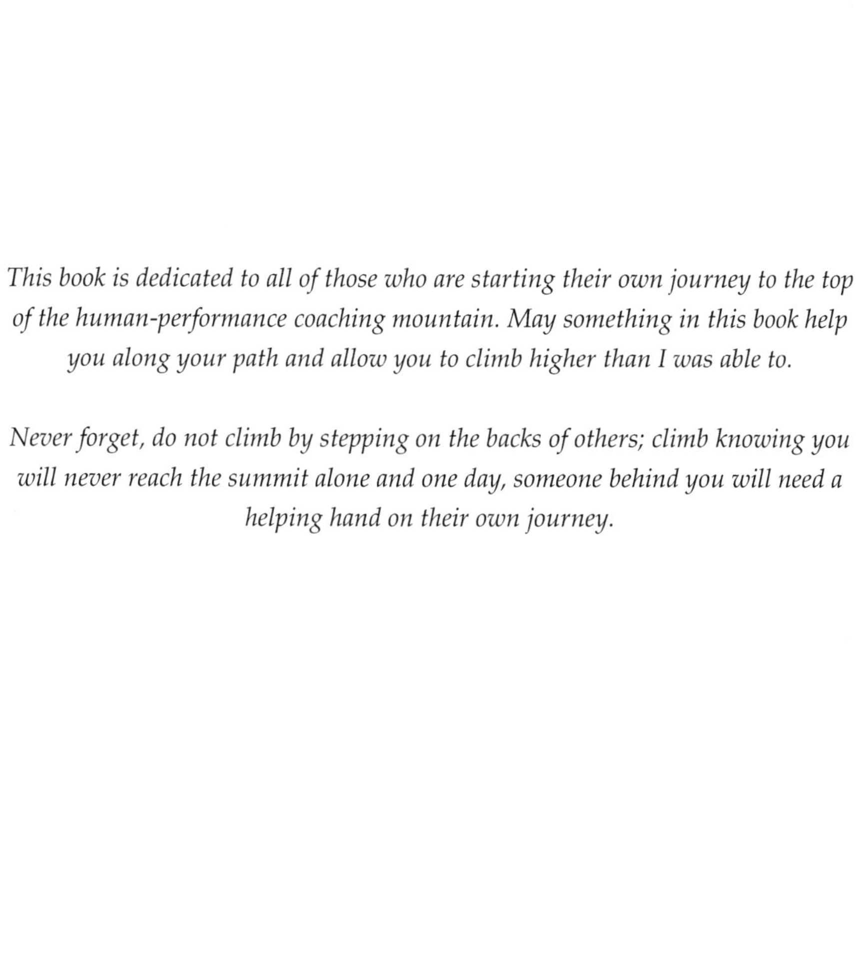

This book is dedicated to all of those who are starting their own journey to the top of the human-performance coaching mountain. May something in this book help you along your path and allow you to climb higher than I was able to.

Never forget, do not climb by stepping on the backs of others; climb knowing you will never reach the summit alone and one day, someone behind you will need a helping hand on their own journey.

DISCLAIMERS

Please consult with an appropriate medical professional before engaging in any physical activity. Anything mentioned in this book should be discussed first with an appropriately educated and competent professional. If you are unsure if the professional you seek is qualified, find a new professional because they most likely are not.

This book is a memoir. It reflects the author's present recollections of experiences over time. Some names and identifying details have been changed, some events compressed, and some dialogue recreated to protect the privacy of individuals—due to the writer not having the memory of an elephant.

All ideas, content, concepts, or insights from this book are purely informative and based on the perspective of a single individual and their personal experiences. Use common sense and your own best judgment in assimilating and considering applying the information into your specific situation or context. The author, publisher or anyone else for that matter is not liable or in any way shape or form responsible for what you choose to do, say, etc., or not do, say, etc.

No individual, business, company or entity paid for any endorsement or acknowledgement in this book. Nor do the views within reflect the views, positions, or official stances of any individual, business, company or entity that has or has had a business relationship with The Zenta Group or the main contributing author.

Finally, yes, there are some things in the book that seem to be left out. While there are many resources, examples, and specifics, there are also many things mentioned but no clear path shown—only a high-level touch is given. This is intentional. Some will understand, some won't.

AUTHOR'S NOTE

I'm sitting here putting the finishing touches on this book after more than two and a half years of working on it in earnest. Ten years, technically speaking, since many of the core elements came from the journals I kept going back to 2009 when I first was paid to work in the strength & conditioning (S&C) world.

It has been a long road to get to this point. And it has been not only a cathartic experience but also a grounding one. I had no idea it would take this long, having started in June 2017 as a way to decompress. About 80% of what you will read was written between June 2017 and December 2017.

From there it took two years to put the finishing touches on things; many a long night sitting at my dining room table in front of a screen, often with a beer or margarita in hand, to make the appropriate updates, add needed depth around a nebula of an idea, and work with others to prepare this for someone else to be able to read. A journey that while I enjoyed, I'm also pleased to be done with. I'm ready now for a new challenge to undertake.

As I work through this final proofread before moving to publishing, I can say these two things for certain.

First, the landscape of athletics has shifted across numerous areas discussed in this book from when I started writing to now. Some changes are positive, others negative, but all are a part of the natural cycle of growth and evolution when people interact. Enjoy the ride! It is most certainly going to be an interesting one in sports in the next few years.

Second, while this is only the story of my life as it relates to human performance, everyone should take an account of their effort over their lives: journal, document, and then compile. Who knows, maybe one day I will take the journals of notes and experiences I've had since leaving the S&C industry and write about what I've done since: business, family, raising children, and trying to be the person I want to be and my path to get there.

SIDE NOTE—Human performance is something I consider not only the physical side of what I did in S&C but also all the people, culture, and leadership things I did as well. I considered myself a human performance coach because, as you will see, I didn't view my role as simply a matter of developing physical outputs but developing all levels of the human condition for optimal performance. I just used physical means as a way to go about it.

PREFACE

Why write this you ask? After I "retired" from coaching, I was sorting through some of my old files, documents, training programs, and other strength and conditioning (S&C) materials when I realized I had collected a lifetime's worth of valuable information.

Not just on my own, but from dozens and possibly hundreds of other people, who along the way have impacted me in my decision making, my philosophy, my work style, and everything else that has helped make me, me. Whether it was about training or about life, the material covered every realm of the things I had learned, and what wasn't in hardcopies was on numerous flash drives and external hard drives I had collected over the years.

After spending time looking through the material, I felt that I wanted to share all of this "stuff." It was the essence of how I came to be who I am: my journey as a coach and my journey as a person finding purpose in their life.

Some of the "stuff," I saw as I combed through it, came from people who were reticent to share their knowledge openly. Unless you worked directly with them, so much was insulated within the old boys' club dogma of how things operated in the field of S&C. Information was not shared, and left to sit on old hard drives or in file cabinets, and that, to me, had always been a fundamental problem of the profession.

I had always tried to help change that by sharing and giving to anyone who asked, often, even more than the person asking ever wanted or knew could be given. I tried to be as open of a book as I could with everything I had collected, and from that, I began to realize not only had I collected a lifetime of information from others, but I myself had something to add to the collection.

That's how this morphed into a much bigger, much larger undertaking. Something I thought would take a few months to write out, now spans three years of effort, countless hours of refining my writing (with help), and hundreds if not thousands of conversations with others in order to help me hone in on exactly what I wanted to say and the way I wanted to say it.

Along my journey, many people suggested that I write a book. I kind of laughed at the thought of it and never took it seriously. Then I read Ron McKeefery's book *CEO, Strength Coach.*

After reading his book, one of the things colleagues and I would always talk about was how we wished we had a book like his when we were interns. I wish someone told me these things back then and gave me both a dose of perspective and a tangible resource to reference.

While there are some that may disagree with Coach McKeefrey about his philosophies on training, I have yet to find anyone who does not applaud him for what he has done and still does to move the profession forward. He recognized a long time ago helping build future professionals was more important than just adding weight to the bar, and for that, I along with countless others are indebted to him.

I've connected with Coach McKeefery a couple of times over the years, at conferences and through phone calls, and he has always been generous with his time—even being gracious enough to Skype into one of the classes I was teaching as a guest speaker. I have a profound respect for the lengths he has gone to enhance and advance the S&C profession, and while I'll never be able to replicate the impact Coach McKeefery has had on the development of the industry, I hope to give whoever reads this book some insights for their own journey.

It made sense to me that if I could pour all of my knowledge, lessons learned, and experiences into words on a page, someone else could use that information as a launchpad to jumpstart their own careers, and we could raise the bar of the profession as well.

Additionally, as I transition out of one career and into yet another new role, it has been a cathartic experience to put everything down on paper. I am a firm believer that much like a computer after software updates, you need to hit the reset button and let the new programs take effect.

To that end, to have the chance, in a sense, to reboot and start-up again —after internalizing the lessons and appreciating the experiences to best see the positives while learning from the negatives—has helped me in ways I still can't fully articulate.

It was in this process that I could truly start to understand how everything I did in the first decade of my professional career has affected me, my family, and those I worked within the big picture, while setting the stage for the future.

While there are both positive and negative stories within this book, my use of the negative interactions is to illustrate the learning process, not to disparage any one individual specifically. While not everyone I have ever worked with is someone who I built a personal connection to or shared mutual affinity toward, all of those people in good times or bad did help, influence, and develop me in my journey.

There will most certainly be pushback from some readers who will disagree with some of the things I discuss, the intensity of emotion I have, or the perspective I take on certain situations, and I welcome it.

Let it foster dialogue, conversation, and moments of thought among people to a productive end.

I'm not here for a popularity contest or just to be polarizing. Many people will agree with the things I say, but I also accept that many will not. That's just part of putting yourself out there and a key reason why some people never go for it; they are more concerned with the way people will look at them afterward.

Finally, I am certainly not here to say I am absolutely, unequivocally right and everyone should listen to me or that the things discussed within this book and my opinions are absolute, indomitable dogma that must be followed. This is my story, my approach, and my context. If you can't distill it with a grain of salt or disseminate what is and what is not useful for you and your given context, then it doesn't matter what I say because you were never going to hear me anyway.

PART I

CLEARING THE LAND

I've come to believe that all my past failure and frustration were actually laying the foundation for the understandings that have created the new level of living I now enjoy.

—Tony Robbins

INTRODUCTION

Always dream and shoot higher than you know you can do. Do not bother just to be better than your contemporaries or predecessors. Try to be better than yourself.

—William Faulkner

"Be Better Than Yourself" is tattooed on me as a constant reminder, helping me keep perspective. Sitting along the right side of my rib cage, the words curve above and below a tribal designed sun and an "old man" moon sadly staring at the sun. The words represent the quote above and the design is a tribute to the classic fable of the sun and moon.

In brief, the story goes that the moon longingly looks at the sun dejected in the belief that it will never have the ability the sun has of powering life on earth with its radiance. One day, as the moon casts its gaze upon the earth staring at the sea, lost in its desire to be anything but itself, it notices that the ocean tide ebbs and flows by its own path across the sky and that indeed it has the power to affect all of the earth, just like the sun, but in its own way.

We are all amazingly capable people with an unlimited amount of potential but hamstrung by our own fears, doubts, and often desires to be someone else, when all we really need to do is be the best version of ourselves.

The Post Cliché-Quote Introduction

My name is Joseph Staub; most people call me Joe. I was born in Massachusetts and come from a great family. My parents and sister are wonderful people: caring, loving, and supportive of everything I've ever done. Growing up in a small, middle-class town, I was lucky to have had many opportunities and support in all areas of life from my family, friends, and colleagues. Looking at it with the experiences and world view I have now, for all of my life I have faced nothing but first-world problems and day-to-day frustrations.

Acknowledging how fortunate we were and helping others were always things instilled into me across all levels of my family. If I had to guess, I think my upbringing helped guide me to want to be a coach and to give back because I was fortunate to have so much.

From an early age, I saw that not everyone had the environment or level of support I had, but they did have the potential to be as good or better than me if given the nudge they lacked. I have had a lot of little and sometimes not so little nudges to help me get to where I am, in addition to a few huge kicks in the ass that we all get in life. Some I will discuss, others I will leave for a conversation over a cold beer and good tequila another day.

How Athletics Fits into Things

Athletics has been a part of my entire life. I tell people that my first daycare was a Gold's Gym, but I'm not joking, that literally was the first "daycare" I went to when my mom and dad went to work out.

I've always liked being competitive, and I've always liked being physical.

Within that, physical skill was always something that came easily to me. Whether it be running, jumping, sprinting, or any physical combination of skills, I was always athletic. All that stuff came very naturally to me. If you asked some of my friends who have known me my whole life, they would say that I always identified as the athletic guy because it just came naturally to me.

I was not only identified as a jock by my peers but I also followed suit with my social behaviors, many of which fit the associated stereotypes of people in that realm. It wasn't until college that I started shifting towards becoming an academic of sorts, even becoming classified as "nerdy" by some. It was an interesting change to say the least.

While I've always loved the act of participating in physical activity, the people closest to me know that I read books, and more recently listen to podcasts, even more than I watch or follow sports. I generally only watch and follow sports if I have to for work-related purposes, if I know someone competing (i.e., a former athlete), or if it's a Boston-based team (I can hear the first complaints from readers coming in now).

I would much rather read a good book, learn something new, or go do something physical than watch sports. Maybe that sounds crazy for a guy who lived and breathed sports for the first thirty years of his life, but it's the truth.

I like doing, not sitting back and watching.

Yes, there is a part of me that loves the process of watching film, breaking down tactics, and learning technique in order to prepare for competition. But even those processes have a means to an end: the competition.

I don't enjoy doing that work and don't seek it out if the goal is not doing something myself. I love being in that type of moment: exerting physical outputs to whatever the task is at hand; feeling the physical and mental toll it takes as you output the effort; and using the purposeful suffering of a physical nature for a means far beyond just physicality. If I can't do that—if I'm stuck on the outside looking in—I'd rather not do it at all.

When I think about it, that is probably a big reason why I geared towards S&C as a profession so quickly and naturally as I did.

It is a constant "doing it" profession: constantly on the move, up and down, push and pull, being physical, being engaged in the moment, demonstrating, applying, and being hands-on. Every day I probably did an entire workout worth of exercise demoing to athletes or planning a session out with coworkers.

Being an S&C coach touched on something I was good at (being physical), allowed me to stay connected to something I had experience in (sports), while giving me an outlet to put my energy into helping others (coaching).

Me on Me

I don't take myself very seriously. I'm more sarcastic than anything and take everything and everyone with a grain of salt.

I've been told I have a skeptics heart and a sailor's mouth, both of which are very true. I'd rather laugh at a good joke and make people laugh than be overly serious and miss an opportunity for a new experience.

I don't need to be a person of extremes just to prove a point, though sometimes I have to go to extremes to prove the point. I've never been afraid to stand up for what I believe and stand up for those who I care about.

I'm also known to be very literal, more often than not direct, (probably more than I should be), quite often come off brash or harsh, and most of the time brutally honest.

Sure, it's got me into trouble a few times but I enjoy my own brand of comedy even if others don't get it.

I once heard it said that everyone wants you to tell them the truth, but when you tell them the truth, you're an asshole, and since then it has made a lot of sense to me. Most of the time, I am that asshole, but I own it and wear it like a badge of honor. Someone else's inability to deal with truth and facts is not my problem, it's theirs.

I would also be remiss not to mention that one of the things that's gotten me a few good laughs but also in trouble a few times is that I often tell people I'm allergic to bullshit.

Why give all this upfront?

Because I want to make sure you get a picture of who I am and where I come from. Why I'm a coach, and how I know who I am and what I stand for. And by knowing that, I know what I want in this life; and I can tell you it has nothing to do with the results in any competition.

1

EARLY LIFE SHAPING MY STYLE

THE FOLLOWING ELEVEN EXPERIENCES, WHILE NOT ALL-ENCOMPASSING IN MY life, are the critical elements that helped shape and form the foundational elements of how I approached working as an S&C coach and working with people in general.

There are numerous individuals, family, friends, and co-workers and countless other experiences that also played a role, but there had to be some things that didn't make it past the editing room floor. Those stories and the lessons learned we can save for another day.

A Billboard About Justice

I'll never forget being a little kid—maybe six or seven years old with my family driving to my grandmother's—and seeing this billboard on the highway:

> "An injustice somewhere is a threat to justice everywhere." —Martin Luther King, Jr.

Once I saw it I couldn't get out of my little brain. The message had an impact. I often thought about it but I never discussed it with anyone. That summer, whenever we drove to my grandmothers, I saw that billboard. And thinking about it every time we drove past, I came to realize that it wasn't just a billboard advertisement representing Dr. King's words and the issues he championed.

It was that someone had taken the time to make those words have power by giving them tangibility on that billboard.

Once we have written words down and they are no longer just ideas floating around in the space of our own head or just words spoken out loud, written words become literal artifacts, creating not just a figurative tangibility but a long-lasting and enduring bond forever tied to the one who wrote them. They become irreversible once written. Words give you the power to put forth your position, draw a line in the sand, and stand for something.

I realized years later, as I pondered over that quote from time to time, that something deep inside me resonated with it. Life is not always fair, and we all have the ability to go on the offensive: to speak up, stand up, and defend what we believe is just.

SIDE NOTE—Certainly, we could dove-tail in a whole other book worthy of a dialogue on what is justice, injustice, and the moral and ethical concerns related, but that's not the purpose of this book.

Blue-Collar Mentality

One of the driving factors that got me into coaching and developing people was I was never naturally gifted. I had to do a lot of extra work—and I mean countless hours of extra work—to be competitive.

Now, let me qualify that statement. When you talk to some of the people who knew me in my youth or in high school, I was naturally gifted because it's all relative. I was naturally athletic and comparatively more athletic than most of my peers during my youth but I knew that I was average compared to those on a larger scale. I had to work for every inch of my progress because I knew that when I got to bigger and bigger stages, I was going to be average. There was always someone who did less and was still better than me.

I was fortunate to have parents that instilled in me from a young age that you get what you work for. There was no shortage of being spoiled at times and I never went without, but there was always a strong undercurrent that you have to work for what you want—there are no handouts.

I had my first job when I was thirteen years old, working at a children's indoor activity place. From there, I bounced around a bunch of other small jobs while in high school, everything from general labor to washing dishes to ringing things up at cash registers.

This continued on to when I was in college, even while being a full-time student and athlete. I always had a job. It didn't matter that my time was very limited and I had a lot of things on my plate. I always worked, always was on the grind, and always had some level of cash flow.

I had things I wanted to do, and I found ways to accomplish those things, often by simply pouring more effort and focus into things when others wouldn't or couldn't.

In addition to having a blue-collar mentality, something that was also drilled into me was the lunch-pail work ethic: show up and do what you're supposed to do until it is done. You didn't do half of the job and then say, "Oh, I'm going to take a break," or "Oh, you know it's time to go do this."

When you make a commitment, you stick with your commitment until the end. There was no other choice but to finish what you started and do your best when you did. Taking it easy, half-assing it, or not finishing something that needed to be done due to laziness were not options.

Although, it certainly took some time for me to get the importance of this through my youth.

It's this specific part of me I credit for getting me a job offer in one instance, which is the same job I write about turning down in a later part of this book.

Towards the end of an interview, which had gone well from my perspective, the S&C coaches were cleaning up and moving old equipment out of the weight room to make space for new equipment that was being delivered later in the week. During our conversation, we had started moving the equipment, and at one point, the S&C coach I was interviewing with looked at his watch, looked at me, and said, "Hey, man, you are good to go. You don't have to do this with us. Besides, it's going to take a while."

I looked at him and without hesitation said, "Well, it will go faster with another set of hands, and besides, we already started so we might as well finish."

He stared at me a bit sideways for a second before eventually nodding. I doubt he thought that was what I was going to say after being there for eight hours on an interview and having to drive a few hours home. We proceeded to spend a couple of hours moving equipment and talking shop, well beyond just S&C related topics.

A few days later, when he offered me the job, he specifically mentioned a key factor that helped make me his top choice: I stayed to put in the work to see something through, even when I didn't need to. As you will later read, while I would have enjoyed working for that person and know I would have learned a lot from them, I ended up turning that particular job down for totally different reasons.

Reigning in the Hustle

While I always knew the value of hard work and understood I had to hustle, I also had to learn how to reign it in. Intensity and passion are both powerful drivers but if left unchecked, they can lead to a lot of problems.

Operating at a high velocity with high intensity is sadly abnormal in almost every "normal" situation these days. Not many do it, nor can they, and for some reason they tend to view those who do as "too much."

When I was little, a friend of mine was an altar boy at our local church. One day, when we were hanging out, he told me that he got paid to be an altar boy and he got to have a sip of wine during the services. I remember thinking in my little third/fourth-grade brain, *Hey, if I do this, I can make ten to twenty bucks and have the money to buy whatever I want.*

The drinking of wine didn't really do much for me at the time, but I inherently knew it was a cool bonus. I remember leaving to go home that day thinking to myself, *That was a pretty good idea,* so I mentioned to my mother on the drive home, "Hey, Sean is an altar boy. Did you know he gets paid? It would be cool. I could go to church and get paid to be there. I'd even be able to sip the wine! I'd go to church every Sunday!"

I remember her looking at me funny with this sideways look of both amusement and horror, saying, "Well, I don't think that's the purpose of being an altar boy."

While I was a little too young to understand what it meant to be an altar boy in terms of ceremony and the religious aspects (even at a very young age I didn't associate with religion), I remember not understanding why my mother didn't see how much sense it made to monetize having to spend time in church. Especially something that my mother wanted me to do and I had no interest in (outside of now being able to get paid in the process).

This moment stuck with me. I couldn't reconcile my mother not wanting me to do something she told me often she wanted me to do and be able to get paid to do it.

It was the first time I realized something that would come in handy over the years: just because you can do something and just because you can get a certain outcome, it doesn't necessarily mean that it's a good idea.

Trying to leverage being an altar boy to generate money instead of being an altar boy to serve the religious aspects of the role wasn't the appropriate motivation in that environment. While I had the intensity to do it, that didn't mean I should have. Although, I have to say, I still think it would have been awesome to get paid to go to church and drink the wine and it would have saved my mother decades of trying to get me to go. But I never followed through in trying to be an altar boy.

Train Smarter Not Harder

While I understood the concepts of hard work, being consistent, and putting in the time to hone my craft, I also understood that I needed to be the most efficient version of myself because just working hard and "getting after it" wasn't going to be enough. I needed to train smarter. I needed the best coaches, teachers, and mentors I could find if I was going to get to where I thought I could go.

I vividly remember one day when I was in the sixth grade. It was a Saturday in the summer and I had asked my dad to kick the soccer ball around with me so I could practice some things I had just learned at a soccer camp. He was 100% invested in helping me work on my skills, as well as getting to spend some father-son time with me, so he happily obliged.

Being a lifelong athlete and having played football in college, my dad understood the competitiveness, mindset, and drive that was needed to be successful in athletics. What he didn't have, however, was anything beyond the basic knowledge of how to play soccer. Sure, he had read books, bought cleats, and took a few coaching courses, but the level of refinement I was starting to need had eclipsed his knowledge.

So there we were, doing drills, having fun, and getting after it but in the middle of doing a drill I had a question about the technical aspects of what I was doing. While it was somewhat rhetorical, I looked at him awaiting an answer. Without much hesitation, he said plainly, "I don't know. We're going to have to find someone who does."

It was as if a light bulb suddenly clicked in my head. There was my dad, the huge athletic guy that my entire life always knew everything, could do anything, and had all the answers, and he said he had no idea.

He was one of the smartest, savviest people persons I knew (and still know), and without much of a pause, not only said he didn't know but added one of the most important things you can when you don't know: that we should find someone who did.

It was at that moment that I realized all the extra work, all the effort, and all the motivation would never take me to where I needed to go if I didn't put myself around the right people in whatever it was I wanted to be better at.

It wasn't just one's internal drive but also the external environment that allowed anyone to achieve their highest level of ability. At that moment, I recognized that much like competing in sports against those who are better than you, I needed to put myself around the best, most creative, most tip-of-the-spear people if I wanted to learn how to take myself to the next level.

At the time, however, I didn't know that surrounding yourself with leaders in your field was only a part of the secret. The quality of the leader would ultimately prove to be just as important as the knowledge they possessed.

Expertise is Good, but Great People Matter More

Up to that point in my life, I always had great supportive people around me. I could name a dozen names of parents, my dad included, who helped coach my friends and me when we were kids. People who sacrificed their time and gave their effort (and sanity at times) to help us excel. There was even an instance of a father quitting his job so he could coach our local town team when his boss said he couldn't have time off.

It's hard for people to understand how strong a community of support there was and I've come to realize now that sadly it was an unusual environment to be a part of, not the norm.

However, while these parent-coaches were great people and tried their best, none of them had the level of expertise to show us the technical and tactical skills to achieve our utmost potential. Shortly after that summer day with my dad, I was approached by a coach who would forever help, shape, and guide my approach to coaching.

His name was Tom. He was one of the soccer coaches at the camp I had attended, and he coached the age-group team that I fell into at the time. He had seen me at the soccer camp, called my house, and asked if I wanted to try out to be part of his club team. So, in short order, I showed up to tryouts and made the team. It helped that I was the only goalkeeper that tried out but I like to believe I was the only one Tom asked to try out.

Tom was a phenomenal guy. He was fair, he was honest, and he was up-front with everybody. He would praise you when you did well or exceeded his expectations but he also would also let you know when you didn't live up the potential he saw in you.

He was a tremendous coach and motivator, and he had a passion for not just soccer but getting us to become better people through soccer.

He was someone none of us wanted to let down as the energy and commitment he put into us was awesome to be a part of, and even at a young age, you knew it meant so much to him to be able to impact us positively. He was the first real example I had of someone who wasn't just a great person but had the technical and tactical expertise to bring me to the next level.

Tom's first year coaching the team was the year before I tried out, and the team had seven losses and had not won a single game. It didn't deter him, and if anything, it only made him give more of himself to help make the next year great. We went on to have something like five wins and two losses and moved up a division to play more competitive teams. Then the year after that, we were playing for the championship having gone unbeaten with seven wins and we most certainly didn't do it with raw talent.

We were more Bad News Bears than the Yankees.

We were able to achieve that success because Tom was able to craft an environment where we all wanted to play for him. We wanted to learn, he put us in positions to learn, and he helped us learn how to put ourselves aside and embrace the role we each played for the team.

He got the best out of us because he gave us confidence.

He put us in an environment where we could all grow and get better and also where we could fail, fail again, learn, and not be discouraged. He kept things fun, but he was serious.

He even brought in some of his friends who were former college/pro soccer players to help us train, teach us new things, and push us to improve. He understood the power of a different voice or idea in order to help us keep improving if we got stuck.

It was an awesome environment to be around, and the lessons I learned helped me not only in soccer but in other areas of my life.

Looking back on it, sometimes I took it for granted—I was a twelve-year-old after all. But I have realized, as I have gotten older, it was a tremendous experience to be a part of.

I owe a lot to that guy.

Unfortunately, like most instances when someone is doing well and being successful, the other coaches at the club got jealous. They started to think that they had the answers to push us to even higher heights and that Tom did not.

Given the politics of the situation, he was removed from coaching the team in favor of one of the club's higher-ups and his protégé, who both came from a radically different school of thought and with a radically different approach. While the argument could be made that this new coach and his minion did have a deeper level of tactical and technical soccer knowledge than Tom did, it was immediately apparent they lacked the key element that made Tom successful: he had no ego as a coach.

It was at this time that I saw firsthand how disastrous it could be if selfishness and ego get in the way of doing the right thing.

That's exactly what Tom did not do and that's exactly why we succeeded.

He knew how to establish roles and get people to embrace them; he knew how to build confidence. It was a pay-for-play team, it was supposed to be competitive, and we were. He allowed all of us to compete. Everyone. No matter what. Some played more than others, but everyone got their chance to contribute in the way they could.

Everyone knew they had a role to play as well as how to play it; that was Tom's true genius as a coach.

When the new coaches came in trying to reap the glory and take the benefit, they lost sight of that.

I remember one particular meeting after practice, the week after our top defender—whose mother was also deeply involved in team operations—left the team. The meeting became about how good they were as coaches, how we as the players weren't good enough to be a part of what they were trying to do, and how they would be trying to recruit us out of the team if we didn't try harder.

It was a sad attempt at motivation and one we all saw right through. The impetus shifted from developing and empowering the people who are there to be worked with—the players—to instead becoming an ego-stroking competition for the two coaches. At one point, they even made disparaging comments about the player's mother for not being good at the role she was voluntarily helping with. One in which she was very good at.

As a team that once had such a strong culture, we use to have almost-full attendance for voluntary practices in the snow during the New England winters, where no one would consider missing it or not giving 100% effort. But it became an environment where skipping practice and lying about scheduling conflicts with school and family became common.

The culture shifted to apathy and lack of interest for what was being taught among the players. No one knew their role and everyone walked on eggshells unsure of when the next temper tantrum from the Coaches would come, resulting in menial punishment conditioning.

It was sad to see because, within twelve months, everything that Tom had built into the group and team culture over those last three-plus years dissolved. It became a contest of ego for the new coaches who were in charge, and they destroyed the entire team dynamic with multiple players leaving and the team itself ultimately dissolving.

This was one of the key defining experiences in my life and one my father years later reflected on and said to me "I wish I took you out of that sooner. I didn't realize how caustic it was until it all fell apart." I replied to him, however, that while it was terrible to be a part of, it was an amazing learning experience.

I learned the true aspects of what learning from someone else was all about. It had nothing to do with if they had the knowledge or expertise in order to be a teacher or a coach. What was most important was the kind of person they were and how they treated people while sharing that knowledge and expertise as a teacher and coach. Could they be a mentor?

Learning to Deal with People

As you will notice throughout this book, there are often quotes or phrases tied to each section or as part of a story or deeper explanation of a topic. Over time, I've come to realize that I naturally connect these tidbits, quotes, or saying to the principles and philosophies that guide me. This next one is one of my favorite quotes of all time and applies universally to every situation humans are involved in. It's a quote that I have had hanging in my office or framed on my desk with every job I've worked in and will continue to have:

> "There's nothing more difficult and dangerous or more uncertain of success than an attempt to introduce a new order of things in any state. For the innovator has for enemies all those who drive advantages from the old order of things, while those who expect to be benefited by the new institutions will be but lukewarm defenders." —Niccolò Machiavelli, *The Prince*

It's something that stuck with me, ever since I read *The Prince* when I was going into freshman year of high school, and started to open my eyes to interacting with people in the real world beyond my friends and family.

I'm not going to dive significantly deeper into this particular topic right now, because as I have tried over the years, it is certainly more a thinking point than one to explain.

Stop. Read the quote again, slowly.

Let your mind bounce it around and think about it for a few minutes before you continue.

Ask yourself, *How does a quote hundreds of years old explain many of the professional situations you've been in?*

Let yourself drift around with it in your mind for a while longer, rereading it a couple more times.

Ask yourself about the different perspectives of the people referenced in that quote and how they each feel regarding each other.

The more I've reflected on that quote in complex professional situations, the clearer some of my next steps seem to come.

It probably seems strange to have this particular quote from this particular person in this book as *The Prince,* and Machiavelli himself, each have certain stigma and connotations associated to them. But as it relates to understanding culture, political influence, and playing *The Game of Thrones* —if you will—it is spot on to human nature.

While there is also a place for pragmatic thinking, essentialism, and certainly a few more perspectives—each having a place and purpose —some we will touch on in this book, others we won't. No matter how much I learn from those other schools of thought, all of which have place and purpose, I always come back to this specific quote.

Pursuing Wisdom

If knowledge is power, I also quickly learned that being educated is only one piece; I needed to take that education and connect my knowledge to my experiences; and through application, gain wisdom.

Using the context of weightlifting, but applicable to any situation, anyone can be a walking encyclopedia with limited experience "under the bar."

Anyone can have all the experience in the world "under the bar" but lack the knowledge and ability to articulate what is happening beyond simply the act of doing it.

Anyone can know a bunch of stuff, but if you can't apply it, connect it, and use it, it doesn't matter.

This dichotomy helped me realize that the path to having wisdom was what would allow me to become a great teacher, coach, and mentor—not just having the knowledge or the experience in isolation.

In middle school, there was a brand-new teacher, having just graduated from college, and she spent more time trying to impress us with her knowledge of the subject matter than teach us about it. She would cite and reference all kinds of examples and chastise us for not being as well read or worldly as she was.

One day, as she was explaining something, one of the kids in the class raised their hand and challenged her lesson. My classmate's point of contention was that the teacher was wrong, as their father worked in the specific field doing what was being discussed, and he would always say when the subject came up at home that, "People who've only ever read the textbooks get this wrong all the time, as it is a much more dynamic and complex process than how it is explained."

The teacher then started in on a tirade of spewing knowledge, sensing her authority on the subject was being challenged. Feeling like there was something to this and not being afraid to step in, I raised my hand and asked point-blank if this teacher had ever personally done what she was teaching like the other student's father did.

There was a brief moment of silence from her, and she flushed a bit, as she sheepishly admitted she had never done what she was explaining. I then turned to the girl who had originally spoken up and asked if her dad ever explained what the context was of him saying what he said. And she was able to give a pretty solid rational answer given the complexities of the subject in question.

Even the teacher, who while still a bit emotionally vexed, was impressed with the answer. And while I'm sure it pained her, had to admit to everyone that it was, in fact, plausible that there was more to know than just what she was aware of.

While this teacher had boundless knowledge, she lacked the experience and "time under the bar" to have a true grasp on her knowledge and be able to "connect the dots."

In contrast, at a later time in middle school, I remember going to the home of a friend of mine whose father was an electrician. We were in science class together and we thought it would be cool to test our newly learned knowledge of electric things by going to his house and messing around with all the stuff his dad had in the basement.

My friend's dad had all kinds of wires, resistors, switches, etc., lying around and we tinkered around trying to build a flux capacitor. When his dad got home from work and saw us messing with things, he laughed at our rudimentary effort and showed us some cool tricks.

My friend started asking him about resistors and voltages, amps, and current flows. His dad nonchalantly brushed off the questions with, "Those are questions for the engineer guys. I never have to deal with that stuff."

Being young and naive, my friend then asked his dad why he wasn't an engineer and what the difference was. His dad then said that he never went to college and joined the union out of high school like his father had because it was good pay and good hours. And all he had to do was follow the plans the engineers made, putting things in the right places the right ways, like a Lego set. He never had to worry about all that other stuff.

Besides, he said, even if something went wrong, as long he did what he was told to do it wasn't his fault. It wasn't his job to make sure things were designed properly; it was just his job to build it as the plans said too.

These two examples illustrated the stark contrast between knowledge and experience to me.

Sure, my friend's dad had all the experience in the world, "time under the bar" per se, but he lacked the ability to communicate in the appropriate level of detail what he was doing beyond the physical steps of doing it. He did not have a clear understanding of why things worked, or how they worked together, but only that they worked.

My teacher, on the other hand, having read every book on the subject and able to quote authors and articles hand over foot had never been "under the bar." So, with her lack of experience she was as good as dust in the air when it came to getting things done.

Why is all of this relevant, you ask? Why these two stories?

Isn't it obvious? It's knowledge versus experience.

But that isn't what I'm getting at because that is only the first layer of the onion (shout-out to Westy). What I learned from these experiences and later connected was the second and third layers of the onion: the ability to gain wisdom or to "connect the dots."

We, as a society, are often told and have the construct ingrained in us that learning and expanding your knowledge base is what matters and that you have a fixed time to do so, while you are young.

That the more you know, the better you are at things.

Generally, this idea centers on academic instruction and having earned your knowledge through completion of some kind of degree or certification. We are then told that experience can only come with time, and lots of it, and that wisdom is best reserved for the long-experienced and learned, chronologically older, adults.

However, chronological age is no longer a marker of knowledge or experience, just like it has never been a marker of mental maturity, in addition to a litany of other things.

The combination of technological innovation, changes in

communication (internet, smartphones, etc.), access to information, ability to capture the lessons learned from others' successes and failures, as well as discussing anything in real-time has allowed individuals to gain knowledge and experience far beyond what was previously capable, at speeds never previously imagined.

The research into this phenomenon is very interesting and worth reading. However, this accelerated curve to knowledge and experience comes at a cost: the lack of being able to have wisdom due to the critical skill "connecting the dots" not being developed.

> "Wisdom is being able to connect the dots between your experiences and education, allowing you to create a cumulative net of knowledge you can draw and learn from, show others, and guide you in your own decisions."
> —My Dad (seriously, he says this all the time)

To gain wisdom, one first must go through the internalization process of understanding oneself. Then, one must take the knowledge one possesses combined with one's external experiences to leverage the two in any manner that suits the given context.

It's not just about drawing on what you know but taking what you've gained internally and melding it with what is external; learning from others, constantly drawing from other's experiences, asking questions, and having dialogue to gain fresh perspectives, new approaches or insights in order to constantly refine the internal ability to externally use all that you have ever done.

The speed of collecting knowledge and experience has radically increased, but the process to convert it to wisdom can only move at the speed you are capable of handling.

Paying Attention

I've often been asked how I came up with an idea, had an insight, or was able to anticipate and react to something that hadn't happened yet. The answer is a pretty simple answer: I pay attention.

You have to understand that I'm not trying to sound like an omnipotent, all-knowing being and that I have all the answers, because I can tell you more often than not, I fail and I'm wrong.

I pay attention in the sense that I'm always looking, listening, trying to understand what's going on in the spaces around me, both near and far. There's never a moment where I'm just sitting and not trying to take in some level of information about something.

This annoys my wife to no end.

And this is where it gets tricky because most people find it difficult to filter the outside noise and best disseminate the information into useful material outside of their personal bias or emotional response.

It took me quite a long time and a lot of practice to be willing to listen to the second, third, or even fourth opinion in a situation. But just because I'm willing to listen it doesn't always mean that I will, or if I do, that I will believe the information I gain.

Never forget we often find answers to our problems in the least likely places, from people who we may discount, and when we are willing to be open to finding an answer outside of where we expect it to be.

Self-Mastery First

Just like in training, context and situational awareness define the outcomes, as well as the goals and tools that you'll use to get to those outcomes.

You first have to master yourself before you have a chance at being able to understand people.

Generally, most people consider having mastered themselves some sort of physical mastery or spiritual mastery. And don't get me wrong, those two aspects are very important in the process. The physical mastery is often the hard skill, whereas spiritual mastery is often the soft skill.

The key is the combination of both: where you can internalize and reflect on your emotional and non-emotional responses to understand how the emotions and thoughts that you create and bring with you to any physical activity affect the outcome, just as much as the steps that got you to it.

You have to be willing to detach yourself and see your life as a long continuum. Only when you simultaneously view yourself as someone on the frontline fighting in the trenches, overseeing the battlefield from the hilltop, and looking down from the clouds from a global perspective are you able to appreciate yourself as well as internalize your own actions and machinations.

I've spent a lot of time understanding my biases and my own flaws, of which I have many, and I am constantly struggling in the battle of self-improvement versus self-destruction. I don't know if that ever ends.

Secondly, you have to understand the role you're in and the positive and negative ways that affects you and your interactions with people. How can those interactions be adjusted, manipulated, or purposely used to derive other outcomes?

One of the most important characteristics to any developing leader/coach is able to follow someone else.

You have to be able to take orders.

I don't mean that in the strict military cliché of charging a machine gun on an open battlefield because your superior told you to. There is a time and a place to question poor orders and push back against poor leadership. I've never been afraid of doing that but there's also a time and a place to understand that it might be your role to shut your mouth, be disciplined, and do as you're told. Again, a skill that I continue to work on and be challenged by, especially when dealing with subpar leaders.

Because if you can master your own thoughts and opinions while helping and following someone else, you will then be in control of your own thoughts and opinions when someone else is serving you.

Listening, Not Just Hearing, What is Said

Effective communication is not just a matter of listening or speaking to someone else when you need something from them.

Taking time to speak with and listen to someone else, while being open enough to understand how that person's cumulative experiences and viewpoints drive their thinking, allows you to better understand their logic structure.

This, in turn, gives you the general idea of how to best approach them and speak with them at a level that they will be receptive to or is within their functional limits.

You have to have some context as to what drives and motivates them as well as their experiences and personal history. Often, people subconsciously react and act to certain stimuli or situations due to where they come from and how they've developed over time, regardless of the present situation or context.

Having some grasp on that—not only for yourself but for others— and being willing to listen to gain perspective, will allow you to facilitate better communication and act more effectively.

There is no specific example here as life is the example. How many times could you have had a better outcome in whatever it was you were doing had you asked one more question, known one more fact about someone, or had one more moment to absorb a tidbit of information.

Dealing with People, CYA

Anytime you are in a customer-facing role or any time you're interacting with people in a direct way, you will have friction among people.

> "Everywhere you go, no matter the situation, it's always the same problems or people with different faces. You have to ask yourself then, what type of person and type of problems do you want to deal with."
> —Unknown

There was one specific instance when I was in high school that made me realize even when things are going well and there isn't friction, you always need to cover your ass, because you never know when a situation will come up that if you are not prepared, you could be caught in a bad spot.

In high school, I was voted captain for track and field, and at the beginning of the season, we wanted to have warm-up tracksuits for the team made. So, a couple of other guys and I got together, picked out a tracksuit, created the logo design, met with a local embroiderer, and got it all set up to go. I was in charge of collecting all the money and keeping records of who ordered what sizes and everything.

It was an awesome learning experience because I was put in charge of a couple thousand dollars since they were seventy dollars each and we had about 100 people on the team.

Being in charge, not wanting to make any mistakes, and knowing that I was holding other people's money (mostly from my teammate's parents), I kept pretty meticulous notes in a notebook and then transferred them to an Excel spreadsheet every night when I got home.

I wrote what the name on the check was, what dollar bills they gave me if it was cash, what person it was for if the last name on the check was different than the last name of the team member, what size they wanted, what day they gave me the money, and where and what time they gave me the money.

Maybe being an S&C Coach for me was meant to be as I had a knack for Excel even then.

Remember, there was no online banking so I couldn't just pull check images or statements whenever I wanted.

Fast forward to a few days after the tracksuits were handed out. We were in the locker room after practice and a younger teammate came up to me and said he paid but didn't get his tracksuit, and he seemed pretty upset by it.

For a moment I thought, *Oh, shit, this is my fault.* But it was quickly replaced with, *No way, I'm good.* I said, "Hey, man, look, you're not on the list," as I grabbed the final printed document out of my locker. "I don't have you here. I have no record of you giving me cash or check. I have no record of you giving me money because I wrote down everything. I have names, dates when people gave me money, the location they gave me money." I showed him on my alphabetized spreadsheet, that must've had ten columns of info per person. I made it a point to take that spreadsheet and put it in his face, like, *Look, you're not on the spreadsheet.*

He tried to complain and tried to say his parents gave him money and such. All I could reply was, "Look, man, I don't have one for you." And he walked away, putting up a pretty weak fight.

Later that night, I got a call from this person's father who was obviously upset and said, "Hey look, I gave my son seventy dollars in cash for a tracksuit and now you're saying he doesn't have one. He said he gave you the money." I said, "Okay, this is the situation. I have this spreadsheet where I kept track of all the information—a lot of information. I'll happily send it to you for you to see. He is not on it, and it is not a mistake."

As I explained it to him, he was filling in the blanks. He realized I had my ducks in a row, I had a good deal of information to solidify my position, and I wasn't just pissing in the wind.

He said, "Wow. You did all that?" And I said, "Yeah, specifically so this wouldn't happen." I said, "Now, you may have given him money but he never gave me money. So, I don't know what you want me to do. But something doesn't add up and it's not on my end."

I found out a couple of days later from another person on the team that this kid ended up admitting he took his dad's money and spent it on a new video game instead of paying for the tracksuit.

He was going to try and lie and say he paid because he didn't think I had kept such good records. When he realized I did, he tried to pretend it didn't happen. But his dad, knowing he gave him the money and there was no tracksuit, started asking questions and led to him calling me—to the chagrin of the kid in question because he knew he was found out.

It reinforced to me that you have to cover your ass and you have to be very meticulous, especially when you're dealing with other people's money or people who may not have altruistic motives. A clear, factual, and provable track record is key in preventing yourself from getting into major trouble, putting assholes in their place, and most importantly, protecting yourself from blowback others try to put on you.

2

MY JOURNEY

It's interesting when you start to reflect on long stretches of your life experiences. As I sit here in this period of transition in my life, I have the opportunity to take the time and write (this sentence was written in 2017).

Everyone always says, "You should write a book." But it's often one of those things that people say they will do but never take the time to do. When I was feeling out this undertaking within my network, one of my good friends said, "It's one of those things people always say they're going to do but don't do. You just have to shut up and do it. So, stop talking. Start writing."

So here I am doing it.

It's kind of tough and weird to talk about yourself in this setting. You do it briefly in one-minute elevator conversations with people you meet or your three-minute interview pitch.

It's generally a few words on the different parts of your life, perhaps who you are and where you came from, and you cut it down to a couple of paragraphs of information that can cover 10–15 years. But to try and draw it out and distill out the key points that are relevant to a specific part of your life with significant substance is a lot tougher than it sounds—at least for me. I'm pretty good with words coming out of my mouth but to write at this level was a challenge.

It is definitely something you should try and definitely something to include in the journaling you should be doing (more on that later).

Supposed to Be a Soccer Player

Growing up, I did every sport you could think of.

I had good enough raw athletic ability to run, jump, throw, etc. And although I could do a bit of everything well, I gravitated towards soccer; it just came more naturally to me.

While I played all the positions as a youth, I enjoyed playing goalkeeper the most. It was an odd sense of detachment being a goalkeeper in the soccer field because you're only called into action, or hopefully only called into action, only a few times in a game. If you finished a game as a goalkeeper totally physically spent, that meant things went to hell in a handbasket for your team.

There is also the possibility that for the entire game you're not called into action at all. You're riding high on adrenaline with your body and mind on full alert but all you're doing is communicating and organizing elements throughout the game.

It was a position I naturally gravitated towards both from the athletic standpoint and the intellectual side of the game. I liked learning the physical skills and the tactical side of being a goalkeeper—helping play my part in the chess match of strategy during the game.

Like anything in any sport, there is a lot of tactics that go into it, but being a goalkeeper in a soccer game, especially when you're playing a team that's better than your team, is a very mentally demanding task to organize and influence all the moving parts.

It's a constant tug of communicating what is happening, both where the ball is and where it is not, in order to keep everyone on the same page. It's like being a point guard or a quarterback in a lot of ways. Most people would think that the central midfielders on a soccer team would have that field generalship—and they do—from an offensive standpoint. But from a defensive standpoint, and also in some ways offensively given the full-picture view of the field, it's the goalkeeper.

Adding complexity to the dynamics, by being able to use your hands in a confined space as well as being expected to make physical contact in a way that isn't always allowed for other positions, it was basically the ultimate puzzle. How does your physical size, reactive capabilities, and mental acuity, in conjunction with all of those qualities of your teammates, influence if you go for the ball or not, catch, or deflect?

I got to the point of playing soccer where eventually other sports started to fall by the wayside and I was playing on multiple teams at a time and training and playing year-round. By the time I turned sixteen, I had specialized so significantly and developed enough to be considered very good and on the college scholarship track.

Unfortunately, I was also pretty burnt out.

It took me a long time to realize what was going on, only understanding its significance much later in college when I had coursework related to the topic: playing and practicing year-round at a high level and traveling around both domestically and internationally made me start to resent playing.

My heart was just not in it the way it needed to be.

Soccer had become a very privatized aspect of my life compared to my "at home" or "in town" life.

It took me all over the map, I met all kinds of new people, and it was a phenomenal experience. It laid the foundation for me to have experiences that helped build certain skills and abilities later on in life. But I sacrificed a lot of my social development when I was younger. Although I was still able to get to parties, go to friends, and get to experience most normal things my age, I missed out on a majority of those types of things because I was always doing soccer. If you ask a lot of my friends, they'll tell you the same thing. I was always around, but I was never around. It's actually been an undercurrent throughout my entire life, even now, especially with some of my childhood friends, that I'm always on the periphery—around but not around.

Because of the demands I had from soccer, then from being a college athlete, and then from my professional life working in college sports, while I've tried my best to "be around," I've missed a lot of key defining moments for people. And I've had many friendships I wanted to continue drift away due to the demands I was placed under (albeit, I choose those demands, so I guess at the time those other things weren't as important).

As I started to feel the pressure of being burnt out during high school, in order to get out of playing soccer and do something different, I had given serious consideration to quitting soccer at the high school level and trying football.

Our football team wasn't very good, and we didn't have a big team, and I had thought I could significantly help given I was athletic and physically bigger than most.

On the flip side, in my four years of soccer, we had only lost three games. We had sixty-two wins, three losses, and seven ties with two state titles and a loss in the state championship.

So, three out of the four years, we're playing in the state title game, whereas our football team, unfortunately, I don't think won a combined ten games in my four years there.

We always joked that if our soccer team suited up in pads, we would probably beat our football team just because a majority of the most athletic guys in the school played soccer.

While I gave it serious consideration, I was too scared to quit soccer, to be honest. I was too scared and too worried about what people thought. I wasn't strong enough yet within my own skin to not let outside influences bother me. It would take a few more years and a lot more failures, second-guessing, and constant work in my own head to be comfortable enough with myself to push aside the judgment of others— even those who opinions I truly valued.

SIDE NOTE—Don't get me wrong, it's not like other people's opinions and inputs don't matter to me; I take feedback into consideration in making decisions. I respect my wife's opinion, my family's and friends' opinions, but at the end of the day, I've gotten to the point where I'm no longer scared to make a choice because of what other people think. I make a choice based on me. I make a choice based on the best information I have, at the best point in my life, for the best reasons I can, whether good, bad, right, or wrong. I'm okay living with the consequences and moving forward.

It's a powerful internal feeling when you are no longer self-limiting due to others' outside points of view.

Knowing what I know now, I wouldn't have played as much soccer when I was between twelve and sixteen years old. I would've done other sports or found other hobbies, and I certainly would have taken more time off to recover mentally and physically. And before we go down that rabbit hole, which is certainly a book within itself, I will say I am a huge believer in not specializing until as late as possible (a conversation to be continued another day).

While I had the potential to play soccer in college and had offers too, I was so burnt out from it by the time I graduated high school that I didn't want to play anymore. I've felt no loss ever since and haven't even played recreationally with friends ever since my last soccer game in high school.

Track and Field

In a school of about 800, there were about 120 boys on the track team and a significant number of people were acquaintances or friends.

So, I joined the track and field team during my sophomore year for outdoor track. While I had no intention of doing it seriously, I was athletic enough to do most of the events and physically trained enough to run. Plus, I had my friends around me and I didn't just want to play soccer anymore.

The first day at track and field practice was the first time I was ever coached by one of my first mentors in physical development outside of my father.

Obviously, my mother and father played a huge role. So too did my aunts and uncles, and my sister who was always playing sports. I grew up with being active as being normal. But the first person who I had as a coach from a physical development standpoint who had deep knowledge and a deep personal experience was Coach Powers.

Coach Powers was the gym teacher at our high school, and he was also the football coach and the track coach.

He was a strict, no-nonsense, no bullshit, clean-cut, straight-up guy who loved his job. He had passion for what he did and invested his time, effort, and energy in helping us get better as athletes and as people. He spent his own money on equipment to help make us better. He did everything he could to try and get the most out of us.

I know dozens if not hundreds of other people who worked with him throughout their time at Stoneham High and all reflect fondly on the positive impact he had on them and on so many others.

He was the first person who I learned from that showed me there was a science and a purpose to human performance.

It was not just show up and train. It wasn't just lifting as heavy as you could only in the lifts you liked. There was a stepwise process to better yourself physically, and—coming back to how I liked the strategy, tactics, and the mental side of the sport—I naturally gravitated towards learning the rationale of training.

It was like learning the ultimate game of chess. Anytime I asked him for articles, books, or anything related to learning more, he was always there to help me learn. I probably read more training-related information through high school than I did any subject I was in class for, something my friends can attest to as I got into trouble more than once for reading something unrelated in class.

Outside of being a resource and providing resources to help teach me about training, Coach Powers was always there for me as a coach and mentor.

He was the coach I needed in high school to push me to be my best because he demanded that. He demanded discipline, accountability, and mental toughness. He put us in physically difficult situations in order to push us physically but also give us the mental tools to overcome adversity beyond just preparing for a sport.

The value of what he did for me, I will never be able to repay. It's something I've come to learn over the years—when someone truly adds value to your life.

The first two weeks of the track and field season, he had everyone who joined the team in their first season practice all the different events and eventually "compete" in a handful they showed the most promise in.

That way, you had to try a little bit of everything. Coach Powers could see what you were good at, what you were bad at, and the areas you naturally gravitated to.

One of the first days at practice, I remember I got to high jump. It just made sense. I just knew how to do it. State qualifying was five feet eight, and I jumped five feet eight that day on a hard basketball court in running shoes, flat backing, no arch, from four lefts (track lingo—you know it, or you don't).

Then later that day I ran the 110-meters hurdles. I ran somewhere in the twenty-second range, smacking hurdles and almost crashing a few times. About a week or so later, I had to run them again, but this time was in the seventeen-second range. By no means a world-beater but enough of an improvement that I became a high jumper and hurdler for the next few weeks.

At the first meet of the year, my third timed race ever (with the first two being those early season assessments), I ran in the low sixteen-seconds. So, the third race I ever had, I was among the top three fastest guys on the team and close to qualifying for states. It just came naturally. Track and field just made sense to me, and coming off of the negative experience I was having in soccer, I put a lot of effort and energy into the sport.

In my junior year in high school, I started the winter playing basketball. We were terrible at basketball. I was one of the tallest people on the team at a whopping six-foot-one. At that point, I was a starter on the varsity team. Three games into the season I quit.

Yep, you read that right. I quit.

It took a lot of people by surprise because I had played basketball my whole life: sixth grade, seventh grade, eighth grade, ninth grade, and tenth grade. I wasn't good. I was, in fact, a terrible basketball player.

When I first started in sixth or seventh grade, I could barely make a free throw and I would miss layups—wide-open layups. I just wasn't good at basketball and it was never a sport I wanted to be good at. But what I liked about basketball was the intensity, playing defense, and the back and forth working as a team—the chess part.

I was scrappy and I competed hard so I could play pretty good defense. I lacked a lot of the skills, but I was athletic enough and I was intense enough that I kind of made up for it. Let's just say that people weren't looking for me to score buckets. They were looking to me to get rebounds and play defense because I had no problem getting physical and getting after it.

But I quit. It wasn't because I had bad teammates. I had great teammates—most were the guys I played soccer with. We had a good coach who was a good guy. He did his best with what he was given (which wasn't much).

It just wasn't for me. I needed to make a change. I needed to step out and do something different, and having some success at track that past spring, I had a natural affinity to see what I could do. I had jumped into it on a lark and wanted to see how far I could run with it (enjoy that corny pun).

So, I quit. Selfish yes, but I was okay with it. I quit for a reason. I was leaving one opportunity to pursue a different one. And pursue it? Did I ever. I trained all winter, every day, even most weekends and got ready for outdoor track. That was the year I made a big breakthrough and when I realized, *Hey, I'm good at this* and *Hey, I could do this in college.*

I started to be much more competitive at the state level. I got into the history of track and field, learning the science of training and development with Coach Powers, and doing plyometrics and Olympic lifting.

Before YouTube was a thing, I watched hours of old VHS videos and read books and magazines to learn to get better, and it paid off.

I was able to improve my junior year significantly. I set a couple of records and came close to setting a few more. It was fun and it was competitive.

Fast-forward to my senior year and I put a lot of extra time in. The whole winter of my junior year I put a lot of extra time in. But this was on another level—like having a key to the school to get into the gym and the weight room to train after-hours kind of level.

A good friend at the time, CT, joined me in my training. We did all this extra stuff in the hallways in my high school after school and late at night. We'd put in countless extra hours of work and effort to become better. Hell, we even used those crazy platform plyometrics jump shoes . . . you know, the ones Jimmy wears in *Seinfeld* before Jimmy goes down.

That's one thing I'll always say. I always had awesome training partners, from high school to college and beyond. Any time I went through an interesting point in my life where I was trying to develop and get better, I normally had tremendous mentors like Coach Powers, but I also had key training partners who may or may not have been physically better than me but were always willing to grind it out with me.

SIDE NOTE—Big thanks to anyone who has ever grinded it out with me. You pushed me more than you will ever know, even if I was the one making us do one more thing after we already did one more thing.

The Decathlon

Coach Powers kept an updated list in the locker room, decathlon-style, of what each person's score was in each event (based on those first couple weeks of practice and meets). For each event, there was a rank. He did this because Massachusetts held a state decathlon where each town could send three people to do the decathlon. Instead of pole vaulting, we would triple jump because pole vault, at the time, wasn't a certified event in Massachusetts.

So, at the end of my sophomore year, I did a decathlon. I didn't do that well in it because while I was athletic, I don't know what I was doing. Let's just say I ran my 1500-meter race in sprint spikes and came out of the first 400 meters sub-sixty seconds when I was at best a six-minute miler at the time. And I'm pretty sure I out shot put my discus throw. Needless to say, I had no idea what I was doing.

Onto my junior year, I had the opportunity to do decathlon again, and because I had worked on my craft and taken that winter to just train, I was able to do a lot better. I believe I was top five in the state.

Then, come my senior year, I invested the time throughout the year to be ready to get after it at the last decathlon. I practiced disc throws once a week, did some extra running, and figured I had a real shot at winning the whole thing. I ended up coming in second by a handful of points, which I learned later turned out to be a two-second difference in the 1500.

This is where following in my sister's footsteps takes a hilarious and ironic turn as my sister went to the University of Connecticut (UConn). Through her time there, she ended up living off-campus, as many students do at UConn, and my family went down to help her move to her new place.

In the process of helping her move in, her landlord showed up. He gets out of his pickup truck, chats us up a bit, and after a few minutes he gives me a once over and says, "Hey, you wouldn't happen to be Joe Staub from Stoneham who does track and field?"

I said, "Yeah, that's me."

He replied, "I'm Greg Roy, the track and field coach of the University of Connecticut." To which I replied something to the effect of "cool" and went back to moving stuff for my sister. The interaction lasted maybe a solid twenty seconds, and I didn't think anything of it as he then went to talk to my sister about all things related to living in his property.

At the time, I had no idea if UConn was good in track and field (T&F) or not. And besides, it's not like he had offered me a scholarship on the spot or anything.

About a week later, I had a recruiting questionnaire in the mail from none other than UConn. Shortly after that, I went on a day-long visit to campus for an unofficial recruiting trip. Having been there a couple of times to visit my sister I knew what campus was like and knew that they had the major I wanted to pursue (and were top in the country at that). And after visiting, I just had a good feeling like I belonged there and gained some understanding of what UConn T&F was all about.

After that visit, I committed to going to UConn and never looked at other schools.

Sometimes you just know. Well, I knew.

It was the best choice I ever made for a lot of reasons—meeting my future wife being number one. When you know, you know.

Coach Roy, if you've never met him, is a phenomenal track coach. He'd been in the business at UConn for over thirty years at the time I'm writing this and he runs a great program. I spent most of my time with Coach Miller, who was my direct event coach. That poor guy had to put up with me for multiple hours, literally every day for ten months at a time, four years in a row.

I need to get him a medal or some kind of award for that. I owe them both more than I can repay.

When I met Coach Miller and Coach Roy on my visit, it just clicked. I liked them. I liked their demeanor. I liked their style. I liked their no-nonsense attitudes. I knew they had a track record for helping people get better and taking athletic guys like me and making them win. They had a track record for being successful in their conference and in the region. They had a track record for helping people who are raw like me develop into better athletes and better T&F athletes, so it was kind of a no-brainer.

While I could dive into my personal athletic experiences for easily 100 pages, I will sum it up like this: I learned a lot while being a member of the T&F team at UConn, had amazing teammates, worked hard, played hard, and have some pretty crazy stories.

Most of all, the most important things I gained from the experience made sense to me after I had graduated. Some things clicked years, and years later because I wasn't ready to grasp everything at the time.

That I believe is what Coach Roy's ultimate coaching power is; he not only knows how to help you get better in the "now," but how he does things helps you improve in the future, well beyond your time on the track —you just have to be open to realizing it.

3

MY COACHING CAREER

In this last part of "clearing the land" for the foundation and the building that is coming, as it relates to everything else I seek to cover in this book, I wanted to touch on the trajectory of my coaching career.

In this 10,000-foot view, I aim to give the final bits of context for my ability to pour that foundation and build that building; someone who has found success and also failure, while also constantly evolving along the way.

UConn

With T&F helping drive my commitment to UConn, it also happened that the top program for kinesiology was at the University of Connecticut.

I started out in physical therapy because, at the time, that was what I thought I wanted to do. I was going to get my undergrad through the exercise science department and then work on my doctorate in physical therapy (DPT). At that time on the national stage, the master's in physical therapy was being phased out. There was only a doctorate moving forward, and UConn was in the middle of changing the program and having all kinds of other internal shakeups to make the DPT program a reality.

I was caught up in the middle of it all from a timing standpoint. There was a lot of uncertainty about what I was going to do and if I was going to have a spot in the program moving forward, due to the uncertainty around the requirements of the program.

It was approaching January of my freshman year, and I had taken the passion for the science of training I had learned from Coach Powers and funneled it into an exercise science degree to pursue S&C as a path to a career, not just as a prerequisite to the DPT.

It availed me a huge opportunity because I realized that I could work in the weight room for credit. So, I started spending as much time there as I could, probably to the annoyance of the S&C staff at that time. I was young and while I knew more than the average person, I had no idea about anything related to training and coaching.

I observed, watched, and trained. I asked for material. I read books and articles. As I closed out my freshman year of college, I started beginning to learn two things:

One, I knew nothing, and no matter how much I learned, I still knew nothing. A lesson that, in fact, has never changed since that day.

Two, I wasn't as durable as I thought I was.

I had started to have some injuries, and ultimately, I needed shoulder surgery going into my sophomore year to have my rotator cuff fixed. It was the beginning of a never-ending story, of how while I had the physical ability to get myself to a certain point, I never had the durability to sustain a high-level of performance; that in turn, only made me further want to learn and develop my training knowledge and all things related to optimizing performance in order to maximize my results of getting from *A* to *B*.

It was at this point where I dove into the academic portion of my UConn experience.

Being surrounded by the top researchers in the field and learning in a fast-paced, high-intensity environment was awesome. Dr. Kraemer helped bridge the gap for me between the classroom and the weight room, showing me how to disseminate information, use common sense, challenge the norm, and always consider the context when trying to improve performance.

Countless other professors and their graduate students, a who's who in the exercise science/human performance world, were also key teachers and mentors in my academic development. We were being taught and exposed to things easily 4–6 years ahead of their wide knowledge and acceptance in the rest of the field.

I am not kidding. I was learning about things that wouldn't be published and accepted as "truths" for years.

I also had access to piles of books and information and professionals in the athletic training and physical therapy (PT) side of things as well. I learned about and gained deep insight into the continuum of possible physical outcomes: from the rehabilitative theories used to help regain previous ability level, to what it takes to far exceed current ability, and the costs of those adaptive mechanisms and theories behind them.

Also, at this time, I was fortunate to be given opportunities to stay in the summer and work a variety of jobs at UConn (shout out to the equipment room!) and volunteer with the S&C staff. I was able to learn from some of the best people in S&C. The five coaches on staff at the time each played a huge role in my development because, like any young impressionable kid, I was able to learn from, imitate, and duplicate results off them.

That set the bar immensely high, given they are all in the top 1% of the field. Imitation is the greatest form of flattery after all, and I've been guilty my entire career of being a byproduct of better coaches and people I've been able to learn from and spend time with. I considered myself extensively average compared to the giants I walked among.

UConn S&C

Coach Gerard "Jerry" Martin was the traditionalist of all traditionalists in S&C.

He was one of the O.G.'s of the field, especially on the East Coast.

He was a no-nonsense, no-bullshit kind of guy, who was one of the most intense people I've ever spent time with.

But he was also one of the most willing to teach and wanted to help people more than I think they realized. Although his personality and style didn't always benefit his heart, and some just simply didn't understand him, to me, his heart was always in the right place.

From an S&C standpoint, he was a man ahead of his time. Simply put, he was a genius. He was an innovator and looked at things in a way that was so complex that it was simple. We were doing velocity-based training and power development in 2004–2005 about twelve years before it became a big thing in the US.

I could go on for pages about Coach Martin and the things I learned from him: the times he took to talk with me about all things training-related, or simply life-related, like being a dad and having a family. The latter was a conversation we had a few times because he knew I was dating another athlete (who eventually became my wife). And he thought the world of her, always asking me how she was doing, and chatting her up when she would come visit me in the weight room.

One of the things that stands out in my mind anytime I think of him was one day in the summer of 2010. It was the first time he gave me the whistle to run football conditioning and the first time he ever addressed me as "Coach."

It stands out so clearly because, on that day, I knew I had earned his respect.

He allowed me to take the lead of the group, run the show, and set the tone for the athletes, so I was no longer "Joe" the intern or guy who helped —I was "Coach Joe."

Now that may not seem like a lot to some—a sixty-minute summer conditioning session—but for those of you who knew Coach, it meant volumes.

It was so significant an event that after the session, a few of the football guys who were more aware came up to me and congratulated me on it. One of the joker, comedian-type guys who was always good for a gem comment hit me with, "Aw shit, you a made-man now, Coach Joe. Like the mafia in the moves. Don Martin has said you are a made-man now, Coach Joe!" with a heavy emphasis on the word "Coach."

Unfortunately, we lost Coach Martin a few years ago, but his coaching legacy lives on in the dozens of professionals who worked with and learned from him, as well as through a National Strength and Conditioning Association (NSCA) fund named in his honor.

It's a fund that will receive a contribution from every sale of this book and a fund I hope every reader considers contributing too. Google "Jerry Martin NSCA" to find the page where you can donate.

One of the interesting things about Coach Martin's staff was everyone was a former college athlete and brought something different to the table; not a single one of them was a duplicate in any way of the others.

My main mentor was an extremely successful former athlete herself and has an extremely intense, powerful, and dominant personality.

She also happened to be my S&C coach as an athlete (my wife's as well) and was my first real "boss" in the field, providing me with massive opportunity for learning, growth, and development from a professional standpoint.

She always challenged me to read and learn, to think critically, and expand my capacities as a person, not just a professional. She was always willing to have conversations, challenge thoughts and ideas, and be willing to be challenged. I think that was one of the single greatest things I've ever learned from her—that she was willing to be challenged. She wanted people to come up with new ideas to challenge her and make her better. She never wanted people to listen to her like she knew everything. She always wanted someone to play devil's advocate, even if it aggravated her to no end at times, which I was guilty of and still am.

She always wanted someone to force dialogue so she could better solidify her philosophy through the argument and had to justify and support everything she thought.

It was truly one of the greatest experiences and greatest office environments to be a part of during a critical time in my own development. To her, I'll forever be grateful for the time, effort, and energy she put into helping me (and still does). She was and is the true definition of servant leadership.

The thing she did for us as athletes were numerable. The things she did for us as people innumerable. She's someone who's been invited to quite a few weddings and other important events by many athletes she's worked with. She's someone who always gets a holiday card and that kind of acknowledgement from me because of the value and the impact she's had in my life.

I am honored to consider her a friend just as much a mentor.

SIDE NOTE—While I'm happy to report this is rapidly becoming a normal occurrence in the field of S&C, at that time during my career, it was a noteworthy phenomenon. I was trained by and worked for women. My collegiate S&C coach, who was also my primary mentor, and the first boss I had in a full-time S&C job were both females.

Switching gears to some of the other staff, one of the assistants was probably one of the most creative, imaginative, and wild thinkers I've ever dealt with. Talk about seeing the world in a whole different way; he is the epitome of a mad scientist.

I remember going in and learning about how he was looking at anthropometrics and lever systems, and calculating tonnages for guys relative to their unique biomechanics.

He was doing stuff with heart rate before doing stuff with heart rate was a thing in the college world.

He was so far ahead of the curve in his thoughts, theories, and training that every time I talked to him about a training program, to even understand what the hell he was talking about, was an entire semester or textbook of knowledge I had to learn after the fact.

It was always great to shoot the shit with him, see what he was doing and where he was coming from, and try to gain an understanding of his creative and imaginative process. It was this willingness to get creative while applying the science of training that helped me understand and value never getting locked into the structure of the textbook or research while designing training programs.

Far too often, coaches get lost in the textbooks, the research, or in the specifics of the methodology and lose the creative and imaginative parts of pushing physical performance beyond what it's currently capable of. They don't harness the concepts and mold them as needed to get the results they desire.

The other female on staff was also a phenomenal coach and an amazingly genuine human being (it was also rare at the time to have two full-time females on staff). As someone who was athletically gifted, she could walk the walk and talk the talk.

The most impressive thing, though, and what I learned the most from her was how she made connecting with everyone from coaches to athletes and everyone in between so easy. She was a calm, easy-going personality on the outside with an underlying hyper-competitive streak on the inside.

Her ability to connect, build relationships, and develop trust and buy-in was truly remarkable. It was so intuitive for her; it was like she wasn't even trying. It was cool to see. It helped open my eyes to understand how to attempt to navigate the politics and personalities with the coaches and athletes.

The football assistant who I only worked with in a limited capacity, because he was mainly on the football side and I was mainly the Olympic, showed me one of the more interesting facets of how someone can operate as a professional.

He was two separate, exclusive people and the two never did meet at work.

I never knew him as a person. I only knew him as a coach. And that dichotomy and how he operated was a cool learning experience for me to see how to detach and separate.

Not to say he was antisocial or wasn't willing to connect with anyone. He was a great guy who, when he had the time, would go out of his way to teach, educate, and push us to get better, and I learned a lot from him.

But the way he went about his process of being a coach and building connections was radically different than the others, so it was a good learning experience because it was so different than the others. It helped me understand the need to create boundaries between my professional and personal life and how to best manage the work-life balance that was often non-existent in our jobs.

I'd like to think that as a coach, I have certain elements of all five of these people. During a critical development period for my own professional career, it was probably a one in a million shot to have such highly successful, highly competent people all working together synergistically.

All of them are still in the field, each at the highest levels, and I am forever grateful to them for spending their time, effort, and energy helping me at UConn as well as after I left.

Becoming an S&C Coach

As I progressed, I was afforded the opportunity as a senior in college—through some hard work, perseverance, and good timing—to inherit the opportunity to train two teams. Yes, you read that right.

The graduate assistant (GA) at the time had recently left to pursue an opportunity in the NFL, and I was tasked with helping take over their team assignments.

It goes to show you the changes and the shifts in the landscape of how the industry works, because I obviously wasn't certified yet. I hadn't even earned my degree, and I was in charge of two varsity teams training at the University of Connecticut; I was a senior in college and still competing on the track and field team myself.

To say it was a cool opportunity is the understatement of the decade for anyone looking to be an S&C coach. It allowed me to step up and get experience. And I was fortunate that Coach Martin and his staff trusted me and allowed me to do it. It was a combination of luck, timing, and hard work or, as I will conceptualize later, "opportunity meeting desire."

At the end of my senior year, I had been accepted into graduate school to continue at UConn and get a master's degree under Dr. Kraemer.

UConn was still the top kinesiology program in the country, so to stay on working as an S&C Coach, add responsibilities to what I had already taken on previously, and continue to learn from the best in the business was a no-brainer.

It was a tremendous opportunity and rare experience. It afforded me the chance to get in the trenches and do everything I wanted to do at the time and learn all kinds of new and interesting things across the academic and real-world spectrums of human performance.

This is where I started to develop an appreciation and knowledge for the political landscape and the issues you had to deal with when working alongside people you may or may not get along with, for a variety of reasons. I had plenty of failures in this area as well as a few successes.

I was exposed and challenged as much as I rose to the occasion.

It was awesome.

As my time at UConn came to an end and I started to interview for jobs, I thought I was going to get a job quickly. I thought that I was going to go out there, put my applications out, and someone would just hire me —full-time assistant, good salary, benefits—the whole deal.

I thought I had done all the networking: I had called and emailed dozens, if not hundreds, of people, I went to the conferences, and I built a solid reputation in my circle.

I had responsibility at UConn far beyond most any GA, probably anywhere else in the country.

Yet the day I graduated, I had absolutely no idea what I was going to do next and did not have a single immediate opportunity. I didn't understand my place on the list—another concept I will put to words later on.

Interviewing to Be Full-Time

Within a couple months after graduating, I had numerous phone interviews and a half-dozen ones in person.

Some were courtesy phone interviews, simply because I had the right references, but the jobs were filled before the phone even rang. It was just an HR checkbox. Of the in-person interviews, there are two that really stick out, mainly because of how bad I did in them! A third one is a lesson that, to me, many in the profession need to learn: never take a job if it doesn't make sense.

The first interview was for an entry-level assistant position in Olympic sports at a Big Ten school, working for a director who had the exact assistant spot a few weeks earlier before the previous director resigned and they had been promoted.

I made a huge mistake—a mistake of inexperience on two fronts, technically.

First, I tried to tell the people I met with what I knew and how good I was as an S&C coach, and all I did was make myself look like I was trying to take my boss's job. I came off as an arrogant, cocky-ass clown.

Not a good look, especially when the role I was interviewing for was a low-level assistant, a cog in the wheel who was the accomplisher of the director's vision, not the person who set the vision.

I had tried to sell my vision and philosophy, instead of humbling myself to be a part of someone else's. A big no-no.

Secondly, while I heard what was said, I didn't listen to the situational factors of the department and the administration. I didn't see beneath the questions I was being asked to understand the dynamics at play.

I thought that everything was on the up and up, and I took everything everyone said at face value, letting it go in one ear and out the other before they even finished. I was already planning on where to live in my mind and not being in the moment enough to realize I should actually run from this job!

I was ignorant of the facts that I had done a terrible job interviewing and that the dynamics at the school itself were really bad. They were so bad that in the next five years the school would go through two athletic director's (AD's), dozens of sports coaches, administrators and support staff, and accrue multiple NCAA violations.

Needless to say, I didn't get the job, which was a blessing in disguise as the S&C staff got cleaned out twice in those five years as well and would have included me.

The second interview I went to was at a school where the person who was supposed to replace me at UConn was working at the time. He ended up doing such a good job at the school he was at that the administration let go of his boss and promoted him as the head S&C coach instead of letting him leave to become a GA to get his Master's degree.

Given it made no sense for him to come back to UConn as a GA and now needing an assistant, he called me and said, "Joe, I'd love to have you come to interview for this position." So off I went!

All was going well in the interview and I felt as if we had clicked. And I clicked with the administrator overseeing S&C as well. And towards the end of the interview, I sat down with the AD and had one of the more interesting conversations I've ever had at an interview.

She went on to say that she thought extremely highly of the person who was now the head S&C coach and as a former sports coach herself, she could tell how successful he was going to be. As we began to discuss more of the philosophical side of athletics and the progression of S&C in college as a whole, from her days as a sport coach to now, she let slip what I knew was the nail in the coffin for me.

Judging by her expression, she realized as soon as she said it as well, and we both knew at that moment I wasn't getting this job.

We were discussing different ways to train men versus women and how, in my opinion, I didn't treat female athletes any different than the men in terms of standards, accountability, or the underlying, fundamental parts of being an athlete.

Obviously, some things will differ between men and women—generally speaking from a physical development side—some of the X's and O's of what we will do in training, as most men have trained more than women and are familiar with resistance training, plyometrics, etc.

We went into the social-cultural norms and stigmas that are unfortunately put on women who, while no less capable than men, often start at a lower point physically by the time they get to college and how often they have additional mental barriers to overcome as it relates to lifting.

She then went into how there was a need for more females in S&C. She talked about how women often look at the weight room with a negative connotation because it's generally men who coach them and the men in the weight room are perceived as unintelligent meatheads, screaming, cursing, and making women lift heavyweights.

She expressed to me how she would like to see more strong, confident females in S&C and was keen to hire such individuals.

Right there was the nail in the coffin for me, the average, nothing-special guy being interviewed.

After a few weeks of radio silence, I get a call back from the guy and said, "Hey, Joe, we went in a different direction. It is what it is. Thanks, see you around."

A few days later, I saw that the person they hired was a female. The argument could have been made that she was less qualified than me but a few years pass and she is the head S&C coach at the school, she does an amazing job, and she is respected by her athletes and peers.

So, while I was a good fit on some levels, there was a bigger piece of the puzzle moving at that school, and I just wasn't the right person for the job, regardless of qualifications or how good I had done interviewing.

Looking back on it, the conversation with the AD makes a lot of sense, but at that moment, it was a tough pill to swallow.

Sure, I wanted a job, but the reason I bring this up is because at no point in time did I bash, denigrate, or talk shit about this particular coach or the school. Although I was upset and felt I could have done an equally good job, I simply wasn't the right person for it.

There was no reason to dwell on the fact that the AD had a plan in mind and I was not part of it. I knew that if I had expressed my emotional response outwardly to others, I would have probably shot myself in the foot and ruined a lot of relationships and future possibilities. This, as you will see, is the perfect example of when opportunity does not match desire.

So, there I was, June has passed and I was at home living with my parents with no job, savings starting to dwindle, and student loans on the horizon—and boom—a job opportunity come up.

I drive down and have a great time.

A couple days later, I get a phone call and am offered the job.

Hurray! I'm all good, right? A decent salary of $45,000 with benefits and all that stuff.

The only issue was it was in a major metropolitan area where the cost of living was insane.

I would have had to sell my car and rely solely on public transportation to get around (Uber didn't exist at that point), and I would have had to pay over 50% of my monthly salary just on rent to have somewhere to live reasonably close by work.

So, while I would have had a job, I would also have put myself in a precarious situation personally and financially.

While it was humbling and great to be offered a job, especially after not doing well at some interviews, when I made the pros and cons list for the role, it wasn't a great opportunity.

Now some of you might say, "Suck it up, deal with it, earn your stripes." And part of me felt that way too.

But looking at it objectively—working with 8–10 Olympic sports teams 12–15 hours a day, having to navigate through a major city to multiple facilities, having limited resources to further myself outside of just coaching every day, and spending all my money to just sustain and not grow—made it a terrible job opportunity.

There were limited resources for professional development; there was limited opportunity for tuition remission or any other kind of career advancement outside of coaching.

I would barely be able to pay my bills and would've lived month to month on the redline, where every month I stayed I would be getting closer and closer to creating a catastrophic personal and financial situation. And obviously, that would have blended into my work that in turn would have affected my work performance.

Seeing that, I turned the job down.

Thanks, but no thanks, and people thought I was crazy!

There I was months after graduating school with loans coming in, no money in the bank, living at home, and offered a job for pretty good money in the scheme of things. My mother was upset with me, my father understood but was still hesitant because he saw the impending bills coming, but I knew it wasn't the right thing to do.

It was a bad precedent to set—that the value I brought to the table was going to be abused in that fashion. Now, that might be a harsh thing to say and let me say the head S&C coach and the assistant are both still at that school and are people I am on friendly terms with and have a lot of respect for. They are good at what they do and would have no doubt done their best to help me, but the job was a dead-end, and I believe since I turned it down, there have been three to four people in that role in ten years.

There are times when you're going to have to make sacrifices, and there are times when you're going to have to take one on the chin, but those should be strategic and purposeful plays you make for a specific reason. But that should not normally be how you navigate your career path.

I did not feel that the opportunity provided enough value for me professionally and personally. A lot of people aren't going to like that, but that's their opinion. I chose not to put myself in an unbalanced situation.

A few more weeks go by, and then I get a call from Andrea Hudy at the University of Kansas (KU).

Becoming a Jayhawk

"Hey, Joe, we have a job working with track and field and golf," was how she opened the call. "You interested?"

It was a call that took all of five minutes and then a few days later I was on a flight out to Lawrence, Kansas for an on-campus interview.

Having been through the wringer the last few months, I felt the most prepared as well as the most relaxed at this interview. I had learned much from my previous experiences and said to myself that if I checked my ego and expected nothing beyond the moment I was in, I would be in the best position possible to succeed.

As I sat in the airport waiting for my flight back home, I reviewed the day in my head: I felt solid with Coach Hudy and her staff, I thought I handled my own with the administrators and did well coaching a baseball session, and I gained insight into some of the underlying dynamics with the sport coaches—some of whom I thought I had good conversations with —others I wasn't so sure.

As the process at KU was unfolding (and I would learn later just how significant those underlying dynamics where), I also started looking at private training facilities in my area. Although I wanted to be a collegiate S&C coach, I was also getting to the point where I needed to start making money to pay bills and get my life going. So, I put my name in the hat for everything from a private facility to the Globo Gym in town.

I figured I'd taken a long enough break from coaching and any longer would have started to reflect poorly as a giant gap in my résumé. I wanted to get into the workforce in some capacity and start to have something that I could continue to build experience and credibility with while being able to pay bills.

The private training facility I had reached out to was owned by someone who I used to work out with, when he first opened the facility while I was in high school. About a week or so later, he offered me the director of S&C job at his facility.

I would oversee a staff of five, I would make a pretty good salary with bonuses, and I would have a lot of autonomy in developing the program based around the vision he had for the business as a whole.

Now my heart was set on being a college S&C coach, but it was a damn good opportunity along with working for a guy I believed in. I told him I would get back to him in a week about it.

I let Coach Hudy know I needed to know if KU was a reality or not, and a few short days later I got an offer from Kansas that I accepted.

Turning down the role at the private facility was tough. It's a private facility that still exists and is one I often recommend to anyone who lives in the area to go train at. The owner and his staff do a phenomenal job and have an awesome thing going just north of Boston.

I signed the paperwork on Tuesday, I emailed it back, and on Thursday, October 6, 2011, at 6:00 a.m. I flew out of Boston to Kansas City to start work.

I flew in, got picked up, drove to Lawrence, did my HR paperwork, and then coached my first group that afternoon around 2:30 p.m.

I slept on a co-worker's couch for two weeks and lived out of one bag of clothes, until I found a place and had the rest of my stuff shipped out. It was a do-whatever-it-takes-to-succeed, failure-is-not-an-option moment for me, and it was awesome.

My wife, at the time my girlfriend, had just started physician-assistant (PA) school in New Jersey, so she was going to be there for the three years. While it was tough to leave everything and everyone behind, I had to chase my dream. At that moment, I wanted that opportunity more than anything else in the world, and I seized it with two hands and never looked back.

My time at KU was eye-opening. I started to understand there was a big difference between the name that Kansas represented and the success and history it had, versus what was happening in some of the individual sports.

I found out in the following week or so that there were some interesting dynamics going on among the administration, the S&C staff and the sport coaches. Without going into too much detail, I'll say that during my time at Kansas, I learned more than I ever thought I was going to: what to do, what not to do, how to play the political game and how to fail miserably at it.

I had a significant share of failures in that job, and looking back at it now with what I know now—having learned from those experiences and others—I would approach many of the same situations differently.

I would be much more measured, much more tepid, and much more open for a bipartisan solution versus the "it's our way or the highway approach" we took at times. I guess that's what learning is, right? You go back, you reflect, you internalize, you learn, and you get better to not make the same mistakes again.

In addition to my failures, I also had some tremendous success in Kansas. I was fortunate enough to play a small part in helping an athlete win an Olympic gold medal in the 2012 games. I was fortunate enough to play a small part in helping numerous athletes set school records, personal bests, and all-time Kansas bests and help the university win their first national championship outside of basketball in the last thirty or forty years. I was even a finalist for the NSCA assistant S&C coach of the year in 2014. I didn't win but to be in the conversation was very cool.

I was able to play a part in building numerous programs from the bottom of the barrel to once again be competitive at the conference and national level, some of which was a by-product of new head sport coaches, in conjunction with building relationships, and being allowed to maximize my role due to that relationship building.

I worked with some tremendous sport coaches, some of whom I still talk to this day and some of whom I was fortunate enough to learn a great deal from and gain insights into how they became successful coaches.

In terms of the S&C department, we were a meld of different people, personalities, and ideas, and it allowed for a dynamic that made one of the best staffs I've ever been a part of.

Coach Hudy did a tremendous job picking the right people for the right roles, although I'm sure if she reads this, she will get a good chuckle. I was definitely a pain in the ass to her for a good chunk of my time, with everything I had to deal with and she then had to deal with, outside of the coaching of the athletes.

I look back on the opportunity she gave me and I know that I'll never be able to repay her for what it did for me in my personal and professional development and by simply giving me the chance.

Every day I walked into my office my colleagues challenged me to get better, challenged me to be more knowledgeable, and challenged me to be the best at my craft. All I can hope is that I was able to do the same for them.

I learned more in my three years at Kansas from the people I was around and the experiences, conversations, and material we created than I had in all six years at UConn.

That's no knock-on UConn, it's just a testament to how there are levels to development. And while I had the ability to get so far ahead compared to most others during my time at UConn, my time at Kansas was at a whole other level.

Finding My Place

Towards the middle part of my time working at Kansas, I took my USA weightlifting (USAW) certification and met a guy who was a former collegiate S&C coach turned CrossFit coach. He had left the college side, got into the private setting, and moved into CrossFit as it was starting to takeoff. He was a nice guy and had a lot of knowledge and experience. In those couple of days doing our USAW certification, I spent quite a bit of time talking to him.

In our conversations, he made two comments that stood out to me. The first was that collegiate S&C on the Olympic side was often glorified babysitting because you were generally not allowed to do the best programming or what was actually best for the athletes. This was due to being in such a large group with limited resources, equipment, space, time, and having to bend to the will of sport coaches who often had no idea how to train effectively. He made multiple valid points and cited personal examples of how, in his role in the private setting, he had more control, stronger opportunity to truly help, and got paid significantly better.

The second thing he said was to make sure that you knew what your values were versus the values of the job.

As we discussed things, he made it clear that the value of doing the job was both from a financial standpoint and a personal standpoint relative to your own personal values.

Sure, money mattered but one of the things he couldn't reconcile was spending so much time trying to do a good job and then on a whim getting the floor pulled out from him by different people: a sports coach whose practice changed, an uneducated athletic trainer, and an immature athlete. So, the value of what he was doing didn't line up with his values because he knew that he wanted to spend more time building his athletes holistically at a deep level and put more into them than a surface-level of "training" that he was doing.

He continued to say that his values didn't align from a personal standpoint because he was spending so much time at work that he was missing out on his personal life.

He was already in his mid-thirties, never had a serious girlfriend, but wanted to be married and have children. He knew that if he stayed in college S&C, he would never be able to put the time, effort, and energy into that part of his life, and he felt that the window was closing.

He wanted to do what he loved; but he didn't want to do only what he loved.

Flash-forward to what would be the end of my time at Kansas and I had gotten engaged. My future wife was just about done with PA school, and we were looking toward the future. I had a good job at Kansas, and while I had some headaches and caused a few as well, it had some pretty good upside. And most importantly, I was able to do the thing I wanted to do professionally—coach and train athletes.

However, I was also getting to the point where some of the sacrifices of working at that level and some of the things you deal with at that level weren't aligned with my personal values. Thus, the choice was made to find a way back to the East Coast to be closer to family and start a new chapter, with a focus on my role as a husband just as much as my role as a coach.

I started to look at opportunities in the summer of 2013, and I was offered an opportunity to go back to a smaller school in Connecticut to be the school's first director of S&C. In the process of negotiations, having learned significantly more about the politics and the dynamics within the collegiate system, there were too many red flags to take the opportunity, and I turned it down.

I later learned that I was the first of multiple people to turn the job down for similar concerns, and it wasn't until the school committed to addressing those concerns that they hired a competent, capable, and high-quality S&C coach.

Flash-forward to the week of Christmas and I am sitting in New Jersey with my soon to be wife. We discuss our plan moving into 2014: how when she graduates in May, she will need a few months in order to get licensed to get a job; how I will leave Kansas in the late summer to maximize cash flow, regardless if I have a new job or not; and how we will start our lives together somewhere on the East Coast.

While my wife was extremely supportive and understanding of the challenges in working in the athletics field, given her background as a collegiate athlete, she didn't want to move every 2–3 years for the next twenty. She was willing to hop on and off the train at a few stops but not forever —and nor was I the more I thought about it.

There was a recently posted opportunity at Hofstra University in Long Island and, low and behold, the athletic director and the deputy athletic director were the same two people that were in those roles when I was at UConn. The deputy was a person who I had spent a good amount of time with in the later part of my time at UConn and I had even gone to his house once to help him cut down trees and clear land.

I sent out a few feelers and did the usual rattling of the bee's nest across my network, as is customary when you're looking to make a career move. And on the morning of Christmas Eve, 2013, I sat down and wrote a cover letter, adjusted my résumé a bit, and sent it out to Hofstra in order to put my name in the ring for the director of S&C role.

Director of Pride

After a few weeks of not hearing anything, I thought that the opportunity had gone past me. But as I was boarding a flight back from the Titliest Performance Institute (TPI) certification I had just done, I received a phone call from the deputy athletic director at Hofstra and he said, "Hey, Joe, I got your résumé. I'm interested in talking with you about the job."

He went on with some of the details and asked me point blank, "Is this something you want to do? Are you sure you want to leave major Division I to come to a small Division I school, take a pay cut, and not have football?"

I couldn't say yes fast enough.

The search to that point had been focused on more veteran professionals who Hofstra either couldn't afford or simply just didn't want the job. I believe I was the fifth or sixth candidate seriously interviewed for the job.

February came and I went on the interview. I thought I did well and that I would have a chance. A couple weeks after that in March, the deal was done and I was off to Long Island from Lawrence. I had seven days to leave KU, get to Hofstra, find a place to live, and start a new job as a director.

Most people thought I was crazy leaving a high-powered major Division I, especially with the success we previously had, for a small Division I (more Division III) school, especially for an area where the cost of living was almost triple compared to Kansas.

What they didn't know was that I was leaving KU in June regardless and this move helped me get back to the East Coast slightly sooner than intended, while still being within the career sphere I wanted to work in.

My wife graduated in May, and in August, we got married. Taking the Hofstra job brought me closer to home and allowed my wife to stay close to home and work in a geographical area where opportunities in the PA field were astronomically numerous. For her, it wasn't a question of if she could get a job—it was a question of what job she wanted (ah, the beauty of working in medicine).

Taking this job not only allowed me to work at a school where I could be for 5–8 years, but also seize two key opportunities beyond the job as an S&C coach.

First, being an adjunct instructor and teaching at the undergraduate and graduate level and secondly, having amazing tuition remission. I could start taking classes immediately and take up to twenty-four credits a year for free.

While Kansas paid me more in terms of dollars in a paycheck, Hofstra paid me more in terms of opening doors outside of athletics. That, for me, was critical because I knew my time in athletics wasn't going to last forever. I always viewed being an S&C Coach as something I did, not something that defined who I am. I went into the industry knowing I had a shelf life.

When I looked at the total package of the Hofstra job simply from the trench level—the quality of athlete, resources, and the salary as an S&C coach—it was a massive step backward.

From the vantage point of a higher perspective, however, I won in four major categories.

First, I was able to enhance the salary from teaching. It was also a nice résumé-booster and door-opener.

Second, I could quickly and at little to no cost out of pocket start an MBA—a savings of over $50,000 per year (Hofstra is not cheap).

Third, I was able to live in a geographical area that was close to where I wanted to be with family and friends a drive and not a flight away.

And finally, it allowed my wife ample opportunity to build her own career, while not—for the foreseeable future—having to chase me around the country for mine and constantly having to start over.

SIDE NOTE—Hofstra's benefits package, much like Kansas, was also absolutely phenomenal with retirement benefits to health insurance and everything in between. We were newly married and wanted to start a family and benefits like that took a ton of stress off the table. When we had our daughter, because of all the incentives and benefits from the insurance plan, we literally paid nothing out of pocket.

Let this be a lesson to you: salary is not the only way to define a job's compensation. Look at what you get in the big picture and how much you have to spend on things as life happens.

Now, looking back at my time at Hofstra again, with the multitude of factors I knew and the multitude of factors I didn't know—if I knew then what I knew now, would I do some things differently? Obviously.

Would I do some things the same? Absolutely.

Do I think I succeeded more times than I failed? Yes.

Did I fail? Yes, every day and in every way.

I went to work and every day I tried to do the best thing I could for the athletes. Not for the administrators, not for the coaches, and not for myself —but for the athletes I had in front of me and those that would be coming in the future.

Sure, I did have to do things that acutely impacted the experience of the athletes that I had in front of me, but it was to set a precedent beyond the moment for those that were to come. That foresight and having to take action on it weighed heavily on my conscious every time I did so.

Two Lasting Lessons

I came away from my time "sitting in the chair" with two distinct yet equally important lessons.

When you strip away every trapping of excess, all the bells and whistles that have become the norm in the college athletics arms race, and limit yourself to the minimum, can you still get the job done to a high standard?

Can you only be successful with the "extras" or can you get the job done with the bare essentials? Does adding in the "extras" make a difference or does it make a perception of a difference?

As I stripped away all of the excesses, some by choice and some by necessity due to lack of resources, and worked within the fundamentals only, I found myself more capable and actionable in my foundational philosophies of training and coaching.

I was able to more firmly set forth and create action without hesitation because I truly knew what I brought to the table. My programming was simpler, cleaner in a sense, yet so purposeful for the context of the situation. Although, the programs themselves will never be useful to anyone else as the moment of their usefulness has passed.

The second lesson was it's not worth surrounding yourself with negative and complacent people every day.

Don't get me wrong, we are all going to have to deal with difficult people—that's part of life. Anytime there's more than one person involved, there's going to be an issue at some point. However, on an everyday basis, if you surround yourself with people who are inflexible, unwilling to grow (or worse yet are not aware they need to), and do not operate with a growth mindset, you yourself are going to stagnate.

I felt that stagnation to the point where I asked my boss, that while it was my job to lead and develop my staff, where I got to look to in order to grow and develop myself?

He genuinely replied that he was neglectful in helping me due to being overwhelmed himself with work and it was probably best I sought outgrowth on my own time outside of work.

That was probably the most lucid and honest conversation the two of us ever had in my opinion.

My own stagnation, while slowly creeping in, was slowed due in large part to the tremendous staff I worked with. I had two equally different but equally competent staff members, who I still to this day text or talk to numerous times per month. I even officiated a wedding for one of them (yes, I am technically an ordained minister . . . seriously).

But even with great internal dynamics of our staff, a combination of factors across the entire department and the school as a whole slowly became disenfranchising and wore away at me, taking a toll on my ability to coach as effectively as I could.

It was at that point I realized change was needed and the change was not going to be the growth of the program, the athletic department, and the individuals in it. The change was going to be me stepping away because I no longer had a passion for being an S&C coach and it was unfair to the people I worked with, to the athletes I trained, to my family, and to myself to continue working there. My expiration date had come and it was time for me to go.

Around January 2017, my wife and I put together a plan to move to Connecticut to be even closer to family and help realign our lives to be more on our own terms. Shortly after the end of the spring semester in 2017, I walked into my boss's office and submitted my resignation. I walked out and never looked back.

SIDE NOTE—I'm extremely happy to say that Hofstra, from an S&C standpoint, was taken over by the right person, who truly should have been the person to have the job originally instead of myself. I would be willing to make a safe bet, that for the rest of his professional career at Hofstra, he will lead that program to a level it never before thought possible given its resources and natural limitations of being a small fish in a big pond. Keep up the good stuff Hames, and always put hot-sauce on a quagmire. (The H is on purpose).

Moving Beyond S&C

One of the things I ran into early in my career was achieving a level of success and growth that put me on a path where the only continued professional outcomes I would have would be cyclic.

I was fortunate to work with amazing athletes, be a small piece of their success, and help drive the training of all-Americans, national champions, and even an Olympic gold medalist.

While I certainly was going to have a personal impact on the individuals I worked with, the main outcome I was being judged by from my employer's perspective had nothing to do with that part of the job.

And the collegiate athletic system, especially at the highest levels of revenue-producing sport, does not value that part of the job. If it did, many coaches who had losing records but graduated their kids into the world, developed children into adults, and provided true personal growth opportunities would still have jobs. But it doesn't and coaches get fired.

Since we keep score and there is a lot of money involved, all that truly matters is winning and the dollars that come with it.

If that is something that offends you, don't fill out your bracket in March and try not to watch one of the dozens of pointless bowl games that are simply dollar generators for a select few to pad their pockets with.

Everything I would ever attain and designated "successful" in that system would just be repeating the same outcomes I'd already accomplished.

If you're willing to go into that cyclical success model, what else could you develop and earn as a collegiate S&C coach? National championships and Olympic gold medalists pretty much top out the level of maximizing your trophy case.

Everything after that is an A/B test where you're repeating the same three to four-year cycle over and over again with small refinements in your approach relative to who you have to work with and the sport coaches and support staff you deal with.

I recognized this early on. And instead of falling into that cyclic approach, where after two or three cycles of either having my head in the sand for so long I left more doors closed than opened—or worse, creating massive burnout and mental fatigue, which happens to far too many S&C coaches at all levels—I tried to step outside of those pitfalls and do something different.

That's where I pursued a path that would put me on a new course that wasn't cyclic.

I leveraged the skillset and knowledge I learned and developed a plan to open as many doors as possible and not become defined by just being an S&C Coach. I earned my MBA with a focus in management as well as additional certifications in human resources and other non-athletic related disciplines.

I tried to do other things to build and develop myself, translating what I knew from one industry to help me in others. As I moved forward, I knew that I needed to diversify my skillset outside of that cyclical journey, so when I chose my line of tangent, I had options.

Much like someone transitioning from the military or transitioning into anything different from what they've invested so much time, effort, and energy into, I wanted to have secondary and tertiary skills to fall back on, to know how to transfer those skills that I had, and to value them appropriately in other industries and sectors.

I had most of what I needed already. What I found was that I needed to learn the language of those other industries, learn to reapply skills in a new way, and learn to leverage my experiences to continue to open more doors for myself.

It saddens me to see individuals who've invested so much time, effort, and energy in the S&C profession to be lost towards the later stages of their career when they should be in stronger positions.

There are few—but thankfully more with each passing year—S&C coaches who over the time in their career have pushed outside of the weight room and into administrative or advanced leadership roles not directly related to the training of athletes.

Many coaches, both young and old, have to step outside of the cycle by getting outside of the weight room and getting away from standing at every practice. They are wasting time throughout the day pretending to be busy and fooling themselves into thinking they are on "the grind" and that it makes them better. They perceive themselves to be "doing things" but in reality they are wasting their own time.

The "grind," when you get to a certain point, is a waste.

Yes, you need to put in the time, effort, and energy to become competent and capable. It's no different than anything else. But just like everything else, there is a point in which "the grind" is no longer needed. And if you stay in it too long, you will get lost in it.

You will wake up one day and wonder where life went, feeling guilt and shame for what you missed out on.

The "true grind" you need isn't one of solely effort; it is one that forces you out of your comfort zone—to continue to develop yourself as a practitioner and professional in other avenues and constantly open doors professionally and personally for yourself—regardless if you choose to walk through them or not.

The "true grind" also has a *huge*—and I cannot overstate this enough—a *huge* emphasis on taking time and setting boundaries for you to have a personal life—to be involved with your family, community, religion or whatever you the person, not you the coach, uses to help define your own self. Because that's the thing, you need to define your own self. Failure to do this can literally be catastrophic to you down the road.

I was on the phone with a high-level S&C basketball coach and he had just gotten back from a two-week family vacation, the first one he had taken with his family in a handful of years.

At one point in the conversation he mentioned that during this two-week vacation the head coach had called him and said a recruit was coming in and he wanted them to meet. He had to tell the coach he wasn't coming back to meet with the recruit and interrupt his vacation. And he knew he was going to catch shit for not being around, even though he had told everyone months in advance of his plans.

As we talked further, he expressed how when he was younger he most likely would have flown back for a day or two and sacrificed the time with his family. But with his experience and given he never really got a break from working with the athletes like the coaches do during the off-season, he was going to take his time, enjoy his vacation, and set that boundary for everyone else to accept. They could either accept it or fire him. He wasn't going to budge. He said he slept better that night than he had in years, knowing he finally had drawn a line in the sand, for himself.

The Pull

I had spent the first part of my career in the trenches of the collegiate sports world: researching, coaching, teaching, developing others, and building champions. I knew that while I was done in that specific sector, I still had a passion for teaching and developing others.

I could feel the pull—that's the best way I can describe it—telling me that I needed to help others achieve what they have always been capable of but had yet to achieve.

After a decade as an S&C coach, I recognized that my best contribution was applying the knowledge and experiences that I had into the development of other professionals and providing them the scaffolding to build their own confidence to then go on their own path and one day lead others to find theirs.

From seeing individuals in the trenches of whatever sector of industry they worked and wanting to maximize the leadership skills of the executives in charge of those individuals, I started to feel my passion for being a coach being replaced with a passion for helping align and achieve strategic goals and objectives on the hilltop and in the clouds among the decision makers.

I started to first feel the pull when I was in Kansas.

There was one specific instance when a high-level executive had flown in to work with us that forever changed the course of my path. He came to us looking to get help with the simplest problem in the world—he wanted to dunk again.

He recently turned forty years old, and in addition to staying in shape, he wanted to be able to dunk a basketball again. It was something he had always been able to do in his youth but had slowly been losing the ability to do, given the high-stress, sedentary lifestyle associated with the kind of work he was doing.

It was during lunch between training sessions that we started talking about life and family. As we exchanged our stories about his wife and children and my fiancé and our goals to have children, he said something to me that I'll never forget. He looked me dead in the eyes and said, "Joe, one day, someone is going to pay you a lot of money to work for them because you're good at what you do. I can see how you've translated what you do as a coach into the business side of things. The question you're going to have to ask yourself is, what are you doing to be able to seize the opportunities that may arise?"

It was this pull that I continued to feel through my time at Hofstra as well. I was fortunate enough to be asked to provide insight and guidance to numerous individuals, organizations, and teams both in the athletic world and outside of it as a consultant. Some of that was simply a matter of being in the New York metropolitan area, where there are so many people and so many opportunities, while some were being referred by those I had previously helped when they had a need for someone like me.

I became known as the person who was often asked to lead team-building and culture shifts, deal with the most difficult people (which I barely survived myself at times), and create processes to achieve specific outcomes

While I wasn't always successful and certainly not perfect, I took the same effort and strategic skillset I used in solving the puzzle of developing people into athletes and put it into helping achieve the big-picture goals and aspirations of whatever team or organizational leaders I was dealing with.

Giving Myself Time to Fail

I was able to take on this new challenge and parlay it into numerous opportunities because I was, and still am, constantly challenging myself with projects of all sizes—totally outside the boundaries of what I know.

While desire is easy to have—opportunity, as discussed, is not—so I seized every opportunity I could when I was able to.

To best capture the concept, take Richard Branson's words to heart:

> "If somebody offers you an amazing opportunity, but you are not sure you can do it, say yes—then learn how to do it later!"

You will never be "ready" for the next step, but you can prepare yourself the best you can and take the leap. Not to put too many inspirational/cliché quotes in a single paragraph, but becoming comfortable in being uncomfortable is a requirement if you are trying to do more than you currently do.

It is by this deliberate and purposeful effort of "doing" that I have been forced to learn new skills, apply the skills I had in a new way, and most importantly build my skills in failure and in winning.

It also gave me a great break from the monotonous grind of having such a singular, all-consuming focus. Joe Rogan often talks about this when he speaks about comedians who start having airport jokes in their routines. Because they travel around the country performing standup, their worldview becomes limited to their experiences of traveling around the country in airports doing comedy shows. He started to notice that comedians that fell down the path of talking about people in airports were beginning to crash and burn in their careers and generally never recovered to their previous level of success. It's the same thing for S&C coaches who never get outside of the weight room; their world view shrinks to practice times and counting reps.

I started day-trading on a whim. I always wanted to understand that area of the financial world so I dove in.

Five hundred dollars, downloading the Robin Hood app (I highly recommend that platform), some classroom knowledge, a few recommended books, and a couple of YouTube videos was all it took to have my own small portfolio.

I would day-trade during my free time from my phone, instead of wasting time on social media or playing mindless games to pass small bits of time. I would be looking at analyst reports and the news to understand the climate of the market. Eventually, I went further down the rabbit hole: I started playing with options and even shorted a few times as a way to play the long game and add complexity to the entry-level knowledge I had.

While I never earned a million dollars, I was forced to learn a new skill set—applying what I already knew and was learning in my MBA classes—to do the best I could. And with a few well-timed moves, I earned my beer money for over a year. Money, I am happy to say, that was spent on some of the finest craft beers in the USA.

Intensity and dedication are easy to transfer when you have the ability to output a lot of effort. But they're useless if you don't know how to refine all of the other knowledge and experience you have into managing time, processes, and people into driving efficiency.

As you approach your new journey, you need to give yourself time to fail in order to succeed.

Much like the intern effect, where you learn by doing and failing and "drinking from the firehose," you have to allow yourself the opportunity to be unsuccessful.

Failure is the greatest learning process for success. Just like winning is an acquired skill, failing is also one. And once you learn to harness failure as a skill for your own development and forward progress, you have the opportunity to learn the skill of winning.

When I started to recognize that I was slowly shifting away from being just an S&C coach, I started to apply to jobs and seek out opportunities that I often wasn't qualified for.

While I took numerous interviews in all sorts of fields and positional levels, putting my best foot forward and legitimately trying to be hired, I didn't get—nor did I truly expect to get—any of the jobs.

The reason I put myself in those situations was to learn how to interview in a different way, to learn how to communicate in a different way, to learn how to tell my story in a different way, and get the experience I needed to best direct myself as I moved forward. Failing over and over gave me the insight I needed on where I needed to improve, what I needed to learn—and most importantly—train my mind to be okay with just getting my ass handed to me along the way.

Every industry has its own language.

Now, that may sound funny, but it's not that it's a different language in terms of English to Chinese or Chinese to English. It's a different language in the sense of how people operate their industry-specific variables—in the context of words they choose or don't choose to use. When you talk return on investment (ROI) to a business person or a sports coach, you are essentially discussing the same thing. How will what you do create a positive return afterward?

But in sports, that's wins.

In business, that's dollars.

My Exit Letter

I love the collegiate S&C sector, and I'm grateful for what it allowed me to do and experience. There will be people I'll never be able to thank and repay for the opportunity and the professional development they gave me.

I was able to travel, have amazing experiences, and meet all kinds of amazing people. I learned from, grew with, impacted, and was impacted by the people I was around. My journey was also financially positive (something I consider abnormal compared to most of my contemporaries) because it allowed me to have a nice quality of life, be able to pay my bills, buy a ring for my wife, get a dog (a really big dog), have the roof of my choosing over my head, and support my first child.

This is the letter I wrote and put out publicly shortly after I resigned from my position at Hofstra. I did it to create a tangible artifact to close the door on one chapter of my life and acknowledge in a real way the things I just spoke of above.

> *As one journey ends and another begins, it took me quite a while to start writing this because I both had to settle my thoughts down into some kind of coherent form as well as work through the process and transition I was going through in my life: leaving one career path for another, moving and buying a house, etc.*
>
> *Most of you now know I have chosen to walk away from collegiate athletics and the field of S&C and pursue other professional opportunities. While this course of action didn't come quickly—as I have a true passion for coaching, teaching and mentoring others—it did come easily as it was in the best interest of my family and our combined future on many fronts.*
>
> *My family and I were fortunate enough to move back to Connecticut, buy a house, and be geographically in the place we wanted to be moving forward. My wife*

has a great job, my daughter has her grandparents, aunts/uncles and cousins close by, and we all have a much deeper network of friends and extended family that we wouldn't have had if we had not made this move. It was a slam dunk (pun intended) for our family and something we couldn't pass up.

Over the past few weeks, I have received numerous calls, texts, and emails from former athletes, colleagues, and coaches with kind words of support and appreciation for my efforts when we worked together. While I am extremely grateful and honored by those words, it is I who am the one who must thank all of you.

The purpose of writing this was to try to express and create tangibility with words how grateful and humbled I am to have had the opportunity to work with and have a positive impact on so many people throughout my time in S&C and athletics. Being an S&C coach was truly a remarkable time in my life—one that provided me with innumerable opportunities professionally and personally. And to hear that for many of you I had a positive impact beyond sport is worth more than any game or championship ring we won.

To have had the opportunity to be the person that others were willing to put their faith in, listen to and trust to help achieve their goals was a profound responsibility and one that I took great pride in doing to the best of my ability. Although the "Coach Joe" moniker will fade as time goes on, playing a part in helping others grow and develop—not just physically, but as a whole person—during a critical period of their lives is something I will always cherish.

As I look now to the future, I may never again work in collegiate athletics or S&C again, but I do know that coaching and developing people, helping them build confidence to aspire to achieve things previously thought unattainable, and watching as their set goals are achieved will always somehow be a part of my work.

Thank you for allowing me to be a part of each of your individual stories as you all are a part of mine. Don't ever forget: be a savage, remember it's not rocket science, and most importantly—enjoy the process.

PART II

HAVING A SOLID FOUNDATION TO BUILD ON

. . . keep silent, for the most part, for there is great danger that you will immediately vomit up what you have not yet digested.

—Epictetus

4

BUILDING A PHILOSOPHY

Having been in competitive athletics all my life and all of my professional life, I have had the opportunity to be coached by, work with, and learn from a significant number of coaches from a variety of disciplines within athletics. As would be expected, I've had both positive and negative experiences with these coaches.

Fortunately for me, I've been lucky enough to have had more positive experiences than negative ones.

Even more fortunate for me, I've been able to have experiences with some truly great coaches. Great in the sense that they were able to translate their craft in the exact way the athlete needed, help the athlete mature as a person outside of sport, and have consistent, repeatable results with anyone they worked with—regardless of what the goal was (athletically or in personal development).

These coaches never have an off year or a year when they think, *I just don't have the athletes this go around*. Goals that were set were always achieved time and time again, although the approach may have changed to accomplish them.

I looked back on these experiences and tried to understand how the great coaches I had been around—all from significantly different backgrounds and having widely varying expertise and education—were able to achieve consistent and measurable results. I came to the conclusion that the fundamental makeup that allows a coach to transcend from average to good and good to great is their ability to meld together their personal, training, and coaching philosophies and honestly reflect on how those three philosophies interact and affect them as they work with their athletes.

By continually developing themselves personally and professionally, while giving time for meaningful internal and external reflection about their ability to better their athletes and impact who their athletes are as a person, great coaches are always able to better those they work with.

Take the time to build a solid foundation and make sure you do regular maintenance on it because if you don't, you won't be helping those you coach as well as you can.

This is a tough and difficult process for many to undertake on their own because you need to be—and receptive to be—constantly challenged externally and reflective internally to develop your own philosophies.

You need to have established philosophies even to begin this process; they need to be tested and exposed in difficult conversations and put into action consistently and without hesitation in the real world to make sure they are truly acting as a barometer for future decisions.

In the simplest terms, in order to get what you want, you have to have the vision.

In order to have a vision, you have to have a mission.

In order to have a mission, you have to have a clearly defined philosophy of yourself at all levels to find the mission that suits you.

Lack of purpose and alignment at the core foundational level will eventually be the downfall of whatever you put on top of it.

You Can't Build on a Sinkhole

One of my favorite concepts and analogies to use is, "You can't build a (fill-in-the-blank) on a sinkhole because, eventually, it will all fall into itself."

This may be obvious: any time you're trying to build a structure you have to have a solid foundation. No matter what you're doing or what you're trying to do, if the foundation is inappropriate to build on, whatever you're trying to build will eventually fail.

Additionally, when you start to build and develop a solid foundation, you have to have some plan and objective for what you're trying to do beyond the next step. You need to have the next four or five steps in mind in order to achieve the desired goal.

For example, if you have a solid foundation and build a first-floor wooden structure, and then on top of that wooden structure choose on a whim to try and put two or three more levels of bricks, the weight of those bricks will crush the structure.

Although you have a solid foundation, the concept of a solid foundation for just the base level is not enough. You also need to take into account having the appropriate structural balance and integrity for each further-developed floor. The foundation for a 100-foot skyscraper is a lot different than one for a Ranch-style home in a new suburban development, though the fundamental idea is the same.

Often, you'll see people who have muddy foundations with wooden structures supporting concrete or steel. This illustrates how it's inappropriate to layer further levels of development on underdeveloped foundations. In training, it is often the idea of putting a load on top of dysfunction as it relates to the musculoskeletal system.

All structures, all systems, and all aspects of life are like that—not just the body or muscles specifically.

It took me years of thought, learning, and reflection to truly appreciate that the deep guiding principles of optimizing the development of the human body were the same across all things in life as well.

It was at this point I truly began to understand the words of Mushasi:

"To know the way broadly is to see it in all things."

The Philosophy Development Cycle

The "philosophy development cycle" was something I created to help coaches and leaders I worked with further develop themselves; to lay a foundation for continuous, critical self-assessment, in order to stay true to themselves, and better develop their athletes and/or subordinates as they progress in their own career. It's a great way to start to build your different philosophies, show development, and cultivate confidence.

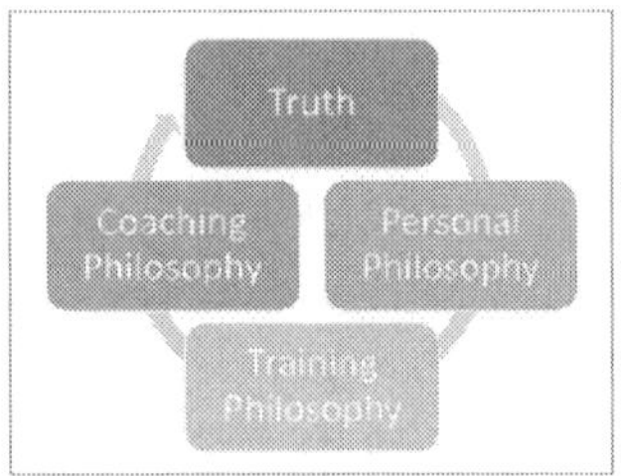

The cycle is initially broken into four parts, each building upon one another and forcing the next layer to adapt to changes of the previous one. This is the most basic visual of the cycle. Each philosophy will begin to develop deeper and more expanded parts relative to the role you are in and the demands placed upon you as a leader. Not everyone will lead or coach others, so you may not even have to truly break down and evolve those philosophies at anything beyond a surface level.

My personal and coaching philosophies, which we will dive into in the next section, have expanded to include approaches to leadership, teaching, coaching and mentoring with unique depths to each one. Those are the hats I've had to develop in order to have a solid foundation necessary to be successful in the roles I have taken on.

Please note that I work through this paradigm with the mind frame of being a coach in an athletic context. Clearly, this can be easily adapted and scaled to whatever role or profession you are working in.

For example, I have evolved a "customer-facing" philosophy for work that relates to managing customer relationships. I had to dive deeper into the standards and style I would use to accomplish tasks in sales, relationship building, and representing businesses as a consultant just the same as I have had to create a framework for working with business owners, CEOs, and other internal stakeholders. While it is beyond the purpose of this book to get in to it those facets, I will say this: it focuses on transformational relationship building and limiting purely the transactional focus that is easy to get lost in when you are providing a service or product to another person or entity.

Remember, "Concepts Over Content and Context Over the Construct."

The Personal Philosophy

The "personal philosophy," or the core ideological makeup of who the coach is as a person, is the first step in the cycle.

In this piece, the coach must answer questions such as, what do they personally value, why do they value those things, and how do those things impact their ability as a coach and to coach?

While simple questions, they are often the most overlooked, and in turn, can cause the greatest conflict with the other parts of the cycle.

Without first properly identifying who you are, you will never fully be able to help another person.

For many, such a deep introspective dive into their own personal motivations and innate and ingrained dogmas will be nearly impossible to do by themselves.

While well beyond the scope of this book, there are numerous places to look at this topic and begin this journey. From an athletics standpoint, it is my belief that Paul Chek has the best approach to this compared to a more traditional, academic and clinical self-improvement ideology like that of Jordan Peterson (whose views and opinions I do not agree with all of the time, but I recommend his self-authoring program and book *12 Rules for Life* as tremendous resources all the time).

The Training Philosophy

The "training philosophy," or the technical/tactical methodology that you use in order to create improvement in physical outcomes as a coach, follows the personal philosophy.

At this point, the questions shift away from the internal machinations of the coach themselves and what drives them as a person and shifts into how the coach is employing specific external training modalities to achieve the desired outcomes and why?

Why do they believe these training methods are the ones they should use?

How do they rationalize the meat and potatoes of what is being done compared to the constant barrage of superfluous methodologies? What is their process for cutting through the muck and gurus to disseminate useful information?

Failure to rationalize this part of the cycle often leads to arbitrarily incorporating methods or jumping around without purpose from methodology to methodology with the belief that because it was successful for others, it will be for them as well. There is a lack of understanding around the structured growth concept of "what am I doing today so I can do what I need to do tomorrow in order to achieve the goals I have for the day after that, and so on, and so on."

This is the part of the process that, metaphorically speaking, cook's become sous-chefs, and sous-chefs become chefs.

The Coaching Philosophy

The "coaching philosophy" is the sum total of skills and strategies that you employ to teach the training philosophy to those you work with. This last part of the cycle draws together the two previous parts to define how and why the coach will connect with those they are working with.

It considers the structural piece of what is to be done, when from the timeline side of things, as well as the methodological manner in which the coach imparts knowledge upon the athlete in the learning and mastery processes.

Without definition here, a coach is often only successful with those who "fit" their coaching and training style; they have —at best—a vague notion of their own "why" and aren't able to adapt how they train for different types of people across different contexts. This is a common flaw often seen in technically or tactically knowledgeable coaches whose athletes aren't able to "get it" the way the coach instructs.

Knowing how you learn and communicate is only helpful if you are able to adapt it to the way another person learns and communicates in order to impart your knowledge. If you can only transfer your knowledge in one manner, then only people who learn in that one way will be capable of learning from you.

Truth

The last part of this cycle is "truth," or taking the time to have an honest, objective review of the situation. This is done through both introspective self-reflection and external evaluative mechanisms to better understand what was done, how doing it that way was positive or negative, and to evaluate which of the three philosophies needs to adapt or change.

This is often the easiest for people to consider on the surface but the hardest for people to put into action. Often it is because there is conflict within their "personal philosophy" compared to what they are doing in their "training philosophy" and "coaching philosophy."

While there are many manners to discuss this phenomenon, "true north" is by far the most widely known and also the title of a great book. Joe DeSena of Spartan and Ben Bergeron of CrossFit New England are two people to seek out if understanding how to align your values with your actions seems like an impossible task with the external pressures of life trying to influence you or otherwise. There are numerous others in all areas of life—Stephen Covey stands out across all domains, for example—but those two I have studied intensively, met personally and believe in wholeheartedly within the domain of physicality.

Lack of alignment in internal values to outward action is a catastrophe waiting to happen.

Where and when it will manifest is the question, not if. If you feel yourself spiraling, please seek help. I promise you there is always someone who will listen and lend a helping hand.

If you can look at what you did and say that what you did was the best you could do—with the best intentions at the time of when you did it—that's all you can ask for.

Use the experience to better yourself and your skills and whoever you work with moving forward.

Always try to work from the intelligent defense standpoint by being able to explain what, how, and why in an articulate, intelligent manner. If you can't do that, you're going to be in a world of hurt, and most likely, your athletes will be feeling the physical hurt, regardless of which philosophy you are talking about.

Working through the "truth" leads back to the "personal philosophy," allowing you the opportunity to redefine, break free from, or reinforce yourself so that when you begin the process anew, you are coming from a more focused and refined position.

SIDE NOTE—This cycle is truly never-ending. Take my writing this book for example: a decade from now, there will certainly be subtle and even seismic shifts in what I think, how I explain things, and where I stand regarding everything in this book. For me or anyone to think otherwise is to think foolishly.

The Four Lenses of Finding Truth

You have to have four internal lenses: two which create the range and two which refine that range in order to evaluate and view the "truth."

The first is the "optimist lens."

Most everyone knows what this means in terms of seeing the positive: the glass half-full and not the negative half-empty, and constantly being willing to move toward a positive direction, hoping for the best possible outcome.

This lens sets the positive outcome boundary.

The second is the "pessimist lens."

The pessimist viewpoint needs to see the worst-case scenario, and it prepares for the negative effects and consequences that could happen from any decision. It goes beyond seeing the glass as half empty to the glass breaking, spilling its contents, and never being able to be used again.

This is the second range boundary, or as I like to call it, the "when shit goes sideways" part of the equation.

While it's imperative to have a grasp on what both of these lenses can show, to help set the range of the possible outcomes, you cannot lose sight that all they represent is a range of possible or probable outcomes.

The interaction of variables within and outside of your control often make things fall somewhere in between the range. Being able to refine the view relative to these boundaries is critical.

The third lens—that is the first lens of refinement—the "realist lens."

The realist looks through the optimist and pessimist lenses and based on real-time situational factors and information, as well as previous experience and knowledge, make judgments and assessments as to what the expected outcome will be.

This lens never gets too high on the hope and never gets too down on the possible; it waxes and wanes slightly in each direction.

The last lens, that is the final level of refinement you need to have, is the "introspective lens."

This is where most leaders fail because they are either overly optimistic or pessimistic and don't refine their viewpoints realistically enough and never look at how they affected the outcome by being involved.

Conceptually, you can look at it like a modified Schrodinger's paradox: a leader can consider the range of possible outcomes and refine that down to what will most likely happen based on everything at hand; but if they aren't considering their own involvement and how that affects things, they will never be able to understand why things happen, because their involvement influences the outcome.

If you cannot detach from, evaluate, and judge your own decisions and decision-making processes to consider your own personal biases and limitations, the truth will always elude you. Thus, your decisions will be inherently flawed.

Cognitive dissonance, anyone?

Perspective is in the eye of the beholder. Anything looked through each of the first three lenses or a combination of the three lenses will always be slightly flawed and askew. This is because there isn't an internal lens looking inward to find, understand, and negate personal bias and develop a stronger sense of purpose to the outward action.

Creating a Tangible Cycle for Yourself

The first step to get started in the philosophical development cycle is putting words to each of the three philosophies. It forces you to create tangibility. This simple, yet powerful act of creating tangibility via the written word allows you to take up the challenge of peer review. And it creates your own philosophical contexts to reflect on over time, allowing you to compare them objectively in a concrete manner and not just subjectively in your own mind.

Remember, the greatest flaw we have is that in our own minds things always make sense.

It is only when we communicate our thoughts to another person (in whichever medium) that we truly know if what we think makes sense or not—not only to ourselves—but to whoever is listening (or reading) as well.

We've all had that moment talking with someone about something that's been on our minds for a while—thinking that we're making sense—only to watch the body language of the person and their other nonverbal cues tell us something is amiss long before they verbalize back that we aren't making sense.

The following is a basic template I use as a launch point to help get people to put their philosophies down on paper.

- Why do you want to be a coach/fitness professional?
  - What is your mission as such?
  - Why is that your mission?
- Who impacted you the most in the field?
  - When?
  - How?
- What is your philosophy on training?
  - How did you come to it?
  - Who impacted/mentored you?
  - Why did you come to it?
- What is your philosophy on exercise programming?
  - How does who you work with change it?
  - Why does who you work with change it?
- What are your personal principles/values?
  - How do they affect & effect your professional ones?

From teaching students in the classroom to working with interns in the weight room, usually these are the first three questions I ask:

- What methodology do you use to train?
- How do you coach athletes?
- In what ways are the above two things influenced by your own personal beliefs, morals, and biases?

Most are pretty quick answering the first question, giving me a brief rundown of the methodologies they use, their rationale to using such methods, and most importantly showing they have a grasp on "what it takes to get better." Few are able to delve into how they coach athletes and apply these methods beyond the customary motivational "rah-rah" tactics.

Not many get into the deeper understanding of how they have to adapt the presentation of their methodology due to the following:

- Individual athlete makeup (physical and mental maturity, training experience, gender, etc.)
- Sport-specific historical/cultural factors (i.e. overhead lifting in throwing sports, baseball versus javelin,)
- Managing intrinsically versus extrinsically motivated athletes

Only a handful of people have ever put into context how their own unique experiences and who they are as a person have shaped their approaches and how their personal beliefs significantly impact what they do and how they go about doing it. There's no way around the fact that you, as a person, drives how you, as a coach, are going to be.

Before you continue on from this section, I challenge you to take a month and put pen to paper (or keyboard to screen) to create a tangible artifact that represents your philosophy.

Set a specific time, on specific dates, three to five days apart and make sure you stick to those dates and times regardless of what life has thrown at you.

Write down your initial thoughts—use the guide if you are having trouble—but try just to let it flow. Take thirty minutes to an hour the first go around, save it, and don't look at it for a few days. Go back, reread it, edit it, shape it, spend no more than thirty minutes on it, and then leave it alone for a few more days.

Save each updated copy separately from the previous one, even though much will be redundant initially. Every time you refine it, save all previous work as its own version. This might seem cumbersome at first but in the ensuing years, as the you make adjustments at longer and longer intervals, it will be an amazing collection of longitudinal data to understand your path.

Repeat this process a handful of times during the month and after every time, also take note of the mind frame you are in while working on it and consider how that impacts the adjustments and thought the process you have while working on it.

You aren't always going to want to work on it at the assigned day and time but make yourself do it anyway. You need to see how your personal biases influence what you perceive your purpose to be. Think of it almost like a session-RPE (rate of perceived exertion) but instead of effort, your state of mind and state of emotion.

Do you have a bad day with other staff? You expand on the professional relationship thoughts and might have some venom in your words.

Do you have an amazing session with athletes and get the results you wanted? Any surprise you doubled down on the strength of passion you write your training philosophy with?

By the end of the month, you should have a pretty clear version to start from moving forward.

This will be the scaffolding you can now spend the remainder of the year on, 1–2 times per month for 35–45 minutes Work on it; expand and contract it.

By the end of the year, you should have a firm grasp of who you are, the journey and experiences that you've had to get there, and most importantly the ability to use "truth" to see if the words you claim are representative of and aligned with your outward actions.

5

PROFESSIONAL PHILOSOPHIES

FOR PERSPECTIVE ON MY PERSONAL PHILOSOPHY, INCLUDING STRONGER INSIGHTS as to what drives me as an individual, please read the chapter "Early Life Shaping My Style."

In order to set the stage for running through my professional philosophies, I think it's important to first discuss what I've found to be the universal professional perspectives.

When I look at myself and try to understand my global behaviors, beliefs, and values, I define myself as a dealer in truth.

I would rather tell someone the truth and be honest then bullshit them. I'm okay with dealing with the consequences of having to tell someone the truth, even if they're not ready to hear it.

I'm not okay dealing with the late-stage repercussions of pulling the wool over someone's eyes or sugarcoating it and then having to deal with the snowballed issue in the future.

Maybe it's a lack of inhibition due to concussions and head trauma or it's simply just not being afraid to draw a line in the sand, but either way, facts are beautiful things even when the person you are telling them to can't see the beauty.

SIDE NOTE—That remark on head trauma is not a joke. I do often consider this a variable about myself—my impulse control, and lack of filter at time— given my personal history of having had multiple concussions.

I also define myself as a builder of confidence because, to me, by helping facilitate the internal growth of confidence in any individual or group of individuals, they can have the self-efficacy needed to achieve the apex of their abilities.

Belief is a massively powerful thing.

To be believed in by others externally and to believe in yourself internally is literally a life-altering condition well beyond its application to sport competition.

Understanding Roles

Having professional respect sets the tone for everything you will ever do with other people.

We no longer live in a world where you can insulate yourself from everyone else in the professional setting and be in a silo forever.

Understanding each colleague's role relative to your own helps provide an environment that breeds trust and success. The less you encroach on other people's turf, especially when the person is competent and you have trust issues, the more likely they will *want* to help you rather than *have* to help you.

That little bit of semantics can make all the difference in how fast or slow things you need done get done.

Respecting space, boundaries, and roles, while being vulnerable, will allow the team to develop efficiency and effectiveness with the resources at hand and streamline operations and processes. Much is written on this topic. Authors like Stephen Covey, Patrick Lencioni, and other similar writers are who you should read to learn more about vulnerability and its place in leadership.

Cross-departmental and collaborative communication is paramount because members of different areas or specialties each have different skills, knowledge, and expertise.

If you are not asking yourself, *What are people currently doing over there that we can adopt or adapt to maximize what we do over here?* then you aren't doing it right.

That question conceptually also needs to be asked outside of the people around you: it's a micro question to your world and a macro question to the external world.

Why waste time, effort, energy, and money ground flooring something that has already been made into skyscrapers. A few minutes of effort asking questions and looking for answers can save you an untold number of hours, days and even years.

Even if it's "what not to do," everything can be a teacher if you are willing to be a student.

Some of the greatest lessons I've learned and the most valuable experiences I've had are from interactions with people who might as well have been from a different planet because of how dissimilarly we operated and how poorly their choices and actions manifested outcomes.

Remember, regardless of their style, ability, or knowledge everyone has the potential to contribute something.

Don't get me wrong, I'm not saying you have to get along with everyone, be friends, and have cookouts together. There are some people that will be the fire to your gasoline and it will be difficult to work with them. I can certainly think of a few people who I felt that way about, and I'm sure they felt that way about me. And while you may be better off not working with them for longer than you need too, they can still provide you something as you move forward.

Situational Awareness

The critical skill of having the situational awareness to read between the lines and evaluate interactions among people is something you must work on perpetually. You never know what may be driving someone at any moment in time.

Pay attention to the dynamics at play; look at the broader implications of what precedents have been set or could be set. It goes back to the idea that "just because you can doesn't mean you should."

When you take the time to step back and understand the dynamics at play, you will gain perspective and better understand if you need to take immediate action or let things play out before making a move.

Every action or inaction creates a ripple that could affect many interlinked pieces. The same issue may be minor to one person but significant to another. Do not underestimate the impact minor issues can have.

Not every partnership needs to be formed, and not every position needs to be filled. Sometimes decisions are made because the view from the hilltop shows something completely different than the view from the battlefield, and only by constantly assessing the situation, asking questions, and gaining insight from multiple perspectives will you stand a chance at operating effectively.

Feeling Like an Idiot

A few years ago, I was at a national conference and I saw a former colleague. He was speaking with someone else, so as I passed by I said, "Hey, man. I'll catch up with you later?" He gave me a quick handshake, nodding in agreement, and went back to his conversation.

Later that night, at one of the social events of the conference, I saw him again. So, I went over to speak with him. After some brief hellos, he said that he needed to talk to the person he was speaking to alone because the conversation was private and he would find me later to chat.

Not wanting to interject further and without thinking much about it, I asked him if he had seen another colleague we used to work with. He informed me that this person was over near the bar in a separate crowd of people.

I assumed he was giving me the right directions and I headed over to the bar. And after taking a few minutes to look around for our former colleague, I realized she was nowhere to be found.

As I was circling back around, I walked by my former colleague again and he gave me this weird look—a kind of "go fuck yourself" smirk. I thought to myself that it was odd because I'd seen him do it before. It usually meant he didn't like whoever he was looking at and up until about three minutes before, I had thought he and I were on good terms.

I'll admit, I couldn't help but think, *What an asshole. Why would he tell me she was over there when clearly, she wasn't? I guess we weren't on as good terms as I thought.*

The following day, I ran into a different mutual friend and mentioned the interaction the night before and made a comment about my former colleague being what I perceived to be an ass.

This mutual friend informed me that those two people recently had a falling out and weren't on speaking terms. This was news to me because back when we all worked together they were close—to the point that their spouses and children spent a lot of time outside of work together.

So, by not taking the time to talk, communicate, and understand the dynamics, I had no idea there was a shift in their relationship. And in my ignorance, I was left thinking that this guy was an asshole, while he was likely thinking I was an asshole for asking about her.

Since we all had worked together, and we had all kept in casual communication over the years offering advice, encouragement, and best wishes during times of personal or professional achievement, he probably assumed that I knew they had a falling out and was being a smart-ass for asking about her.

It was a total failure on my part to understand the dynamics at play, and I almost created a false narrative in my own mind about this person simply because I didn't understand the situation.

Being Open to New Perspectives

This is probably the most difficult thing for people to admit they struggle with, myself included. Besides showing professional respect and maintaining awareness of the interconnected and interdependent nexus of actions or inactions of others around you, you must actively stay alert to learning, not shy away from taking on new ideas that are not your own, and detach emotionally in order to logically argue new perspectives.

Yes, that is a mouth full.

So to simplify—you must be open-minded.

You cannot strike down an idea before you first internalize it well enough to take it or its opposing side as your own.

If you can't make the argument for the person, then you shouldn't make the argument against the person.

Only then, after having confronted the perspective with logic, reason, and objective thinking, can you truly cast it aside (if that is, in fact, the appropriate action).

Additionally, in order to maintain an open mind, you must also take time to be as critical of yourself as you are of others.

Don't get lost in your own perspective or it will become your reality. The outside world has a funny way of looking the way we want it to.

In the world we live in, it's unacceptable to not explore other perspectives. At a minimum, you have to accept that there are different viewpoints and yours may or may not be "right"—and that "right" is fluid and relative in most cases. There are very few true absolutes.

Perspective not only allows us the opportunity to see the same thing in different ways but also allows us the chance to grasp the context of a person's situation better. And we can use that context in the future to build our own well-positioned viewpoints out of those experiences.

That is one of the key things that having an open mind allows: being able to learn from others' experiences and viewpoints without having to have them ourselves.

While there are many different manners to explain this idea, I personally prefer the illustration from Stephen Covey's book *First Thing's First* with two people on the opposite sides of a curve: one sees convex and the other sees concave.

SIDE NOTE—Aside from this one book you should read (as I have mentioned it twice in the last few pages alone), Mr. Covey has numerous additional materials that you should dive into.

With that said, remember, "concept over construct, context over content." Never get lost in someone else's dogma, no matter how much you believe in it. I'll reference Jordan Peterson here again to reinforce this point. I love a lot of what he promotes but also disagree with a lot as well.

Use what you learn to shape your own worldview—not adopt someone else's. And never lose sight of having your own philosophy while being able to understand others will have theirs. Don't be one of those idiots who preaches openness and inclusion only to force people into accepting your position and slamming anyone who disagrees or has their own differing view.

Operational Capacity and Complacency

"Operational capacity" versus "operational complacency" was originally a concept I used to help describe the differences between people who had shut down in their work-life to the minimum required effort compared to people self-motivated or empowered to expend their full ability and grow to enhance it.

Terms like growth mindset, driven, and high potential—they all encompass people maximizing their operational capacity. In this vein, "operational capacity" is defined as the current level of ability someone has to bring to any specific objective they're trying to accomplish.

This is a flux state because it can grow or shrink depending on a multitude of internal and external factors.

"Operational complacency," however, is when individuals intentionally self-limit themselves to the minimum required extent of their abilities to barely complete or sometimes fail to achieve the intended objective/outcome.

It's typical in human nature, both in our underlying physiology and in our mental state, to gear down.

From a training standpoint, think "size principle." You naturally gear down to the lowest-level of motor units needed to complete the task in order to accommodate a basic principle of life: do not waste energy when you do not have to—you never know when you might need it.

This is not only a physical phenomenon but it's also a cognitive one. People naturally shift down in an effort to streamline their output, especially when they lack the challenge or incentive to do anything more than the absolute minimum.

Often there is a lack of "why" that causes the mind to lack focus and purpose.

For any individual to operate at their maximum operational capacity, there is a high cost. It's a physically challenging and emotionally draining function given the high-stress state it imposes on the system. As such, people are not able to operate at that maximum output for a long period of time.

They need methods and manners to both recover and replenish themselves and the others around them from outputting at that level.

Everything has a cost.

Often, in S&C, you see coaches drive themselves into operational complacency by downregulating and simplifying the tools (methodology, equipment, cues, etc.) that they could use. They continuously touch the same tools without using other tools, whether it be due to lack of effort/imagination, lack of mastery, or lack of willingness to do something new because what they did was previously successful.

The same training program is done year after year after year because there isn't any room in the situation for the coach to grow and develop.

Whether it be lack of career progression, financial incentive, departmental resource improvements, or a litany of other possible factors (often all working in tandem), after a certain period, they fall into the cyclic nature of the profession and the path of least resistance. They simply do what was done before and this is especially true if it at one point, it was successful.

One of the best things you can do to offset the shift to operational complacency is rebuild your knowledge base and constantly challenge yourself to find situations where you can implement this new knowledge. Give yourself more tools in your toolbox to draw from and more experiences relative to your work, and most importantly, more reasons to use your imagination to find solutions to problems you had not thought of before.

When you deal with operationally complacent people or people who have become operationally inefficient or ineffective because they've lost their willingness to put forth effort beyond the minimum, you start to see this insulated, narrow-minded, and self-centered viewpoint that reinforces them to be closed-off, unwilling to be challenged, and unimaginative.

It is a vicious feedback loop they often don't even realize they are in.

They often create these dogmatic bonds that are bigger than they truly are. "Oh, we can't do that because . . ." or "Oh, this can't happen because . . ." or "It's their fault because . . ." It's this, and it's that, and it's all these other things—other than what truly is the problem.

They've built an insurmountable mountain in their own mind of the issue and they're not willing to go beyond it.

Awareness of this is also critical when you get into a change in culture. The situational context in which you manipulate someone's environment matters as most people are in their little groove and they don't want to be taken out of that groove because it's become easy for them there.

Operating Defensively or Offensively

"Operating defensively" is when you're directly limited by outside confounding factors that you are not in a position to directly change. Factors such as people, resources, space, or equipment can all put you on the defensive, having to be reactive instead of proactive.

However, "operating offensively" is when you're able to work at a full or near-full operational capacity, you're able to take the entire set of your skills to the task, and you're able to draw from a higher level of possibilities. This creates a cascading effect, allowing you a greater chance to bring all your skills and all the skills around you to continually drive positive outcomes.

The interesting thing about operating defensively, however, is you have to recognize that what you perceive to be outside confounding factors are self-limiting—in the sense that they will only limit you to the level you allow them.

Often, people coach defensively or operate in an entrenched defensive position because they lack the confidence to see that they—and only they—have the ability to influence their own perspective.

While there are times where situations are really out of your own control and people, places, and things will limit you—you have to decide if you will allow them to be a confounding factor.

The moment you feel yourself being pushed into a defensive coaching position from someone or something, first re-evaluate whether you're truly on the defensive or not. Adjust your own outlook of the situation to create a more operationally efficient and offensive coaching strategy, and with this repositioning, avoid falling into a defensive position unnecessarily.

Jocko, one of my go-to persons on this topic, has spoken on this idea significantly, albeit with slightly different terms. And between his books and podcasts, you can gain significant insight. Google "Jocko Good" for a starting point.

If you're not open to being challenged and having courageous conversations, you're never truly going to unlock the ability to operate at a high capacity. Eventually, those outside factors will beat you down.

Have a system. Be flexible. Adjust as necessary. Remember more than anything, your perspective and mindset position you offensively or defensively and allow operational capacity or operational complacency.

Trust the Process

These days there is far too much emphasis on quick fixes and shortcuts. And there are way too many gurus telling you how fast you can get great at something without putting in the work to truly deserve to be great. Filtering through the detritus is a skill within itself and a critical one.

Those that have worked with me for any length of time know I say certain things repeatedly—and by repeatedly, I mean literally thousands of times over the course of a college athletes career: "It's not rocket science," and "Wow, it's like I get paid to do this," or "Stay safe, don't get arrested, and if you do, don't be wearing school-issued clothing!" But the expression, "Trust the process," might rank highest on the list for things I would say the most.

What most people come to appreciate but often overlook is that consistent, purposeful work day in and day out and taking pride in accomplishing your objective from start to finish is what will help provide them a stronger sense of purpose to their actions. It helps reinforce self-confidence and belief.

Sometimes it's enjoying the process and being an active participant in the journey—not googling the life hack that can make things quicker and simpler in the long haul—that allows you to actually gain what you wanted from the experience in the first place.

While much more could be said here, I do believe everyone grasps this concept and attitude differently as the process means and is different for everyone (figuratively and literally).

I am going to leave it with how I internalize the idea: there is perfection in the imperfections of the process.

One prized gift that has hung in every office that I've had since I received it is the artwork pictured below, given to me by an intern I worked with named Ashlee.

Learning How to Learn

One of the most important things you can ever learn is to learn how you learn.

This meta-learning process is probably the most important thing I've personally experienced from the development-of-self standpoint. When I learned how I learned, it allowed me to not only gain knowledge and synthesize material and experiences but connect them into a large web that I was able to draw on at any moment, at any time.

The meta-learning process is different for everyone, so this outline is simply how I went about it and how it made sense to me. There are many different ways and methods. I would suggest poking around things by Maudsley, the originator, and Tim Ferris to gain insight on where to start.

First, I had to understand how to defy distractions.

I had to learn how to position myself so that external distractions wouldn't take away my focus and ability to remember the material. When I work, I like to do it in a quiet environment and listen to low volume background music like jazz or classical. That is my most optimal setting; I operate at my highest capacity like this. I'm quickly and consistently able to enter a degree of a flow state. Add in a moderately hungry stomach, a touch of caffeine, and a slightly uncomfortable chair and I'm the Picasso, Shakespeare, Mozart version of myself creating masterpieces.

However, I know that in non-optimal settings I can still get things done —just not at the same pace. I know this because I practiced a lot in all kinds of environments and paid attention to my effectiveness.

I can work in places where I'm constantly being asked questions, being called, or being texted—or even in a loud environment—I'm just not nearly as effective as I am in my optimal setting. I plan accordingly if that is the case and I don't try to cover as much ground as quickly. What I would only need an hour for in an optimal setting, I know I need almost three hours for in a non-optimal one, and five in an extremely suboptimal setting.

While this seems obvious, test it out and see in what way you optimally perform. It might be the loud room with a lot of noise and not the library—or it might be the other way around.

The second thing was I had to incentivize myself appropriately.

I had to learn what incentives worked and what didn't. We all naturally crave an outcome for our effort. Think about it from a physiological standpoint; the body down-regulates to spend the least amount of energy for the greatest return. If you put energy into something, it must serve a purpose.

For example, physical activity incentivizes people to look good in their bathing suits or to have an extra piece of desert. Incentivizing yourself is a critical motivator and self-efficacy tool. It helps create an acknowledgment of and tangible validation for completion of a task. It's a critical thing to do. If you keep doing things and don't take the time to acknowledge or have some type of anchor for the completion of a task, you can easily get into a negative feedback mechanism and not complete tasks because there is no associated value.

> *SIDE NOTE—You don't have to finish everything you start; purposeful quitting has a place. Sometimes not going down with a sinking ship is a good idea, no matter how noble the idea is. Sunk-cost theory is real. Just as real is throwing everything into the sunk-cost theory, excuse bucket. Be cautious and take purposeful time before you "quit" anything.*

I've incentivized myself with both external rewards and internal awards. External awards being I can go out and do something once I complete what I'm working on: I can't go to the new brewery until I finish this because I know that if I go over and drink a few beers, I'm not going to want to do it when I come home; finish first, then go.

External incentives can be small, everyday things or can be big things. It doesn't matter. The trick is keeping them in a similar scale. Doing the laundry doesn't mean you've earned a two-week vacation. Completing your dissertation deserves more than hugs from your circle of people.

The key is a nice balance of the reward compared to the effort.

Additionally, the internal incentive is also critical because it helps build the internal self-confidence and the internal efficacy to know that you can accomplish tasks.

This might be one of the most underrated parts in the development of behavior change for people who don't know why they can't change their own behavior.

For myself, I create tangibility and create an anchor when I've completed a task. Or when I have achieved a certain result that I've set a goal towards, I will take a minute and look in the proverbial mirror at myself and say, *You did X* or *You accomplished Y*.

I will go on to tell myself a bit of a narrative relative to the experience—it may have taken longer or it may have been quicker—but whatever the situation may be, I give myself that one-minute introspective look at what it was and how I got there.

I give myself positive affirmations like, *You didn't give in to a difficult situation* or *You were able to achieve what you wanted to achieve* if things were particularly hard or difficult to accomplish.

Taking that moment to internally reward yourself and affirm that you're confident and capable of doing the things you set out to is a strong internal motivator and a strong confidence builder.

It's something, sadly, many people don't do as they only validate their effort externally and never reward themselves internally for doing the work.

Next, I had to learn to focus my attention on a single task.

Everyone always talks about multitasking as being a difficult skill but being able to single-task is actually much harder. The discipline needed to say "no" to other things in your own mind as well as to other people and put all of your bandwidth on a single task for a period of time is not as easy as it seems.

Things to look at if this is a foreign concept to you—or one you don't understand because you think multitasking is more vital than single-tasking—are mindfulness, stoic philosophy, and centering yourself.

One of the things that I like to do when I'm preparing to get into the mindset to do something creative (like write or draw) or any kind of learning is a minute or two of breathing, finding my breath, and focusing my mind.

Whatever stress of life it may be—family, bills coming up, meetings, issues with your significant other—slowly start to peel those layers in whatever way you want to get them out of the way and open up the emotional and mental capacity of your mind to the single task in front of you.

Lastly, I had to learn to go beyond the technical and tactical constraints of whatever knowledge I was trying to learn. I had to open my mind to draw from other experiences that could allow strengthening and better synthesis of the technical and tactical material I was trying to learn. Analogous thinking is the precise term.

Having the ability to be open-minded is tough. Anytime you get good at something, you often tend to see through that lens in all situations. You aren't always able to detach from what you know and be open to new possibilities or connect the unconnected that you may not even know yet.

We all naturally self-narrow and thus become self-limiting. Down-regulation is a natural phenomenon across all aspects of being human.

As we get better in our fields of work or study, we narrow our focus and become more receptive to seeing answers we want versus leaving open the possibility that it could be something else. When you go beyond the technical and tactical, you have to be willing to step outside of the specialty and knowledge base that you have and be open to the possibility of other answers with different implications than you may understand. You have to be willing to flex your imagination—something that is sorely not taught enough and given enough emphasis these days.

You must be able to connect different experiences and knowledge into other setting even if they do not make sense initially.

For example, one experience that made me better connect and create buy-in with athletes that I worked with was the customer-service-orientated work I had done when I was younger. I spent time in restaurants in customer-facing sales positions where I had to engage and connect with people directly. I had to get them to do or buy something I wanted them to, while listening to them, adapting to their needs, and providing for them—not for myself.

While those jobs have nothing to do with coaching athletes, it has everything to do with connecting people, which is much more complex and easily carries into working with athletes.

Over time, I've started to see that the knowledge and experience I've gained in seemingly unrelated areas has helped me more significantly in the development of the people I worked with as athletes and professionals than some of the technical or tactical knowledge I learned about human performance directly.

There's a lot to be said for taking the time to learn the psychology of training and the psychology of people. While clearly, he was influenced by many others, Brett Bartholomew is on the forefront of this in the human performance landscape with his book *Conscious Coaching* and additional resources he's created.

There are several subject areas outside of human performance that need to be investigated to maximize human performance. They include but are not limited to behavioral psychology, cognitive behavioral psychology, general psychology, sociology, systems theory, systems modeling, stoic philosophy, essentialism, and pragmatism.

Becoming an Accountant

I heard a fable from one of the smartest S&C coaches I was fortunate to learn from and work alongside. We shared an office together for a few years. While I'm sure he got it from someone else, I heard it from him first and have stolen it ever since.

The story starts with a guy who wants to run his own business (in the version my friend would tell, it was to run a gym—fitting given the context).

So, our future gym owner sets out to get the advice of the most successful person he knows. What this successful friend tells him is, "For the next two years, become the best accountant you can be and then open your gym."

Our future gym owner doesn't quite understand but accepts the advice of his sage-like friend. He sets out, for the next two years, spending his time as an accountant, learning everything he possibly can, and doing the best possible job in the roles leading up to and being an accountant.

The day comes when he's ready to open his gym and his wise friend shows up. The new gym owner says to him, "I get it now. It took me until a few weeks ago to get it, but I get it. I had the passion for working in a gym, the knowledge about how to train people, and the equipment I needed. But what I didn't have was the knowledge of how to own a gym. I had to go and learn everything else I needed to know—outside of what I wanted and was passionate about—in order to be successful in what I truly wanted: this gym. I had to become an accountant first. There was no way I was going to make this work had I not done that." At this his wise friend smiled and nodded. The lesson having been understood: do what you need to do now, so you can do what you want to do later. Because if you want certain things, you must do things a certain way.

In an unfortunate example, I had a former intern who had all the passion, drive and desire to be a great coach open a gym. He outfitted it with top-of-the-line gear, poured his sweat equity into the place, and did everything he could to try to make it work. But he failed miserably.

What he lacked was the knowledge of how to run a gym: from choosing a location and establishing a presence in the community; to differentiating among local competitors; to overbuying equipment and not having a client base. He followed his passion without understanding how to "do the job." Unfortunately, he had to close down within months of opening and liquidate almost all of the equipment to cover his debts.

I will say though, he has gone on from this to find success in his new endeavors and is someone who I'll always admire for his unyielding positive attitude and never-quit mindset.

Acknowledge Success

When you set a goal and achieve it, take a moment to acknowledge the accomplishment. That doesn't mean you're going to stop or not continue on to the next thing because you accomplished this one.

What it means is that you are going to step back, detach from the action of life and say, *Hey, I did this*. It can literally be that simple, or it can be something more outward, like going out to dinner or buying yourself something. Create some kind of moment where you create a tangible anchor in which you say, *I did it*.

I worked with a guy one time who had gone through a rough patch in his life. He was fighting a combination of personal demons and a handful of external issues brought on by them. In the process of talking to him, he mentioned how he wanted to get a job, get back on his feet, and get his life going in the direction he wanted.

He was making significant headway personally and professionally and the main objective he had was to get a steady, solid paycheck, which would help facilitate the next steps for him.

In the next few months, he did exactly that. It wasn't anything crazy, but it was nonetheless a full-time job with benefits. And it was the launchpad he needed to help drive his life in the direction he wanted.

Knowing it was a big moment for him but that it also meant he now had even more to accomplish, I could sense his tension building in order to attack the next step and keep charging. It was great to see his forward momentum and desire for more, so I made it a point to give him a gift card, told him to buy a steak dinner, and—while not to settle on the success of the moment—said not to forget to stop and pat himself on the back and tell himself, *Good job*.

There will always be work to do and things to "get after," but sometimes you need to stop and enjoy the moment. Those kinds of moments are fleeting so catch them while you can.

Learn from Failure

Success has been an accumulation of failures for me.

My belief, shared by many across a litany of areas, is that one of the best things you can do is fail, miserably, especially in a controlled environment.

Failing gives you the chance to see what needs to be done to be successful and how you need to go about changing (adjusting, removing, enhancing, etc.) things moving forward.

If, that is, you're willing to pay attention to the lessons the failure provides.

One of the first things I taught when working with an athlete lifting weights is how to fail.

While knowing how to fail lifting wasn't the desired goal, I wanted every athlete to have the answer to the following question: how do I safely and effectively get myself out of the way when things go wrong?

Lifting, especially in an intense and progressive manner, can be a highly complex, highly variable endeavor, and even if you do everything right, still may not go as planned. And I'm not talking about doing tricep kickbacks with pink dumbbells here; I'm talking about "worshipping at the church of iron" where you're pushing yourself in ways you never have been before.

It's similar to life in that respect.

When training, you're often in a semi-controlled state trying to recreate an effort you've already done but at a better-quality output or do something that was previously undoable. A lot can go wrong in that situation; you need to know how to get away and live to see another day.

Don't get me wrong, there will be times when you need to ride the line of staying the course and risk getting hurt to accomplish the task—a competition, for example—but not every day should be like that.

On the flip side, however, if you succeed in everything you do and challenges never surpass your abilities, you can be lulled into a false sense of ability because you never fail or face the challenge of overcoming setbacks.

I once had an athlete who cried when she failed her lifts during testing.

Now, you might say this isn't anything out of the ordinary—an athlete showing emotion in the midst of defeat—but what struck me that day was what she said to me after I told her to stop crying and try again: "Coach Joe, I never fail at anything—ever. I just don't understand why I can't do this."

It hit me. She was a 4.0 GPA student and everything across her history of sports, academics, etc., was accomplished at a high-level relative to where she was compared to lifting. She was a novice in the gym, having never stepped foot inside one in any serious capacity until she came to work with me.

In the macro, she never failed to accomplish anything before. She was always the big fish in the small pond and what she thought was "hard work" had always been enough.

Now, however, she was just a small fish in the ocean and it was starting to get scary because there were a lot of pointy teeth out in that water. She was, at best, an average athlete and never had to work that hard to be the best given who she had been among.

She was academically intelligent but was also sheltered by the academic system (a conversation for another day). She had no concept that the real world worked differently; that even with your best effort—doing everything right—you still are guaranteed nothing.

I knew in those nanoseconds of understanding, that in the next months I had to help her learn how to fail—and be okay with it—before we had a chance to make real progress. I even adjusted our training in order to let failure be okay and encouraged failure in certain moments.

Because failure is okay when it's purposely used as a learning tool. Failure when the stakes are real and there are real consequences—that's when winning is the only option. That requires a totally different kind of training, mindset, and process; the "swim or swim" mindset I like to call it.

If you have the chance to fail in a controlled environment—for the sake of growth and if it won't comprise you in a "real" negative way—fail away, fail often, and become better because of it.

Stand Your Ground

As you go through "the process," and you've worked on being an accountant, acknowledged successes when they happen, and learned from as many failures as possible, there comes a time when you need to stand your ground when you are right.

Doing so will help you build your confidence in a different but equally important way. While this may seem obvious, it's something that not many people realize.

One time I was covering a preseason team for one of the S&C coaches who was out having just had a baby. I had met with the head coach a few days prior in person to confirm the schedule and also provided my cellphone in case there were any last-minute changes, something that often happened with this particular coach.

Come the day of the first session, which was supposed to be at 8:00 a.m. in the midst of eating my breakfast, a few minutes after 7:00 a.m. I got a call from the very angry head coach, who had a reputation for being a little abrasive and a little unwieldy.

"Joe, where the fuck are you?" the coach said, "We're starting at 7:00 a.m." They continued on colorfully, making it a point that I was at fault, clearly stupid, and questioning if they wanted me working with their team.

I said flatly, "Okay. I'll be there in a second." And as I grabbed my stuff to jet out the door, I looked at the schedule I had been given a few days before and it clearly said 8:00 a.m. So, I took a deep breath and slowed my pace a bit.

When I arrived, the athletes were already doing the testing. They had taken a key to the weight room from the head coach, taken the equipment they needed, set up, warmed up, and proceeded to do the testing.

After seeing this and making a note of it for another day and different conversation, I went directly up to the head coach, and shoved the calendar packet into their face. While keeping direct eye contact, I said, "Hey coach, this is the schedule I have that you sent me a few days ago."

The coach was clearly mad before I raised my challenge and I could see them now boiling over to a higher level of anger. But suddenly, they paused, looking at the papers in front of their face. The words slowly coming out of their mouth, "Oh, I never sent you the updated schedule." They went on to say they had sent out an updated calendar to the team the previous night around 9:30 p.m. but had forgotten to include me.

The breakdown in communication was simple and was clearly the coaches fault. I was sure as hell not going to back down or apologize for being late, especially after being treated that way. I was going to get an apology.

Before the coach could speak further, I said coolly, "We'll talk about this after the session," and turned back towards the athletes to finish out the session.

The coach and I met afterward, went over the schedule, and made sure we were on the same page. I made it a point to mention how I had double-checked the schedule days beforehand, purposefully provided my cell number in case of this exact issue, and I did not appreciate the tone or attitude during the phone call earlier as they were the ones who had dropped the ball and not the other way around.

The coach looked at me slightly confused. I don't think anyone ever stood their ground to them. But recognizing I wasn't going to back down and that I was in the right, I got a half-hearted apology. Knowing that was the best I was going to get and it wouldn't serve any purpose to salt the wound further, I let it go.

SIDE NOTE—Now, this isn't a tactic I would use in every situation. There is a time and place to take your lumps, close your mouth, and keep your opinion (right or wrong), to yourself. There is also a time to take ownership for your own mistakes and have no one to be mad at but yourself for miscommunications.

But there is also a time when you are right and when you did what you were supposed to the way you were supposed to and should not have to tolerate poor and abrasive treatment.

You need to stand your ground and prove your point.

This can be a razor-sharp edge to walk and one you must do so smartly and with purpose—not full of reactive emotion.

Could I have kept going after the weak apology I received? Sure. Would that have been proactive or purposeful in any way? No, it would have just been for my own ego.

The point had been proven. I could let it go after that.

6

LEADERSHIP PHILOSOPHY

Facilitate. Don't complicate.

- Be an Advocate
- Drinking from the Firehose Can Be a Good Thing
- Delegate
- Foster a Culture of "Us" and "We" Instead of "I" and "Me"
- If All You Know is What Those Around You Know, You'll Eventually Know Nothing
- The Goal is Not to Have to Say No, but Saying No Can Be Okay
- Ask the Person in the Trenches but Help Them Understand the Battlefield
- Maintain a Positive Work-Life Balance

LEADERSHIP IS TRICKY.

Everyone has their own opinion on the how's, what's and why's.

When people ask me about being a leader, I often talk about my leadership philosophy or how I empower others while avoiding operational complacency as best as possible.

And then I see their eyes roll as the sarcasm oozes out of their mouth, "Wow, that sounds great Joe. Really catchy and deep but you didn't say anything."

So, what is my leadership philosophy?

Facilitate Don't Complicate

Well, it's "Facilitate. Don't complicate."

And now I can imagine you saying, "What the hell? How did you go from a thirty-word explanation of your leadership philosophy to just three words and a strategically placed period?"

It's part of being a leader (insert wink emoji).

Although I have all of these things written down, from acronyms to catchy descriptions, I do not inundate people with everything at once.

My goal as a leader has always been to give those around me the chance to maximize their own contributions while receiving the least amount of guidance from me along the way.

I try to facilitate opportunities for them to bring their full skill set to the task.

I also strive to not add layers of complexity or redundancy to their tasks as that will switch their focus to inefficient tasks and will bog down their ability to contribute.

Now, what that entails are different for every person, role, task, and situation. But in order to have a standard model to work off of and a foundation to build on, I've formed a list of concepts I use and constantly review in order to adapt and adjust.

I ask myself if I am doing enough to "facilitate, not complicate."

The first fallacy of leadership, in my opinion, is believing that you are infallible as the leader and that you can always fix things because you're the leader.

Often times, getting out of the way will help solve problems faster than inserting yourself into them.

If you are leading others, at some point you will not be with them. Do you want them looking around for you to tell them what to do? Or do you want them to act to the best of their abilities within a framework of what they believe is the best thing to do as if you would have done it yourself?

Be an Advocate

What I mean by this is be an advocate for the people both above and below you. It's not just about supporting, giving a "rah-rah" speech, providing resources, or putting someone in for a raise at the end of the year.

Being an advocate goes far beyond what most view as a standard oversight role.

It means consciously putting in effort to let those around you know that you are on their side, that you believe in their ability to do their job, and that you view them as competent and capable, even in their failures.

You must give them the freedom and autonomy to work on themselves or help develop them to that level of competency. By creating an environment that they return to each day knowing they have someone who will go to bat for them in their good moments, you empower them to want to put forth effort.

They also have to know you'll hold them accountable and you will dole out the appropriate level of discipline at the appropriate time.

Being an advocate for someone might mean giving them a kick in the ass to step their game up when they need one.

It also means that you share and communicate with them in an honest and frank way.

You cannot be an advocate for someone by telling half-truths, sugar coating things, or hiding information in order to protect them or yourself.

Certainly, there are strategic pieces of information that do not need to be available to everyone at times, but if those who work with you don't know the real narrative, they will create their own in its place.

This is one of the most dangerous things that can happen if you are trying to lead others.

Drinking from the Firehose Can Be a Good Thing

I often look at things with a "swim or swim" or "failure is just not an option" point of view.

That, however, is a point of view that has been harnessed over time and with significant failure along the way.

All too often, those who preach leadership preach perfection. They espouse the ideals of no failures, no mistakes, and grind, grind, grind. They push the idea that if you fail, you were unprepared and that you should have done better to begin with. But if you're not allowed to fail, how will you ever learn?

Most people have tried to drink water out of a garden hose on a hot summer afternoon. Well, imagine if that was a fire hose. Not many people would want to put their face in front of that.

However, sometimes the only way to learn and the only way to be better is to put your face in front of the fire hose , try to drink from it, and not drown along the way. The only way to take advantage of the "swim or swim" mentality is to give someone a controlled environment to get overwhelmed in.

Allow them to fail and fail over and over again, even when they are not as prepared as they possibly could be. As long as they are in a controlled environment—one where failure will not be catastrophic—they will have the opportunity to learn from the experience.

Drinking from the firehose can be a good opportunity to allow someone to be in over their head before you put them in an uncontrolled environment where getting drowned by the firehouse could be disastrous for business and not just their health.

I would often do this with my interns when it came to working with athletes. After basic competencies were established, I would give them the reigns for a part of a training session. I would set the stage for them: you're going to do this, this way, at this time. I would also give them some degrees of freedom to add their own personal touch to things.

I would then let the athletes know that the intern was in charge and unless I had to interject that they were "the boss" at that moment.

Often times, the first experience was a disastrous failure for the intern who was "the boss." But it was okay. That was the point.

We were able to spend time unpacking the experience—the good, the bad, the lessons learned—and create a new framework for their development. So, the next time an opportunity arose they were better prepared and better equipped to handle the moment.

Delegate

Learning how to delegate and outsource is a critical staple to anyone who wants to lead and manage.

You have to balance the centralized versus decentralized command structure; knowing how and when to delegate and outsource to those around you as needed.

Balancing when to interject and take control is vital. Sometimes "taking over" can stifle the growth of those around you because it can let them think that they have a safety net in you and creates a dependency on you "making it happen" for them if things so sideways.

This can also spiral quickly into an environment that breeds operational complacency due to resentment.

If you read Tim Ferris' book *The 4-Hour Workweek* and similar books, you learn that managing and being effective with time means, in certain situations, leveraging those who have specialized talents to complete tasks for you instead of taking the time to do them yourself.

Instead of trying to design a book cover and having to learn how to use Adobe Illustrator, I just found someone who could do it for me and paid them to do it. I provided a vision, gave some boundaries to what I wanted, and got the hell out of the way—having no more input until a draft was ready to be looked at.

Understanding when you need to delegate and when you need to "be an accountant" is one of the toughest challenges leader's face.

I honestly believe that leaders who are not effective delegators lack true knowledge of their own personal philosophy and have massive malalignment in their own value structures and competencies.

I have yet to meet a leader across any spectrum who was a poor delegator that didn't also have a massive gap in understanding of themselves at a deeply personal level.

While there are a multitude of reasons for that lack of self-knowledge, I have seen the key reasons often being their inability to be confident in who they are as a person and their inability to appreciate their own uniqueness and weakness to empower others who are better than them.

Fostering a Culture of Us and We Instead of I and Me

Whether I'm consulting for a business or doing a project of my own, you'll often hear me use the terms "us" and "we" to refer to myself and the people I'm working with. Even if I'm simply in a one-time conversation, I change the wording from "I" or "me" to "us" and "we."

Most people don't notice it, but it's the ones who do that I know are going to have the deepest insights or perceive the greatest slights.

Instilling a group mentality is the number one priority as a leader.

In the group dynamics of good leadership, one plus one equals a lot more than two.

If you stand together and have some type of unified bond, even if it's just the social construct of considering yourselves a team, you'll be able to influence the group's mindset and you'll have a better chance at aligning their actions.

You can build some degree of altruistic behavior simply by constantly reinforcing "us" and "we" instead of "I" and "me."

Often, in teams or with businesses that are struggling to find cohesion and a unified vision, the key point of collapse is an individual with a key role having an "I" and "me" mentality—even if they aren't directly saying those words.

Their lack of cohesion in the unit drives a wedge between others in the group and either breaks down the team at large or worse—creates siloed cliques within the team.

The scariest situations are when the leaders themselves don't even realize there is such a division. In their own minds, everyone is a "team" or a "family" because those on the team act that way around the leader but act in opposing ways once the leader isn't around.

Without going too deep into groupthink and social identification theory, can you think of an extremely successful team that was able to outpace everyone around them time and time again but had no connected purpose, no shared vision, and no sense of strong bonds between members at any level?

Let me know when you do.

I'll wait.

If All You Know is What Those Around You Know, You'll Eventually Know Nothing

Another fallacy of leadership is that, as a leader, you must know more than those around you.

The problem here is simple if that is the case: cut the head off the snake and the body will die. In a sports analogy, the body being assistant coaches who have no idea what to do if the head coach is not around.

Sadly, this happens all the time. I would often see assistant coaches (and middle managers) who made the monstrous mistake of only learning from those who they worked for and not understanding the "why" behind what they learned, only the "what".

This is an extremely risky proposition because if the person you are working for doesn't have a growth mindset and isn't exposing you to more than they themselves know, you won't learn anything beyond what they have limited themselves too.

You need to ask yourself, is the person you are working for actively participating in your growth and development or are they simply using your efforts to help them achieve their own goals.

Rank your current professional abilities required of you on a scale of 0–100, and if every six months you are not an improved version of yourself, then you are not being developed properly from a professional context.

The goal isn't to hit 100 in six months; the goal is to be in constant improvement. Even an increase of one is an increase.

How can you be expected to provide more value and better outcomes in your role/job if you are still at the same level of ability as when you started?

Learning from Others

I had to have a rather difficult conversation with an executive recently where I had to explain to them that the fourfold growth in sales they had projected for the coming year was not going to happen.

Why was it not going to happen? Because they, as well as the rest of the leadership of the company, had put no time, effort, or money into improving their staff.

How could they expect their staff to have the skills and abilities to create a fourfold result if they were still at their original level of ability? I put it in simple math terms for them; they were a $5-million-dollar company and wanted to be a $20-million-dollar company. How could they expect $20-million-dollar results from people who only had the skills, knowledge, and abilities to be $5-million-dollar people?

I went on that only if their staff had put in time, effort, and energy on their own, outside of work, would they have improved their abilities and had the chance to help achieve this lofty goal.

This executive flatly didn't understand what I meant and unsurprisingly the company did not come close to achieving its fourfold goal.

There is a famous business proverb, as it relates to developing a company, that encapsulates this idea in all of its simple elegance. Who said it first I do not know, but it goes something like this:

The CFO says to the CEO, "Why do we have to spend so much on training employees if all they do is eventually leave for better jobs after we paid to train them?"

To which the CEO replies, "What if we didn't do anything to help make them better and they stay?"

The Goal is Not to Have to Say No, but Saying No Can Be Okay

Often, people say "yes" simply to avoid conflict. They don't want to say "no" because it's easier to go down the path of least resistance than to take a stand.

Especially in a service role, where you are trying to provide something to a customer, often when "no" should be said "yes" is said instead. It ultimately creates ripples that eventually can become tsunamis in other places.

I'm sure you've heard it said in a million different ways:

- "The customer is always right."
- "Never say 'no.'"
- "Do your best to make them happy."

Generally speaking, there is a lot of truth to those expressions. However, saying "no" can be okay as well if used properly and for a purpose.

Saying "no" in the right situation can allow you to provide better quality and level of service if it's said for the right reasons.

For example, saying "no" can be okay if you are drawing a line in the sand to make things appropriate, fair, and equitable in a situation where a boundary needs to be maintained and someone else is trying to fudge that boundary.

Also, saying "no" can be okay if you are asked to go against your moral values or ethical beliefs or if you are asked to do something so far beyond your capacity that you risk causing harm to yourself or others by doing it.

While the above is seemingly obvious, many times, a "yes" is still given when it shouldn't be.

Depending on the situation, saying "no" can often allow you to say "yes" to an improved outcome down the road compared to a lesser short-term outcome.

There are thousands of examples of this across a multitude of professional dynamics but be careful to saying "no" simply due to laziness, complacency, or a lack of effort. If you're in a leadership position saying "no" in that way, that is the ultimate failure of leadership.

There are dozens of great resources on the idea of essentialism and other "no" empowering ideologies.

If you don't understand the general concept that saying "no" can be okay and can actually lead to a better "yes" in the future, I cannot help you here further.

It's something you are going to have to experience to truly understand.

Ask the Person in the Trenches but Help Them Understand the Battlefield

Often, but not always, those who make decisions are levels removed from the people who have to carry them out.

Regardless of hierarchical structure, those making the decisions need to disseminate a clear and concise version of what is happening to those who are "doing."

They also need to take the perspectives and input from those who are "doing" to make sure they are aware of trench-level, situational factors that may be changing/affecting the bigger picture goals and outcomes.

As a leader, you need to understand the "temperature" of your people and the context they are working in. This is invaluable information as you will be able to gather insight as to why people are getting "cold," "warming up," or "on fire" as it relates to the goals you are trying to accomplish and how they interact with you.

Having a context to the environment they are working in also provides clarity as to some of the factors that influence their "how" and their "why."

Perspectives from the Battlefield

The trench, the battlefield, the hilltop, and the clouds—these four perspectives (or positions) are what you must consider when dealing with anyone above and below you in your professional career. While there are often more organizational hierarchy layers than four, these four qualify and quantify all the possible strata in between. It's just a question of how granular you want to go breaking down the layers into sublayers given your specific context.

Anyone in the trenches is someone who's specifically working on the front line of the job. It's someone who's living in the thick of the situation day in and day out. And because of this, their perceptions and perspective are often skewed towards the real-world implementation and execution of whatever service or product you're trying to provide as they are the arm of action.

Their viewpoints are often pragmatic and directly linked to their own situational benefit, given their immediate level of engagement and experience. This information is a double-edge sword as it can both help the overall battlefield but also draw in and waste resources unnecessarily given its limited global view. This position has the most blind spots.

Across the larger battlefield, however, is usually the middle manager or some of those who come out of the trenches to move position across the landscape.

This slight shift in perspective, because of some level of mobility in a designated area or a static position with multiple areas in view, allows for a somewhat bigger viewpoint of the encompassing space. However, it is still limited because of the chaos of what's going on all around them and their lack of control of what is beyond their view. They still have blind spots—just at a new reference level.

Since there is more happening than they can control around them, anyone in this role is critical as their perceptions can significantly influence outcomes or cause breakdown in alignment and coordination of those in the trenches.

Anyone in the trenches or on the front lines of the battlefield will not always have the totality of information, access to information, or decision-making responsibility to make a large-scale impact beyond their immediate scope but their influence can create massive impacts on that global picture for those above them. Failure at their level can be critical across the battlefield without them even knowing they had that impact.

When you have a battlefield viewpoint, you're often overwhelmed and limited by everything going on in front of you; that minimizes your ability to truly see what's happening outside of your field of vision.

It creates a demand for a hilltop view, which is usually the first level of commanding positions that have the ability to see the entire battlefield. The caveat here is that because of a more expansive view, they often lack the ability to see within the trenches or see more than a single area of reference at a time. There is still a blind spot, albeit a different type.

Consider yourself being on the hilltop and there'll be multiple trenches, multiple positions, and multiple angles below you. As you look down, you'll only be able to see in or out of certain areas; although you'll be able to see all the areas, you won't be able to see the nuances and slight differences within each unless you adjust your position on the hilltop.

You might not see the mud in the trench on the right-side slowing people down and the need for the resources (boots or drainage) to get things moving fast again because you can see directly into the left trench and that issues do not exist there.

That is where the information being passed back up to the hilltop from those on the ground is vital. There could be a missing piece or a lack of perspective from those on the hilltop, such as the muddy situation on the right, that they don't take into account because it was either not communicated to them or it was simply just not viewed as important enough to be communicated.

This is where the fourth and final position is needed—the cloud-level view. This detached viewpoint allows you to see all things at once. It allows you to understand the operational structure of everything going on that allows you to make better decisions to those that oversee the hill, the battlefield, and then the trenches.

The key to this, however, is you cannot stay at the cloud level for any length of time as it is a skewed viewpoint. And to truly understand what you are looking at from the cloud viewpoint, you have to have experience each of the previous three positions.

Oftentimes, leaders have the battlefield view and can't rise into the clouds because they lack the ability and knowledge to truly understand what defines the levels below them.

Their own perceptions and faults limit and convolute what they understand to be happening in that environment. They either aren't listening or simply don't understand the impact their choices are having.

Starting from the Mailroom is a Strategy for a Reason

I recently met someone during an interview, and we found so much common ground and stylistic similarities that he wanted to continue our conversation about leadership and management post-interview.

He had recently become a regional general manager overseeing around fifteen restaurants in the chain that he worked for. It was a position that was considered to be a "suit and tie" role and something he had no experience in.

He shared with me his story of how he ended up being in this role.

He started at eighteen years old, washing the windows on the weekends and doing general unskilled maintenance—the only thing he was qualified for, given he had not finished high school at the time.

In the course of ten years, he progressed through every single position within that original restaurant, from the starting point of a part-time, twelve-hour per week window cleaner to a full-time general manager running the entire restaurant. At the same time, he also earned his GED, college degree, and was doing an MBA at night because, in his words, he was never going to be limited in his growth simply because he hadn't checked a box.

He oversaw three restaurants because the town he lived in was a major metro area and had the population to support three within a four-square-mile space.

And he was moving onto becoming a regional general manager overseeing the profits and losses of approximately fifteen restaurants, which totaled over $13 million in sales.

There were numerous people above him who couldn't figure out how he was so successful, some looking to learn from him, and others discounting his success. How was he able to have the best employee-retention rates, the best customer satisfaction, and numerous other top-notch marks across the KPIs (key performance indicators) the parent-company higher-ups kept?

As he talked, it was clear that his ability to understand the trench, the battlefield, and the hilltop gave him the ability to have a cloud-level perspective when he needed it. At times, it gave him an eagle-eye ability to find the exact spot at the correct level where he needed to focus his effort to create the outcome he desired.

He had more self-doubt than he had faith in his ability to do the role because of his path to get to there. Something we talked about at length and something I helped him address. I'm happy to report, after two years of being in the role, that he has turned his region into the most successful one across the entire company nationwide.

He was recently promoted to become the national training coordinator, and along with a few of his protégées, makeup the company-wide management training team.

A funny coincidence to note, every one of the people on his staff have very similar paths; each having worked across multiple roles from the bottom to now the top of the food chain (pun intended), although they all have different personalities, styles, and growth patterns.

Help Maintain A Positive Work-Life Balance

In order to maintain operational capacity and minimize complacency, there needs to be some kind of work-life balance.

With that being said, in order to become better at your role, you have to be asymmetric in your professional development compared to outside life at some point in time. For how long you need to be this way is relative to both the profession you are pursuing, your own abilities, and what level of expertise you seek to have.

Likely in the early stages of development or at planned intervals, you will have to invest the time, effort, and energy to develop the skills needed to be a master in your craft.

You will need to "become the accountant," and this will require a temporary imbalance—but ideally, a short-lived one (for each stage of development). This deep and intense shift of focus can be hard and seem unfair in the moment, but it ultimately allows you the freedom to find greater balance longitudinally.

Look for ways to break free from unnecessary work, useless hours, and overall waste of time.

Being "on the grind" is a waste of time in most cases as being busy doesn't mean you are effective.

I often hear S&C professionals, as well as others, discuss how they are too busy to do anything but their job. Too busy to meet, too busy to talk on the phone, and too busy to help others in the profession.

That's scary.

I've never met anyone who is that busy—in any field, doing anything—and I'm talking Fortune 500 CEOs not just S&C coaches.

Inefficient and lacking in the ability to place things in the appropriate order of magnitude? Sure. But *that* busy? Not a chance, especially in athletics.

There needs to be an exorcism of the idea that the 100-hour work week somehow makes you more committed than someone who works 30–40 hours.

Putting in hours is a tricky thing. If they're productive, it can be an amazing way to get an edge, build relationships, etc.

If they're ineffective hours, then you are just missing out on other things you could be doing instead.

Here's a big secret: if your 100 hours isn't efficient and productive, you probably are spending 100 hours on only 30–40 hours' worth of work.

Imagine if you could streamline your effort—not take shortcuts or use life hacks—but simply be more effective with your time and free up 30–50% of your time.

There are plenty of ways to do that. I'm not going to give them all to you here. I will provide some ideas with the "order of magnitude" and a few other tidbits across this book. But you need to go figure out how to manage your time, manage your responsibilities, and manage your effort better. I don't remember where or when I heard it but the CEO of Dropbox had a great perspective on the 100-hour work week.

What I will add here, however, is a question: once you have created efficiencies to your effort and freed up time that was once busy, what are you going to do with your newly acquired time?

Be Careful How You Reinvest Your Time

This specific instance is related to a college S&C coach who I had previously worked with and was taking a new job that answers the question above—in the athletics context—but again, conceptually it can apply across all professions.

This person had just taken a new job—technically a lateral move—and went from having seven teams to work with to three teams to work with.

Their hourly load, total athletes to work with per week, and numbers of coaches/support staff to engage with was more than cut in half. From an hour per week standpoint, they had thirty hours back on their plate to divvy up as they saw fit.

In a conversation about what to do with the time now freed up, I said not to fall into the trap of reinvesting all of that free time into the job.

"You may want to take the thirty extra hours you have and put ten hours more into each team you work with. Think about what you could accomplish with ten hours more per group of athletes per week. *It would be amazing, right*? Wrong." I said.

I continued, "Think about it. Why not give each team five hours more per week and take the remaining fifteen hours for yourself? Improve your personal life relationships and be around your significant other for meals. Better yourself through education and development, get another degree or certification to open more doors, and maintain a growth mindset. Build a more balanced, well-rounded life all the while adding a good chunk of more time to the groups you are going to work with. Adding five hours a week to the quality of work you already do with the seven teams you had in this job is going to be a huge upswing for your three new teams in your new job."

One additional note of reference here is being developed by those you work for, a common theme I have mentioned numerous times.

A mentor once told me, "On any given day, your boss may ask of you more than they give, which is part of life and something you should expect to happen. On a monthly average, if they are asking for more than they are attempting to give back, give them six months, and if the balance is still out of whack by a large margin, find a new boss. They don't understand how to make you better or—even worse—aren't willing to make you better. If all they do is ask of you and don't focus on making you better than when you first arrived, working for them is going to suck the life from you. And no amount of money, title, or anything else is worth that imbalance in your life."

You need "you" time.

What are you doing to improve yourself?

What are you also doing to rest and recover from the advancement? Find a time every month to do something for yourself by yourself. Decompress. Detach. Shut off the phone and ignore emails and texts. Do you.

Don't let anyone get in the way.

If you've earned it in your own eyes, you won't think twice about it. If you haven't earned it in your own eyes, you will question yourself the whole time while doing it (that's an obvious sign you need to evaluate your situation better and the dynamics *not* that you shouldn't be doing it).

Pay Yourself First

This one comes straight from my grandfather. Pay yourself first; you did the work.

Every time you get paid, take a small piece (I go with 2% now, but previously I would go with five dollars) and do whatever you want with it, guilt-free.

You did the work to earn money, you get the first cut.

There will always be bills; there will always be costs, there will always be (fill-in-the-blank) for you to have to pay.

Whatever you do, *do not spend it on someone else. It is for you and you alone.*

Find the value in that and you will start to value yourself more, and you will be amazed at how that bleeds out into other facets of your life and how much more effective you are with your finances as well as your time, effort, and energy.

Chase the F-U Life not the F-U Money

Get to the point where you have aligned your values with your actions and your purpose with your effort. And chase the "F-U life" not F-U money.

Build the life you want that allows you to stay above the bullshit, the negativity and not just be able to have the material stuff. You'll be surprised that when you get to that point, the value is far beyond anything money can buy.

You can use a material thing as a driver to help you focus your efforts on an outcome. Everyone has the "poster on the wall" of a materialistic thing they want when "they've made it." Check out Andy Frisella's MFCEO Project podcast for more on this idea and other takes on using materialism as a driver to help you at times.

When you get to the point where you're working towards the life you want—not just the next cool toy—there will be a lot of things that just seem to fall into place for you. Call it whatever you want (karma, fate, etc.), but it's funny how the universe seems to respond.

7

KEYS TO SUCCESS

THESE ARE KEYS TO SUCCESS I'VE FOUND THAT SEEM TO HELP UNLOCK THE impassable doors both personally and professionally.

Most of them are honestly common sense, in my opinion, but as the first one explains, the obvious isn't obvious until it's palpable in the real world.

- Create Tangibility
- Know What You Know and Know What You Don't Know
- Concepts Over Content and Context Over the Construct
- If You Want Certain Things, Do Things a Certain Way
- Help Those Who Help You, Up and Down the Ladder
- Listening is Just as Important as Speaking
- Don't Force it if You Don't Need To
- Opportunity and Desire
- Everyone is New at Some Point, and Everyone is Replaceable
- When You Can, Sleep on it
- You Get Out What You Put in

Create Tangibility

By creating tangibility, I mean writing “it” down, speaking publicly to others about “it,” and creating an edifice that makes “it” real.

Most people don’t realize that things can sound wildly different in their head than when spoken aloud (even if it’s the exact same words you thought internally). What makes sense in our heads when we repeat it to ourselves, generally sounds or comes out totally different or doesn't have the same message compared to when we speak it to another person or write it down for someone else to read.

To stay on message and to stay in line with what you're trying to accomplish, one of the key things you need to do is create tangibility.

Tangibility helps build trust because it creates structure and a tangible artifact to go back to in absolute and relative terms over time.

This not only applies to personal growth and development but also in professional settings where you need to cover your ass and document situations.

A paper trail of texts, emails, and notes of meetings is a way to create tangibility. Just make sure you’re using them in a positive and productive way instead of just creating an additional burden.

There are a lot of times when you can create tangibility negatively or accidentally influence someone's perspective in a negative way because they may not be comfortable with things being “tangible.” Many poor leaders do not like to leave a paper trail because they can hide and defer blame better that way.

You have to be aware of how and why you’re doing certain things and then what perspective and dynamic they're creating.

Words written down or recorded (think video on your phone) are extremely powerful, and in this day and age, digital content is influencing people’s livelihoods in ways unthinkable two years ago, never mind a generation ago.

Always be aware of the tangibility you are creating. Some of it will last forever and can either haunt you for all your days or empower you to amazing heights. Check the “Hilarious Stories” chapter at the end of the book for a funny example of this.

Know What You Know and Know What You Don't Know

I knew I was on to something with this idea, not only that day playing soccer with my dad, but when I got to UConn and had the chance to learn from coach Jerry Martin.

Coach Martin, who sadly passed away in 2015, was a legend in the field of S&C. His genuine intensity about coaching, teaching, and mentoring those around him—not just physically, but as people—is still unmatched in my eyes. He was a tremendous mentor to me: someone who I learned more from then he probably realized he was teaching and someone who I would never have been able to repay for the opportunities he gave me.

SIDE NOTE—Let's be honest, the only reason Hudy ever called me, when she could have hired literally anyone in the industry, was because of Jerry. It was never said directly to me but I like to think because it was that obvious and no-one thought I was that dumb to believe otherwise.

I remember the first time I heard this phrase as clear as the day it happened, which was the first day I ever worked with Coach Martin for a football session.

About an hour before the session, I was in his office going over the plan and our conversation veered off course into a chalk talk that started with him saying, "Know what you know and know what you don't know."

As he covered the whiteboard with marker and I tried to scribble as much as I could down in my notebook, the highlight that emerged went something to the effect of, "It takes a much stronger person to admit they don't know something and to ask for help than for a lesser person to think they have all the answers and hide in fear of looking weak."

It was at that moment I knew that this recurring theme was one of the true keys to success and something I always needed to keep in mind.

When you know, you believe, and you're confident, stand your ground.

Always remember though, things change, sometimes faster than you expect. Your strong footing can become loose underneath you if you don't pay attention.

It's not possible to know it all; there is just too much.

I know more about the science of the body and developing human physiology than most people. I can say that fairly confidently given my background.

I can also say without a doubt and would be willing to bet my life on it, that in the grand scheme of things, I know about one-ten-thousandth of 1% of what there is possible to know on the subject. And every day someone is out there learning more than I ever have or will on the topic.

Every day I become more and more average in my knowledge and stronger and stronger in my position of knowing that I don't know anything.

What makes me dangerous is I learned how to learn and I am too dumb to quit.

Concepts Over Content and Context Over the Construct

This one I am going to keep simple. Look to learn from, adapt, and apply the concepts you learn and experience. The construct that they are packaged in is situation-specific and often not directly transferable to your "world."

Some of the best concepts don't necessarily apply to the context you might be in. Often, the conceptual framework you're working on needs to be readjusted to benefit the contextual framework you're working in.

The amount of information you can gain from listening and watching is staggering. Even in the digital age, if you know what to look for and know how to disseminate certain concepts and contexts in situations, you can always gain a better understanding of any person's situation or process dynamic.

If you're willing to listen, not just hear, watch, not just see, and have the patience to let things develop and have a manner to internalize all of the information, you'll be able to not get lost within the specifics of a construct and the semantics of content.

If You Want Certain Things, Do Things a Certain Way

This is a global concept that can be applied in micro and macro situations.

Be wary of trying to do things the same way to achieve an outcome. Be hesitant to lower the standard of what you do and expect a higher-quality outcome.

While many things can be repeated to achieve continuous forward outcomes, there will always come the point of diminishing returns.

You have to be willing to try something new, something different, or something that previously did not work but could work now.

Never operate from the framework of "we've always done it this way" or any similar sentiment. If you work with or for someone who says those words or are the person who say's those words, look around you for the rider on the pale horse, he can't be far away.

Help Those Who Help You, Up and Down the Ladder

I wouldn't be here today if it wasn't for numerous people who helped me along the way. They provided me with opportunities, resources, etc., to be successful. There are too many names to list, although some do appear throughout this book.

Far too often, people focus their eyes up the ladder and only put effort into helping those that can help them on their ascent.

Unfortunately, when those people fall, they have only left a pile of stepped-on individuals beneath them—none of whom are likely to help them.

While the people above you may give you your big break, remember that it's the people below you who give you the chance to be successful.

No one has or ever will do it all alone.

No one is that good and no one ever will be.

Always take the time to be appreciative and thank the people at both ends of the spectrum. It comes back to professional respect: everyone plays a part and everyone has their role.

At a previous job, I counted among my favorite colleagues a friend who I would talk to about our team's games, debate individual players' potential, and trade craft beers with. This guy wasn't my boss, a colleague, or someone I supervised. He was the building's custodian.

Many people we worked with wouldn't give him the time of day as if his role was beneath theirs. Little did many know that this guy owned multiple businesses, hustled his ass off, and had a clear vision and purpose in life. He worked at the school specifically to get his children the free college education offered to employees.

He was my go-to barometer for what someone in the department was truly like as his interactions with them always revealed their true character. Any time I had to get a better read on someone or know how they had been the past few days, if I hadn't seen them, I would ask him. More than once, he let me know someone was in a good mood and helped strike while the iron was hot; or on the other hand, if someone was having a bad day, and it probably wasn't the moment to spring whatever it was I was planning on springing on them.

I specifically chose this example because, while I could have gone into helping interns and those you directly work with, I think that is an obvious and standard part of the job.

If they work directly under you, you should be taking care of them to the best of your ability; developing them to be better than when they came to you and set them on the path to being better than you. That's the baseline.

The question is are you willing to do that to people not directly under you?

Are you willing to take the time to always look to build those above and below you regardless of their connection to you?

What do you want your legacy to be with those who only knew of you — not just those who worked for you?

Listening is Just as Important as Speaking

At times, you need to stop and listen.

Just be aware that listening is different from hearing.

Let that float around in your head for a while and then ask yourself, *Am I listening to people, or am I just waiting to speak in return*?

Some of the most powerful leaders I've ever studied or had the benefit of working with could accomplish more with a look or gesture than many others do with a million words. It was because they listened to what was said and knew better than to add their own words to what had been spoken.

Don't Force It if You Don't Need To

This one, while extremely obvious, I find the hardest for subpar leaders to understand—especially ones who can't delegate effectively.

There will be times in life when a lot of things are happening at once. And your best bet is simply to pause and listen to the drumbeat and feel the ebb and flow of the situation before acting or choosing not to act.

I think a lot of people are unaware of or aren't willing to pay attention to that kind of nuance in situations.

People often don't take even a single breath to try to see the impact of the choice they are about to make. Instead, they act immediately and try to force an issue to prove their position or just make a choice.

Having control and discipline is not only a personal attribute, it's also related to how you operate around other people.

Yelling at someone and pulling the "chain of command" card are two ways you can interact with others as a leader, but often, it's best not to.

One of my favorite examples of not understanding this concept involves two head coaches that I worked with previously.

They both always had the same approach to problems; they always had to push people's buttons to get their way—no matter the issue— serious or trivial.

They had no diplomacy and no compromise. Even though they didn't need to create conflict, they always did simply just to make it known how they felt, what they wanted, or what they felt they lacked (actual or perceived).

They both created a dynamic where it became a "cry wolf" scenario. A lot of people didn't want to help them because they constantly "complained" and when something was actually wrong, most everyone let things stay wrong or were slow to address the problem just to spite these two coaches.

It was sad to see, but also enlightening, because it hammered home the phrase, "Just because you can doesn't mean you should."

While this example has a negative framework to it, bear in mind that that this can also be related to positive efforts.

There are plenty of things you can do to create a positive outcome in the short term, but you always have to remember what kind of precedent that sets. Not every short-term, positive precedent creates long-term, positive outcomes. Can you think of something in this vein related to your current role?

Sometimes you have to leave an acute issue unresolved, and thus not set a precedent that is unsustainable or unfavorable, to allow the longer-term positive outcome to be realized in a more viable and sustainable manner.

Sometimes doing the right thing in the moment is not the right thing to do for the future. Seeing that is critical if you are trying to accomplish a larger vision.

It's the difference between chess and checkers.

Opportunity and Desire

In order to be successful, there are two things you need: opportunity that may or may not always present itself and desire, which can wax and wane over time.

If you don't have the desire, you aren't in the game, you can't play without it.

If you're not truly invested in what you are pursuing, you should stop pursuing it. Eventually, the misalignment will catch up to you, beat you down, make you jaded, and tarnish the experience. It will cause you to lose "operational capacity." Purposeful quitting has its place.

So how do we best define desire to make sure we can create positive alignment with our actions?

In this context, desire is the willingness to do what's necessary and being prepared or preparing for whatever undertaking you seek to accomplish. This happens regardless of whether the opportunity to realize that desire is or ever does become available.

So many people miss out on the opportunity because they weren't prepared to the level they needed to be even though they had some level of desire.

Opportunity is fleeting and uncontrollable.

You never know where, when, or why an opportunity will present itself.

If you don't have the desire to be prepared as best you can, which may still not even be enough, you'll never have a chance to seize the opportunity if it arises in whatever form it does.

To quote Coach Martin, "If you're successful, it's your fault. If you fail, it's your fault."

Preparation and It Not Being Enough

You may need help and you may or may not get it.

You may ask for help and may not receive it.

Sometimes, it's sink or swim, and you still may not be able to do everything that is asked of you.

You may not always have the skills and ability to meet the challenge and overcome the obstacle but you'll have to try to do it anyway.

Even if you're doomed to fail, know that you don't stand a chance, and the entire attempt is pointless from the outset, you still have to convince yourself with the utmost belief that you can—and that no matter what happens the apex of your abilities is the only output you will put forth.

At that moment, where you're willing to go as far as you can go even though it may not be enough, that's when you will truly see what you are capable of.

Working Smart vs. Working Hard

As I've mentioned before, if you're not working hard, then you're not even in the game. One of my favorite ways to explain the difference between smart and hard work is using the example of "the ladder." Say you're in front of a wall (an obstacle to overcome) and you're trying to get over it. Well, what most people do is throw up a ladder and climb up it as fast as they can to get over the wall.

What smart work entails is first asking yourself, "Is this the right wall?" There is nothing worse than putting the ladder on the wrong wall. You'll have done all the work to put the ladder up and climb to the top before realizing it was all for nothing. All of the time, effort, and energy you spent was a waste. You ended up "here" when you needed to be "there."

As you better understand the manner in which you calibrate your effort to maximize efficiency, the next thing you should ask yourself is, "Do I even need a ladder? How high is the wall?" Because if the wall is only three feet high and you throw up an eight-foot ladder, you've put in a lot more effort than was needed.

Those last questions are the true essence of being on the path to working smart. The final step is getting to the point where you ask questions like, "Should there even be a wall?" You could spend all your time finding the right wall to climb or the appropriate ladder to use; but this third layer of the onion is where you realize that you could spend all your time trying to get over a wall, trying to find the ladder, and planning the appropriate processes to make that happen, but if what you need to do is walk over a little patch of grass, there wasn't even a wall to begin with.

Everyone Was New at Some Point, and Everyone is Replaceable

This comes from a card I received from a colleague when I was just an intern trying to make my way and he was leaving for another job. Matt, who was a GA at the time, was someone who had a profound impact on me in just a couple of months we worked together.

It's no surprise that he's doing tremendous things working with the military population because, even at a younger age, he had a keen sense of what it took to be successful, in regard to work ethic and understanding his role up and down the ladder.

Written in the card, which also came with a small food gift card (Matt understood the way to my heart as well as the need to feed poor interns) was, *Come in every day like it's your first day. Always act like you're the new guy.*

I didn't know it at the time but that phrase was something that would always stick with me. It was something I reflected on numerous times when I would be organizing my desk and find it again.

Act like you're new but also know that you are replaceable. Never get complacent and never go into cruise control.

Have the first-day-of-work passion every day you go to work.

If you don't, find new work.

Also, part of the lesson I learned from Matt, given the way he treated those underneath him, was you also always have to be willing to educate the new person and be educated like you're a new person (even if you are not).

We all were, at one time or another, inexperienced and unknowledgeable.

We all were the new person at some point in our careers.

Be willing to teach, coach, and mentor when appropriate; and also, be willing to be taught, coached and mentored. Because if you won't or don't, someone else will. And soon you'll find yourself on the outside looking in.

Everyone Is Replaceable, Even Family

Once there was a sports coach and an S&C coach who were brothers-in-law. The sport coach fired the S&C coach because he didn't want the S&C coach to do a lower-body workout one day and the S&C coach did it anyway.

There is obviously a lot to unpack in that example, such as having too rigid of a framework instead of a flexible one, but let the bigger lesson sit: if even family is replaceable, then you are too.

When You Can, Sleep on It

This one is a classic.

Take time to think about decisions. Take a reasonable amount of time to think through the process and understand the effects your choice could have.

"When you can, sleep on it," isn't just an internal maxim, it can also be discussing the decision with someone else to gain perspective and valuable insight.

Often, an outside perspective can help you think through things.

Be aware of giving yourself time to emotionally detach, especially if you become heavily charged and influenced by your feelings (regardless of what they were) in the process of coming to a decision.

Far too often, people make decisions in the heat of the moment with a high emotional charge even when they don't need to. If they had given themselves a little longer to work through things, separate their feelings from the situation, and a gain better perspective, they could have made a better, more purposeful decision.

There are certainly times when had I been able to be more of a scalpel than a sledgehammer, I would have made things easier in the long run. Hindsight is twenty-twenty.

On the flip side, you also have to be able to make quick decisions if they are thrust upon you.

There are times where you do have to make an immediate choice with lack of evidence or context, mounting pressure, and unexpected situational factors.

You need to have the confidence and skills to do that. It's a skill that takes time to be good at.

And you shouldn't just paralyze your decision-making process by delaying action in order to "sleep on it" when a decision needs to be made quickly.

"Sleeping on it" in a moment of immediacy may be a five-minute detachment to get a cup of coffee or listening to a favorite song. Something that helps you quickly detach, literally slow down to breathe, and figuratively gather and compose yourself to best move forward.

I can think of no better example of incorrectly using the "sleep on it" approach than an administrator who I worked with previously.

This person, in some circles, is regarded as a significant figure in the athletic world, having the paper résumé to back it up. But when you look at what they've accomplished, the track record of action just isn't there.

They're infamous for and so inept at making decisions in a timely manner—and making effective decisions at all—that it was openly a running joke among all staff that he ever worked with, across multiple jobs.

It got to the point where the staff's attitude, unfortunately, split into either take action first and tell him about it after or—worse—take no action at all, because it was viewed as pointless to try to do anything, since he wouldn't make a decision on anything.

In other words, it was easier to ask for forgiveness than permission, which created a whole slew of other problems.

For those who chose to ride the "operational-complacency" bus, another set of equally problematic issues for all involved would arise.

The individual would pass the buck and defer responsibility up or down the chain of command by not deciding until after an important date or milestone. And then it didn't matter what the decision was, because the critical juncture had passed.

They used this both as a delay tactic and a complacency marker, allowing themselves plenty of time to "work on things" and often "not remember" previous conversations even happened.

It was funny how "he would take such great notes" during a meeting to only not remember the meeting and have no record of those notes a few weeks later.

He was the ultimate example of the phrase, "Just because you've done something for twenty-five years doesn't mean you've done it well."

You Get Out What You Put In

This one is fairly simple. What you put in is what you get out.

If you don't put the time, effort, and energy into things, if you're not consistent and committed, dedicated, and disciplined, you will never be successful.

How you define success can vary. Not everyone's goals are the same, and the path may wind differently to the same end point, but no one ever accomplished anything by not doing anything (lottery winners still technically had to play).

One of my favorite lines to use in this context is, "You cannot Febreze your way through things. Eventually, people will smell the stink."

The fastest way to enhance your own bullshit detector is do the needed things to be successful in your endeavors and spend time with people who are even more successful than yourself, in whatever they are trying to be successful in. Elevate your circle as they say. You'll quickly be able to smell and tell those around you who have a Febreze stash.

8

TEACH, COACH, MENTOR

A LEADER MUST SET A HIGH STANDARD FOR THOSE IN THEIR PURVIEW. However, you cannot just set a high standard and hold an employee or a team accountable to that standard; you have to guide them to find their own path and eventually create their own high standard.

Leadership doesn't stop with you setting the standard and asking people to reach for it.

Leadership begins there. It's within the classic mantras such as "What you tolerate, you encourage," and "If you raise the bar, you lose the losers. If you lower the bar, you lose the winners."

Setting and maintaining the standard is important. But the next step is encouraging that person to create their own standard and manage their own performance because just accomplishing or living up to your bar doesn't do anything for them when you are no longer there.

A true leader (we'll get to more on this later) must be able to affect positive change on that person after that person has moved on from the leader. In a sense, helping establish a lifestyle built off the legacy of how they were led.

True leaders instill an almost religious zeal in those that learn from them; it truly becomes a dogmatic shift in their thinking (I'd venture a guess and say it also creates measurable changes in their bodies across multiple systems directly impacting their physiology).

The core elements of developing those under you to be more operationally efficient is made up of three pillars:

1. Teach: show the how and where
2. Coach: provide feedback on what and why to develop a system of self-sufficient skill development in the fields taught
3. Mentor: offer guidance for further mastery via gaining wisdom

A leader is someone who is a teacher, a coach, and a mentor.

You can be a teacher. You can be a coach. You can be a mentor. But if you're not all three things, then you'll never be a true leader.

Leading is part teaching, part coaching, and part mentoring while also knowing when to do neither.

Teaching Philosophy

Would you rather be a cook, a sous chef, or a chef?

A cook takes a predetermined recipe (predefined methods), gathers the necessary ingredients, and follows the instructions given to recreate the original to the best of their ability.

A sous chef, while more adept than a cook and at times able to stand in place for a chef, can add their own flair to the chef's recipe within reason. Sometimes the sous chef makes something unique but is still bound by the demands of the chef.

A chef is someone who has a level of mastery in the culinary arts that allows them to create an original recipe at any moment in time using whatever methods they choose from any combination of ingredients.

While the cook, sous chef, and chef are all making dishes and they're all using the same ingredients and equipment in the kitchen (a knife is a knife after all regardless of who is holding it), it's the knowledge, intent, and purpose that defines the role and utilization of tools.

This is a universal idea and one that is important from a teaching standpoint.

You have to start as a cook. You have to follow a recipe, and you have to take other people's work, and you have to make dishes to the best of your ability. Take tier system or 5-3-1 or triphasic: do it as prescribed regardless of situational factors, throw it on the menu, and see if it sells.

Being a cook gives you the time—whether it's time in the kitchen, "under the bar," in the saddle, or whatever you want to call it—that you need to build and develop the critical skills and experiences (successes and failures) necessary to be able to take the step then to become a sous chef.

It also allows you the chance to embrace your role and learn how to empower yourself by building confidence. You learn that each recipe, while having a purpose and making sense in the way they mixed ingredients and used tools, can always be slighted adjusted to keep the essence but adjusted to the specific context of your situation.

As a sous chef, you have some mastery, some skills, and some experience.

You probably also have a forte—you're pretty good at one thing or another—and the reason for that is both the time you have invested and the depth of your experience.

Because you've taken the time to try and replicate so many other things, you've started to hone in on what you're good at and what you bring to the table.

Throw in a splash of 5-3-1, a pinch of Westside, shake it up with some triphasic, and cap it off with a tier mesocycle with an Olympic lifting focus. See how it tastes and either look to put it on the menu or go back to the drawing board. But at this point you are no longer following the method only. You're taking the essence of what the creator intended and applying it to the situation you currently face as best you can using their principles as boundaries.

As you improve, though, you know that the end goal is to become a chef. To reach your potential, the first 85% of the work is up to you.

You can be a cook all you want, but until you have exposure to a higher level where you can experience the palpable difference in your abilities to those you are up against, you will never move much higher than 85%.

At that point, in an effort to achieve that level of ability to get to 95%, you need guidance. And that's what being a sous chef is: you have the opportunity to learn from a chef and you get to advance your practice with the guidance of a true master or masters.

While a great teacher can get you to 95%, they can't push you over the edge to 100% of your ability.

To get you from sous chef to chef, and this is where a lot of people struggle, is not about specialization anymore.

Being a sous chef is what's allowed you the opportunity to specialize in something that you're good at. To become a chef, or in order to get that last 5%, you have to believe in yourself, you have to go back to the basics, and you have to become a master generalist capable of owning the skillset—not just having it.

It's kind of like an hourglass. You start at the top of the hourglass as a cook with a great many other people. As you learn and improve, you trickle down and become a sous chef at the smallest point of the hourglass. And at the apex of the funnel is where a lot of people get stuck in the mindset that they have to be so specific, in control, and dominate a tiny little space.

They don't realize that they have to broaden their scope again to pursue ultimate mastery and become a chef.

That's why they are so focused and often falter. They don't realize it's no longer about only knowing "how to cook," but using all of their skills and all of their experiences and all of their knowledge in a variety of ways, adjusting and adapting when needed and at their own whim.

Have you ever watched the cooking shows on the Food Network?

I think so many people enjoy watching Food Network shows because they like to watch a master at work. Viewers learn that the people who are successful aren't necessarily the ones who say, "Oh, I've worked with this ingredient before," or "Oh, I've made this already."

It's the chefs who may not know the ingredient but have a keen understanding of all the different methods that they could use on the ingredient; they draw from past experience and use analogous thinking to create. That's what being a chef is.

The path to mastery: following and replicating as a cook, taking some level of ownership and adding some specialized flair as a sous chef, to finally having the autonomy and the intuitiveness to be able to create at any moment as a chef.

The chef knows when to use their internal abilities, when to seek external ones, and most importantly when to take controlled guesses.

Your goal as a teacher is to establish those three developmental processes because learning is not enough.

It's no longer about just being exposed to ideas and content but understanding how to use assessment and critical feedback to evaluate the metrics that drive the purpose of your effort.

You need to have the ability and scope of the human element in order to blend the art and science of being a teacher; to teach the appropriate level of technical development and refinement in the manner best suited for the student.

As a teacher, your way isn't the only way. You have to be willing and flexible enough to adapt your style to transfer your knowledge in a way that your student can understand.

A student can only learn as deeply as a teacher is willing to teach. They can only develop as far as a coach is capable of coaching. And they can only find their own mastery if their mentor is willing to let them without the crutch of the mentor.

Coaching Philosophy

What is the Purpose of a Coach?

The purpose of a coach is to empower others to have the confidence and the skills to meet the demands placed upon them.

The essence of coaching another person is showing them how—and giving them the feedback—to achieve something that they otherwise would not be able to achieve.

If you are teaching someone to do something that they don't believe they can do, the higher mission is to instill confidence. Because when you've created confidence in the individual or group, you've given them the belief in their abilities to produce at their maximum level of effectiveness.

In order to build and develop confidence in another person or group of people, you have to do three things: you must establish culture; you have to understand how to work smart, not just hard; and you have to understand the continuum of opportunity and desire.

Never Put Doubt Where There is Confidence

Understand that the factors that give athletes confidence are the things you must be careful with when coaching. One of the biggest mistakes you can make in coaching is putting doubt into your athlete's mind about something that they have confidence in.

This can be a sharp edge to walk. Because if their confidence comes from something that can negatively impact their long-term development or ability to maintain a high level of performance, you have to seek to limit their exposure to that stimulus while also building and developing their confidence in other tools that aren't as detrimental to them.

If what gives them confidence is a nonnegative exposure or process, then it should not be stopped or undercut; let it happen but don't let it become a crutch for the ability to achieve the desired level of performance.

This is a concept, especially in the Special Operations Forces (SOF) tactical setting, that more human performance coaches need to understand. You don't make it through some of the most grueling and intensely combined mental and physical selection processes ever created without doing something right. Somewhere along the way something worked. It's a question of efficiency (fine tuning) and operational longevity (good maintenance plan)—not radically altering effort due to your own biases as a coach. Clearly there's more to be said on this topic but this was a great example to use given the above subject.

Understanding the Three Levels of Coaching

First, there is the gross-skills coach, someone who knows how to teach and develop the broad skills required for whatever outcome you're seeking to learn.

Gross-skills coaches are best with unmolded clay and are able to bring shape and character to their clay; they take people who have potential but no development and get them to a level of passable ability.

These coaches have a good understanding of the basics but not necessarily a wide variety of teaching skills or real depth to their tactical or technical knowledge. Therefore, they can teach the correct and often most simple way of how to do something and lay a solid foundation.

It might not be perfect and it might leave open the door for a bad habit to form, but they can help you accomplish the "general idea" of what you are trying to accomplish.

The key here as an athlete is not getting stuck with this type of coach when your skillset and ability has gone beyond their purview.

If the coach isn't actively working on bettering themselves (to in turn help you), it's necessary to look elsewhere to take the next step. This should be done on good terms to the best of the athlete's and coach's abilities. If this becomes a contentious point and destroys their relationship, then both the coach and athlete are at fault.

The next level of coach is the developer; these coaches are able to take unmolded or shaped clay and work it into a refined product.

They have the ability to add levels of detail a gross-skills coach simply isn't able to, but they are not able to do this to every facet of the athlete.

As an athlete, this is the kind of coach who you want to work with in your initial stages, allowing you to stay with them longer and over time maximize your development with them.

If you transfer to them after having some level of development under another coach, you may see a performance decrease at first, but over time you should achieve a higher level of performance than ever before. This slight dip and compensation are the same effects found in "general adaptation syndrome" but include not just physical aspects but also the learning and relationship processes of working with a new coach.

Generally speaking, developer coaches are constantly trying to better themselves and purposefully seek to improve themselves to improve their athletes.

But if they are restricted by certain dogmas related to technical or tactical methodologies, the last type of coach we discuss should either replace the developer or be brought into the fold as an additional coach to bolster knowledge in lacking areas.

This last type of coach is a refiner who can only work with well-shaped clay; a coach who works with an athlete who simply needs specific detail work.

They may struggle to teach the basics because their work focusses on a level of technical and tactical-specific mastery. If the athlete doesn't already have those fundamental skills developed, they could significantly struggle to learn the systems of the refiner.

At this level, both coaches and athletes have to truly evaluate the need to chase this level of mastery compared to working on other things. Many athletes choose coaches that are refiners when they're not yet ready to handle that level of technical-tactical development. Many coaches think they are refiners when they don’t have the level of mastery needed to bring someone else to that level.

An athlete not understanding the different types of coaches and what their current needs and actual potential are can have a significant impact on the athlete becoming burned out, washing out of the coach’s system, or having a maladaptation that ruins their careers.

What's more, as soon as the relationship between coach and athlete has more to do with ego than realistic, consistent growth—performance will suffer.

Any competitive athlete and any competitive coach will always want to gravitate towards more advanced and complicated training because they view it as the only way for them to get better and to push harder.

Nothing can be more dangerous than this.

More complex training does not lend itself to increases in performance if the athlete isn’t ready, doesn’t need that level of complexity or the coach can’t properly teach the skills of that higher level.

This is where it up to the coach to instill a specific sense of purpose and process of development into the athlete so that they don't overshoot their training and undermine their growth and development, no matter what level of ability or potential they have.

Earning the Capital "C" Coach Moniker

Coaches with a capital C are the ones who have earned the moniker for a lifetime; coaches with a lowercase *c* are the ones who've earned it for the moment.

Culture

Culture has to be created and maintained every day; it's an ongoing ebb and flow.

Everyone thinks of culture in terms of motivational quotes or some kind of nebulous idea that is important but isn't always something they can impact.

The truth is much like these two quotes that you've likely noticed I use a lot: "If you raise the bar, you lose the losers. If you lower the bar, you lose the winners," and, "What you tolerate, you encourage." Culture involves active participation by the person setting it as well as those participating in it.

This is one of the best definitions of culture I have found, although I don't know who I can attribute it to as it was hastily written in my notebook during a lecture at an event I attended (if anyone knows who said this, please let me know so I can properly cite the source in future editions and work):

> "Culture is the way of life of a group of people consisting of the behaviors, beliefs, and values they accept, generally without question, that is passed down by communication and imitation from one generation to the next."

By this definition, culture is all about fostering positive relationships and creating buy-in.

The key to culture is to set guidelines for people to follow. You should have some type of tangible structure that outlines the approach that should be taken and the expectations you have for the achievements desired.

From this framework, you can then teach and continually reinforce the appropriate behavior within that framework.

That consistent behavior can be measured against the output action and can then help build confidence over time through success and controlled failure. This allows you to build culture.

People often mistake a coach, business, or individual who is organized as having a plan and thus having a culture. People often think that just because they have things in some kind of system (are organized) means they have a strategic, goal-driven, process-oriented approach (a plan) and therefore a culture.

Culture is not having a plan. But you need to have a plan in order to build culture.

Building Culture

One of the first steps in building a culture is defining who you are and how that impacts how you do things. Please see the "philosophy development cycle" in the "Building Philosophy" section for more info related to this topic.

You'll notice that we often go back to the individual as the root cause because their machinations dramatically impact their actions and, thus, the results for the group and for the system.

Next, you have to ask yourself some questions.

What is your mission? And does it make sense for you to try and accomplish this mission given who you are and what you're trying to do?

Also, what is the lasting impact of doing all of this, or the big-picture vision?

This is where people often mistake defining their purpose with having a barometer to navigate future development and growth based on original intent.

You have to ask yourself what the ultimate goal is beyond simply being successful in competition, because if being successful in competition is the only vision you have, then your mission is simply to win.

The question then becomes, what happens when you don't win? How do you accept failure and grow from it if the only thing that matters is winning and you spent no time on anything other than trying to win?

This may be a counterintuitive process to most sport coaches or inexperienced coaches as they believe the true essence and vision of what they're trying to do is win in competition.

In fact, winning is the outcome of having built and developed an appropriate culture around a certain ideal: the "why."

The ideal of what the culture needs to be is relative—there are no absolutes. But as long as the culture is staying true to what the mission is, the vision will eventually be accomplished.

Isn't that success no matter how you define success?

It's building a culture for people to stay on mission and ultimately achieve the long-term vision of what you set out to accomplish.

Culture is as relative as it is absolute. So, the last thing you have to ask to find your culture is how far away or how close are you to the culture you want?

Alignment

If you want a quick primer on how to keep alignment in the culture you create and the importance of tying a group together with passion and dedication, find the books of teams that have long histories of success—not singular instances, but continuous cyclic success.

In the pages of those books, you will be able to disseminate the process-orientated system that was built to last beyond any individual and how that is context and situationally relative.

There is no absolute manner in which alignment is maintained; it is a context and concept-relative action for the given culture, the style of the curator(s), and the focal point in which that culture was created around.

Consider that the manner in which you maintain alignment for a culture may change from one group of people to another group of people over time within the same culture.

While winning or achieving desired goals is often what the culture of the team is built around, it isn't always the inflection point.

If you are lazy, watch the movies of the books—there are plenty.

Just know that you need to have a process to assess alignment and also a process to realign. If you do not, you will come to understand insubordination, resentment, and mutiny. It's just that simple.

SIDE NOTE—This is one of those moments where I'm purposely leaving something out by the way.

With Those Who Work for You

While I often prefer to look at it from the position of "with those who work *with* you," I specifically chose to use the word "for" to give context to the dynamic of responsibility you have in a position of leadership for those who you are accountable for.

In relation to developing culture and professional development with your staff, the goal should always be, "to teach you everything I know, so you are able to push beyond what I was able to achieve while doing it in your own way."

If you are a leader, are you building others up or are you taking from them?

As we have discussed, the ultimate goal is to have them not need you. In order to get to that point, you have to actively put in time energy and effort for them to be able not to need you.

It doesn't just happen if they work with you for a few years.

I always told the people who worked with/for me, "the Joe way only works for Joe." They should seek to take the "Joe way," as well as everyone else's around them, see what they like, see what they don't like, and make their own way. Because if you are not authentic to yourself, then you will never be authentic to those you work with.

You can certainly be an amalgamation of those you have learned from, but at the core, it must be your way (again, see the "philosophy development cycle").

Developing others is more than just going to conferences or giving autonomy for someone to do things the way they see fit.

There are two separate and distinct manners in which you need to develop those around you.

First, it's developing them from an empowerment standpoint: building and developing their self-efficacy so that they are and view themselves as confident and capable while still being willing to learn and grow.

It can be self-rewarding to help build someone in this way, but be sure not to be blinded by doing so. Empowerment is not enough. You need to also give them the hard skills to back up their new confidence so they can *do* things.

Therefore, the second kind of development deals with the hard skills. What tangible, actionable skills have you made them learn to improve their ability to *do* things?

This could be teaching a new modality of performance, such as a manual therapy technique, but it could also be sending them to public speaking seminars so they have more skills in their toolkit to communicate to their athletes and coaches. Work on not only what they lack but also what they have; seek to develop all of their hard skills while providing them an environment to be operationally efficient.

Generally speaking, both types of development bleed into each other and can either create positive feedback loops where one helps the other, but you have to be aware of how they can also create negative feedback loops on each other and stifle growth.

Role Development and Acceptance

Role acceptance is an important part of creating a more operationally efficient versus complacent environment and then allowing for the opportunity for further role development.

Helping people understand what their role is—how it can help in the micro and macro—allows role acceptance to happen. From there, if people know what is required of them, it allows additional responsibilities to be added to their plate when it makes sense to do so.

Have a process to rotate roles for selected exposure. This can help determine the best fit for responsibility based on personality type, physical potential, and demand and not pigeon hole any one person in an area of strength or in an area of weakness.

Let them be good at what they are supposed to be good at before having them try to be good at something else.

Stupid Questions

There are stupid people, and there are stupid questions.

Do not confuse stupidity for ignorance though.

There are ignorant people—some by choice and some by lack of information or experience—both of the latter of which are easily remedied if the person is open to it.

As we've discussed, a level of ignorance is needed at times and in certain contexts because it's important for creativity and not becoming too bound to certain dogmas.

As you gain an advanced level of technical and tactical knowledge, that's all you start to see. You start to try and apply the specific skills and knowledge you have to all situations versus being open and creative in applying new skills and knowledge to different situations.

Success is an Exclusive, Not Inclusive Environment

Not everyone makes it. One of the big fallacies that we've been telling people is that everyone's a winner.

One of the things we need to always remember is that anything that has a performance metric and creates rank is an exclusive environment.

Fundamentally, until we stop keeping score, the score matters. And even when we don't outwardly keep score, many still do internally because it's human nature.

Competition is exclusive; in competition we don't want everyone included. We only want the best. So, one of the things you must do in a competitive ranking environment is create some type of excluding mechanism.

Not everyone can be a part of or be successful in competitive environments.

Some people will naturally weed themselves out.

But some people will rise in that situation.

So, you must be willing and able to create an excluding environment because if it's too inclusive, you will have too many people who aren't able to consistently achieve the level of output desired.

If we keep score, who's better than someone else matters. I think that's one of the ultimate faults in the competitive sphere: people don't make it more exclusive.

You must be willing to cut ties and push people out. That's one of the factors needed in order to drive people to be successful.

Because they are constantly being ranked and evaluated, they must have the mindset that they're not here to make friends. They are there to win.

Everyone wants to be your friend after you win. No one wants to be your friend after you lose or fail.

Or, I should say, only your *true* friends will be your friends after you lose. A great barometer to determine who's truly there to help you versus who's not is who's there during your lowest points. The barometer to see who's fake is to watch them all disappear when you hit your low points.

You must be willing to push away the personal sociocultural need for acceptance among peers to develop a competitive edge.

Anyone who has achieved elite status in their physical performance has had to sacrifice the social and developmental time periods that others had because they were so focused on the training and development of their technical and tactical skills. There's only so much time in a day; if you spent it all training, you didn't spend it elsewhere.

It's not often that you find extremely elite level performers who aren't extremists in some aspects of their lives. Because balance and symmetry do not correlate well with the asymmetrical sacrifice needed to become that level of elite.

It's no surprise that elite-level athletes often have addiction issues, dependency issues, and relationship/interpersonal issues because the extremes in which they operate in their normal day-to-day setting never gave them the opportunity to build and develop the skills necessary to manage or not have those extremes in their everyday life after sport or between sport.

As we will see, there's a radically different mindset between optimum performance and health and wellness.

Building Culture in College Athletics

We are here to win and be successful in a results-driven business (college athletics). But our key focus as coaches is to mentor and develop young people in sport and in life because the following are important to us collectively:

- *Commitment and pride in us (team pride)*
- *Developing and building discipline and self-accountability (altruistic behavior)*
- *Displaying mental toughness and having resilience (strength of character)*

We strive to help build the constitution of character necessary in those athletes we work with to step up to challenges and overcome obstacles that get in their way both individually and as a team.

Why are these things important to us?

Because we seek to give those who come to us the opportunity to become self-sufficient, self-aware people of high moral fiber; people who are willing and able to do the things necessary to achieve personal and team success while representing us in a positive fashion, both during their time with us and after their time with us—in perpetuity—as we will forever be tied together.

Above, is my definition of what a successful culture is in the collegiate athletics setting. It is the sum total of every experience I've ever had in college athletics: the people I've worked with and the successes and failures at every level of both good and bad experiences.

It is a formulated amalgamation of what I have seen work and a rough approximation of an "ideal" (if such a thing exists).

While the ultimate authority on team culture is the head coach, I wrote this from the standpoint of an S&C coach who has the ability to impact team culture either by means of direct or indirect implementation.

Directly, when the sport coach requests them to do so. And indirectly, when the sport coach doesn't know how to do it themselves or chooses not to and the S&C coach needs to in order to accomplish their job. Sadly, this is common because most sport coaches don't know how or don't value the skills and time needed to build, define, and curate the needed culture in college athletics.

Please note that I referenced "in perpetuity" and being "tied together forever" because everyone in the society that we live in seemingly must be labeled regardless of the depth of their affiliation (a topic for a different day).

The first line in a news article and most likely the headline itself will always feature some combination of the following: former *X* school, *X* sport, and athlete name. Like the following: "Former UConn Track and Field Athlete Joe Staub..." Hopefully, it's a positive headline and not a negative one.

Being the Curator of Culture

As the leader of the S&C department you can never forget these things:

- Having done it is not enough, knowing how to do it is not enough. Everything works and nothing works; there are few absolutes.
- There are over 100 certifications, no national or state licensure, and minimal regulation on the industry. I know amazing coaches who aren't certified in anything, and I know terrible coaches with every certification under the sun.
- You must be educated, you must be creative, and you must experiment. But you must stay within a rationale framework. Did you intelligently craft your position with an objective, evidence-driven strategic, goal-orientated plan? If so, you can

never be "wrong"— you just can be philosophically disagreed with.

- You cannot simply make someone do something; you must be able to articulate and explain the "why." You must remember to coach who you have, keeping in mind what their abilities are, and work towards realistic and achievable goals for them.
- You must be a dealer in truth and open to learning from everything—even things not to do. Learn to focus on drawing a positive from everything; you must adapt like the body does to every stimulus—good or bad.

Mentoring Philosophy

Mentoring is the final piece of the teach, coach, mentor puzzle. Your goal should be to mentor those you work with to have the level of self-awareness and intuition necessary to know what needs to be done and the ability to correctly "do" without hesitation when the moment arises.

As a mentor, you should not be seeking to change a person—that's the wrong outlook. Everyone comes and goes at their own time and in their own way.

Instead, you must give them the opportunity, give them the knowledge and critical assessments (teach), and give them purposeful, directed, feedback and encouragement (coach) to develop the self-aware attitude needed for internal reflection.

Because only by internalizing their own development in combination with stimulus from the external environment will they be able to change and spur internal growth to better manage external conflict.

Ultimately, that means they don't need you because they have gained wisdom—not just experience or knowledge.

> "Wisdom is being able to connect the dots between your experiences and education, allowing you to create a cumulative net of knowledge you can draw and learn from, show others, and guide you in your own decisions."
> —My Dad (seriously, he says this all the time)

Growth Mindset

Growth is just another natural biological process of development given certain conditions.

If you never put a person in the right conditions needed for growth, they will never achieve it.

If they're thrust into situations or have conditions placed upon them, but don't have the confidence or skills to meet the task, they'll never be able to overcome the challenge and adapt. Instead, they'll be stuck in their same routine or, even worse, be crippled by the experience and immensely set back. Interesting takes on this idea and similar concepts are seen in books like *Outliers*, *Talent Code*, and *The Sports Gene* in the sport context, among countless others in other industries.

From the viewpoint of an individual, what you tolerate is what defines you. It determines the thresholds and limits of what you say you stand for versus what you act on.

Everyone wants to stand for something and be empowered by a higher purpose. Many don't do or aren't able to because it isn't always an easy path. People will challenge you, push back against you and your "why."

Not everyone is willing or able to stand their ground when challenged in their beliefs, especially if they are contrary to popular standards or norms.

Of those that do have principles, not all will be able to change their perspective or admit a mistake, choosing instead to buck the notion of their own infallibility. This within itself is entirely another issue.

Set standards that give people the opportunity to reach goals and create experiences that will then allow them to develop and grow. Even the things not to do are still things to learn from. Always seek to draw positives out of every situation.

Just like the body adapts to every stimulus, good or bad, you must do the same. You must be able to find the good in the bad and the bad in the good; draw a positive adaptation from it and don't let the maladaptation shape your change.

The Goal is Not to Need Me

While playing soccer in my youth, I once worked with a goalkeeping coach who knew a lot about goalkeeping. He had played at a high level himself and at practice he had a lot of good ideas for drills and theory of playing the position.

However, he thought that "coaching" also meant standing behind the goal during games in real-time and telling me what to do because that was what was done to him.

It took me all of one game to address it with him, and he could not understand why I thought it was burdensome. He thought it was helpful.

I had to explain to him that having his constant input during the game made me question my own instincts and affected my actions by slowing down my decision-making process rather than speeding it up.

I also didn't want to become dependent on his voice as the driver for my actions because he was not going to be at every game for the rest of my career.

I intuitively understood that if he had prepared me appropriately and I had put in the proper effort, I should be able to function without him.

I implemented this directly into how I trained my athletes and my staff. If I was able to prepare them correctly, they would be able to do things without me because I wasn't always going to be there and I didn't always have to be there.

When you develop a level of competency and autonomy within a person by teaching and coaching them, it will mean they don't need you to sit there and hold their hands anymore. You allow the highest level of their own ability to show through because they are the ones truly in control.

Far too many times, athletes are lost without their coach, depending on them for constant input and never developing any self-mastery and self-sufficiency.

P.O.L.I.S.H.

- Professionalism
- Organization
- Leadership
- Intuitiveness
- Stress management
- Hustle

One day I was working with a group of interns and one of them kept interjecting and interrupting everyone else. Not only was their input out of turn, but it was also coarse and lacked even the faintest situational awareness—of the topic and of who else was in the room (sport coaches working out).

Shortly after the session ended and everyone had left, one of my colleagues turned to me and said, "Man, he needs to be polished. He has potential, but he's just so rough around the edges."

While I had often heard the expression "be polished" before and it made sense, I was suddenly struck by an idea. What if "polish" was not only something that people need in their development—what if we could build a framework to do the "polishing."

Shortly thereafter, with some scribbled notes over lunch, this system was officially born.

Given I am looking at this particular portion at a more global viewpoint, I'm not going to drill down into this to from a professional S&C standpoint. Take the concepts and apply as needed to your context.

Professionalism

It's not just about appearance but that certainly places a role in perception.

It's not simply developing the craft but if you aren't doing that, you can't stay relevant in an ever-changing world.

There is a difference between developing your professionalism as a practitioner, as a professional, and as a person. If you aren't doing all three, you aren't going to be competitive for long.

Organization

As simple as it sounds, are you organized? Are you streamlined and efficient based around a repeatable process that you can adapt as needed?

Are you able to put things in their appropriate order of magnitude to maximize your effort, or do you not know how to task orientate?

That doesn't mean you have to have everything in calendars and notebooks because that is only one manner of expressing organization.

Everyone's system is different, but everyone has to have one. And it has to be constantly evaluated to see how it can be improved based on the changing situation and context you find yourself in.

Leadership

Leadership is the essence of "polish," that's why it's smack in the middle along with intuitiveness (this literally couldn't have worked out better when I was making this).

The reason there is a "smack in the middle" is that leadership and intuitiveness are the two things that must be built to create a self-sufficient person.

If you're a leader and you're a teacher, coach, and mentor, how do you develop leadership in others?

Will you give them the opportunity to develop micro-confidence in a controlled environment so they are ready when things are truly at stake?

You need to give them the opportunity to be placed in high-velocity decision-making situations and in low-velocity decision-making positions in order to test themselves.

There are many leadership styles to choose from—find the one that makes sense for you and allows you to help others find their own path.

Intuitiveness

You have to learn mastery of whatever technical, tactical, or strategic objective you need to have.

It's the difference between playing music and creating music.

The level of capacity for intuitiveness is individual. Not everyone will have the level of intuitiveness needed to be a maestro in music or the black swan in ballet. But whatever level you can develop your own intuitiveness to, you'll be able to connect the dots and be more proactive instead of reactive.

Don't mistake this only for the often-used intuition as a "gut feeling."

While there is certainly a part of being intuitive related to that side of things, it is also a learned skill.

Fall down the four-step OODA loop (observe, orient, decide, act) decision-making rabbit hole and see where it takes you.

Stress Management

Stress management is key to everything you do, from developing yourself to developing others.

There are three main components to stress management: mental toughness, resiliency, and hardiness (innate character versus learned coping mechanism versus the ability and will to overcome).

Those are three critical delineations in the stress management process. Understand not only how your own stress management is important but how you outwardly portray stress and what that does to those around you.

If you never thought of how your stress imposes stress on others and how the management of your own stress helps others, then you need to spend some serious time learning about the topic.

Hustle

While pure effort is a piece of the puzzle, it's not simply just that. Like I said previously, if you're not working hard, you're just not in the game. But just because you're working hard it doesn't mean you are either.

So, if you don't have hustle, if you can't grind, if you're not willing to put out, if you don't have the ability to go regardless if the situation is optimal or not, you aren't even in the game. In a sense it's like breathing—sometimes you do it more consciously than other times but nevertheless it's just something you always do.

You also need to be put in situations and among people that force you to build the ability to output that level of effort and experience the cost of doing so.

One of the biggest problems that I have faced, dealing with so many people who ask me how to improve, is they thought they were working hard. But what they didn't realize is that they weren't even scratching the surface compared to others who they went up against.

The reason behind this is the false sense of self some of them have and a lack of perspective. If you think you are a hard worker or doing something out of the ordinary, find a better circle. Because I can promise you there is always someone, somewhere who makes your effort look like their warmup.

Find those people, operate at their tempo, and get their perspective to what hustle is. And that doesn't just mean long hours because quality of effort is not quantity of time. Gather information and find what level of "hustle" you want to have, why you want to have it, and what the cost of operating at that level is. Never forget—there is always a cost.

Optimizing Ignorance

Now, here is a wild concept for most people to grasp.

At times, you need to be ignorant.

Yes, that is a powerful word with many connotations, so let's make sure you understand the perspective and operationally define where it's placed in this context.

There is a level of ignorance (not knowing) that is helpful. Discipline and structure can greatly increase creativity but also destroy it. There needs to be a balance. And as a leader, one of the burdens you carry is purposefully leaving alone those that look to you ignorantly for help.

Why do you ask?

Because by optimizing ignorance, you allow a level of freedom and creativity to exist in a state not bound by information, context, and experience that may bias it. You can actually remove the "paralysis by analysis" effect by optimizing ignorance.

By forcing everything to fit into a standard operating procedure (SOP) or rigid frameworks, you start to take away the ability to do the unorthodox, the imaginative, and the never been done before.

Remember that part where I mentioned how people who spend all their time doing a single thing and see that thing even in places it may not be because all they know to look for is the single thing they know? (Yes, there is a word that summates that. Hit the Google to find it.)

Not knowing or not having a full understanding is sometimes the only way to not be held back from finding the best decision to get the desired outcome versus feeling as if you need the best outcome based on the decision.

One of the key ways to facilitate this is to listen to those in levels below you. Perspective is a relative phenomenon just like knowledge and experience. Take the time to listen to the creative solutions of interns, outsiders, and anyone who does not know your 'thing" as well as you do.

Some of the best ideas I've ever had have come from conversations with interns. They would share a thought they had—which I never would have had given my biases—and with a few tweaks a solution come up that I never would have come to on my own.

PART III

THE TYPE OF BUILDING TO BUILD

Begin with the end in mind.

—Steven Covey

PERFORMANCE OR HEALTH AND WELLNESS?

WHILE THIS POINT WILL BE DISCUSSED MULTIPLE TIMES THROUGHOUT THIS BOOK, in many different contexts, let this be the clear moment when the question is asked.

Are you seeking a performance or health and wellness approach?

Understanding the two and their extreme differences, in both outcomes and effort as well as culture and expectations, is critical for you moving forward and framing much of the content of this book.

Much like my approach when I coached athletes directly, this book was written from the performance-based mindset. It's not a book on general health and wellness nor are the concepts viable in settings were the overall expectations are equality of outcomes. That context does not work when the score is kept and money is involved because there will be winners and losers—those that are good enough and those that are not.

There is nothing wrong with the health and wellness model, mindset, and approach that looks at the holistic balance of the system in relation to its world. It works for its context, and to be fair, there needs to be a greater emphasis on it in certain places that have shifted to a performance model. Youth sports specifically come to mind but that is yet another conversation for another day with the requisite margarita number being in double digits.

Not everything has to be performance-orientated.

Not everyone can be, wants to be, or should be performance-based.

Malalignment of these mindsets at any level is a critical issue and needs to be addressed before charting any course forward.

9

WHAT TYPE OF COACH ARE YOU?

ARE YOU A FORMER ATHLETE THAT HAS TRAINED A FAIR AMOUNT AND KNOWS more than the average person?

Are you someone who took an online certification and attended a couple of seminars?

Are you someone who has an academic educational background but no experience in the trenches?

Are you someone who has just lived "under the bar" or "on the field"—has put in the sweat equity—but lacks the knowledge and language to define what is happening beyond the obvious visual outputs being done?

A few of the most obvious and common indicators of people in the profession or within roles in the industry are education and credentials.

While it's important to have a combination of traditional education-based knowledge as well as practical, applied experience, there are two ends of this spectrum that are worth referencing: "the alphabet soup phenomenon" and "the waste of time" belief.

SIDE NOTE—Seminars where you pay a couple hundred dollars to learn cookie-cutter information, along with a couple hundred other people, are taught by those who often only understand the basics themselves and give minimal to no feedback. They are trying to get as many people in and out of the seminar as possible to make a buck. They only test you on conceptual knowledge and not the ability to understand it at a deep level, or apply it in its truest sense personally or professionally.

The Alphabet Soup Phenomenon

On one far end of the spectrum sits this newer phenomenon that people have been falling for called the "alphabet soup effect." Viewing coaches as qualified and competent only if they have "alphabet soup" after their name in degrees or certifications.

More education is never a bad thing. I'm an example of that personally, as are many others. But when you come across a person in the industry who has almost a dozen or more active certifications, I often question their personal and professional hands-on experience in the trenches, training with live athletes and not classroom subjects.

Between the financial costs and the time commitment to maintain that many certifications, often times you find that they have a lot of knowledge between the ears but very little experience implementing the vastness of their know-how to get real results on the training field or in the weight room.

They often get caught up developing "the perfect program" by integrating a variety of training philosophies and methodologies that may or may not actually work together. Often, what they say they're doing is a vastly different shade of gray than what they actually are doing on a day-to-day basis.

I'm more impressed with those that, while constantly seeking knowledge and developing themselves, have a set belief system and are able to be consistent with how they apply and integrate new knowledge within their base. That person may have had a dozen certifications over their career as they evolved but not a dozen at a single time.

I'm not impressed with anyone who "throws the baby out with the bathwater," per se, and constantly changes their base beliefs around new information they receive on the whims of fads and gurus.

It's a Waste of Time

On the other end of the spectrum, there is this undercurrent of "throw the book out the window" and all that matters is "the iron and the grind." These are coaches who view all additional learning and certifications and such as a "waste of time."

You see this a lot with aging coaches who've either achieved a level of growth in the profession and stagnated or have been recently replaced and don't understand that they don't have the knowledge, skills, or abilities to continue to grow and adapt to the current demands.

They often have only one certification. And they often degrade it and other certifications, saying they only have it because they have too as a checkbox. They preach to all those who listen that nothing in the classroom, in journals, or at seminars is really going to teach you what being in the training environment and doing it yourself will.

Often these are the people who've been very successful in the early stages of their careers helping athletes. They've been "under the bar" but they never learned outside of the training environment. And their athlete's success levels off or worse—trails off.

They often never did anything to continue development beyond the things they already knew, and they are leaving far too much on the table in terms of what they could be doing to improve their athletes (and themselves for that matter).

So, this begs the question: is there a clearly defined prerequisite as to what level of education is enough or how much personal experience or coaching experience someone needs to be competent and qualified?

I don't think there is. And while there are obvious baseline competencies to help show understanding of the basic knowledge base, there is too much variation in the art of coaching that impacts the science of training.

Learning more is never a bad thing, but that growth should not be at the expense of gaining experience by applying the knowledge you currently have to better understand what you currently know.

By balancing both continued learning with practical experience, you maximize your own development over time based on the demands placed upon you and the areas of emphasis you need to improve upon to have success for those you train.

Think of it like this: it's not the size of your library that matters nor is it how much time you spent reading or rereading the books you have; it's understanding and using what was in the books you read, knowing where to look in the library when you need to read more, and using the experiences you have accumulated your entire life to best adapt everything into the lessons you're trying to instill in another.

Unfortunately, in this industry there are quite a few incompetent, uneducated professionals who hold the profession back.

Some of the best S&C coaches in the collegiate world aren't in the NFL, NBA or Division I collegiate football or basketball setting.

I know, *shocking*, right!

Some of the people in those roles are my friends and some are people I know. Some certainly won't talk to me after seeing this—and that's on them. Sorry, not sorry.

If you can't handle that some of the best coaches don't coach anymore or don't coach at the "highest level," you are fooling yourself. And your hilarious, fake reality must be nice cause it is not the real world.

I hope my pointedness isn't lost on anyone here. There are some good ones for sure, just like there are also shitty ones—at all levels and in all things.

Don't Get Stuck Being Just a Strength Coach

If you still consider yourself just a strength coach, take a good look in the mirror and truly evaluate whether what you want to do is just be a strength coach? Or are you an educated, multi-disciplinary, multi-faceted specialist who leverages multiple methods across human performance enhancement to help those you work with?

The field of S&C is shifting so rapidly right now due to technological advancements, the openness of knowledge, and the paradigms of oversight (I'm looking at you medical model). There are going to be so many professionals left behind and so many gurus springing up, making the waters too murky to really be able to determine who is truly helpful and who is hurting the profession.

Lack of Professional Development

One of the biggest disservices to those trying to gain entry to our profession is that we don't teach them the appropriate knowledge and skills to be successful beyond the science of training. And as an industry we fail to incentivize further professional development.

Like a head coach being a CEO and not having the management skills needed to excel beyond the X's & O's of the sport, future S&C coaches are taught the science and the practice of training but often aren't taught the art of coaching. And rarely, if ever, are taught the art of people.

Also, what is the draw of furthering yourself as a practitioner when there is rarely, if ever, a financial compensation tied to your improved skill set?

The entire collegiate system is skewed in the wrong direction. Do you wonder why there are so many coaches beat down by the system and stuck with no skills or ability to do anything else? They never had a path, and they accepted it instead of making their own.

Almost every problem with this profession is self-imposed by those within the profession.

Every curriculum dealing with the science side of training should have minimum requirements in classes related to sociology, political science, cognitive development, public speaking, business development and different styles of management to give context for the skills, knowledge, and abilities needed to connect with people.

It's Always People First

I once had an intern who was a PhD student for one of the most well-known and respected academic leaders in the field of sport science. This person had the knowledge base, passion, and desire, but what they didn't have was basic communication skills.

They lacked the simple ability to communicate and connect with the athletes we worked with.

It was painful to watch someone who was so knowledgeable and competent in the science not have the slightest clue that their inability to land a job and "make it" had everything to do with their lack of communication skills.

This person ended up auditing classes in public speaking, communication, and behavioral psychology during the last part of their PhD program and made massive strides in their communication ability and style.

Ultimately, they have gone on to be a very successful performance coach in the private sector and collaborate with numerous other top professionals and universities in their area of expertise because they developed the skills to share their knowledge.

Additionally, we don't put enough emphasis on connecting and developing knowledge across the continuum of our field and driving the value of continued learning and open-mindedness to future professionals.

Your Starting Point is Just That, a Starting Point

A stark example of this is when I was brought in to an undergraduate kinesiology class that was primarily made up of athletic trainer (AT) and physical therapist (PT) hopefuls. My lecture was to teach the basics of Olympic lifting: from theory to application to practical demonstration in a training setting.

So, off the bat the task itself was impossible, but I tried my best.

We started with thirty minutes of classroom discussion and then we did forty-five minutes of hands-on work in the weight room. Within the first thirty minutes of class, we discussed the differences between the *sport* of Olympic lifting and *training* using Olympic lifts: what are the details that are similar, what could you scale up and scale down when appropriate given training goals, injury factors, etc.?

We went over a lot of textbook knowledge and real-world experience (not just mine, but examples drawn from numerous other professionals at all levels that I incorporated). Granted, it was a crash course in many ways, but I purposefully gave them dozens of reference materials to seek out themselves since we had to stay at a Sputnik-high level.

When we went into the weight room to do some basic competencies, the student's abilities to move efficiently in any capacity was extremely poor. And to make a point, while the group was not helping change the stereotypes of the fitness and aesthetics of athletic trainer and physical therapy students, I now, often, sadly see many hopeful S&C coaches who are motor-skill morons as well.

SIDE NOTE—Part of developing your craft is practicing what you preach. Consistent training with some level of nutrition and recovery will create a certain kind of skin-covered meat vehicle for you to do your job in. It's an unfortunate reality of the profession but those that can look the part, in some cases, can get the jobs before others who don't. You don't have to look like Arnold or be on the cover of Maxim but don't put yourself into the same professional category of the smoking pulmonary specialist telling patients it's bad to smoke. Look around you: do you pass the eyeball test or not? In this profession, it matters.

Additionally, as I was trying to teach, some of the students made light of the whole experience and wrote off the material: how they didn't need to know the information, how they don't train, and how it was a waste of time, etc. It showed they didn't quite get it.

As we approached the end of class, instead of further reviewing technical aspects I shifted gears. I explained to the group that if they ever wanted to make it at any level in the profession working with athletes, then they had better take learning about training and training themselves seriously.

"A lot of you guys are going to get to a point where the level of education you're seeing in the classroom or the textbook isn't enough anymore to be successful in your careers."

I continued, "A lot of you guys are going to face challenges to get to work with regular people never mind athletes because you lack critical knowledge. Don't think that it's enough to have a degree or certification because that only gives you the initial level of knowledge needed."

"How many of your contemporaries at other colleges are learning not only what you are learning here but more advanced knowledge about rehabilitation, technology used in rehabilitation, as well as how it relates to performance? How many of them are putting themselves through the wringer to better understand what it feels like to be an athlete and train day after day with everything else in life going on? If you aren't learning more than what your teachers are teaching and pushing yourself practically, you're not even in the stadium never mind in the game to get jobs."

As they were a smaller institution with very limited resources, I went on to say to them, "Look, you guys aren't being exposed to cutting-edge methodology here. You're being exposed to the best ability of the teacher you have, which you should be thankful for because they are going above and beyond for you. But that means that many things are PowerPoint only, not hands-on in real settings, like some people in other schools are getting. So, for you guys, you're going to have to go out and take additional certifications and courses in manual therapy, in soft tissue modalities, and in laser therapy, and learn how to use new machines and different techniques. Because what you're learning isn't necessarily what the industry is requiring. Ice, ultrasound, stim, and isotonic strengthening are not going to get you the career working with superstars you think you are entitled too."

I continued, "You're going to be left behind at your parents' house if you think you can get a job in college or pro sports because you came to this school and got a degree four years later."

As if I hadn't proved my point, and simply being a direct reflection of who I am, I went on to discuss how you can't possibly rehabilitate somebody to a level of higher performance if you have no idea what things those athletes are doing to improve their performance are.

That doesn't mean that every person must be a gold medalist to coach someone to be a gold medalist. Or every athletic trainer must run wind sprints to be able to rehab a sprinter with hamstring problems.

But there is a level of practical in-the-trench experience that you need to have in order to understand the situational context of how best to use your knowledge and expertise. If you've never pushed yourself in any physical capacity, how can you relate to someone who is? You cannot. And that person is going to go find someone else who can. They won't want to work with you because you don't get what they are chasing after.

It's about learning the theory, the implementation, the biomechanics and the process of who, what, why, how, and when.

How do you use methodologies or tools: plyometrics, strength training, energy system development, etc.?

How can you learn and manipulate those systems and skillsets to better the rehabilitation process?

Because although you're only one part of the sport performance and the human performance continuum, your place on the path leads to improving performance for the athletes you work with.

If you don't have the prerequisite knowledge and understanding of what people are doing to improve performance, you can't possibly rehabilitate or recondition someone to be able to go through those tasks. Don't end up being the athletic trainer who says someone can't deadlift because their back hurts but can Olympic lift and do plyo's full-out (I personally had someone tell me this once at a place I worked).

If you haven't learned enough to have conversations up and down the chain in the athletic world, from sport coaches to orthopedics doctors to everyone in between—you don't stand a chance.

You must be able to teach, coach, and assess. And know how to interact with others, especially with someone who has influence but lacks knowledge, to make sure the appropriate message is getting across in the needed way to maximize the athlete's development.

While this example is related to athletic trainers and other rehabilitative based practitioners, the exact same thing can be applied to future S&C coaches.

How many of them are taking the time learn the rehab side of things?

How many of them truly understand the physical therapy environment and can discuss the differences and similarities between the Janda and Sahrmann dogmas?

How many understand allelopathic versus osteopathic medicine and the models in which most medical doctors (MDs), physical therapists, and athletic therapists learn about physical development and training of the human system?

Do S&C coaches need to be experts in postural restoration, Functional Range Conditioning (FRC), Functional Movement Screen (FMS), Muscle Activation Techniques (MAT), or any of the other modalities?

No. But S&C Coaches should know the difference between Rolfing, Active Release Techniques (ART), and pin-and-stretch message technique so they can be able to understand the level of competence, knowledge and ability another practitioner can bring to the table?

With the oversight of the medical model starting to "reign in" what many in the sports medicine world consider issues stemming from poor S&C coaches, the S&C profession as a whole is at an important inflection point. To be frank, it's one that's going to see a total change of what we currently consider S&C for a few years before most of the medical models fail and a new paradigm emerges. It's a paradigm I'm happy to explain another day over even more margaritas as it's way beyond the scope of this book.

I'm Just as Guilty

Another stark example of how underdeveloped we are as professionals was in a recent LinkedIn post I saw from someone discussing their trouble trying to break into the collegiate performance world. They had not been able to get any interviews because they had limited experience; and the believed their experience was limited because no one would give them an interview.

It was a post that showed a naïve, immature point of view, and I wanted to see where it was coming from and why. So, I clicked on their profile and went deeper into their education and knowledge base. They proudly displayed a 3.8 GPA in their undergrad program but nothing beyond their degree. They had no volunteer or internship experience or experience in any related area (including any performance setting in any capacity). Their only work experience was in a customer service role at a grocery store.

My first reaction was to laugh and say out loud to myself, "No shit no one wants to hire you. You haven't done anything." At least via LinkedIn, they had nothing to show being serious about the profession beyond applying and getting rejected. Although they may have known the textbook knowledge well, why would anyone take them when there were hundreds of other people out there who had invested in their own development in a multitude of other ways?

But as quick as that laugh came out, I immediately chastised myself for perpetuating the cycle. I realized I was ignorant of the context beyond the content.

I took a moment to think on their situation and, in truth, I had no idea what it was. I was just being another asshole in the profession, and while I don't mind being an asshole, I didn't want to be just another S&C coach asshole.

I sat there for a second and let my mind wander.

Maybe they had to work at the grocery store for personal reasons, like they had one car and a family member worked at the store as well, so they couldn't work somewhere else simply due to logistics.

Maybe they didn't even have a car and they had to walk to work. And the closest performance-related opportunities were out of reach because they didn't have transportation to get there.

Maybe they had to make money to pay for school and the only related jobs were volunteer, so they had to sacrifice the time to have the money to pay for school first. I've personally known many who fell into this category over the years.

So instead of laughing at another millennial who "didn't get it," I decided that I would reach out, connect, and see what I could do to help.

First contact was quick. Obviously, they were excited to speak with someone in the field and try to get things moving.

After a handful of email exchanges, it because abundantly clear that this person was one of the most passionate, well-read, and aspiring coaches I had ever met.

The context was in fact that they did have to work at the grocery store because their family owned it and it wasn't doing well as a mom-and-pop against the big chains.

Living at home, going to in-state school close by, and working at the store every moment they weren't in class or at the gym training themselves helped save costs for the family and the store.

They would work endless hours, especially on weekends and holidays, to save their parents' money from paying employees and help keep the store going.

Aside from class and work, when they had free time, they hit the gym and put themselves and also their friends through the wringer. They had reached out to dozens and dozens of coaches at all levels through phone calls, emails, and LinkedIn messages and only a few had responded. And even fewer of those followed through with replies or promises of passing information along.

They were getting nowhere but not because they weren't trying. They were getting nowhere because the people who could help them weren't looking beyond the content and into the context. No one was taking the time.

I felt an immense sadness and empathy for this person because I was a coach who set out to help (teach, coach and mentor) and inspire others, but I had failed them.

All of us—leaders of others, drivers of our profession, the ones who preach that hustle, grind, sacrifice and all that other bullshit is what makes us great coaches—we couldn't get out of our own ways to see this was the exact person we all wanted to be the future of coaching.

They were the type of person we wanted on our staffs and the quality of person who could truly help the profession transcend into its next iteration—away from moldy basement-closets-turned-into-gyms and into an esteemed profession of high-quality, high-caliber people with the knowledge and passion to help others—people who pay it forward.

I took the time, I listened, and I connected them to as many people as I could and pushed them as far as I was able. I didn't do it for the moral dessert.

I take no credit for their current and future success other than saying I did my best to help when I could in the moment we crossed paths. Everything else, they did on their own, and it would not surprise me if one day they were one of the top leaders in all the field.

That's what I mean that we lack professional development and are an underdeveloped profession.

To begin, we don't instill the fundamental skills and knowledge, the art of coaching, and the open-mindedness needed to learn beyond what we know in the science of training to give future coaches the realistic picture of what is required to succeed in the profession.

We also do not place enough emphasis on paying it forward— giving more than we take—in the development of future coaches, seeing the context beyond the content, and empowering each other to drive things forward as a community of professionals.

While things have dramatically improved in the last ten years, there is still too much insulation, too much belief that there are secrets and methods that cannot be shared (sorry to burst your bubble, nothing you are doing hasn't been done before) and far too much segregation among performance professionals along arbitrary lines (football versus Olympic, personal trainer versus performance coach, or whatever other labels are placed upon the different contexts) all trying to achieve the same thing: improved human performance through servant leadership.

Here' a news flash: between the changes being pushed by the sports medicine side of the coin and a few key lawsuits coming down the pipe, things are going to be radically altered across some of these historical delineations, especially in college football.

The textbook is not enough.

"Under the bar" is not enough.

It's a combination of the two with a healthy mix of altruistic action by the previous generation to make the next generation have a step forward. We cannot continue to fight the same battles that take away time from helping the athletes and helping the profession advance.

The Underdeveloped Professional Profession

One of the toughest things about being an S&C coach, in my opinion, is the insulated nature of the S&C profession. Both its historical lack of inclusive knowledge sharing and the jobs themselves, insulate S&C coaches within the physical walls of the weight room itself.

Granted, it's changing due to the emergence of a stronger and richer body of knowledge, access to that knowledge on a global scale due to technology, and more and more coaches and individuals involved in the field being willing to share with others.

However, for most people, the insulated nature of the job itself remains.

S&C coaches might have the willingness to share or help others but find themselves in a situation where they spend so much time solely in the weight room, at practice, or team-related events that they aren't able to go outside of the job to do it. This can be a double whammy, because if you don't have the time to build and develop relationships with the important people around your sphere of influence, you risk having those people stuck with ideas given to them by others.

The field of S&C is unique in that you don't actually need to know what you're doing to be able to be in the field. There is no licensure or constant standard to which people are held.

Sure, there are certifications and there are tons of processes and tons of hoops people jump through to deem themselves and others worthy. But when looked at from the outside; there is no unified structure, theory, and regulatory body coming down and managing the prerequisite skills and experience of those in the field.

SIDE NOTE—And people wonder why the medical model is starting to take over? Let's be honest here, for a long time bad S&C coaches were the problem. People were allowed in the profession who had no business being it in, and it still happens to this day in some ways. Also, poorly educated or egotistical individuals now hamper all sides of the performance continuum, and some of them wield tremendous power and are pushing agendas that are going to radically alter athletics—many of them not for the better. The landscape is shifting—seismically. I've mentioned it a few times throughout this book for a reason.

And there probably never will be a regulatory body, because there are no clear-cut answers to what the best way to train is. There are also no right answers on how to train for a certain outcome for everyone.

The development of physical attributes, much like the development of a person, is a unique, non-linear sequence, and subject to influence from factors known and unknown across the past, present, and future, both internally and externally.

There are certain principles and facts of science and biology that come into play in the overall sense, but in specific and individual levels there are no absolutes.

We certainly can do better, and there are organizations and people trying, but that's the problem. They've been trying for decades with limited success, because they're all coming at it from the same angle. I have given long periods of thought to a paradigm that could help solve this but that conversation is well beyond the scope of this book and would also radically alter the performance continuum as we know it today—the only way possible to fix many of the issues (I'm more than happy to share—just send me an email and we can chat).

S&C as a Lifestyle

S&C is not a career. It's a lifestyle.

It's not something you can do to any degree of success trying to operate like a 9 to 5 job. If you, as an S&C Coach are not willing to live the 24-7, 365-day lifestyle, your values and goals will never be aligned with the lifestyle of the profession.

This is why there's such a high burnout and turnover ratio across all sectors of the profession at large. The lack of alignment can be crippling when you're putting that kind of time in.

So, to understand how to avoid it you first must understand the essence of the job itself.

Coaching, especially S&C in the collegiate sector, is a servant-leadership position.

You are a support staff, playing a small part in a much larger wheel, and everything you do should ultimately be traced back to helping the athletes.

To do so, you must push aside your personal time, your personal needs, and your personal wants to serve someone else. Often, you don't actually serve those you are intended too; you serve someone else (sport coach) who controls those you work for (athletes), or you're at the whim of a person who possibly has limited working knowledge of your part of the continuum (doctor or athletic trainer).

Depending on what level you are at or what team you work with, money-generating or not, you could be asked to be on call 24-7, 365 days a year. You could be asked to travel and possibly do no more than thirty minutes of work per day directly with the athletes when on the road.

Personally, there were times where I had to miss funerals, births, weddings, and all the other life events or experience that I wanted to go to or be a part of. But I couldn't because at that time the work lifestyle took priority.

So, if you're not willing to live that lifestyle and commit to making those sacrifices, you're going to struggle long term.

Don't get me wrong, there will be periods of time when you attempt to find methods to help balance things in order to attend to outside events. But more often than not, you'll have to make judgment calls as to what you can't miss compared to what you will have to miss and sometimes that call will be made for you.

You need to have a strong understanding of your "philosophy development cycle" to truly understand if a career in coaching is something you want for the short term or for a career.

You could be asked to do other things—many of which are outside your scope of practice and create possible liability situations—such as being the team nutritionist or psychologist. You get asked because of limited resources and you have to do them anyway as the job blends into those two areas as well as many others.

That's the nature of the role—at least the accepted one by many— from administrators who turn a blind eye, to sport coaches who want to be like whatever other team they heard about doing it. It has, in some senses, spiraled out of control due to poor oversight from a national regulatory body and poor understanding of the use and purpose of an S&C coach due to the ignorance of administrators and sport coaches (which is why education and communication is absolutely paramount for your success).

The profession is truly hampered because expectation compared to reality is so out of whack.

It's so out of whack recently that with the rise of social media S&C coaches have begun to develop their brands as professionals from the wrestling sports entertainment world. To steal lingo from that world, they develop their gimmicks and cut promos in character to help advance their professional careers.

Most S&C coaches who have adopted this type of "brand development" (if that's the best way to describe it) did so to fit a perception of what they're supposed to be and believed to be by head coaches and the public: they "bring the juice." And in some cases, it's helped them get jobs regardless of their actual skills coaching, teaching, and mentoring or the quality of their character as an individual.

That is scary. But we allowed it to happen; we put the perception ahead of the purpose, so shame on us all. Is anyone really surprised why sports medicine has been in on the long game to take over the S&C industry and is currently delivering what I consider a dim mark on the profession as we know it?

Collegiate S&C is a Young Person's Game

There are not many old coaches who are, day in and day out, in the trenches. And from what I have observed the last few years traveling the country, there won't be many either. I know of a dozen right now, as I write this, actively looking to leave the profession entirely and start new careers—some with twenty years of service. The tacit knowledge alone that will be lost with some of these individuals leaving is going to be detrimental to the profession as a whole. But sadly, no one will even notice. And the next generation will fight the same battles and spend countless hours "creating" things that they could have had someone else give to them by asking, listening, and learning.

And while we're at it, let's qualify what even "old" is in the world of collegiate S&C and, to a degree, professional sports in the US. If you're over forty-five years of age you're geriatric, and if you are over fifty-five you're a dinosaur of a bygone era.

Now there are few, and I could easily name names who are still relevant, who all seem to have been at a single place for over twenty years. But at about fifty years of age is when you start to cap out your career longevity due to burnout or lack of success.

You can only take so many moves, so many new beginnings, or be let go so many times before opportunity dries up.

I haven't even mentioned having a significant other, being married, having kids, or other factors that go into being able to do the job.

So, where do you go? How do you pivot and shift when all you have done is a job that is anything but normal and follows very few if any "standard" career curves? You must have a plan, and you must work on that plan while coaching to prepare yourself for after coaching.

Again, there are always exceptions to the rule; there are dozens of coaches in their forties and fifties who are still the "tip of the spear" and dominant. But I'd argue there are thousands who are not—and even more who never even made it that long in the profession. The norm isn't success at that age.

I have had one of the most successful college S&C coaches, with almost thirty years at a single place, tell me to my face that he had no idea what he will do when he stops being an S&C coach. He knows that day will come but he has no idea what to do when it does. And it saddens him, because he knows it but has no idea how to do anything about it at this point in his life. He admitted that he doesn't know his own children that well or—with tears welling in his eyes—his wife. In his words, he was "head down in the sand, grinding it out like he was taught." It's all he knows and he hasn't tried to learn anything outside of training athletes for decades. The money has finally become good enough to not start over so he said he'll "continue to do this for as long as I can and save as much money as I can so I can retire one day."

To anyone reading this starting their journey—never be that person. Keep doors open and actively open more as you walk your path. And most importantly, if you choose to have family, it means you need to be an active part of it.

The Spiral

Since the profession attracts naturally intense people who often are multiple deviations off the "normal range" and is a heavily siloed ecosystem within the field of athletics, it's easy for someone to fall down the spiral—losing sight of who they are at their core and covering up their own life with the wins in their professional life. Coaches, athletic trainers, any athletics staff member, or anyone for that matter can be caught in the spiral.

Substance abuse—primarily alcohol—mental health issues from the conflict between the person, the pressure (real or perceived), and the job itself, as well as erratic behavior—all have a place in the spiral. Numerous other manifestations and causes exist each just as valid as the next. The spiral can be sped up by having a constantly negative environment surrounding you and an overwhelming feeling that nothing will change regardless of your effort.

We've all been in the spiral to one degree or another. I know I have more than once and I've lost friends to the spiral. Sometimes it hits us for a moment, tossing us around like a rogue wave, and then is gone—just a moment in time. Other times it builds up far away and you don't notice until the tide has abnormally receded and the tsunami wave is already on top of you, doing its best to drown you.

If you feel like you're in the spiral, I want you to know there's always someone to talk to and someone who has or is going through the same thing. You're not alone. You're never alone. There's always someone who cares and someone who can help you—you may just not know them yet. For a starting point please go to https://psychcentral.com/lib/common-hotline-phone-numbers.

The Cycle

As I mentioned before, very early in my career I was able to achieve a level of success and growth that put me on a path where if I continued in the realm of college athletics, my professional outcomes would have would be cyclic.

At a very early point in my career I was able to achieve the highest level of physical outcome for those I worked with and we won. I was very fortunate to work with amazing athletes and be a small piece of their success. I helped drive all-Americans, conference and national champions, and even an Olympic gold medalist. While I never scored a point or won a race, I like to think of it like this: I was not so bad at my job that I prevented them from achieving the success they did.

Everything else would just be repetitive year over year.

Stepping outside the box and thinking about it are the apex of the collegiate S&C coach; major career outcomes from working with athletes that we define successful coaches by (albeit wrongly define them by, but point for a later section).

If you're willing to go into that cyclical success model and be evaluated mainly on competitive success, what else could you develop and earn as a collegiate S&C coach?

National championships and Olympic gold medalists pretty much tops out the level of maximizing your perceived skill and competence.

Pretty much everything after that is an A/B test where you're repeating the same three to four-year cycle over and over with small refinements relative to who you get as athletes and the coaches you deal with.

Therefore, the collegiate level is plagued with people who have entrenched themselves for years doing the same repetitive things over and over, allowing themselves to stagnate and lose sight of continued growth for themselves and for their athletes.

This issue is two-fold, both on the S&C coach for growing complacent and on the system for giving them no reason not to be. There is often little incentive in the profession to do more.

So, very early on I recognized this: I could fall victim to that same cyclic approach and after two or three cycles consuming a decade or more of my own prime years, open myself to massive burnout and mental fatigue. Instead, I came up with a plan to step outside of that cycle and never be self-limiting in my own progress.

I pursued an advanced degree and additional certifications outside of coaching to sharpen my sword and broaden my skillset. And I tried to do things to build and develop myself not related to the profession (conferences, seminars, reading, writing, teaching, and learning) and opened as many doors as I possibly could for myself moving forward with professionals in those worlds not just in athletics.

I networked my ass off, especially with people not in the athletics world.

Gaining Entry to S&C

One of the things that I saw and heard a lot, and still do, from numerous individuals trying to get into the S&C field in the collegiate sector, is that just gaining entry seemed impossible.

It often seemed there where way more people than jobs available. And this *is* the case. I imagine that for every five people trying to get in, there's only one job.

Now, recently, there's been an influx of more jobs as schools and universities have recognized the value of an S&C coach and the demands they place on them. More and more positions have opened, especially in new sectors like high school and tactical populations.

The issue though is more and more positions are graduate-assistant level and professional-intern level without benefits, or underpaid entry-level positions. Schools have realized they need help but they don't want to or can't pay for the help they actually need or the quality of help that is required from these roles and the expectations/demands placed upon them.

The catch-22 here is most of these jobs are starting to require certifications and graduate degrees. Explain to me how that isn't madness and I will buy you margaritas for a week.

What has happened? Schools either fill the positions with a highly qualified individual and pay them peanuts, increasing stress, burnout and turnover as better jobs appear and that person moves on. Or they hire the barely qualified individual who can't effectively do the job, is dumb enough to get paid nothing, and needs to have a mentor (who may or may not be present).

It's a no-win situation before it starts.

How any administrator who considers themselves a leader would willfully, or worse ignorantly, put themselves in this situation is a part of the problem. They set people up to fail from the get-go: they hire overly qualified people and undervalue them, giving them no room to grow or reason stay; or they hire underqualified people and demand more than they are capable of while also giving them little reason to stay.

That is what's happening time and time again and it doesn't seem to be acknowledged by decision makers. This is an issue at the administrative, legislative, and governing-body level.

While a lot could be said on this topic, I will leave it there. A lot of people out there at schools, organizations, and in the private setting are trying their damnedest to address this issue. I thank them and salute their efforts. In time things will change. Currently, we're just in the painful stage of change. And while this is a very negative stance, it is to prove the point.

Change is coming—that's an unstoppable and undeniable fact. You need to have a voice in it or it will be change that takes your voice away forever.

On the other hand, when it comes to the specific individual trying to figure out ways to break into the profession, it starts with getting experience while you're young.

One of the toughest things you can do to break into the collegiate S&C sector is be a middle-level professional, especially, if you work in the non-professional sport sector.

It's very easy for mid-career and senior-career professionals in professional sports to transfer into collegiate sports. It's very difficult for mid-career professionals in the private sector to transfer into the collegiate setting.

For whatever reason—partly being experience, partly being the ignorance of hiring committees, the ignorance of coaches, and the ignorance of the industry itself—there are many people in the private sector, who are better than those in college but are perceived to not be competent and thus don't get the opportunity. This is slowly starting to change for the better.

I can think of one specific example of a person who recently came into the Division I setting, with a background in high school and private training, with business acumen, and with a lot of life experience to boot. He is dominating his role both as a coach and as an administrator.

It's funny how a guy who never worked in the college realm, but has a ton of experience and knowledge across multiple aspects of the performance continuum and is seasoned in life, is orchestrating one of the biggest program turnarounds I've seen in the last decade. Shocking, right?

There is no one setting that best defines or creates the best coaches. There are always good coaches and bad ones in every setting.

While I don't believe there's a specific road map that will get you into collegiate athletics, or to any specific role you desire in the performance field, I can tell you about a few roadblocks and things you can do to avoid them.

Senior Year is Often Too Late

One of the toughest things for anyone currently in college is to not have experience until their senior year internship. You need to get some level of experience in some capacity as early as possible.

If you're not an athlete or don't look the part, you're already at a significant disadvantage no matter what anyone tells you. Welcome to the real world.

Don't let anyone blow smoke up your ass. While it's not the only way people get jobs in the S&C world, especially at the Division I college level, being an athlete or physically looking the part plays a role in who gets jobs.

Get in early, work on your craft, work on yourself, and become someone people need around so they will fight for you to stay when it is your time to go.

My Internship Experience

Personally, I started volunteering in the weight room the summer between my freshmen and sophomore years. I volunteered throughout my time as an undergrad while being an athlete and going to school full time (notice my purposeful lack of the term student-athlete).

During that time, I accumulated over 1,200 hours of volunteer experience and worked part-time jobs throughout college. That allowed me to have a significant leg up on most of my competition.

For example, there was an individual I did my undergrad with who shared many commonalities with me: we both had a passion for coaching and we both physically looked the part—but I was an athlete and he was not. During our senior year, when the opportunity arose to become a GA at UConn and work in the S&C department, this person tried their best to earn that role—and he was deserving of it.

When the time came, I was given the opportunity and he was not. I even heard through mutual friends that he said he thought I only got it because I was an athlete.

While that most certainly played a part, I know for a fact (my boss told me so) that the most significant reason I got the GA position over him was I had put time in over those last *four years* compared to him only doing it for the last semester.

At the time, he was just as good as I was but I had done more for longer. I had known what needed to be done, had built trust with those I worked with, and had demonstrated added value. Had he spent as much time as I had earlier in his career, who knows who would have gotten the GA role.

Now, this person went on to be a GA at another school, worked in the college realm for a bit, and transitioned to professional sports. He has done an amazing job as a coach, as well as a professional, building his personal brand and showing his value along the way, which has helped him climb to and succeed in his current position.

While we are not close friends, we connect once or twice a year and have discussions on a range of topics. More than once, I have sought out the information he puts out to help train the athletes I work with because he is very good at what he does. You could argue he is more successful in the profession than I am, and in many aspects, I would have to agree.

Experience Every Level You Can

I also recommend that you experience, in some capacity, every level of the performance spectrum.

Be a personal trainer at a Globo Gym, be one at a private facility, work with youth, high school, college and pro athletes in some capacity. Train whoever walks through the door.

See the differences in the industry: the level of resources, the level of athletes, and the process of building and retaining a client base.

Get paid by commission, market yourself, and learn how to run the business of yourself in all of those roles and types of situations.

While I only interned one place during my undergrad, I made it a point to spend time with every different coach and reach out to coaches at other schools to talk shop, network, and gain their perspectives. I reached out to something like 200–300 coaches at a variety of levels via phone and email. I was constantly asking people questions and visiting schools/gyms when I had free time.

I once spent an entire spring break traveling to different places on the East Coast on my own dime, meeting S&C coaches across the spectrum of settings so I could learn. In seven days, I visited eleven different places, met dozens of professionals, traveled well over 1,500 miles, and even slept in my car a couple of nights. Some of those connections came in handy 3–4 years later. Some still come in handy now, more than a decade later.

If you don't show the desire to learn and grow, no one is going to take the time to help you. Even then they still don't owe you the help.

If you don't ask questions, bring new things to the table, or show you want to improve, you will not get anyone to mentor you. Even then they still don't have to take the time.

Have a notebook to write things down so you can ask questions at the appropriate time. The key being *the appropriate time*. That's a skill within itself.

I was very fortunate to have great mentors to learn from. Each one challenged me in their own way, and also made me learn outside of them, because they all knew they didn't know it all. I was never insulated in thought and learning, which helped me not only maximize my time spent with whoever I was with but also anyone else I crossed paths with.

There Are Only Two Kinds of Internships You Should Ever Take

Every year, I spend a significant amount of time helping up-and-coming coaches position themselves for their future, and one of the key areas I work with them on is helping them seek out internships.

Previously in the S&C/sport performance industry, the emphasis was always on doing as many internships as possible to show coaches you had earned your place by doing the grunt work—"earning your stripes." These experiences served to do the following:

- Expose you to as many coaching styles as possible, since many places had insulated themselves from sharing with others
- Build your network and reputation as you went from place to place

This process not only educated you in the different ways you could train but served as a method to land a job, either through the grapevine via your new connections and their connections, or by transitioning from an internship role to a full-time role.

The emphasis was more being "on the grind" rather than developing as a professional and practitioner. It was a "learn by the seat of your pants" through "sweat equity" and sacrifice to the cause.

However, with the saturation of the market and a very low growth rate of positions (a topic for a different day) there is a recent trend of many up-and-comers having multiple internships—sometimes upwards of five—on their résumés and no prospects of full-time employment on the horizon.

Additionally, via improved technology and the overall development of the profession (access to knowledge and the body of knowledge), any individual can learn the basics—to some degree many of the advanced aspects—and connect with almost anyone in the profession to discuss these concepts, all from the comforts of their own home.

With so many people qualified at a basic level, even getting your foot in the door is harder than ever if you're not leveraging technology to learn and network. As a result, this makes the major emphasis of an internship, not the exposure to the ideas and people, but the experience of hands-on application in a setting.

How can this be? Isn't the way to getting a job doing internships, grinding away, and proving you're worth it? It seems like every friend you have in every other industry goes about it that way, but why is it so hard for you?

Simply put, about 80% of internships in the S&C/sport performance industry give you little to no ROI and are a waste of your time.

Internships themselves are no longer a viable route for funneling people into the profession. So, in order to get a better ROI out of doing an internship—compared to just getting an internship—there needs to be emphasis on how that internship will differentiate you from the crowd of hopefuls, allowing you to gain true traction in getting full-time employment.

Because of this, there are only two kinds of internships you should take.

The No-Brainer

The first is one, by the name of the place alone, distinguishes and identifies you as competent due to being associated with a specific brand. Examples of this are successful professional sports teams (i.e. NFL's New England Patriots, NBA's Golden State Warriors, NHL's Chicago Blackhawks), top-shelf major college programs (i.e. Kansas Men's Basketball, Alabama Football, Texas) and top private facilities (i.e. Landow Performance, EXOS, P3).

Regardless of the experience you have as an intern, the ROI by having a well-respected name on your résumé is impactful, especially if you're able to get time with their priority athletes or teams. The longer you stay, the better you are assumed to be, regardless what you are doing. It's simply credibility by association.

Where They Invest in You

The second one is a place that, unlike the first, may not have the name recognition but instead has a person (or persons) that are purposefully set up to teach, coach, and mentor you during your internship. They purposefully invest themselves in your development during your time there, not just to make their own jobs easier by adding another set of hands, but to truly help you progress as a professional and practitioner. These are the hidden gems that differentiate you *doing* an internship from you *developing* at an internship.

You identify them by doing the following:

1. Connecting with other interns and coaches who were previously there
2. Asking questions such as the following: do they have an internship curriculum, and do they follow it, or is it just there because it's great lip service? Do they give you more responsibility when you show you could handle it? Or no matter your progression, are you simply there to do errands and setup/clean?

The true identifier of a place like this: they actively discuss and have a process to try to make you better by teaching you all that they know and letting you experience things first hand. So, when you fail, it's in a controlled situation.

Often the "no-brainers" are also these places, but unfortunately, it isn't always the case so be careful: don't mistake a logo for quality.

A Few Other Things

And a couple of other things (did you really think it was just *that* simple).

Never do I mention paid or unpaid. Paid opportunities are rare in the S&C/sport performance domain, especially if you have limited experience. You should expect to do at least one, maybe two, unpaid internships. Any more than two unpaid internships and you need to be rethinking your own career development progress.

The market is so saturated at the "no-brainer" places due to the volume of people who want to intern at them, often the only chance you will have is unpaid. *Never* pass up a chance to get paid for an unpaid opportunity unless the unpaid opportunity is a "no-brainer." You need to create salary history to maximize your own value moving forward.

Get Out of Your Comfort Zone

Get as far away from your comfort zone as possible within the means you have. If you can, go somewhere new, be on your own, find a place to live, get a paying job while interning if you need to, and figure it out. Hell, live in your boss's basement for a while if you have to. That "figure it out" experience will be invaluable to you in life not just your career. There is always a way to make it happen. You might have to sacrifice something, somewhere along the way, but the step back in this moment can help you step forward in the next. If you can't step forward afterward, you wasted your time.

You will only get out what you put in. You need to be competent as well as be confident in what you know and what you don't know. Be a master generalist before you try to be a specialist. Learn by listening and doing not just reading or watching. Spend time on your own developing yourself as a professional and practitioner but take time for things outside of work. Have a balance, establish it early, and never let it waiver too far in either direction.

If you find yourself looking at a place or currently at a place that doesn't meet the criteria of "no-brainer" or "where they invest in you," detach yourself and don't waste time just going through the motions. You'll lose the chance to develop and grow. Detach, reassess, and move forward to a place or person that can truly help you stand out from the crowd.

Doing the Job is Not Special

People often feel entitled to be given praise for doing their job.

Doing your job the way it's supposed to be done deserves nothing more than the compensation you're currently getting.

That's the job you signed up for.

Going far beyond the scope of your job in a positive manner is what *should* (keyword there) foster some type of reward.

Just because you showed up and did what you were supposed to do when you were supposed to do it doesn't mean you should get more.

The Best Recipe I Have for Success as an S&C Coach

You must have a blue-collar mentality and a lunch-pail work ethic.

You must position yourself with thought leaders in the field, who are great people, who will support you, and who will do their best to help you.

From there, you have to continue to learn and challenge everything you know in order to improve and better yourself and those you work with.

Initially, you will need to be asymmetric in your life balance given the time and effort it will take to pursue and accomplish mastery of your craft. You must be willing to accept the consequences and struggles, both personally and professionally, that come with this. However, this should not always be the case. Purposeful effort with intent is not the same as having your head in the sand on "the grind."

The moment you stop improving personally and professionally is the point that those you work with will need someone else to help them further themselves because you no longer can.

Anyone who has sought to be at the apex of their abilities, in any manner, can relate to this. It's a concept of life not just S&C.

Training the Athletes is Not the Job

I would say that the biggest barrier to entry into collegiate athletics S&C, for anyone outside trying to break in, is the belief that what matters is training the athletes —that the program you create and the X's and O's is what will get you the job. In fact, that's one of the last things that matters, because if you can't do the X's and O's you aren't even in the ball game.

Programming and training the athletes is the fourth most important thing that matters.

Let that sink in for a minute.

Training the athletes is not a top-three priority of the job.

If I had to rank them, I would say creating buy-in from the head sport coach is the most important thing. Creating buy-in from the athletes is the second most important thing. And creating buy-in from the administrators and other support staff, like athletic trainers, is the third thing because it can save your job when the first two things fail you.

Like I said, the fourth priority is training the athletes. Because to have a chance to effectively train the athletes and bring all your knowledge and competence to the actual training, you have to have those first three things nailed down tight.

Most people believe it's the other way around.

I had a colleague who got promoted to a new school and became an assistant athletic director for sports performance. He was to work directly in football, but also had oversight of all the S&C for Olympic sports. This colleague specifically said to me in person at a conference, "I don't give a fuck about the administrative stuff or any of these other sports. I'm here to train football. That's all I want to do. The only reason they gave me the title is I make more than everyone, so I must oversee everyone. I don't even plan on going to the Olympic weight room because I don't care what they do. Because their jobs aren't on the line if we're not successful in football. But mine is. So, the only thing I have time for is to help football."

Now, this particular person, after two years and a huge mess of issues outside of football created solely by them and their lack of attention to anything other than football, was let go by the administration. And his football coach who had brought him in originally didn't even go to bat for him when he found out how poorly he was managing his staff and other responsibilities outside of football. The football coach wouldn't dare put his name behind someone who did that bad of a job outside of the weight room regardless of their success in the weight room.

Imagine if he did have "a fuck to give," put a little effort in, and didn't let things spiral out of control. He might still have a job.

The Game of Thrones

Due to this new paradigm in priorities, one of the things that I often tell those I work with and those I speak to in this industry is everything you learned in class isn't going to prepare you to be able to play the political game of people—or as I like to call it, due to the popularization of the books and TV show, *The Game of Thrones*.

You must spend time going to meetings, meeting with coaches, and learning the political, social, as well as the psychology aspects of how to gain influence and network with people.

It goes back to the Machiavelli quote from before.

I would often take interns with me to meetings with sport coaches simply to expose them to the situations, conversations, and issues that emerge outside of the weight room walls.

Also, having an additional person in the room often helped in situations where a witness was needed to confirm that certain things were said or not said (but that's a whole different topic).

If you don't believe *"the game of thrones"* is important, go online, and Google recent articles from S&C coaches who no longer have jobs. They failed miserably at playing "the game" or even understanding it existed and are complaining about it.

10

PREPARING TO SIT IN THE CHAIR

When you're starting out in your career, every day you walk into the office or facility, you should look at your boss's chair (or stability ball) and ask yourself what happens if the person in that chair is not there the next day?

What are you doing and what have you done to be able to sit in the chair until it is filled again? And what are you doing in the "big-picture" to prepare yourself for that chair to one day be yours?

If you look at that chair and have no interest in ever having it (there is nothing wrong feeling that way), you still need to be asking yourself how you're going about maximizing the impact of influence your "chair" currently has?

Define Your Role as a Professional

If you can't be committed to yourself, how are you ever going to be committed to something or someone else?

Let that marinate around in your mind for a while.

To quote Bruce Lee, "The only help is self-help."

You must understand the skills and abilities needed to transition from one role to the next, you must be able to embrace the differences in roles, and you must not fall into old habits that are no longer within your new roles demand.

You must learn how to trust, delegate and manage.

If you cannot learn these critical skills as you advance your role, you will find yourself not being taken seriously by those around you, nor will you find lasting success.

A few of the skills most people can't demonstrate in these situations and why they become this way is that they're not able to respect people's space (professional boundaries) and develop themselves.

They've not been given the critical skills necessary to develop themselves outside of the singular identity they developed while inside a certain role.

They find it hard to embrace new responsibilities and put old ones aside. Delegating responsibility is a paramount skill that needs to be learned to be successful and as you move higher up the chain of command.

It's a skill you can have only if your abilities to build those below you and above you have already started to be developed.

While a select few can radically alter how they operate in just one day, most can't. Giving responsibility to someone else can be difficult if you've always individually borne that burden and have a strong emotional connection to that output.

One way to begin to release responsibility is to see others as equal, not less than, and respect the space of other professionals.

In the context of an up and coming coach, you must see yourself as an equal to those around you. And you must constantly work to build and develop yourself to be able to hold your own with people above and below you.

While you may not feel empowered or experienced enough to be on equal footing—and in some cases, you won't be—you need to have the confidence in yourself that you belong.

It should go without saying—but I will say it here anyway—you must be confident in yourself, yet you must be careful not to let too much ego get in the way. It's good to have confidence but a detriment to let hubris overtake common sense. It goes back to the chapters on "leadership philosophy" and "keys to success"—there needs to be a balance.

You should have a level of self-confidence to believe you can be the person to do the job and do it well, but you must have a counterweight of humility to know that you alone do not have all the answers. You'll need the help of others to bring you to your highest heights.

Don't Get Lost in Titles, We All Have Names

One of the things that I would often do and made sure that I did appropriately, given the context of the situation, was call people by their first name.

If I was in a work setting or around athletes, I would address the person appropriately to their title; Coach, Doctor, Mr., or Mrs. whoever.

But as soon as I was in a private, in an informal situation (around peers, at the grocery store, etc.) or behind closed doors. I would address them by their first name.

This always helped provide me with a subtle reminder that whoever it was, they were just another person, no different than me. It helps the people around you, who know the value of what you are doing, recognize you're aware of the formal and informal nature of being a professional.

It's amazing how something as simple as that helped me develop relationships with others and check egos when needed.

There were very few individuals who I would address with their professional name regardless of the situation. These people often had the moniker "Coach" and had earned the right to be called that title.

Not saying that I didn't respect other individuals who were coaches I didn't always refer to as "coach," but there was something specific about these individuals that help them transcend their given name to be called "Coach" at all times. If you've been around sports for any period of time, you certainly know someone who is just "Coach" and the reason behind it.

Growing and Taking Ownership

You must get out of the weight room.

One of the first things that I teach any intern or anyone who's ever worked with me, is that while being in the weight room is most of your day, it cannot become all your day. It's actually only about 25% of the job.

Now, this may run counterintuitive to what many people think because the hours and time you spend in the weight room training athletes significantly outweighs the time you generally have to do anything else—especially if you work on the Olympic-sports side and have multiple teams.

Thus, the question you must ask is: what are you doing outside of the weight room? How are you talking to coaches? How are you building relationships with administrators and other support staff? How are you taking ownership of your role, making others aware of your competency, and adding value to all those around you? Are you being seen and heard or is the only narrative you have in peoples' minds one that someone else tells them?

You must have the right blend of self-confidence to believe you have value, the humility to know you can't do it alone, and be humbleness to ask for help.

If all you do is spend time in the weight room, you'll never have the chance to change perceptions and write your own narrative.

Keeping Record of What You Did, Not Just What You Do

Because we live in a litigious society, you must cover your ass (CYA).

Everything you do should be tracked, recorded, and managed. How you choose to do that is up to you.

On the one hand, don't get lost spending so much time tracking and recording that you lose sight of the higher goal. But more importantly, don't find yourself in a situation that could threaten your reputation or career without documentation to support your efforts and thought processes.

Many times, I took courses of action because of outside factors beyond my control. So when things went sideways, which they often tend to do—

Murphy's Law and all that bullshit—I had objective, recorded facts to support my actions. I cannot tell you how many emails I sent to myself with something to the effect of *I was told by this person on this date to do or not do this particular thing. I voiced my disagreement and they directed me to do it anyway.*

I never left things to interpretation and subjective perspective, especially when it came to polarizing issues or dealing with an egomaniac who actually had influence.

Notebooks, journals, emails to yourself—however you do it, document everything. Facts and objective data first, subjective opinion second, and assume that everyone will read what you write and only have the context of the words in front of them—not the entire history—so write with that in mind.

Document the highs and the lows and the good and the bad. That way you will always know the who, what, when, why and how of the situation. This always comes in handy when you have to debrief a higher-up who has no clue about the day-to-day goings-on but is the adjudicator of the situation.

Networking and Connecting with Others

Currently, the body of knowledge in S&C has grown to a tremendous depth and with social media, the opportunities to connect are vast.

Tim Ferriss talks about this a lot on his podcast and in his books. When he was at Princeton, he would challenge students to connect with famous people like Bill Clinton or Bill Gates. He would offer a free flight or incentive for them to do it, something like a trip to anywhere in the world or whatnot, and there was always one or two people who did do it but many who never even tried.

It wasn't an overly complicated process. It was simple. Those that succeeded took the time to reach out and communicate and were creative in the ways that they did so. If you spend the time and find ways to reach out, you'll be able to connect to pretty much anyone now. You just have to actually go do it. I can personally attest to this: I 've been fortunate to have great conversations with many "influencers" or "high-profile" people simply by reaching out to them.

So, taking this a step further, when I would teach in the academic setting, I would always have guest speakers for class. And for every speaker I had, I always tried to find their counterpoint—whether it was a true counterpoint, in the sense of a person who had openly dissenting opinions towards them or a person who had philosophically differentiating opinions in their approaches.

It was an opportunity not only to learn but for my students to open a personal line of communication with thought leaders in the field on both ends of the argument.

I would constantly tell the students, "Don't limit yourself to just who you learned from or the school of thought you know now."

Actively seek out people who do not agree with you: listen to them, learn from them, and empower your own growth from them. Disseminate fact from fiction—gurus and trends from purposeful knowledge.

If you limit what you know, you limit who you can know.

If you limit who you know, you limit what you can know.

At Conferences and Events

I get asked this a lot from up and comers: how do I build my network and maximize my time at conferences and events?

The answer is simple. Aside from doing a superior job at your current place of employment, so internal recommendations are there when opportunities arise—at conferences or events don't spend any more time than necessary with people who you know or talk to regularly when you don't have to.

If people you know are connecting you to new and different people, that is one thing. If they are staying insulated among themselves in a pack and acting like high schoolers, walk away and find a new circle.

Listen, it can be awkward, going up to someone random and saying "hi." As surprising as this may be, I'm naturally a very introverted person. It doesn't bother me to not talk to anyone all day long. I enjoy the silence of my own mind. Some of you who only know me through work will laugh and say I'm lying since I hardly ever shut up or don't have an opinion, but those who have known me since I was young know that I have evolved greatly to be outgoing.

It has taken me a lot of time, a lot of effort, and a lot of awkward moments and stupid comments to be able to be the way I am with people when I'm purposely trying to be engaging and dynamic. I often feel fatigued from having to be that that but I do feel empowered by it at times —a feeling that I did not have for years when I first began in the field.

Generating conversation beyond an introduction is a lost art in our society now, not just professional networking.

I learned it's important to go in with the right outlook. And when I realized the following it radically changed how I looked at what some would consider "a social person."

Assume nearly 100% of people are just as awkward about interacting with others as you are—they also want to meet and know new people—but they're just as scared as you are.

Also, assume 75% of people you do try to talk to are going to either blow you off outright or be pleasant and then find a way to get out of the conversation within sixty seconds.

That's okay. Hell, that's half the point. Just get them to know you exist and move on.

Over time those people will see you more and more. They will grow comfortable with you being in the same space as them, and they will begin to know or hear about you from people they know—especially if you're kicking ass at your current job. These people are just the slow play of networking.

For the remaining 25% who do talk to you and give you more than sixty seconds, don't ask for anything outside of contact info (if that is appropriate in the situation).

Focus on trying to show your value to them and add value to what you talk about. If you get on a topic where you have an acquaintance that is better suited to help them or they would like to talk to, connect them. Actively try to work from the framework of "how can I help this person" and not "how can I help myself because of this person."

This will help build your external reputation outside of your current job. A person in any profession who is thought of as a rock star internally by those they have worked with and as a high quality, always helpful, "great person to know and wish I could work with" person by others in their field will never struggle to get a job.

Building Your Salary History and Value

One of the biggest struggles in the industry is the lack of financial incentive relative to the amount of work required.

At the time of this writing, a study came out discussing salary ranges and trends in the profession and they are appalling, in my opinion.

You must know your value and demand to get it.

No one is going to pay you more if you're not proving you deserve it. Asking for more is pointless. Prove it. And that also means leaving to go somewhere else if where you are isn't willing to value you the way you should be valued.

One of the things that must be done if the profession is to move forward and progress in a positive direction, is building a salary history for levels of work you have done and can do to accurately value what you contribute.

More willingness and knowledge in how to negotiate contracts and more specific job descriptions and responsibilities are needed to best position those in the field from being taken advantage of (I recommend to everyone I meet to read Chris Voss's *Never Split the Difference)*.

For example, one of the most common occurrences that a competent S&C coach is tasked with and generally never capitalize on financially is having to take over other teams.

When hired in a role, the duties and responsibilities are often explained in an informal way and not clearly and precisely written into the job description. It's rare that a college S&C job (outside of football & basketball, but even then) specifically and explicitly states the teams you will be working with and the specific scope of the role.

Anyone being offered a position should ask for the job description, including duties/responsibilities and any other information that pertains to the position. Request team assignments in writing that delineates what services are expected and what are extra (nutrition, travel, and being at practice to name a few).

You should clearly understand, upfront and also for performance reviews, both what is expected for the job and what is going above and beyond. There need to be specifically understood processes frankly specified in your contract stating what will happen and who will conduct them. Knowing who holds power over you allows you to hold power over yourself.

So, how does taking over another team play into this? Hopefully, you see the connection. If you are hired to do a certain set of tasks but due to your competence as well as factors beyond your control (another S&C coach leaving, a sport coach wanting change, etc.) you are now tasked with more work—you should, in theory, be entitled to more pay.

That's generally how it works in most settings outside of athletics.

However, due to ambiguous and often antiquated job descriptions, S&C coaches are stuck taking on additional work (diluting their quality work for quantity of work) with no recourse for an improved financial position.

Strictly speaking from a business point of view, if you are asked to take over another team on top of your current responsibilities, you should receive an increase in pay. A good base number to start with is $10,000.

You must make your voice known, either when you're asked or during your evaluation. You cannot let the opportunity slip through the cracks.

This industry like most others, does not care about you and your personal welfare. It's not looking out for your best interests. It will replace you tomorrow with someone less qualified who will do more for cheaper. That's life.

No matter what your administrators, coaches, or anyone else says— it's a take, not give industry.

Do not be taken.

Yes, that's harsh but it's reality. Just like in life, there are very few people who care about you. And the multi-billion-dollar juggernaut of collegiate athletics is not one of them.

Personally, I experienced this at UConn. I was a GA, and the other GA left halfway through the year to take a full-time role elsewhere. I was then tasked with taking over six of their sports (three men's and three women's), one class they taught, and assisting with two other sports they assisted with.

While this increase in responsibility was massive, as well as the trust the staff had in me to pull it off, I set about putting together an outline of what it would look like. After seeing exactly what I was getting into, I went to my boss, and the first thing I asked for was the other GA's stipend for coaching and teaching.

There was no way I was going to take on all that responsibility without some financial remuneration. It just didn't make any business sense, never mind common sense. If I wasn't going to be compensated, I wasn't going to do it. Fortunately, my bosses agreed and I was given the additional stipend.

As you can see by my calendar below, it was a busy semester. I ate while walking between buildings, often sleeping only 3–4 hours a night between preparing for teams, doing school work, and working outside jobs to have the funds needed to be in school. Mind you this didn't include the weekends and depending on what teams were in season or out of season meant multiple sessions on the weekends as well.

Time	Monday	Tuesday	Wednesday	Thursday	Friday
[illegible]			Diving		Crew
[illegible]			Diving		Crew
[illegible]		Golf Makeup - FH	Tennis		Crew
[illegible]		Golf Makeup - FH	Tennis		
[illegible]	Crew	Tennis	Crew	Tennis	Crew
[illegible]	Crew	Tennis	Crew	Tennis	Crew
[illegible]	EKIN	Tennis	EKIN	Tennis	Mac Meeting
[illegible]	EKIN	Tennis	EKIN	Tennis	Mac Meeting
[illegible]	EKIN	Tennis	EKIN	Tennis	
[illegible]	EKIN		EKIN		
[illegible]	Crew	Staff Meeting	Crew		Crew
[illegible]	Crew	Staff Meeting	Crew		Crew
[illegible]	Shenkman Makeups	FH - Makeups	Shenkman Makeups	FH - Makeups	Shenkman Makeups
[illegible]	Shenkman Makeups	FH - Makeups	Shenkman Makeups	FH - Makeups	Shenkman Makeups
[illegible]		Kraemer			
[illegible]	Football	Kraemer	Football		Football
[illegible]	Football	Swimming	Football	Swimming	Football
[illegible]	Football	Swimming	Football	Swimming	Football
[illegible]	Football	Football	Football	Football	Football
[illegible]	Football	Football	Football	Football	Football
[illegible]	Football	Football	Football	Football	Football
[illegible]	Football	Football	Football	Football	Football
[illegible]	Football	Football	Football	Football	Football
[illegible]	Golf	Golf		Golf	
[illegible]	Golf	Golf		Golf	
[illegible]	Class	Class	Class		
[illegible]	Class	Class	Class		
[illegible]	Class	Class	Class		
[illegible]	Class	Class	Class		
[illegible]	Class	Class	Class		

It was an amazing, extremely challenging experience I'd never change. And I was able to improve my compensation for doing a job I was going to have to do anyway, which significantly helped lower the burden of outside financial stresses—like when my truck needed $2,000 in repairs mid-semester.

So why is this so important? Is just getting paid the most important thing? No, though that is important (we do live in a world where "money talks" after all).

The most important thing was establishing and building a salary history. By proving what I provided was worth the money, I was paid correctly at the time (granted it was still peanuts in the big picture). And it ensured that in the future I would be paid more due to the improved competence, experience, knowledge and quality of work I would later demonstrate.

Building a salary history relative to the experience, success, and perceived value you bring to the bigger picture helps generate an industry-wide notion that a certain salary range is required relative to a level of competency and responsibility.

The only way to do that is to properly define what the role entails. It helps you financially articulate what you deserve relative to what you do.

It helps during hiring and evaluation periods to justify a raise or bonus. It also helps to leave behind a positive financial environment for the next person to fill your shoes. If you brought and added tremendous value, which caused you to have an improved financial position, the next person to fill your shoes should have the same if not greater abilities (with a competent hiring committee), thus continuing to build positive impact with whoever fills the position in the future.

Pay Scale

The salary ranges mentioned below are generalized to show the separation between lateral and vertical positions due to the increase in responsibility as you climb the ladder. Geographical factors and pure financial statuses (revenue-generating versus non-revenue generating sports/departments) will have effect on these numbers. Let me be clear:

this is for competent professionals who show the skills and abilities to effectively execute the requirements of the role.

It should become standard that a full-time (FT), benefit assistant-level position, depending on geographic location and level of financial resources, should be between $50,000 to $60,000.

First-tier, mid-level positions such as assistant director (AD), associates, or any other similarly named position should be within the $60,000 to $80,000 range.

Second-tier, mid-levels, such as associate directors, associate heads, etc., depending on how you break things down (mainly being delineated at the revenue sport end or on total experience) should be in the $80,000 to $120,000 range.

True director roles or significant income-generating sport teams should then start at a minimum of $150,000.

This director-level role consists of overseeing up to three staff members. For every additional staff member over three—not only in job description, but in function, and responsibility—salaries should improve. This also trickles down to the first and second-tier, mid-level positions because they would oversee those in lower-level positions underneath them.

Negotiation for Perks

Additionally, there are situations where you must be aware of how to negotiate and leverage all the resources provided to you; to gain value in your role without it being an increase in take-home pay.

A simple example of this is a cellphone. While seemingly mundane or a commonplace and depending on the level of institution, today's professional must constantly use their cellphone to communicate and interact with all those that they work with during work hours and after. Or should they?

It's often easier to text or call than it is to meet in person due to the dynamic nature and geographical restrictions of practice locations, facility locations, etc.

Because of this and because of the demand for the job to use the phone, the job should pay for or provide a stipend for the phone.

If they do not, then you have no obligation to use your personal cell phone for work-related issues. Think about it: using a personal vehicle for anything work-related gets you mileage reimbursements and often requires paperwork or a paper trail. Why should using your personal phone for work be any different?

Try only using your computer and phone at the office for a week and tell everyone you are no longer using your personal phone for work.

Imagine if every S&C coach and athletic trainer did that. You'd get your cell phone paid for damn fast when shit hit the fan, and administrators would be hammered for being cheapskates for hindering their programs if there was an emergency situation.

But remember, if someone is paying for your phone, they legally have a right to the information on it. This is partly why schools *do* pay for coaches' phones—to track recruiting related communications. It's not your phone—it's theirs. Whoever pays for it owns it.

Let's do some quick math: a basic smartphone/cell plan is about $100 a month. For any twelve-month period, that's about $1,200. So, in theory, to cover that $1,200 you need to earn give or take $1,500 pretax depending on where you live.

So, getting your phone paid for, by the company is a great way to take the cost off you and increase your total benefits package.

Similar things such as car stipends, travel allotments, continuing education fees, clothing/gear, etc., can be used to help offset a lower salary.

Remember that whole salary history? Well, consider the following two scenarios.

You could get hired for $50,000 at one job and have no outside perks; you pay out of pocket for everything. As I just mentioned, a cell phone is a quick $1,200 out of pocket expense, never mind clothes, shoes, certifications, etc.

Compare that salary to another job that will pay you $44,000 but provides a phone, , two pairs of shoes, and certification/membership expenses. In this second situation, when you add the total benefits (taxable and non-taxable), it can add up to an additional $10,000, making the package actually $4,000 better than the higher salary job with a significantly less amount out of pocket money required.

Another thing you need to look at is tuition remission for continuing education. It's one of the only reasons that subpar pay can be justified at many smaller schools.

A university or college will pay for both your academic and professional continuing education. One of the main reasons I was okay with taking such a big pay cut when I left Kansas to go to Hofstra was the amazing tuition remission program for Hofstra employees, allowing me to get my MBA for peanuts. It was a key factor for why I took the job.

If you're at a place that doesn't seem to compensate you fairly in salary, look to maximize any possible perks or fringe benefits to remove out of pocket expense and build value in other ways like getting an additional degree. It may not help you get ahead at the place you currently are, but it will certainly help you open doors in the future wherever you may end up.

Getting another academic degree, especially in an area like business, management, or finance for pennies on the dollar will certainly help raise your earning potential and open more doors than it leaves closed.

Information is Free

Something else to consider while working in the university or collegiate system is having employee access to a massive resource of information whether it be journals, databases, etc., because you're at an institute for learning.

One of the things I would always do every couple of months is go online and download as many articles, journals, or other research that I could—especially journals that were costly when bought as an individual not affiliated with the school. I did this, not only because it afforded me the opportunity to build my own body of knowledge, but because it was free.

Find someone in your network who doesn't have access to free information like that and ask them how they acquire it. They will say they do one of three things: they pay for it, they get it secondhand from someone else with access, or they don't seek it out at all.

In the first case, they will most likely complain of the costs but say that it's a necessity; the second case shows a smart colleague; and the third is a clear sign you might need to find a better network.

The Services are Free

Also, given you are on a campus that is geared towards ejecting its graduates into the workforce, there are significant opportunities for professional development with knowledgeable people or actual experts. *And it's free as well.*

A lot of undergrad and graduate students don't go outside of the classroom setting to maximize the free exposure they have to those resources. Employees of the institutions often don't even consider it.

Often, there are people sitting in offices who want to help and don't have anyone to help, because it's like some kind of taboo to actually use the career resources.

Résumé writing, public speaking, basically anything to make you better professionally is available for free at most schools. Take advantage because once you get out into the real-world things cost money.

Résumé work can cost upwards of $300. Make friends with those people and let them help you.

Also, do this before the last few weeks of the semester as that's when everyone else is trying to do it as well. My golden rule is to wait three weeks after the start of the semester and then get in there. Get to know people, get help, and leverage free resources to make yourself better.

Can't Make Them Drink

I once had an intern who asked me to review his résumé. After providing some insight into the basics, grammar, flow, and content, I made the suggestion that he go to the career center and get more in-depth help as well as brush up on his interviewing skills. He said he would and then said thanks for taking the time to help him.

A couple weeks later, I revisited the subject with him and asked him how the career center was. He replied sheepishly that he hadn't even gone yet and that it was "on his radar" to do. I followed by saying, "Make sure you go soon. They're going to be swamped as the semester ends."

A few more weeks later, days from the semester ending, he asked me to look at his résumé again. He wanted to really start applying to jobs because he was so close to graduation and could start immediately. I again said sure, and when I opened the file on my computer, I was stunned.

He barely had made the changes we had discussed months before. I replied to his email asking if he sent the wrong file, thinking that he might just have attached the old copy and not the updated one, something we've all done before.

The next day he came into the office and told me that it was the most up to date file. I asked him what happened to the changes we had discussed and if he went to the career center. He looked at me and said he didn't get too since they were booked up and he had no time.

Stunned a second time, I asked him how he couldn't have found time in an eight-week period to schedule a free service that was specifically there to help him with exactly what he wanted help with. He looked at me and said something I will never forget: "Coach Joe, I just didn't have time between working, interning and trying to have a social life. It just never fit into my schedule."

And it got even better from there. A few months later, in the summer, he came back to visit and said to me something else that I will never forget: "Coach Joe, do you have any idea how much getting résumé help costs? It was like $500 to work with this company in New York that helps recent grads with their résumés and interviewing."

Again stunned, I looked at him and said, "Did you know that one of the senior execs from that company is actually now the director of the career center? They took the job this past semester." It was something I knew because I had been meeting with that person regularly over the year to help sharpen my own resume.

To which he replied, "Really? That would have been good to know when I was still in school. I wouldn't have had to pay for help."

You can lead them to water but can't make them drink.

What Number are You?

A while ago, I was asked by a senior administrator who I knew from a previous job to go to their university and do two things: first, help them best integrate S&C and sports medicine because they were put in charge of the two and both department directors just couldn't seem to get along; and second speak to everyone on those staffs about leadership, career development, and improving the dynamics of their overall team.

So, there I am, in the football team meeting room with about thirty people—everyone from interns to department heads for S&C, and sports medicine, as well as the senior woman administrator (SWA), deputy director and the administrator who brought me in. In the midst of discussing a point on seeking knowledge outside your sphere, I noticed that one of the people in the crowd was starting to doze off a bit.

Employing my best stare-through-you-into-your-soul look I could muster, I stopped and waited for him to acknowledge me. I stared at the person to the point where everyone in the room begin to feel awkward as well. Finally, I said, "Hey, are you okay with me picking on you a bit? I don't want to if you can't handle it or don't feel comfortable. But if you're up for it, I'm going to give you some shit."

This particular person sat up a little straighter in his chair, puffed his chest out a bit, and replied, "Yeah, I don't mind. I have thick skin."

I started with, "Okay, who are you and what do you do here?"

He replied with a bit of bravado coming out, feeling the challenge in my words. "I'm an intern for football," he said, as if working with football somehow ascended him to heights mere mortals couldn't achieve.

I replied calmly, "Cool, tell me your background, education, experience, etc. And who you are in this field in five years."

He told us where he did his undergrad, his GA, that he was in his fourth internship, and after that he was hoping to get a job in football. And in five years he wanted to be the director at a Power Five school.

Pausing for a moment to take it in, my next question came out fast and hot. "Have you ever been paid to work in the field? Outside of personal training and side hustles?"

"No," was the response, "I've only ever done internships."

"How old are you?" I asked before he finished.

"Twenty-seven" was the reply.

I paused and slowly put my foot on the accelerator. "So, you're telling me you have a master's degree, are twenty-seven, have done four internships, have never been paid in the profession, and in five years you're going to be a director of a Power Five football program? What number are you? What makes you so special?"

I paused for effect. The question was rhetorical.

I continue, "Not to be an ass, but at twenty-seven, I was the director of a mid-major, Division I school, traveled full time with basketball, taught in the grad-sport science program, was working on my MBA fulltime, and consulted while my wife had our first child. I consider myself lucky. I was in the right place at the right time, knew the right key people and got an opportunity I otherwise shouldn't have. I was the third, fourth, and even fifth choice at Kansas and at Hofstra. But I was only in the conversation because I had a low number."

I paused again. Everyone uncomfortably shifted in their chairs and the tension in the room was palpable. "Now, while I just took a shot at you, which you said you could handle, let me explain something. You say your goal is to get to that director position in five years. Well, what number are you?"

"What number? I don't know what you mean." His bravado was tempered by me being a total dick to him.

I replied, "For the sake of math, I'll keep the numbers round, but would you agree there are about fifty director jobs in Division I that are Power Five in football? Jobs you'd consider worth having?"

"Sure," he said, playing along.

"Great, fifty jobs with fifty people in them. Fifty people who want the job and don't want to let it go in the next five years, right?" I continued.

Again, his reply, "Sure."

"Okay, so at that level, all fifty jobs probably have four assistants because you can have five full time in football now. So, with fifty jobs that's

200 more people who in the next five years most likely want one of those fifty jobs too, right?

I pushed on the gas again: "Now what about at all the other schools: Division I, II, III, professional sports and private sector. Maybe, there are another 1500 people who would want one of those fifty director jobs? Great, so we are at 1750 people right now in the industry who want fifty jobs."

Without pause I continued on: "In the next five years, between people coming and going in the profession and newcomers, say there are— what —like 500 people a year who have a goal of getting one of those fifty jobs who aren't apart of that 1750? So, in five years you have the 1750 people currently in the profession plus say another 2500 people give or take. Okay, now we are at about 4000 people for fifty jobs."

I flip the switch and hit the nitro giving no time for response: "How many me's are there? People who aren't in the profession but could come back in for a job like that and are way more qualified than you? Say, 300? Cool, so we are somewhere in the ballpark of an ever-changing group of close to 5000 people trying to get fifty jobs from right now this moment to five years from now. The people that have them don't want to give them up, there are people every day trying to get them—some who are climbing over anyone in their way—and there are also people who could have a shot at them but aren't actively trying but could decide to all with more experience than you. So, what number are you?"

I waited for an answer but one never came. "You see what I'm saying? What number are you? Are you the fifty-first next man up getting a call soon or are you 4951—just another person in the blender?"

"What are you doing to improve your number and be one of the fifty in five years? What football coaches know you and will bring you along on their next job, giving you a shot you might not have earned yet? That's a big part of how college football works. So, how are you jumping the line? What do you bring to the table that is going to make you be 'the guy'? Cause I can sure as shit tell you this, falling asleep here and now—you might be the highest number in the room."

There was stunned silence.

I let it sit for a few moments before I pulled back on things. "Hey, man,

I appreciate you letting me beat on you for a bit. But seriously, that's how you all need to look at it if that is your goal."

I looked around to the group, focusing on the youngest faces. "I sat in Dr. Kraemer's office my junior year and he asked me what my goals where in the profession. I said, be a director at Division I, run and build a department and staff, and help train an Olympic gold medalist. You don't just win those by chance. You actually have to know what you're doing to help an athlete achieve that level of success."

I continued my story: "He looked at me and said, 'What makes you so special? Why do you think it will be you instead of the everyone else who is trying to do the same thing for 150 jobs?' In that moment, I had no answer. I had never thought of it with that perspective: putting a number to it and creating a finite boundary to something I imagined thousands were also chasing. It was in that moment that I doubled down on learning, networking, and sharpening my sword. I knew I needed a lower number and I worked towards getting it.

I turned back to the twenty-seven-year-old: "While I was certainly rough on you, I hope this is the moment you see that perspective and do what is necessary to achieve your goal. Let me know how I can help." He nodded his head and I went back to discussing seeking external learning and knowledge.

11

WHEN THE CHAIR IS YOURS

When you step into a job, you're either replacing someone or you're the first coach ever in that role. The latter means you're in the best situation because you can form, develop, and structure the environment—and thus the culture—without any preconceived notions, positive or negative, established by whoever might have been there before you.

On the other hand, if you are taking over from someone, you hope that person didn't leave you out to dry by setting bad precedents. You can only hope that the reason they left was a positive one, and they left you a solidly built foundation to work with. Sadly, in recent S&C trends, this is often not the case with job hoppers chasing paydays and notoriety while leaving a tsunami of physical and emotional damage in their wake for the next coach to clean up.

I have both stepped into that situation myself personally and worked with numerous coaches who did the same. We inherited wildly malformed programs that were built on all kinds of promises, only to be abandoned at the first chance the previous S&C coach got to "move up." It left athletes to have 2–3 sometimes even 4 or more S&C coaches in their careers, sport coaches jaded, and built even further resistance to letting an S&C coach have control.

SIDE NOTE—If you're an S&C coach reading this, take a second and think of being a sport coach dealing with S&C coaches who do this. Imagine if your livelihood—how you put food on your table—and a key part of that being the S&C program, radically changes every couple of years. You think you're just going to let whoever comes in have cart blanche? Hell, no.

You're going to micromanage; you're going try to keep hold of control so you get done the things you know have worked for you previously; and you're not going to let some random new person, who you don't trust and don't know, spew their magic—"the research says so"—sauce all over your program.

It should not be a surprise that head coaches are resistant to new S&C coaches if they didn't personally hire them or at least had their desired level of input in the process.

Imagine you're a head coach who has had dozens of S&C coaches over the years and had mixed results across the board with them. Imagine that you had an amazing S&C coach at one point and since then have only had "slapdicks." Or worse yet you only had "slapdicks" and then get a good one. You wouldn't know what to do: how to trust them and how to integrate what they have to offer. Your only experience was with "slappies."

Gain that perspective as an S&C coach with the head coaches you deal with and I bet your whole approach to relationship building will change.

I know multiple and specific examples of S&C coaches who spent weeks getting a position at a school, were there for less than a month, and then took another job elsewhere. Never mind the countless S&C coaches who spent less than a year at a school, spent a ton of money on equipment, nutrition, and implementing their "philosophy" (that included costly signage for slogans and other stupid shit that they "needed"), and left the school stuck to do the entire process again with the next S&C coach they brought in.

I know of a few schools where changes were in the $100,000+ range one year for a new S&C coach with a different philosophy from the previous one, only to have to change again the next year when that S&C coach left and someone else came in with yet another different program and needs list to do their job, costing another $100,000.

The irony of not having money for certain things, but being willing to drop thousands of dollars for new "junk" with every changing philosophy, is still something I enjoy laughing at administrators for when I inevitably get the call asking why they can't seem to get their programs on the right track.

My answer is often something along the lines of, maybe, if you spent that money on a quality person, incentivized them to stay and build a well-developed, high functioning program, a significant amount of your problems would solve themselves or never become problems to begin with. But I digress.

History Provides Many Lessons

As you step into a role, you must get a history lesson across all spectrums of what you'll be doing. You must take the time to understand the background of the situation and the people (previously and currently) involved.

Often, things are the way they are because people set precedents that made them that way, without realizing that over time ripples turn into tsunamis in different areas.

You should create a history analysis of coaches and staff you must work with: who has influence, what kind of influence do they have, why do they have it, as well as should they have it?

Who among the people you directly and indirectly deal with values the weight room and who does not?

Who wants to help you and who wants you to help them?

Who must you keep on your side? Who can you not afford to lose as an ally? But also, who can you afford to lose as an ally for certain situations or for certain times?

You must remember not every sport coach or administrator is critical to your success.

You cannot always appease everyone. So, you must identify the one or two linchpins in the system, who must always be kept aware of your actions, because of their influence on your ability to maximize your results

—indirectly or directly. This plays a massive role in how you're perceived and how you're professionally evaluated by your superior or their superiors.

I once worked with an SWA who, in a meeting dealing with an out of control volunteer coach in track and field, described herself as being "the winged angel of death, never allowing you to step foot in this facility again." The poor volunteer coach in question responded by turned ghostly white, and I'm pretty sure he was close to peeing his pants.

So, you bet your ass that I stayed on her good side (which was easy for me, as I thought the world of her and she was very receptive to me: lending an ear and providing great insight when we spoke).

Being Evaluated

Speaking of evaluations, all details regarding this should be finalized during the interview process before you take the job. But in case they aren't, a top priority is to find out the following:

- What are the expectations for how you are evaluated?
- Who evaluates you and why?
- Why are you being judged on certain things within or not within your influence and spectrum?
- What objective data sets are going to validate or disprove subjective claims?

SIDE NOTE —Evaluating an S&C Coach has recently been a major topic of conversation, it seems, as many don't seem to understand how to do it. To me it's actually pretty simple. A multifactorial subjective score sets boundaries for what objective data shows to be true. I'm happy to show you how to do it. Just email me, and we can figure out the details.

Understand the Local History

You also must create a historical analysis of the department and facilities for training the athletes.

What is the facility like? Are things clean and organized? Has regular maintenance been done? How has the space evolved in the previous ten years? What has been done, what has not been not done, and why?

What is the staff like? How are things achieved or halted? What level of competency does the staff have? Are they able to operate anonymously or do you need to P.O.L.I.S.H. them?

The history analysis must also include the athletes because they are the customers you're trying to serve. Do they come to the weight room and use it? How much do they use it? How do they use it? What do they need to do there versus what they have been doing/what do they think they need to do?

Once you've developed a pretty firm grasp on the history of the place, as it relates to the things going on around you and how you fit into it, you can then start to make an action plan.

Please note that this history analysis takes time. You might have to be actively moving forward on some things while still gaining your history analysis, because at the end of the day, the wheel still needs to move.

Therefore, a simultaneous, two-pronged approach is required with phase 1-A being called "stepping back to go forward" and phase 1-B called "getting the ball rolling." From there you can move onto phase 2 and phase 3 of "sitting in the chair" and building something beyond what is currently there.

At this point, I'd like to interject with another personal favorite quote. I like to use the Machiavelli quote and this one as the two sides of the same coin related to dealing with people.

From Bruce Barton:

> "Action and reaction, ebb and flow, trial and error, change—this is the rhythm of living. Out of our over-confidence, fear; out of our fear, clearer vision, fresh hope. And out of hope, progress."

This is not going to be an instant, overnight process. Outside of the honeymoon period of being the new person and being able to make quick changes on a few things, the mindset should always be evolution not revolution.

Phase 1-A: Stepping Back to Go Forward

When you first take a job, you must temper the desire to take total control with the need to gain perspective. It's something I've both failed at and improved on with every new place I went.

Sure, there will be things you need to make immediate changes to or take action on (which we will discuss in phase 1B). However, you must also take the time to gain as much perspective as possible. You must go to introductions and meetings. You must get face time with coaches, student-athletes and other support staff directly involved with your role. You need to watch training sessions, practices, and competitions. You need to insert yourself into as much as possible, while being a fly on the wall. Gather as much perspective and knowledge as you can while having as minimal direct influence as possible.

Take notes (as I mentioned, this will freak some people out) and be aware of how your presence is changing what actually happens on a daily basis.

That's why you need to take as long as you possibly can in this stage. Be around enough that people get accustomed to you and act the way they normally do. Then they'll shake off the act they are putting on because you are new there and you'll see what really goes on.

Not everyone is like that, but most are—especially the unconfident ones.

This process allows you to truly ascertain the changes that need to be made by understanding the dynamics at play. It also allows you to build trust and rapport by asking intelligent questions and having deeper conversations with key stakeholders.

And it helps to show that you have the vision and the ability to make change but also the knowledge that growth is a process—that while it can be fast, it generally shouldn't be rushed.

The goal is to always make sure people know that you are there to help them, that their success is your success (and vice-versa), and that the goal of your effort is to add value to and improve their program in an area you're an expert and they are not.

During my first fourteen days as a director, I only coached three sessions but I attended over twenty-five. And I had over thirty meetings, most of the time, dressed in casual business clothing. I was in a situation where I was fortunate enough to be able to detach and create a historical analysis as best as I could to help drive some of the future decision-making.

I had two key frameworks I used when meeting with coaches and administrators. The first was directly from me: "I'm here to help build an S&C department and allow it to help you and your team in ways it never did before." And the second was from the vision of the athletic director: "We're here to be successful in every competition we take part in." Not saying it worked perfectly or that my gathering of facts was perfect—they certainly were not—but that was the intent.

Phase 1-B: Keeping the Ball Rolling

While phase 1-A mainly deals with situational factors, risk management, and "flow" in many areas of the department, phase 1-B is the obvious things that must happen from day one that you can't wait on.

Questions in this context include the following: are there team training programs that need to be created; and are you going to slowly adapt what the're doing to what you want them to do or does the situation allow for total redo?

Administratively, what's the status of the department and the staff? Are immediate changes needed to be made? What other immediate actions do you need to take to both set the tone and leverage the honeymoon period of being the new person?

These could include equipment, scheduling, staffing, team assignments, information collection, etc.

The honeymoon period (the first 4 to 6 weeks) is critical to the success of the longer-term goals and bigger changes you are trying to bring about.

It's key here to get people sold on your vision. Going back to the Machiavelli quote, many will feel the pressure of the acute and mid-level changes you are making—uncertain if they want to help or not—and that's okay, because if you have a decent history analysis, you'll know who and what situation you can and cannot leverage to your benefit.

If you do not have any type of appropriate depth to your history analysis or you fear someone might have deceived you, you should seek to get some level of consensus across key stakeholders and generate a specific tangible record of that consensus for record-keeping purposes. That way, if with more context over time you realize an initial action taken was an incorrect one, you can adapt the strategy as best you can and repair possible damaged relationships. This is most likely going to happen to some extent, so be prepared for it.

I failed tremendously in this respect as a director, and by the time I realized it, I had quite the hole to dig myself out of: who I initially thought was important weren't the people who actually were; the people supposedly in power had no power; the people who shouldn't have had a say held all the cards.

Those three coaching sessions I mentioned were a specific example of a time when I wasn't allowed to step back and ascertain the situation. Instead, I had to insert myself directly.

I inherited a situation where the S&C coach working with a team had developed an extremely caustic and apathetic environment among all the sport coaches and even some of the athletes. Having little more than a day from when I started in the role to taking over all aspects of the final weeks of this teams in-season training, I needed to aggressively commandeer the situation and redefine the boundaries for the athletes and the sport coaches. Things had gotten out of hand.

It took me three days to make a connection with the head coach, who is someone, to this day, I still deeply respect and admire for their coaching career and accomplishments. They are a true legend in the coaching world.

The athletes craved the change to a positive environment and quickly rebounded in their attitude and efforts as it related to changes in S&C coaches and S&C in general. They went on to finish the season with a playoff run—that when I first got there, looked impossible. Now, don't get me wrong, I'm not claiming I caused that playoff run to happen. But what I am saying is I helped change the environment to allow it to be a greater possibility. I merely helped remove stress.

The sport coaches no longer had the mental burden of S&C eating up their time, the athletes brought more energy, effort, and intent to training, and the collective atmosphere shifted. I facilitated their potential and removed an obstacle that was hindering it. In this case, it was a simple personality conflict. Although, it could have been numerous other issues all causing a similar hindrance.

Also, for the record, the S&C coach mentioned is actually a knowledgeable and passionate coach. They made great strides in their career after this situation because they had the ability to do so. They just needed the right situation, which in this particular case was not the best fit for a variety of reasons.

So, what was the "magic sauce" I used to help facilitate this positive change?

I listened.

I heard what the head coach had to say, what the other coaches and support staff had to say, what the issues were in their mind (right or wrong, but mainly just misguided), and I heard and understood what the athletes said the issues were (right or wrong, mainly just a learned byproduct of the negative reactions by their coaches).

I focused on changing the narrative to change their perspectives: we did 90% of what the sport coaches wanted, or thought they needed, and 10% of what I wanted. And day-by-day I changed that ratio 1–2% based on building trust.

In an interesting note regarding this whole situation, the head coach retired following the season and the coach who took over had a very different personality and style. Recognizing the risk for a suboptimal arrangement, I ultimately reassigned the team to a different S&C coach who had a better fit in terms of personality, style, and experience than I did.

I was the wrong person to work with that new sport coach, regardless of my previous success in that sport as an S&C Coach. There was no reason to fit a square peg in a round hole.

Phase 2

There is no specific timeline for transitioning out of phase 1 to phase 2 as phase 1-A could be a significantly longer process compared to phase 1-B or vice-versa.

As a general rule of thumb, you should only shift to Phase 2 when you have been consistent for at least a semester with the training environment and training of the athletes. Depending on the context you are in, it might take three or more semesters to accomplish.

While there will be many superfluous issues that come up, getting into a groove with the athletes leading up to this point should help allow you to branch outward. You should be able to go beyond simply just training the athletes and keeping the wheel rolling.

The following list, while not inclusive of all things, should cover a wide variety of areas to evaluate, refine, and create so that you have the next 2–4 years of process steps in place:

- Staff development and role acceptance
- Team assignments
- Scheduling facility use and facility expansion
- Training plans
- Department usage/impact KPIs
- Facility maintenance/repair issues
- Equipment needs versus wants and the wish list
- Internship program and outreach
- Performance education materials for athletes' coaches and community
- Website/social media print
- Research projects with internal and external stakeholders
- Technology integration/optimization

Phase 3

Phase 3 is when you are actualizing your vision as a director. Generally, this vision is crafted in a very broad framework before you arrive, narrows within the first year, and is what you are "selling" everyone on.

It truly starts to happen by the end of the second year because, at that point, you will have a much firmer grasp on the resources, the needs, and the alignment around you as you engage in building the department and see its impact across the athletes you train (or the inability to do so and thus the need to move on).

Depending on the context, you'll be able to realize this vision within 3–5 more years. This means the general baseline of developing a department and shaping it to the vision you had should be expected to take 6–8 years.

Remember, evolution not revolution.

The key ingredient at this stage—outside of success in accomplishing results with athletes in training, that while not explicitly said should be a given—are that you have had the time to build the necessary relationship capital across all those involved to actualize your vision.

At this point, charting the next course is what is required. In some respects, going back to phase 1 and rebuilding everything into the next generation of functionality.

SIDE NOTE—Clearly there are going to be some football or basketball people bitching about this, saying, "I do this in one year or a semester? We don't have time to wait. We'll get fired if we're not winning right away!"

True, but that's a problem with the industry as a whole (you can win eight games in a football season and get canned a year after taking over a sub-.500 team). And a problem that's only becoming more obvious with every passing year the coaching carousel becomes more and more ridiculous and gimmick-based.

Coaches change jobs within weeks of being hired now when they find greener pastures (generally financially).

Imagine what would happen if the athletes could do the same.

There is chaos, disorganization, and lack of continuity at the football and basketball level because few truly build anything beyond superficial and fake "cultures" that the athletes inherently know can change multiple times in their career based on factors beyond their control.

Is anyone surprised there is such poor effort in many of the bowl games during the football postseason?

I'd be willing to bet football will soon have an eight-team playoff and a couple more bowl games, both for financial milking and increased chance of basketball-like Cinderella stories—the ultimate money maker.

Setting the Next Person Up for Success

When you leave a job, you should write a small report objectively detailing your time spent in the role, which is customary in many other professions but not always required.

A couple of sentences explaining your philosophy, your training style, and your programming, as well as any additional objective information you can share, will help your replacement be two steps ahead. Leaving copies of your training programs and other related materials should be required because it's critical information to understand for a new coach taking over.

Many sport coaches have gotten smart and ask their S&C coaches to send them programs so they can keep a record of them. This is usually because they've had a carousel of support staff. More than once I've had the sport coach *give me* copies of programs because they were smart enough to ask the previous S&C coach for .

In one instance, the program files—which the sport coach never looked at and just saved to a folder on his hard drive—was a giant Word document with the following type of program:

- 11/15—Squat heavy and lower body accessory work
- 11/16—OFF, some kids did recovery
- 11/17—Heavy uppers/conditioning

Take care to not make your report subjective or emotionally biased; "it's all gumdrops and lollipops, and everything I did was amazing" or a low-blow, acid attack of "this program sucks."

You should report on the status, needs and experiences you have had with the team(s) you worked with purposefully detached emotionally and with as many facts and data to support your position as required.

It doesn't have to be long or complex but provide insight and context so the next "you" knows what happened, has an idea why it happened, and also has perspective on what was going to happen.

If you are struggling to do this, keep it simple and print out a copy of each year's workouts and use a one-page cover page that looks something like this to give your brief:

TEAM:

Training Summary:

Training Schedule
(Days / Duration)

Goals / Emphasis of
Training if I was still
here:

Remember, something is better than nothing. If you leave them totally in the dark and absent of all info, you're part of the problem in the profession. Be one of the people that helps raise all boats and tries not to sink other ships.

Professional Portfolio

One of the things that you should do as you build and develop your philosophies over time, if you seek to attain a leadership position, is create a professional portfolio.

As we've already discussed, by creating tangibility and creating an edifice to put those thoughts and concepts into, you're able to better understand them yourself and expand upon them to other people. You may not ever even have to share the portfolio, only parts of it.

Obviously, this is going to be S&C related, but adapt the concept and theory to any industry.

Now, the thing about the professional portfolio is that its relative to the position and level you're in. Much too frequently, you see people sending portfolios that are way beyond the scope or role they're applying for. It shows lack of context and situational awareness and makes it seem like you're trying to take over and instill your philosophy and approach when in fact you're subordinate to someone else's.

Your Résumé is a Biological Entity

As you build your philosophy and start to develop who you are as an individual, as a coach, and as a leader of others, you also must take the time to record and document the steps and processes you've taken throughout journey in a professional format: a résumé/CV. Way too many times, we find ourselves in a crash course trying to put together a résumé the moment before we need it for an interview or to apply to a job.

I always tell people that their résumé is a biological entity.

It should be something that you view as a live, transformative, ever-changing, ever-growing, and ever-shifting entity you constantly refine (your portfolio is the same but we'll get to that next).

When you start to think of these materials in that sense, you'll start to put in little bits of effort over time. And you'll not only have a significantly firmer grasp on what you've achieved and the manner in which you achieved it, but an updated, articulated version to share with others at a moment's notice without much effort to "prepare" it.

Your résumé is where you can show the concrete examples of the success you've had and the growth of responsibility you've undertaken during your professional roles. It's within the personal interactions you have while interviewing or discussing with people about a future role that you can impart not only those metric representations of success but how your philosophy and approach help drive those successes.

One of the things that I schedule in my yearly processes of self-development is setting aside three hours, every three months, to revise my résumé.

During those three months, anytime there was something very specific I wanted to add, I would open my résumé and at the very bottom make a note of whatever it was. I would add whatever context I needed to so I didn't forget or lose those details.

When my scheduled time came, I would start by looking through my journals and the notes I had made at the bottom of my résumé and do a full revision, creating an all-encompassing master-copy.

Because so much of the legwork had already been done in previous iterations, it was just an exercise in formatting, providing clarity, or adjusting the look and feel if I wanted to. After this session, regardless of whether or not I was looking for a job, I always had a well-thought-out résumé presented in a way that I personally felt best represented me up to that moment in time.

If the need arose to hand it out, it was simply a matter of parsing down the master copy to a job/role-specific version, which took minutes and not hours to change and send out.

More specifically, when working in the college world, I would always make sure one of these revisions fell around Thanksgiving. The reason I would do this around the end of November was because the football landscape shifted in December and January, the basketball landscape shifted in March and April, and the Olympic-sport sector shifted in June and July. Thus, I would be prepared ahead of the shifts in case anyone called asking me if I was interested.

Additionally, as I mentioned previously, if you currently work in the collegiate environment, you must make sure you are taking advantage of the career resources and career development tools you have access to. You need to go to the career center/writing center and have outside people work on your résumé and your cover letter. Go to seminars on improving your writing skills and leverage the people around you (*for free*) to help you for the future (*when things may not be free*).

Remember that every industry is different and a lot of the people who you'll deal with in these settings have never worked in the collegiate athletic world. So, while they may not truly understand some key information you need to put on your résumé, they'll be able to give you insight about details that you didn't think to put on your résumé or ways in which you should format or create context for information you already have.

It doesn't matter if you use bullet points, paragraphs, or pictures —or whatever way your résumé is created—if it follows two key rules:

1. It fits the industry of the role you are applying for; every industry has specific niches and nuances to résumés that you need to learn to best maximize your content, visual appeal and emphasis to whoever looks at it. Look at how the book *CEO Strength Coach* influenced résumés and literally set industry trends; school logos on resumes anyone?
2. You have to make sure that you personally know and understand everything that is said and the manner in which it comes across, because it's a representation of you. The last thing you want to do is not truly know what your résumé says about you or the way it says something.

As an Intern

If you are an intern trying to find an internship, you pretty much need a cover letter and résumé and maybe something else that's asked of you—a video of you demonstrating, lifting, etc. Due to the low experience you have, you are not expected to have a very deep or wide-ranging portfolio that covers numerous topics.

That doesn't mean you shouldn't have a master copy you keep for yourself that you work on and refine for the day you need it, but know when to pull it out and know when to keep it hidden, especially at this stage of the game.

Your role as an intern isn't to have the vision for the department; it's to listen, learn, grow, and get experience.

As a GA

If you're an intern trying to become a GA or a paid, non-benefits, part-time, professionally experienced, but not full-time coach (whatever it's called these days), you might need a more comprehensive packet. It should include a general and brief outline of your philosophy, training, and coaching philosophies and how you approach training, just to give a better context to those you would work with.

Depending on the role, you might be directly interfacing with sport coaches, so it's important to be able to communicate clearly and effectively to them who you are and how you can help. One of the most important things to remember is that you're in a subordinate role to the director of S&C; while you may have autonomy in some capacities, it's not your department. Cook if you're a cook, sous-chef if you can, but remember that you're not a chef or a master chef yet.

It's also key to have a framework for answering "situational" and "behavioral" questions that will come up during an interview because at this point, you'll be given responsibility and autonomy and people want to know how you handle things and your chain of logic in dealing with "difficult athletes" or "coaches who are set in their ways."

Recognize that when you're being interviewed, the questions asked often give you much more insight into the dynamics of the role and the dynamics of the department than the people asking them realize.

Most sport and S&C coaches, and administrators for that matter, have limited to no actual training in how to interview someone. Look for the deeper context of what they ask, what it means, and why they're asking it. A question phrased a certain way can actually be a statement. The quality of the questions is far more important than the content of the question—and that goes both ways—since you'll have questions to ask too. Be careful to not get too pointed in asking questions that read between the lines because you might catch people off guard in a bad way.

Never forget it's a two-way street. They have to want you and you have to want them. Keep in mind that if you accept the job, your livelihood is dependent on working with them. Surrounding yourself with people who you want to be around every day is something to consider.

Moving to a Full-Time Role

If you're trying to become a full-time assistant in an entry-level position, you need to expand your portfolio to include some deeper sample training programs and add density to your philosophies and approach. It helps provide credibility and context that you're able to step in and be fully autonomous.

You're starting to become a sous chef; you need to show that you can stand on your own feet and do the job when the boss isn't around but still understanding how to play your role.

Becoming a viable and useful part of that director's staff is 95% of what you're trying to do. Make sure you align with and are able to work within their philosophy.

A key here is starting to better be able to answer questions for people who don't have the technical or tactical knowledge of the profession. You must be able to translate and transmit information to an administrator or to your sport coaches—directly interfacing with people at the highest degree of your career so far.

Sitting in the Chair

As you look to transition up to a director role, one of the things you must remember in your portfolio is that you're no longer meeting and talking to S&C coaches.

You're the S&C coach that's going to be in charge and lead the department. You're the subject matter expert. You're going to be the one building and developing other staff members.

Your philosophy will oversee the department and those underneath you, as well as provide the vision to build and develop the department moving forward. You must make sure your vision and philosophy aligns with those you'd be working for.

It's one thing to have different opinions on training strategies and be able to discuss that; it's an issue of a different kind to have a vision in direction *Y* and work at a place whose vision is to go in direction *K*. It becomes more of a question of the leadership, vision, and the philosophy that guides the school and the overall athletic department, than it does the specific X's and O's of how you train the athletes.

If you are interviewing for a director position, you couldn't possibly have got to that point in your professional career if you were unable to execute the X's and O's of training athletes, creating training programs, etc., (at least I hope). While you still must have those things in a broad, general sense because they are the fundamental tenets of the job, you need to have the relevant information prepared for the audience that's going to be making the decision.

The person who's going to hire you is going to be a high-level administrator or the AD themselves. Often, they lack true understanding of the demands of the role and the depth of knowledge you have, but that's why they're hiring you. They have a handful or more of "you" who report to them on the different pieces of the athletic department as subject matter experts of their own areas.

It's worth noting there's a massive shift to being an advocate for your people and your department at this level. Far too often, people take on the director role but they fail to realize that no one else loves S&C as much as they do. And it's their job as the director and department head to advocate the vision and advance the implementation of growth for their department.

Not stepping up to the plate and championing issues in a politically savvy and viable way, will only stagnate your department and create deep frustration. If you, as a director, are spending more time talking to your staff or coaches about what you would do if you were allowed too, you need to instead spend more time talking to your administrators and fundraisers to actually do what you've been saying you would. If you end up trying to do so and end up talking to a brick wall, it might be time to look for a new job. You might not be the right person to champion the cause or you might not have an effective leader above you to help you.

How I've Changed

I've often looked back at all the different examples of my cover letters, résumés, philosophies, and portfolios. And I've seen a significant change over time as I've gone from someone who was being led, to someone who was leading, to someone who is making the decisions about leadership. Those demarcations are critical because it's an internal growth process for you to look back, reflect, and see your thought process to understand how you went from one stage to the next.

An insight I gained from this: I've always been actively preparing for more responsibility in order to be ready when an opportunity came along. Similar to the sayings, "dress for the role you want in the future," or "act according to the role you want, not the one you have," you need to constantly be pushing forward in your development to best prepare yourself for the next step.

Far too frequently, I've worked with coaches and up-and-comers who are trying to take over an open position or move on to a position somewhere else, and they're not able to get the job, because they aren't perceived to have the skills to do the new role regardless if they actually do or not.

Instead of growing and stretching themselves in a long-term process, they're trying to seize opportunities at the last second and in a haphazard manner. The most obvious way is fixing a resume in the eleventh hour and asking for references from people you haven't spoken to in months—if not years. And, unfortunately, they often get passed over or left behind because they haven't shown key decision makers their ability or haven't developed in the way they need to versus the way they have perceived themselves to.

12

DEVELOPING AND SUSTAINING TRAINING CULTURE

WHY, YOU MAY ASK, IS CULTURE SO IMPORTANT IN THE TRAINING environment?

It's because the physical demand of goal-based training requires a consistent environment in order for it to get results; training is different than "working out." In this particular environment you're asking individuals, both personally and as part of a group, to do things they've never done before, things don't know how to do, things they don't want to do—and in most cases—things they believe that they cannot do. The S&C coach has a massive influence on the "culture" simply because they are the purveyors of the shared experience and effort of athletes in a demanding way; through physical activity

However, while the S&C coach is the primary driver, training culture is actually a dynamic continuum of five relationships. These relationships have nothing to do with the specific S&C coach in the role, although the individual clearly influences each in unique ways.

When viewed as global relationships, the perspective then comes about understanding a successful department and not just an individual. That's something missing in the current climate and what has led to some of the change coming down the pipe.

The department itself needs to be consistent outside of any individual.

No individual S&C coach should be able to entirely shift the core elements of the department with their arrival or departure. If this is the case, to put it bluntly, administrative leadership is lacking and the culture of the athletic department itself is most likely average to below average.

Everything bleeds out into everything else. It's no different than the athlete who skips class and can't figure out being on time for practice. To quote one of the all-time sport classics *Remember the Titans*: "Attitude reflects leadership, captain."

SIDE NOTE—As we've discussed, training is far more than just lifting, but I'm going to use the term "weight room" to act as a focal point for where training culture emanates from. I find it mentally easy to visualize and for you to use as an anchor in your mind during this discussion.

While the individual may change who the physical extension of the weight room is—forcing changes to the dynamics—the five dynamics themselves never change. For this reason, everything in this section is written from the perspective of being a college S&C coach. Adjust, adapt, and apply for any context.

The five relationships are: the weight room to sport coaches, the weight room to other staff, the weight room to the athletes, the weight room to the sports-medicine/athletic trainers, and finally the weight room to itself.

I'm going to start with "other staff," one of the most overlooked relationships that can quickly make your life significantly easier and give you allies who have influence. From there we will cover the other four, in no particular order of importance. All five interrelate and bleed into one another. Never forget they are always a dynamic continuum all affecting each other in ways you can and cannot see.

In Relation to Other Staff (Becoming a Master of the Human Element)

Be seen. You cannot build relationships with people if you only spend time in the weight room.

Talk to other staff and talk to other coaches, especially those you don't normally interact with. Do it to get to know them and to understand them; not to try to get something from them. They are living breathing people too with their own "stuff". Don't ever forget that.

Get out of the office, walk around, be friendly, and engage. Do not let for one second the only perspective people have of you be what they hear from the athletes or sport coaches.

Ask yourself, do you really want your professional reputation to be based solely on the perceptions and communications of 18 to 22-year-old's? Or sport coaches who may have needed to retire (or be fired) fifteen years ago?

Can you trust anyone is accurately and effectively translating the things you say and do to other staff members in full context? No, assume it's always a game of telephone in kindergarten.

You also need to allow people to see both your educated side and your human side.

You are most likely just as educated—if not more, in your respective specialty—as others across the entire athletic department (most often more than the sports coaches themselves). You need to show them that level of education and competency you have in your subject area (without being overly prideful or boastful) and that you can be functionally useful to them beyond just helping them win.

You also need to demonstrate a unique blend of deep nurturing and human connection that you can develop in those you work with in your role as a teacher, coach, and mentor.

However, if you're a "lunatic," don't try and hide it. Embrace and play with the stereotype that you're an unhinged person who lives in a dirty, gross training environment and only wears grey sweatpants. Think Deadpool breaking the fourth wall. You need to be lucid enough to understand how to leverage this as a tool to help you; not just embrace the gimmick and cut promos while "bringing the juice."

If you physically look the part, you're probably best known as the meathead, a yeller, or an overly intense, unpolished individual. You can leverage that at times as well. Just like how you can leverage not physically looking like the stereotype. The key, as always, is being honest to yourself first. Don't pretend.

Just try your best to manage the intensity you bring, keeping it at a level relative to those who don't understand that kind of mindset. Few people understand the intense and consistent mindset needed to be the "tip of the spear": constantly growing beyond current capacity, embracing adversity, and getting "shit" done at all costs.

Do you love training more than your athletes? Do you often operate at a different tempo and intensity than your other athletics staff peers (and most other in society)? If you answer yes to both of those questions, you need to manage yourself, because you're the minority and they're the majority. There are a lot of more average people out there than tip-of-the-spear people.

Everyone has a place and a purpose. You're not better than them. You're just different. But just because you're a "lunatic," it doesn't mean you can ruin it for the next S&C coach after you and the profession as a whole. To paraphrase a good friend, "Don't be an asshat even if you are in fact one."

Additionally, it may be helpful in outside projects and events to get people to see you want and can be helpful beyond just contributing to the scoreboard.

Show them that the vision and mission you have is beyond just "W's" and watch the alignment and support for what you do magically increase.

In one of my roles, I would make it a point every week to walk up into the academic space and all levels of the building that I was connected to and say "hi." At first many of the academic support staff were perplexed as to why I was trying to communicate with them. There was no emphasis on our synergy in helping build the athletes as people not just performers. Sadly, a common thing at many places.

Over time, by having those informal conversations to discuss the individuals we worked together with or just see how people were doing, I had built enough relationship capital with those other staff members that allowed me to navigate difficult situations in the future or have allies when certain situations came up. People knew who I was, they knew what I was about, and they had heard it from my mouth directly. And they felt comfortable and confident sticking up for me when others attempted to shift the narrative in the wrong direction.

You must also think what kind of additional value you can bring, not only to your staff but to the department, both to benefit the weight room and your own personal growth.

Whether you're good with logistics, ideas, editing videos, or creating websites, whatever skills you have you can help others with them. Even helping with trivial things like seeing your supervisor struggle with Excel and asking if they need help because you're pretty with it can go a long way for you.

For example, by helping someone to simplify formulas, streamline visuals, and simplify documents they were using to try to create the overall athletics budget, not only do you gain credibility for knowing more than just your subject area (excel for this example), but it gives you an inside look into the backend of department financials (information you have to exercise good judgement on whether to share or keep to yourself).

It helps build a reputation that you can be asked to help with a bigger scope of projects than simply just what you do and that you'll assist while maintaining professional respect, staying in your lane, and keeping information confidential.

Open Gym for Staff

Working on being seen and providing value is important, but just as important is bringing people to you.

Have an open hour at the gym for staff but recognize not everyone wants to train, likes to train, or knows how to train. Don't try and convert other staff, coaches etc., into becoming devout regulars, "worshiping at the church of iron." *Field of Dreams* it: those who will want to come will come and those who don't won't.

On the other hand, be keen to not let your weight room become a health club for staff; it's not a twenty-four-hour fitness gym. There should be a designated time and space that it is allowed for staff to train and there should be designated times and spaces where they are not allowed to train. This will help solve 99% of the issues that relate to ineligible athletes using your facility as well.

Be careful getting into conversations with groups if you have a sport-coach guru in the group because many sport coaches feel as if they are masters of training, nutrition, and psychology. And while they sometimes may have some knowledge, they are often off base or misapplying the knowledge when it comes to ideas outside of their sport (or in their sport for that matter). Having to undercut them or put them in their place in front of a group can hurt the dynamic in ways you may not realize.

Be helpful if someone needs or asks for help but be wary of constantly giving advice or getting lost in spending more time writing programs and training staff than getting them to figure it out for themselves.

Give pause to how you treat everyone and what everyone thinks of you. You never know who you'll be working for one day or who has the ear of the person who can affect you having a job tomorrow.

In Relation to the Sport Coach (Building Relationships, Having Respect, and Creating Value)

A sport coach's lack of or unwillingness to support the S&C coach work as an important piece of their program is the number one killer to weight room culture.

If the sport coach doesn't value it, the team won't value it. Period.

You must provide clear communication, education and explanation to the sport coach in ways they can understand. You must determine whether they're a process-driven or results-driven person and tailor the metrics and discussions about the development of the athlete and team appropriately.

I once worked with a coach who would constantly belittle me due to his belief that his athletes had not improved—even after I had shown the hard data of objective metrics proving positive change.

He actually handed me the information back, said he didn't care about that "number stuff," and he needed the guys to do better in other ways—which he was not able to define. His career .500 record was a strong factual metric indicating he knew little of how to make a team better.

It was at this point, I realized I needed to shift gears. I started to build and develop a different type of assessment—not only based on objective fact, but on a subjective value score—one he could relate to because it allowed him to constantly change his stance without fear of having a position the facts didn't line up with.

I used a subjective rank scale based on the athlete's character traits and their development, combined with objective facts, to reference how the specific individual had or did not have the elements the coach thought he required of his athletes.

The Head Coach-CEO Conundrum

The idea that the "head coach is a CEO" is one of the biggest issues facing the collegiate realm right now. Head sport coaches have been deputized by the NCAA and other governance structures to "control and be accountable" to everything and everyone related to their program.

Additionally, they are constantly under social scrutiny by society at large—especially if they have large salaries—to "control their program.".

While these pressures are valid and make a lot of sense conceptually in the given context there is a problem. Head coaches are given this responsibility and task of being the CEO of a business, yet they often lack the management savvy and knowledge of how to run a business.

SIDE NOTE—Let no one fool you. College athletics, while embodying an attempt to maximize athlete experience and personal development—at the end of the day—is primarily a financially driven business unit that focuses on "keeping up with the Joneses" and maximizing the athletic talent to build revenue and notoriety for the university.

If you don't believe me, wait until you are filling out your March Madness bracket this year or watching college football playoffs. Is it really about the athletes? No, it's a multi-billion-dollar industry entrenched in multiple other multi-billion-dollar industries that won't ever let it fail. The NCAA has no chance against that juggernaut. It's already starting to lose grip across a variety of landscapes if you are looking in the right places.

The head sport coach is now a CEO of a business, and there are some who are very successful at this. But the issue lies within what it takes to be a sport coach; a college degree and the experience in the respective sport.

Technically speaking, if you use "alternative facts" on your résumé it doesn't even require a college degree to be a head coach. You can get the degree *after* you had the job, try to get another job, get found out, and then get your original job back while you finish your degree (seriously, it happened in the 2010s).

Aside from having played the sport (sometimes even this is not required) there is no prerequisite for the education, knowledge, or ability in any of the major functions of the job including the management aspects of leading others.

Now, with that knowledge of sport coaches, take a really good look at what we've done for all the support elements related to helping a program in the collegiate space. We've specialized everyone related to the athlete except the sport coaches (in the sense of being a CEO), and we've also asked the coaches to have a skill set that most of them don't have (being a CEO).

You can see why there are so many issues with sport coaches who lack the managerial savvy or leadership capacity to lead people who are so specialized. The specialists may have a better grasp on some of those functional areas and may have a better way of integrating those subspecialties into the program than the sport coach does.

Being a head coach at a major program these days generally means you're no longer in the trenches or on the battlefield. You're either on the hilltop or in the clouds.

Even in the lower-level college setting, while you may spend more time in the trenches because of resources, head coaches are also asked to fundraise and do all of the other business-related aspects outside of simply coaching X's and O's.

To put someone in that position without requiring them or giving them the opportunity to learn, be educated on and develop these skill sets is just a recipe for failure, conflict, and malalignment across the entire community of people they associate with.

It's high time that not only do we try to develop the student-athletes, but that administrators and other leaders actively provide management training, time management, organizational development, business development and other key skill sets to sport coaches (assistants and head coaches). Because if they did not learn those things from previous experiences outside of coaching (academically or personally), they will not be receiving them from the job.

The worst thing we can continue to do is let future coaches learn at the feet of head coaches who are incompetent and ineffective in these areas. And the scary thing is there are *a lot* of sport coaches out there that fit into that box.

A recent phenomenon—there are some places that are actively developing processes and programs to help educate coaches and staff. They're using their leadership development staff to not only develop their athletes but also their own staff; it's something that should be a requirement at every school.

One of the areas that I get asked to consult with are building and implementing these programs for schools; helping better develop the head coaches into CEOs and give the midlevel staff a mechanism to reach their potential.

Below is an example of a staff development program (at a very high level) that I've adapted and implemented based off a program that is currently being implemented at a major state school. The CEO program for head coaches, aspiring head coaches, and department directors is entirely different and is more individually intensive rather than group focused.

Yearly Career Staff Development Program

Goal/Objective:

Provide selected staff members with direct experience to the administration and management of intercollegiate athletics functional areas and additional leadership experience for personal development and preparation for future opportunities.

Applying:

- Please complete the application and submit with a current resume no later than July 1.

- Applications will be reviewed and all applicants will be notified no later than August 1.
- Applicants should expect to participate in an in-person evaluation.

Eligibility:

Applicants must currently be a full-time employee and have a minimum of two-years' experience and no more than six years of experience within intercollegiate athletics and not be a head coach or department head.

Curriculum Includes:

- Professional development such as leadership development, national experiences, regional experiences, guest lectures, interviewing and hiring processes, meeting with key stakeholders, and participating in senior staff meetings
- Personal development such as a reading series, public speaking, networking experience, and interview prepping/resume writing

---

Presenting Information

As mentioned at the beginning of this section, I gave the adjusted report (on the following page) to the head coach.

While he was overwhelmed with the information and didn't have the skills necessary to truly understand what I was giving him, I never really had much difficulty with him again as it related to objective data. He eventually recognized not only was there progress but that one of the fundamental reasons there was a lack of development in certain areas had nothing to do with the physical training but everything to do with the depth of character he recruited.

Name	Height	Weight	Wingspan	Period
Player 1	6'10"	231.4	6'10.25"	SPRING

Weight Room Scores	#	Current x BW
Bench	245	1.06
Squat	365	1.58
Deadlift	405	1.75
Snatch	135	0.58
Clean	175	0.76

EXPECTATIONS	Bench	Squat	Deadlift	Snatch	Clean	
[illegible]	.5 x BW	1 x BW	1 x BW	.5 x BW	.5 x BW	
Needs Improvement	.75 x BW	1.25 x BW	1.25 x BW	.6 x BW	.75 x BW	
Minimum Expected	1 x BW	1.5 x BW	1.5 x BW	.7 x BW	1 x BW	
Expectation	1.25 x BW	1.75 x BW	1.75 x BW	.8 x BW	1.25 x BW	
High Level	1.5+ x BW	2.0+ x BW	2.0+ x BW	.9+ x BW	1.5+ x BW	

Performance Test Scores	
No Step Vertical (in)	30.1
Moving Vertical (in)	33.5
Broad Jump (ft-in)	9-2
3/4 Court Sprint (Sec)	3.41
Lane Agility (Sec)	11.2
Stadium Run	13:06

EXPECTATIONS	No Step Vertical (in)	Moving Vertical (in)	Broad Jump (ft-in)	3/4 Court Sprint (sec)	Lane Agility (Sec) *College Court	Stadium Run
[illegible]	Under 22"	Under 24"	Under 7'8"	Over 3.56	Over 11.00	Over 12:00
Needs Improvement	22-25"	24-27"	7'9"-8'2"	3.55-3.46	11.00-10.66	12:00 - 11:31
Minimum Expected	25-27"	27-29"	8'3"-8'10"	3.45-3.36	10.65-10.26	11:30 - 11:01
Expectation	27-30"	29-32"	8'11"-9'5"	3.35-3.21	10.25-9.86	11:00 - 10:31
High Level	Over 30"	Over 32"	Over 9'6"	Under 3.20	Under 9.85	Under 10:30

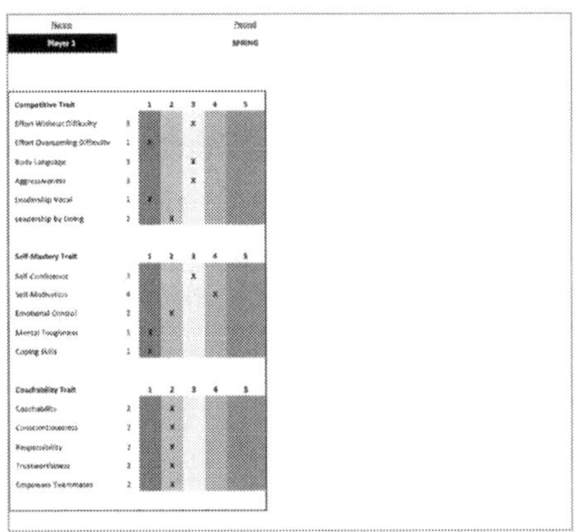

Name	Period
Player 1	SPRING

Competitive Trait		1	2	3	4	5
Effort Without Difficulty	3			X		
Effort Overcoming Difficulty	1	X				
Body Language	3			X		
Aggressiveness	3			X		
Leadership Vocal	1	X				
Leadership by Doing	2		X			

Self-Mastery Trait		1	2	3	4	5
Self-Confidence	3			X		
Self-Motivation	4				X	
Emotional Control	2		X			
Mental Toughness	1	X				
Coping Skills	1	X				

Coachability Trait		1	2	3	4	5
Coachability	2		X			
Conscientiousness	2		X			
Responsibility	2		X			
Trustworthiness	2		X			
Empowers Teammates	2		X			

Some of the best conversations I had with him were philosophically-based discussions about how we ranked his athletes on the subjective part of the scale. It helped us develop some common ground to work with each other on. It was easy to agree athlete X was an immature, "slapdick" impeding their own development in all facets of training. That set the stage for the common ground of, "He doesn't get it at practice either—not surprised he's a pain in the weight room for you too."

The interesting example I was able to show during those conversations was the "bleed out effect: athletes who were late to practice, unprepared, skipped class, or were otherwise not mature enough to be self-accountable (often reflected in my rankings as well) were also the ones who were failing to be successful in the training setting and often also in competition (i.e. not knowing the plays, making the same mistakes, etc.).

I spoke to an intern about this correlation when we were putting this information together saying, "I don't understand how it's an amazing revelation that if you're a shithead on your own time, you're 99% likely to be a shithead on everyone else's time."

SIDE NOTE—To all you sport coaches reading this, if you want better culture on your team, don't look to the S&C coach or military-style, gut-check sessions.

Recruit higher character people and consistently hold them accountable to a high standard at all times—from the moment they walk in, to the moment they walk out. Indoctrinate them into the required culture and cut them free if they can't toe the line.

It's that simple. Seriously.

Understanding the Way to Share Information

This then brings us to determining what kind of information and what level of information you need to share. You need to understand how knowledgeable your sport coach is relative to the performance side.

If your sport coach is knowledgeable, take time with them, listen to them, gain their insights and their slights, and incorporate what you know into what they do and strive to push things forward in a positive direction. Don't be afraid to let it roll since they have experience. Consider yourself more of higher-quality spice adding flavor to a dish that has already been prepared. Don't try to "reinvent the wheel" and totally change what they've already been able to accomplish.

If your sport coach thinks they're knowledgeable but really isn't, work on educating them: talk to them, show them information in a way that makes sense to them, and get them to understand you bring value they don't have and that you want to help them be successful. You should be telling them that regardless but, in this case, you must reiterate it often. Don't overpower them with your knowledge; use your knowledge to build them.

I've mentioned this before and I will multiple more times—I had to say this to multiple coaches when we hit our first friction point working together: "Coach, do you think I'm trying to hurt every one of your athletes and prevent them from getting better? Or do you think I'm trying to find the best possible way, given our situation, to get your kids to the best of their ability so we can win? We may disagree on the specifics because we each have our own knowledge, experience, and expertise but we both want the athletes to be healthy, improve, and win."

In this situation, you must act more as a sous chef by helping to prepare and trim the ingredients to be put into the dish and help add in the correct blend of spices. Don't be afraid to stand your ground and express your beliefs with logic, evidence, and objective data but understand that it may not sway opinion.

Remember, no matter how the conversations go, it's very hard to argue fact. And if you can stick to facts in your presentation, over time you generally can get people to come around to see the trends—both positive and negative—of what's happening.

Also, please for the love of whatever deity you believe in, don't be the idiot that says, "The research says . . ." or "We know from the research . . ." That's the fastest way to kill a relationship with a sport coach who has strong opinions on doing things their way. Build a relationship first, get them to believe in you, and then work on evolving the training.

Most importantly, once a sport coach's athletes—especially their favorite athletes, who they give special privileges to—say they like what you're doing from a training standpoint and that it positively impacts their performance, that sport coach will magically give you a longer leash.

One time, I magically became a competent S&C coach in the eyes of a head coach who previously thought I wasn't. Before, we weren't lifting as heavy as they thought we should or doing what they were used too and what the national team of their sport did; then a key senior athlete's knees no-longer hurt and they told the head coach they had never felt better in their career.

Granted, all we did was correct the person's technique in almost every lift, not overload them all the time, and train consistently with a plan for the few months I had been working with the team. But none of that mattered. What shifted the dynamic for me was that kid, for whatever reason, speaking to the head coach that day.

Now let me be clear, I'm not saying for you to plant information in the athlete's ear for them to be your mouthpiece to the coach. That's a dangerous game and one you should never play. It's like playing with fire and gasoline; you'll eventually get burned, badly. What I *am* saying is if you do a good job and have a positive impact, the athletes will tell the coach and the coach will take notice.

Head Coaches Need to Leverage the Relationship Capital of Support Staff More

It's actually pretty simple. Just read the screenshot:

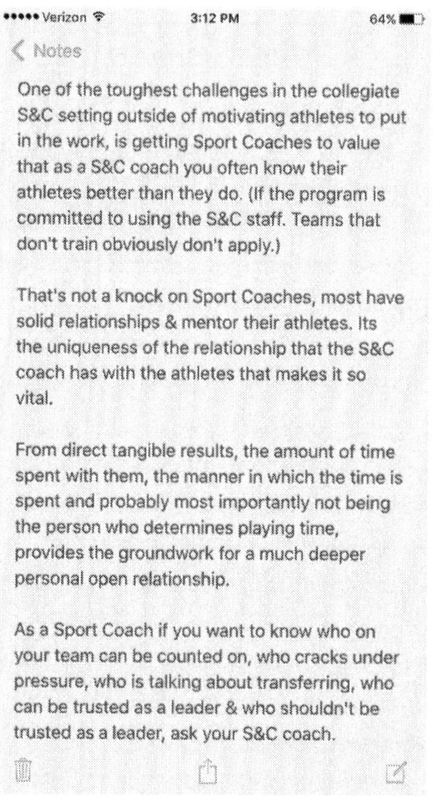

•••••Verizon 3:12 PM 64%

< Notes

One of the toughest challenges in the collegiate S&C setting outside of motivating athletes to put in the work, is getting Sport Coaches to value that as a S&C coach you often know their athletes better than they do. (If the program is committed to using the S&C staff. Teams that don't train obviously don't apply.)

That's not a knock on Sport Coaches, most have solid relationships & mentor their athletes. Its the uniqueness of the relationship that the S&C coach has with the athletes that makes it so vital.

From direct tangible results, the amount of time spent with them, the manner in which the time is spent and probably most importantly not being the person who determines playing time, provides the groundwork for a much deeper personal open relationship.

As a Sport Coach if you want to know who on your team can be counted on, who cracks under pressure, who is talking about transferring, who can be trusted as a leader & who shouldn't be trusted as a leader, ask your S&C coach.

Training is Practice

Training with the S&C coach, whether it's in a facility or on field, needs to be viewed the same as regular sport practice with the head coach. Ideally, the head coach and S&C coach should be synergistically integrating their respective specialties into practice when possible. Nothing is more powerful to an athlete than seeing the integration of effort from everyone they work with.

Imagine taking a week's worth of speed development and agility work from S&C, then tactical work at sport practice, and having a session where both the sport coaches and S&C coaches were on the field integrating the skills into actionable development.

While this is an ideal, and one not always tenable for a variety of reasons, it should be something to shoot for.

This brings two big issues to the forefront: standards and distractions.

First, you as the S&C coach must understand what is acceptable and what is not acceptable by the standards of the head coach.

Far too much, S&C coaches beat their heads against the wall trying to hold teams accountable and instill discipline to their own set of standards that are not reinforced by or during their time with the sport coach.

While you must have your own standards (bend but not break), you also have to be cognizant of the individual dynamics of each sport and sport coach and how their teams are operated.

For example, if a soccer coach doesn't care about players starting behind the line and not jumping ahead of the beep on the beep test or won't support you after you try to hold athletes accountable to it, you're going to drive yourself crazy trying to hold the athletes accountable to those standards when they're with you.

The question then becomes, should you even be running the test if that is the case? There are two sides to that question for sure and room for more conversation elsewhere.

Look at a team that operates with different practice times within the groups or subsections of the team. Athletes will come into the training environment at different times and you must be able to be okay with that.

Not every team will train as a team (though they should, at least once a week, simply for a shared experience as a culture-builder).

Cross-country is the easiest example of this. Multiple athletes may start practice together but finish at radically different times, which means if they're coming to the weight room right "after practice," they could be 5–30 minutes different in arrival time. One athlete may have a two-mile cooldown and others have a five-mile cool down after completing practice together. If you don't understand that natural time discrepancy and adjust for it, you will drive yourself crazy trying to get everyone to "show up together" and "be on time." If you can't adjust for that time discrepancy due to scheduling and other demands, change the training session time. Stop trying to fit a larger, square peg into a smaller, round hole.

The second part of S&C training being treated like practice is limiting distractions, specifically from the actual sport coaches themselves. Until sport coaches can play in the competitions for the athletes, they don't need to train with the team in the weight room.

Let me be very clear here, in sport practices—especially team-based sports—coaches and former athletes are likely needed to help in practice simply due to not having enough bodies to go through certain drills and situations or players being unable to maintain the level of output needed.

An easy example of this is basketball: you need someone running the drills, getting rebounds, etc., to maintain both a high tempo and get the required reps in efficiently. This can be a very new concept for some sport coaches who don't understand that what goes on in the S&C realm and what goes on in the sport-specific side are not the same.

When people are "involved" in practice they naturally want to be "involved" in training. This is where you need to have some rules and regulations for what sport coaches, managers etc., are allowed to do when they come to watch S&C sessions.

You wouldn't go to a mandatory team practice and get in the way of drills, talk to athletes while they were in the middle of the drills, or try to coach things you don't know, would you?

I would be willing to bet the sport coaches would get pissed off fast and tell you to stop or leave altogether, so why would it be any different for you?

You can try it next time with a coach who does it to you. You can interject yourself in their practice the way they do in your S&C sessions and see what they do. Then you can have the same response to them when they do it to you in the weight room—and you can have a nice chat about it.

SIDE NOTE—Disclaimer: Be careful if you do this because you could get fired. This generally is not the best strategy to undertake, but it's an option among countless others. This just happens to be the fishing with dynamite option; it could blow you to pieces but could also help you get dinner fast.

There is a balance asking coaches and staff to watch and see what's going on to give context and credibility to your efforts. You also have to be willing to ask them to leave if they're lounging around, being a distraction, or creating an environment that takes away from your ability to develop athletes.

Now, let's break this down into a couple of pieces. There are situations where you're going to ask the athletes to do extremely intense and difficult things, whether it's competitions, hard workouts, testing etc., where you want the sport coaches or important staff members to come and see the results and outputs achieved at these critical times.

You should personally invite the coaches to discuss why you want them there and the importance of having their support. Even go so far as giving them specific directions on what to do (i.e. stand here, watch X, etc.). Or if you have a coach with a low level of ego, have them write things down or keep track of something to engage them.

The key here is to get the coach to feel the "juice" of the environment and the success of their athletes improving. A key to note here is not your "juice," but the vibe of the athletes and the dynamic *they* create. Be careful to not get lost in talking about the specific improvements in the moment with a coach after an athlete does something because the time for crunching and discussing data will come later. In this moment, the goal is to help the coach feel and value the ebb and flow of energy from their athletes in relation to their training.

Let the coach know how it can help to put a little more pressure on the athletes to perform because they know they're being watched by the playing-time decision maker. And that you can help show who steps up, who steps back, and who the real leaders are—not just who's perceived to be a leader.

However, this arrangement must be tempered because if the sport coaches are always there and the athletes always feel that scrutiny, it can often create a caustic and negative environment even if it's not intended to. I once had a team I would take outside to do warmups, cooldowns and any other non-weight-room based "stuff" I was going to do. I would traverse them all over the athletic fields in a seemingly random manner to specifically keep a large distance between the coaching staff and the athletes. The coaches could never be "on top" of the athletes because they simply couldn't keep up or know where I was going to next. The athletes often appreciated the "air" it gave them from their extremely domineering coaches as well as a chance to openly talk to me without their coaches around.

You should strive to have a balance of the sport coaches being there and getting out of the way. The great coaches do this instinctively. The good coaches just need some guidance. The bad coaches—let's just call them the "helicopter coaches"—they bring a lot of associated noise and kick up all kinds of crap every time they land close by.

Sometimes, asking coaches or other staff to leave—while difficult— is critical. If a coach is lounging around, sitting or being lazy with their body language, on the phone and generally not engaged in watching the training session—get them out!

It's one thing if they're there working on social media or video chatting a recruit to show them the session; it's another thing to be sitting in the corner haphazardly being a distraction by talking about unrelated things or with eyes glued to their phone looking at Barstool Sports Smokeshows (it actually happened—see the "Hilarious Stories" section).

Sport coaches often fail to realize that their athletes take their cues as to what is appropriate behavior. It's no surprise that the sport coach is the number one influence to convince athletes about the importance of the training outside of the S&C coach themselves.

Also, the athletes have a good level of awareness when it comes to bullshit—they are after all 18–22 years old with the world literally at their fingertips. They're quick to know who's real and who's fake.

I give an example of a coach who fell asleep later in this chapter. Her athletes tore her apart after she left and for the next few months after. She had eroded her credibility with her athletes due to her actions. And it took years, after all those athletes had graduated, for her to be looked at in a higher professional esteem again by her team and not to have that story told about her.

Asking a Coach to Participate

There *is* a time to ask a coach to participate in workouts with the team. But it should only be used as a mechanism to drive two specific purposes, and it should only happen during the off-season when the stakes are low and the ability to prove a point and build off of it is high.

The first purpose is when the sport coach is physically incapable of participating in the training but views what the athletes are doing is "easy." You can prove a point to the coach that their perceptions are flat-out wrong by "taking their soul" as David Goggins would say.

Or conversely, if the coach is physically superior to the athletes you can prove a point to the athletes that what they think is enough is flat-out wrong if their coach can dominate them (or show the coach that the athletes just aren't at the level they think they are).

Now, for the record, if you're putting someone in over their heads, have the appropriate medical support available and don't do something crazy for the sake of it. Do what you normally do with the athletes and just show how it's not actually easy (keep the egos in check).

Also, keep an eye on the sessions (in both situations) to make sure the coach doesn't lose too much credibility with their athletes or you aren't losing credibility or any relationship capital you need to keep.

Sport Coaches at Training Sessions

One of the biggest issues I always dealt with from a coaching dynamic standpoint was sport coaches at training sessions.

Now I'm not talking about coming down to say "hi" or talking to the team after a session. I'm talking about standing in the weight room or physical space while training is going on and wasting their time—or worse—distracting the athletes, being a distraction themselves, or trying to coach athletes during training when they shouldn't be.

The most successful teams I ever worked with and the most successful coaches I've been around never came down into the weight room or the training room to stand there and watch, unless they were explicitly asked to by the S&C coach. And even then, they often only stayed for a few moments, leaving to spend their time doing more productive things like recruiting, fundraising or planning sport practice.

This goes back into head coaches being CEOs: managing, delegating, having the confidence and trust to have a decentralized command structure, and being operationally efficient with time. Many times, the ineffective or unproductive sport coach will sit in on training sessions pretending to evaluate their team and actually hinder development.

From a detached point of view, what are they doing?

They're taking up space and wasting time. Sometimes they're taking away attention from the training environment. Sometimes they're talking to athletes who should be task-focused and objective-orientated during training. Sometimes they're on their phone or talking among each other if there are more than one of them.

Or the cardinal sin of all sport coaches; they try to coach the athlete but are flat wrong in what they are saying. I've seen it happen in both a training session with an S&C coach and a rehab session with an athletic trainer. And when that happens it's often because they lack the knowledge and context to understand what's going on, have low self-confidence, and/or feel challenged by your ability to get better outcomes then them.

It's their team. They're the CEO. They can come and see what's going on. But think about it in a business context: would the CEO of an extremely successful business sit on the line in a manufacturing plant or in a salesroom, or a marketing department every day and oversee the small front-line operations by having a say in every single micro-action? Would the AD of your school or the owner of your team both run the overall business and be in the weeds in the day-to-day operations of a single functional area of the business?

No.

Sure, they may go down from time to time, see what's going on to get a feel of the pulse of things, gain perspective, enhance alignment, hear someone out, or get their hands dirty in something they used to do for old-time's sake . But they would then move on to the higher-level functions of their role after that brief moment. All those things just mentioned are tactical moves to leverage the larger strategic focus their job requires.

If they were to try to be the decision maker at the micro-level every day for hours at a time, they wouldn't have the time to address the higher-level functions and demands of the company. Their order of magnitude and their scope of how to be a CEO of a business would be out of whack and viciously ineffective, which would create negative ripples across the company.

All of the time wasted by coaches "watching" training could be spent recruiting, building their skills in other areas to help their program or themselves as a coach, meeting with other people, or planning and organizing all of the additional responsibilities on their plate.

If you, as a leader, don't have any trust to turn your back on people for them to do their job, you're doing something wrong.

The Sleeping Assistant

I once trained a women's team, in conjunction with a head coach who wanted to but didn't know how to, and I was trying to slowly build their physical development and training culture. Over time the group started to embrace the change; they actually loved "getting after it." They listened, they loved being pushed, and they craved the drive towards improvement —not complacency.

A newly hired assistant coach came to a morning training session that started at 6:00 a.m. We were on a field doing some movement prep and general conditioning; a very basic general prep—nothing flashy, fancy or enjoyable to watch.

As the session continued, she went from standing to sitting. Then she was on her phone with her head down and lost in the screen. I walked over as one of the drills shifted into the space she was in, and I noticed as she was actually asleep.

She sat cross-legged on the ground with her hands holding her phone with her head down and out cold. She might as well have been tucked into her sheets in her bed.

I didn't think the girls had noticed yet, so I called out to her. She was startled and shook herself out of it, at which point I said to her, "Hey, don't be here if you're going to be asleep. I'll come talk to you later." And with that she acknowledged me, got up, and left—still somewhat ensnared by the fresh cobwebs of sleep.

Well, within ten minutes of her leaving, every girl on the team was taking jabs at her and berating her: how it was pathetic; how if she thought she could be asleep during training, she shouldn't even had come; how they wanted to be sleeping too but they were there trying to get better.

And they had pointed question:

"What kind of message does it send that she fell asleep when we were here working out?"

"What if we fell asleep at practice?"

"What would you make us do Coach Joe?"

As the voices started to die down, one of them turned to me and said, "Well, you should make her do burpees. You would have made us do burpees."

I said, "Well, you know what guys, I get it. I understand that's not right. I understand it's not the culture, the attitude, and the effort we want to adhere too. I'm going to address it with her after. Obviously, I don't want to take time away right now because you're all here and we have things to do. But don't worry. I'm going to address it with her later."

A couple of them gave me interested looks that said, *Oh, okay. Can't wait to see how that goes.*

Reading their body language, I said, "It's not going to go any other way than me telling her that's unacceptable, don't do it again, and if you do it again there'll be a consequence. It's not rocket science."

We finished the session and a couple of hours later I went to my "sleeping" assistant coach. We talked about it. I said something to the effect of, "Hey look, here's the situation. Here's what we're trying to do: accountability, culture, etc. It's not the place to be falling asleep. I understand you're tired. I'm tired too. I don't want to be up at 4:45 a.m. to be in at 6:00 a.m. at work. But that's the job: the energy, the attitude and the effort we bring helps dictate theirs."

I continued. "As a coach, as an influencer of young people, or as anyone for that matter, you have a tremendous impact in how your attitude and body language impacts the attitude and effort of those around you. We can talk more another time about how you can modulate your impact and you modulate your intensity to drive the group and build culture if you don't understand what I mean. But let's be clear—don't ever let it happen again."

She seemed to be receptive to it but sort of laughed off the conversation in a not-so-serious manner even with my pointed ending. And we left it at that.

Later that night, however, as I was running through my day, I realized I was at fault for not having done a better job explaining to her (as the new person) what the expectations and rules are beforehand. And while it's a given for me to bring a level of intensity and expectation in how I present myself and operate, I can't assume that other people have the same level of intensity and expectations I do.

I needed to create a greater level of tangibility for her to operate in that manner. I could not assume it was a given.

Coaches Trying to Coach

In another direction, and one of the issues that's always tough to deal with, is the sport coaches who want to coach training sessions (particularly in the weight room).

I can think of a very specific example of a sport coach who—again lacking any type of CEO level skill set—created a very negative and, at times, caustic situation with the S&C coaches they dealt with.

Specifically, in the weight room, she would often try and coach the technical aspects of the training as well as the effort part, with little to no understanding of why things were being done (the progressions being used to get from *A* to *B* and that not everything has to be "all-out-all-the-time").

The team's athletes were awesome. They were very purposeful, and liked the training setting.

But this coach often tried to trump the S&C coach who was currently working with the team. She often interjected her thoughts and opinions in the middle of training, stopped training, and even had full-on verbal conflicts with some of the S&C coaches she worked with over the years.

While she did have some good thoughts and opinions and she wasn't always wrong, she was almost always off base in the application of her thoughts. She didn't understand the building blocks and processes that were needed to get to where she wanted to go. She understood the end product on the surface level and even at the secondary level from a physical development standpoint because she had taken the time to learn some things.

But that was the problem—she learned "some" things—enough to know a few things but also enough to be dangerous. She didn't understand the tactical process to achieve the strategic goal; she confused strategy for tactics. She was inflexible in thinking outside of her own ideas, and she viewed anyone else having a better idea or being better at a role than her as a threat to her. She was not willing to delegate and de-centralize because she thought total control would allow her success and no one but her could "make it happen." And she had to assert dominance over others—to tuck them under her wing to be in control.

She didn't see how trying to be the stronger voice than the person who was coaching (the S&C coach) broke down their credibility and how it took away from what this highly specialized coach was trying to do with her team from the standpoint of physical development. The S&C coach's work would have allowed her, as the sport coach, to maximize the improved physical outputs of her athletes for the demands and training to play the sport.

SIDE NOTE—Given the times, I want to be clear: sucking as a sport coach or athletics-related professional has nothing to do with gender, race, religion or any other characteristic individuals can be labeled by, as, or with. There are frauds out there regardless of labels.

Coach-Centric to Athlete-Centric Dilemma

One of the biggest changes at every level of all athletics in the last decade has been the subtle shift from coach-centric programs to athlete-centric programs.

This change has happened not only in sport but all our sociocultural dealings with the current generation of youth.

In sports specifically, it's due to numerous factors such as the notion of early specialization, parents wanting more influence, the politics involved, "pay-for-play" teams, as well as the significant cost associated with specialized training, development, and the perceived need for specialized training-related equipment.

We've progressed to a point where many coaches must answer to and manage so many outside influences that many of them are actually handicapped in running their programs the way they want or should.

It's also why we see so many older coaches, who've been in the business for a long time, straying from what made them successful—or not adapting at all and having to retire early or "leave to pursue other opportunities" due to issues with their athletes.

Don't Work with Coaches Who Will Get Sued

Often, S&C coaches are removed from working with a team due to the sport coach's personal biases and not for a valid reason.

Very rarely have I seen S&C coaches take action to step out of working with a team because of a philosophical disagreement with the way in which the head coach operates or a philosophical divide. Most S&C coaches just "find a way" to grin and bear it.

That's going to be one of the biggest changes we will see in collegiate athletics in the next couple of years and it goes back to the head coach-CEO conundrum and some of the new performance models springing up.

S&C coaches are so specialized and knowledgeable now that they will no longer want to work with certain sport coaches because their philosophical disagreements disrupt and minimize their abilities and create operationally inefficient and complacent environments.

If a sport coach you work with is using negligent and ineffective training methods, promoting pseudo-science performance approaches, and risking the health and wellness of the athletes—or just an overall poor leader who is any combination of verbally abusive or creating a hostile environment—document, document, document.

Put it in writing to your superiors, make sure the right people understand the problems, and keep a paper trail. When an athlete or staff member takes legal action, you won't be the scapegoat the weak leaders that allowed the situation to happen in the first place will look for.

Any time I worked with someone who was that bad on the training side or in the workplace, and the leadership of my superiors was weak because they weren't addressing the problem, I always came at things from the view of being deposed by a lawyer and having a very strong paper trail to show the fact-based timeline of what was happening and what was allowed to happen (it's scary to have to think like that but many of you reading this know exactly what I mean).

In Relation to Sports Medicine (Is it the WR vs. SM or is it the WR with SM?)

SIDE NOTE—I just want to preface this part of the book with, "Oh, a former S&C coach talking about athletic trainers. Someone get the popcorn. This section is going to be really, really, really good."

I'm going to put this as bluntly as I can: the undereducated S&C coach and the undereducated athletic trainer are cancerous to athletic development for the individual athlete, the team, and the department.

Feel free to exchange or add any of the following words to the word "undereducated" in the above sentence: egotistical, overconfident, unwilling to learn, master of all methodologies, or whatever else you would use to describe the cause of bad relations between those these two people working with the same team.

Typically, there is a large divide between the people "who know what it takes physically to do things" and the people "who know the how behind things physically happening."

The stereotypes are the athlete, who was the strongest, but not the best in competition becoming the S&C Coach and the unathletic, athlete wannabe becomes the athletic trainer.

That statement was true for a long time. Fortunately, it's becoming less true every year. Although there are *a lot*—and I mean *a lot*—of people on both sides that need to step their game up.

In the landscape now—and ever-increasingly as the fakes and jokers of the profession (on both sides) get fired or retire—an S&C coach must know "what it takes to physically do it" but also must know the "how and why of it." And the athletic trainer must know the "how and why of it" and also must have a reference as to "what it takes physically to do it."

Having a rock-solid relationship with athletic training is the only way to have a successful S&C program. The only way to have a successful athletic training program is to be aligned with your S&C program.

The greatest ally to an S&C coach is their athletic trainer and vice-versa. You can either be a "two-headed fire breathing dragon," dominating the space you work in, maximizing forward progress, and cutting off coach and athlete bullshit before it stinks; or you can spend your time trying to climb over each other, preaching what each of you think is the "best way," and causing division and fragmentation among the coaches and athletes.

I've seen it both ways and worked in it both ways. Not surprising, the most success I ever found was when we were a "two-headed dragon."

Fix the Issue or Replace the People

I had an SWA at an Atlantic Coast Conference (ACC) school ask me how to best get the S&C staff and SM staff to work together. My response: "Put them in a room and tell them they have five weeks to come up with a plan: to solve the problems, to communicate better, and to improve the athletes' experience and overall health and wellness.

And they need a factual, data-driven structure to confirm this objectively like objectives and key results (OKR) or a KPI model. If they can't, tell them they will be fired and you will find people who can find a way."

Want to know fundamentally why there's often a disconnect? It has to do with the way the regulations related to scope of practice are. Due to recognized licensing, the athletic trainer is always superior to the S&C coach.

Sorry S&C coaches, legally, no one gives a shit about the alphabet soup you have after your name with certifications from non-nationally licensed entities. No, the course you took in whatever mumbo jumbo that a person used, who turned "their system" into a monetized certification, gives you little to no legal standing.

You know what does? Being a licensed athletic trainer: doctor of chiropractic (DC), doctor or physical therapy/physiotherapy (DPT), doctor of osteopathic (DO), or medical doctor (MD).

Why? Because they are a nationally recognized, legally licensed clinical certification. In our legal system, and the NCAA itself, the licensed athletic trainer can *always* dictate when, what, and how an athlete can participate in physical activity. They have the unchallengeable right compared to S&C coaches and sport coaches.

I'll leave discussing why the medical model is going to fail and how there are three different paradigms that will be flushed out— mainly focused around two key things: sports that generate revenue, those that don't, and the shift in allowing athletes to generate money ("pay for play" and income off their name, image, and likeness, etc.). But that is a conversation for another place and, yet again, numerous margaritas.

I personally witnessed a GA athletic trainer with six months of experience and literally *no idea* what training for performance was, trump an S&C coach with over twenty years of experience who is considered one of the foremost experts in S&C in the US. The GA thought it best to "let them take it easy, because they were sore." All the S&C coach could do was acquiesce to the request; they had no choice because they had no power to do otherwise.

It was amazing to watch and it taught me very quickly who ultimately had control in the dynamic: the licensed professional with the larger scope of practice.

Because of how this hierarchy works—to prevent these possible moments of friction and long-term disagreements as well as build professional respect and rapport—both people must always be on the same page. Very good S&C coaches have an entire set of knowledge that very good athletic trainers and MDs simply don't have and vice-versa.

The athletic trainer & S&C coach must review injury reports together, plan training adjustments, and have a consistent message to sport coaches and athletes.

They need to collaborate, share philosophies, teach and learn from each other, train and prehab with each other, and combine the best of each part of their continuum to maximize the situation, the context, and the people they share in the moment.

Anything less is simply just going to cause problems.

I've dealt with tremendous athletic trainers who I was able to build great relationships with, and I've dealt with extremely incompetent, lazy athletic trainers who shouldn't have had jobs never mind an athlete's welfare in their hands.

I have also unequivocally seen the reverse; inept S&C coaches who should never have been allowed to train anyone ever again and the high-quality, top-notch athletic trainers who must compensate for their counterpart's stupidity and often negligent training methods.

For every good there's bad; for every up there's down. You don't have to always get along and conflict can be good if it has purpose and facilitates positive, forward action.

You don't have to become drinking buddies and be in each other's weddings,(though it has happened).

I had profound respect for one of the previous athletic trainers I worked with as a person and as a father outside of our work environment. He was an honest, straightforward, good human being and I cannot say a disparaging thing about him as a person. As a professional, he had slid into a deep hole of operational complacency due to a combination of his time in service and lack of resources.

In our time together, he was always willing to communicate and discuss his position. Although we disagreed and didn't always see eye to eye, we got on well enough and were always able to serve the athletes the best we could—the ultimate purpose of our jobs.

So, while we were never able to truly optimize collaboration of our departments, we were at least able to have some forward momentum compared to previous staff dynamics.

If you're a certified athletic trainer (or a PT, MD or whatever) reading this, understand where you are on the continuum and know what you don't know.

Train yourself in whatever way you want but do it with passion, intensity, and a level of discomfort. If you don't understand the difference between soreness, pain and injury, you'll never actually help an athlete.

If you don't understand the mental side of coming back from an injury —pushing beyond what you were capable of before, to be able to achieve even greater physical output—you'll never actually help an athlete.

SIDE NOTE —*Bet that wasn't what you expected. Now get a napkin and clean off your hands from the popcorn. Don't sully the pages with your greasy fingers.*

In Relation to Athletes (Creating Buy-In and Building Up Another Person)

Want to hear some corny shit that you've probably heard a million times but you're going to read, think on, and create action in your daily interactions this time around?

If you can show the athlete you care, show that athlete you're serious about them becoming serious. If you're consistent in your approach and have framework to work off, that athlete will buy-in.

Are You Coaching or Encouraging?

There's coaching and then there's encouragement.

What feedback are you giving and why?

Are you simply a megaphone in human form; a walking hype machine only there to "bring the juice," encourage effort, keep count of reps, and have the music loud? Or do you have a purposeful way you use motivational tactics to direct effort, provide feedback to elicit change in movement, and understand the art of leveraging chastisement and praise to achieve a certain response?

Walk in Their Shoes to Understand Their "Why"

For your athletes to get you, you must get them. It's a two-way street.

Educate yourself about what's going on today on a personal micro level and in their overall life on the macro level. And be able to communicate about it.

That includes understanding social media, music, pop-culture, and social injustice. It's exploring whatever depth-of-level athlete you have. You must be able to understand the challenges they face today and across the spectrum of their life because those challenges, while in construct will be different in each case, are conceptually the same problems everyone else is challenged by in life when they grow up.

It's not hard to learn names, majors, and the basics of their "what." What are they here for? What drives them? What scares them? Who do they want to be?

It's another level to take the time to learn about what they have going on and tying it into the world they live to gain critical insight as to how and why they do things.

While you certainly need to understand the macro, you must always temper and maintain a professional rapport with the micro.

The Balance of Being Available vs. Being a Therapist

Due to current technology and shifts in social norms—never mind athletes who sacrifice so much "normal" life experiences to train and compete—and living sometimes solely in the "athlete" bubble, many do not have strong interpersonal skills.

As an S&C Coach (or any coach, teacher, or mentor) for that matter, there is a dichotomy of being available—not just for extra training— but to be a person with an open door to bounce ideas off of and have discussions in a nonjudgmental way, while not blurring professional boundaries that should exist and crossing into murky waters for both parties.

Clearly, in the current climate, there's a going to be concern for what I'm talking about from a sexual harassment and abuse standpoint. That is an obvious concern and there clearly needs to be—if there are not already—policies, training and education in place for both sides to make sure the power dynamic of coach & athlete isn't corrupted in that manner. What I really want to talk about here are the blurred boundaries when a coach becomes an athlete's therapist—going too "in-depth"— and the athlete being allowed to create dependencies on the support of the coach.

Now, there are more instances than I can count in my career that I had athletes come to my office and tell me about an extremely deep, personal issue, challenge or situation, and looked to me for guidance and support.

From medical situations, mental health issues, disordered eating, domestic abuse, death and divorce in the family—you name it—I had, at one point or another, an athlete come to me to talk about it.

I would imagine most S&C coaches and athletic trainers are nodding in agreement right now, thinking of how this also happens to them on a daily basis.

These athletes trusted me to share that kind of information with me and wanted my opinion and guidance.

Having this happen to me, especially early in my professional career, has strongly affected how I approach dealing with people. You never know who is going to look to you in their darkest moment (or what they perceive to be their darkest moment at the time) and the level of impact you can have by being available to them in some capacity. It literally can save someone's life or forever change their future path.

SIDE NOTE—Please have the contact info of the resources in your specific place available and ready to give to athletes who need them. I challenge everyone reading this to not only have that info but to go in person go find the people on the other end. Meet in person the mental health counselors, etc., learn from them, and get to know them. You never know when your athletes or you yourself might need them.

For a starting point regarding national hotline numbers and other resources please go here: https://psychcentral.com/lib/common-hotline-phone-numbers

The key here is, more times than not, I had to refer the athlete to other professionals I worked with both due to the law (mandated reporting) or being personally unable or qualified to help in the manner that was needed.

Depending on what I was told, my response was generally something to this effect: "I know this must be very difficult and I appreciate you being willing to discuss this with me. Now, I do have to share this with person *X* because (insert reason). Let's go see if we can find person *X* and we can discuss what you just told me together. I'm here to help you however I can and that means showing you who can help you more than me."

It's not that I didn't want to help—I did. But I knew what I could and should help with and what I wasn't equipped for.

On the flip side, there were also times when I kept certain things in confidence, whether it be about teammates, coaches or circumstances, and helped provide counsel and mentorship on the decision-making processes or life situations the athlete was struggling with during a critical moment in their lives. One of the easiest examples to reference in this vein is a new athlete having doubts about participating and looking to quit or transfer.

One of my favorite stories is of a basketball athlete who was struggling mightily his freshman year trying to find his role on the team. He had gone from a superstar in high school—the head coach's favorite player, who rarely if ever was subbed out— to being a backup in college. And it was beating him down mentally to the point where it impacted his ability to execute at practice. He constantly found himself in the doghouse with the coach and that limited his minutes even more, creating a massive, negative feedback loop the player got stuck in.

We were in the early part of the season at a tournament in a destination locale. And ninety minutes before tip-off, as I helped guys get ready, stretching and keeping things loose, he came over to me and dropped the idea of transferring saying things just weren't clicking on all fronts.

I looked at him and said, "You're just Aaron Rogers backing up Brett Farve right now. Whether you like it or not, that's just how it is. Learn as much as you can every day and be the best teammate you can. Because when it's your time you'll be ready to take over."

I went on and said, "Aaron Rogers had every reason to want to get out of Green Bay his first couple years. Hell, the media even talked about how Farve didn't take any time trying to help him or mentor him. He was in a tough spot. But what did he do? He did his job, he did it well, and look where he is now: Super Bowl winner, huge contract, superstar. Long way from a guy who didn't play a down because he was backing up a legend at the time."

He looked at me and I could see the comments made sense to him. It helped shift this thinking in that moment, turning his perceived negative into a more plausible positive and something he could build around.

This athlete went on to not only dominate college basketball, scoring more than two thousand points in his remaining three years, but has a level of maturity and ownership of himself that will surely see him through a long professional basketball career. I have no doubt he "makes it" in whatever he chooses to do.

However, while it can be a very humbling and self-rewarding feeling to be the person who can "help" someone with their "problems," I have seen many S&C coaches and athletic trainers overstep boundaries and take on trying to help an athlete when they were not properly equipped, legally able too—or worse—sharing what should have been confidential information with countless other staff or even other athletes.

You ever want to see a professional kill their career quicker than it could start? Discuss the confidential, personal challenges of an athlete with other people in the department who have no reason to know such details.

Simply put, you must know what you are capable, qualified and able to help with and help bridge the gap to connect the athlete with the correct professional they need but have not yet talked to on their own.

This is yet another reason to get out of your own world training athletes and get to know other staff. If you don't know who can help with what, how can you help an athlete find the right person in a moment of crisis?

Define Expectations: People Naturally Seek Parameters for Their Behavior

As mentioned before, you must clearly define rules and expectations.

An athlete may not remember what a specific exercise is or how to do a certain drill, but they won't ever forget when someone else gets away with something that they didn't. It's just human nature.

If you are familiar with Jocko Willink and Leif Babin's book *Extreme Ownership*, they talk about the idea of "commander's intent." By giving clear direction as to what you want, you can let others have parameters to guide their own actions.

Whatever word you choose to use (parameters, guidelines, rules, policy), semantics aside, it all means the same thing: you must have structure with purpose, relative to the context of the situation, that drives positive outcomes. Be careful here. Don't have rules just to have rules—it can slow things down and create unnecessary friction points.

While there are many layers to all the different "rules" you can have, there are two main types that we'll discuss for the training setting.

The first and most obvious set of rules are those for general safety. These can include not having jewelry on due to the risk of injury it can pose. While these "rules" exist to keep a safe environment, they don't really have much direct effect on the physical outcomes of the training efforts. They may seem trivial, like not using glass water bottles, but they can also serve a bigger purpose.

When it came to jewelry, I would get athletes that would question why they were able to wear necklaces, rings, and earrings at practice or in their sport but not when they trained with me. They thought it was burdensome to take off and put back on their "bling."

I would explain that it simply came down to safety. Because if we could help mitigate risk—even low-probability risk—in training, then that allowed the opportunity for them to compete, which was the goal of why we trained.

I would further reiterate safety with stories: seeing an athlete degloving their finger because their ring got caught on a cable column pulley or an athlete doing burpees who had their necklace impale them just under their collarbone that led to an MRSA infection and hampered their entire season that year.

Those kinds of stories always helped in the short-term, pushing off the questions for a few weeks. And there was always someone who inevitably didn't follow the rules, which added another story to the docket.

The second set of rules, which bleed out of the first set of rules, help curate culture. They set the standard; they were the line in the sand.

They helped show me who had character, and it helped clarify who was accountable to the little things that could easily get overlooked.

They allowed me to create a climate of expectation and attention to detail—and repercussions if they were not followed. They melded with the more significant parts of training, all combining to create the culture of the team.

When these second set of rules was understood, I generally never had to explain them again, beyond clueing in the freshman at the start of a new year and pushing the senior members of the team (not just the seniors) to instill the rules into the freshman before I had too.

Being Here is a Privilege Not a Right

Due to culture being a flux state, it's constantly being adjusted and adapted based on the behaviors and beliefs of those involved.

Rules that focus on this area include the foundational concept that training is a privilege and not a right. There can never be a sense of entitlement related to training: athletes are not entitled to use the training environment and they're not entitled to win just because they "prepared."

To maintain this fundamental concept and help mitigate an attitude of entitlement (which can quickly bleed out into areas beyond training or from other areas into training), the rule I adopted was a three-strike policy. I started with the standard use of extra work—generally, conditioning—and also added in flares of making athletes clean (one time in weight vests, while having to do burpee's every time the whistle blew). And while those things helped to some degree and failed in other ways, it can to be clear that inspiring people actually took more of my time than anything else. It began to be counterproductive and take away from me helping the people who actually wanted to be there.

If an athlete couldn't maintain the standard (show up on time, follow the policies, etc.), the athlete would lose the privilege of training that day for the first strike.

While this acutely impacted the ability of an athlete to get better, it laid the groundwork for that athlete, as well as others, to see that the rules were not simply lip service without value. One of the biggest cultural mistakes you can make, is the "do as I say not as I do" style of leadership.

For strike two, the athlete lost the privilege of training for a week or seven-day period.

For the third strike, that athlete lost the privilege of using the facility, working with staff, and being in the training environment for the rest of the semester.

It's also worth noting that an athlete who lost the privilege of training for a semester was welcome back the next semester with a clean slate.

First, this helps tip the balance in favor of the athletes who are doing the right thing and not taking your time away from them to deal with the "slapdicks."

It also helps to remove cancerous elements from the training environment and prevent them from spreading and infecting others. Thus, it allows you to control and manage the culture and consistency of what you're trying to establish.

While removing someone from training for the semester is an extreme example, and I don't mean to offend anyone by the using cancer as an analogy, it's an easy illustration for athletes to understand. By cutting out the damaged area before it has a chance to spread, you have exponentially increased the likelihood of survival compared to mitigating the damage once it has taken over the entire system.

Set the Expectations on Day One

I worked with a team where the sport coach did not care if his athletes used the S&C department services or not. He actually told me in a meeting that he had his kids show up twice a week for a few weeks in the off-season to simply check a box. And that when he met with the AD, he wouldn't get in trouble for not using the resources provided. He simply just didn't believe in S&C being a worthwhile part of his program.

The athletes themselves were a mixed bag: some wanted to train, some were impartial, and most didn't think it was important taking their cue from the coach. Funny how that worked.

So on day one, after I reviewed the rules and expectations of training, I said, "Look everyone, if you don't think you can hold yourself to these standards, come here to improve, and have the right attitude— don't come. I cannot waste my time babysitting those of you who come to dick around and take away time from those who actually want to get better. Let me be clear: this isn't a come-as-you-want-when-you-want kind of deal. This is— you commit today to sticking the program and following the rules. You are either all the way in, or all the way out."

After I paused to let it sink in for effect, I closed by saying, "There's no punishment for not coming. I'm not going to try to convince you if I see you. You simply choose not to use the resource, and you have no one to complain to if you do not accomplish the goals you have for yourself. This is what taking ownership is all about. 'If you fail, it will be your fault. If you succeed, it will be your fault.'"

While we had a handful of athletes that chose not to participate in that first off-season, the number dwindled each year to eventually all taking part by my third offseason with the team. And when I left, they had gotten to a point where they were physically one of the strongest pound for pound teams in the department and, I would be willing to bet, in the conference for their sport.

What helped shift numbers over time? Was it because those that trained had a higher chance of being starters in future seasons? Or was it that those who trained were less likely to miss games due to soft tissue injuries or have season ending injuries? Factual numbers like that are tough to deny after all.

Maybe it was simply an improved team culture related to training; a head coach that gave the S&C Coach a longer leash because of developed working relationships and positive results to the athletes who committed to being consistent to training. Who's to say? Correlation is not causality after all.

Define What's "Cool"

People naturally gravitate towards the popular trends of the group. Because of this, seek to create exclusivity.

Competitive sports are exclusive and not inclusive. So long as we keep score, there are winners and losers. And not everyone is equal at the end. If your aim is a performance-based model, that's okay. If you model is health and wellness, then this doesn't matter because you're not looking for optimal performance—you're chasing optimal longevity.

Use recognition boards and other public displays of success and reward winners with some type of tangible artifact to create and reinforce that exclusive environment.

Those artifacts could be trophies, T-shirts, socks, or a dinner. It doesn't matter what it is, whatever you choose, the key is to acknowledge accomplishment and success by differentiating athletes in a way that is both consistent and fair.

The group dynamic should be one that socially views accomplishment and the "reward" as "cool" and a "status symbol" within the team.

If you can properly build exclusivity into your culture it will naturally align the athletes to want to achieve the standards that are set because they're viewed by the group as worthy of putting effort into.

The critical aspect is you must be careful to set expectations and standards that are both realistic and attainable. If benchmarks are skewed in any direction—blatantly unfair or showing a high degree of favoritism to a certain subclass—you will create dissension and devalue the dynamic.

Clear guidelines, with purposeful articulation as to what, when, where, how, and why things can be achieved, must be created and tested to make sure they hold in real life. Just because it's a good idea on paper or in the office doesn't mean it's a good idea applied to a group of athletes or multiple teams. Many good ideas to help team culture have actually hurt it significantly when implemented.

Also, you must be fully transparent and clear in sharing where individuals stand by having objective, quantifiable metrics accessible for all, in a central location like a bulletin board or group chat. This makes it very difficult to argue whether recognition has been earned and deserved based on the parameters initially laid out.

Stay away from subjective recognition because it will create dissension;

the perceptions of individuals and the discrepancies among personalities will cause friction and have some feel slighted. Subjectivity will erode the value of whatever recognition you attempt to bestow.

Mistaking Athlete-Driven for Athlete-Centric

I previously worked at a place where we created a chart for the athletes to understand the interrelated departments and people who helped them succeed. There was their head coach and assistants, the athletic trainer, physical therapist, student-managers, video coordinators, media coordinators, ticket coordinators, S&C coach, and whoever else they had directly working with them.

The web of people grew to be almost two dozen people, all with unique specialized subspecialties. Academic counselors, special learning service coordinators, and tutors also had a place in this intricate web of success that literally covered an entire piece of paper and, in a way, looked like spokes on a wheel with the individual athlete being at the center.

We did this not to only show the resources athletes had available to them but to show what these services would cost in the real world, at an hourly rate, if they had to pay them. Just the S&C and athletic training services alone ran close to $1,000 per week if paid for privately—let alone all the other specialized support services and other free benefits they had.

The point was to hammer home the impetus on the athlete to use those services to the best of their ability.

It was not the staff's responsibility to hand-feed services and babysit, because it would have created entitlement and a lack of ownership among the athletes.

The success of the athlete had to be driven by the athlete.

In a situation with all of those resources, if they were successful it would be their fault; if they failed, it would be their fault.

Create an Environment Where It's Okay to Ask Questions

I will be the first person to tell you there are such things as stupid questions. They exist. No matter what smoke got blown up your ass in your life by someone who wanted to shield you, stupid questions are real.

They're real when you lack the ownership and maturity to let critical information slip past you and you find yourself uncertain or in a position where you make others think you are certain.

However, if someone does not understand the rules or is uncertain how to properly go about a task because you as a leader failed to communicate clearly and effectively, you are the stupid one and not the person asking the question.

It's your responsibility as a leader to let people know that it's okay to ask questions but to hold them accountable to listening as well.

You don't want athletes following you like robots or assume they understand what they're supposed to do when, in fact, you didn't direct them well enough in the beginning or, worse yet, they do something wrong simply because they didn't think or feel comfortable asking for clarity.

As a leader, you shouldn't yell at or reprimand someone for something you have not explained or was not clear about. That is your fault.

You must consciously give the athlete the option to ask questions if they are uncertain about things and give them the opportunity to learn. This can be accomplished in numerous ways: from making athletes explain things to you, quizzing them, etc. But be cautious here so the process of training does not grind training to a halt.

I have seen many coaches so willing to "explain" that they fall victim to athletes asking dozens of questions simply to slow the session down. These athletes take advantage of the coach's desire to make sure everyone is on the same page.

If you sense someone is truly not grasping what you are trying to accomplish, don't stop the training session. Instead, let them know that you will explain it to them more thoroughly after the session and for in that moment they must do the best they can. Given their uncertainty, you should monitor and adjust this person as needed to keep them safe or minimize risk. That way you can allow the session to continue and the goals of the day to be accomplished.

Never Play Favorites

As an S&C coach never play favorites with your athletes. Demand the same thing from everyone: male or female, freshman or senior. Have a consistent line in the sand that everyone knows is there.

One of the ways that I tried to do this was showing acknowledgment and acceptance when athletes made mistakes.

The focus was never on the mistake itself: false starting, doing a drill wrong—whatever it was—it didn't matter. The focus was on the athlete being accountable and taking ownership of the mistake, while simultaneously moving forward and learning from the mistake. And I purposefully held myself to that standard as well, to the amusement of the athletes and often with a lack of understanding from other staff and sport coaches.

If I improperly explained something, gave the wrong directions, or otherwise made a mistake, I would stop, take ownership of my mistake, admit I did something wrong, and knock out a few burpees. The physical task was not only relevant to the context of the situation but something the athletes and I could create a shared experience around.

It was amazing how that simple act of "walking the walk" dramatically changed how the athletes responded to me, both in the moments they made a mistake and while we worked together over time.

Could I have played off any missteps and pretended I didn't make a mistake? Sure. And I did do that at times—everyone does and there is a strategy for it—but more often than not, I owned a mistake instead of faking it.

It helped set the stage so that the athletes always knew where they stood. They knew if they did a good job, I would point it out and be the first one to give them a pat on the back. If they did a bad job, I'd be the first to reinforce that they could do better—that they needed to own their success personally not accept less than their potential.

While I certainly raised my voice, swore, and was at times a savage, I never yelled at an athlete to mistreat them or personally demean them for making a mistake or doing something wrong.

I yelled at them and pushed them because they weren't achieving their potential, weren't being as serious as they should be for the situation, or refused to take personal ownership of their own development. I tried to never let them be complacent in their growth.

There were only two exceptions to this in my career as a coach: when an athlete did something so dangerous that it could have either caused serious bodily harm or death to themselves or someone else. The section below called "Serious Mistakes" will shed further light on this.

How to Push an Athlete with Intensity

With the current climate of society, not just athletics, you must be careful when creating emotionally intense situations and giving people critical feedback.

The underlying message should always be positive; instill in them that they can accomplish what they did wrong or failed at—and most importantly—reinforce your belief in them.

There is a very big difference between yelling at someone who made a mistake and saying, "What the hell! You're smarter than that. Focus. With your skills you shouldn't be making those kinds of mistakes." Compared to saying: "You, dumbass! You keep making these mistakes and you will suck forever."

One of my favorite lines to drop on someone when I had to hold them accountable was, "You are better than that! When you start to believe you are as capable as I see you, you will make some serious progress. What you just did shows me you don't believe you are as good as I know you are."

Letting someone know you believe in them and that you perceive them as capable and competent is a huge confidence builder. I focused on speaking to my athletes and my staff from the perspective of who they had the potential to be—not who they were currently. After all, that was the entire point of training right; to become a better version of what you already were.

Are You Wasting $20,000 Every Day?

One particular way I pushed high-potential athletes, who could go on to play professionally in their sport, was asking them if they were saving or wasting $20,000 every day? At first, they would look at me confused and wonder what the hell I was talking about.

I would explain to them that since they had potential to play their sport professionally, they should consider themselves as having a chance to earn $10,000,000 in their career post college. But in order to get to the point where they had the ability to earn the money, they had to do the work. In their 3–4 years of college athletics they would roughly have 500 training sessions each worth $20,000.

If they seized the day, did what they were supposed to as they were supposed to, and did the right things outside of training, they would be keeping their potential earning power at the ten-million-dollar mark. If they didn't, they would be dropping their future financial potential by $20,000 a day.

There was nothing worse as a coach than to watch an athlete who had that kind of potential have more days where they let $20,000 slip out of their fingers than keep in their bank.

The F-Word in Training

In training, the f-word is for some reason the most misunderstood and mistreated word of all time.

Fun.

You must be willing to have fun.

Now there are two types of fun in training: there is the fun that sets the stage for the culture and environment you are trying to build and there is the fun needed to decompress from that culture and environment.

Both of these types of fun are told over food and drink, in hotel rooms during trips, over the summer and in numerous other situations among the athletes. All of these things help define what is okay and normal within the group dynamic and help newcomers understand the way things work and their place in the tribe (speaking of which, read *Tribe* by Sebastian Junger—great book).

The first kind of fun are things such as team competitions, making bets, or other little nuances that you bring to the training environment. To help drive all the key buzzwords of getting the group dynamics honed in.

These days still have a technical or tactical focus, helping drive the development of the larger goal, teams just add a slightly different "fun" element that helps make them seem different than regular training and helps reinforce the overall culture.

The second kind of fun is what helps decompress stress, fosters strong peer relationships and allows people the opportunity to step away from the "grind" of working towards team goals. I would often refer to these kinds of days as "kickball days" because we would play kickball or other similar activities to shake things up.

Knowing when to use a "kickball day" is an art form within itself. If you can't get the temperature of the athletes (feel the push-pull momentum and pressure training puts on people) you can easily misapply this kind of "fun" and turn it into a caustic negative in the team culture or it just feels gimmicky. Yes, I'm looking at you sport coaches who schedule mandatory "team-building" activities on off days and put strict boundaries on them, guaranteeing no-one will enjoy them.

Understanding when to step away from the seriousness of development or at certain critical junctures (before major competition, during hard training cycles, or after an unexpected defeat) and insert a "kickball day," helps far beyond what's going to be missed in any tactical, technical, or strategic training session.

If you find it hard to grasp this important concept as it relates to team dynamics, it's much like understanding the energy of a game. It's like tapping into the tangible energy of the moment—the flow of momentum —to determine when to call a timeout in order to directly manipulate and influence the game.

Think of the great sport coaches who knew exactly when to call a timeout, knew what players to switch out at the right time, and knew what to say or what not to say to each athlete, in certain moments, to achieve what seemed impossible. It's the same idea but applied to training.

If this still makes little or no sense, you need to enhance your emotional intelligence, better understand how to leverage human capital and, most importantly, learn from a coach who everyone considers peerless with how they connect their people.

Do You Need a Navy SEAL?

It still amazes me that, even to this day, athletic programs use extreme physical discipline and physically rigorous activity from the military and other similarly styled groups to try and instill acute culture change. Brandon Marcello wrote a great article on this a few years ago and I would suggest finding it online and reading it. The only people that benefit are those in the company running it because they are charging thousands and thousands of dollars to come in for a few days.

I've sat with multiple coaches and said, "Pay me instead and we can do the "Joe-gram." I'll get you the same results because we do that every day. And not only will we do what we do every day, but we will reinforce it both inside and outside the training environment."

That last part is the key element in the whole process and is something these acute, intense, culture-building attempters (AICBA) aren't able to do since they are only present momentarily and follow up sporadically: bringing the experience full-circle.

I worked at one university with a sports psychologist to address this exact issue: a lack of follow up and continuity to the shared ideas and experiences from the AICBA. Shortly after the AICBA left, the lessons they taught and the skills they tried to impart were often not kept up by the head sport coaches or the athletes because there was no follow-up effort. They were one-time experiences: not debriefed experiences, not lessons learned woven into the new cultural fabric of the expectations, and not required actions. However, the consistency needed to reinforce the actions behind training culture principles is not a one-time thing—it's an everyday thing.

Serious Mistakes

Unfortunately, in my time as an S&C coach, a few serious mistakes did happen in training. While I was extremely lucky to not have anyone (athletes, coaches, interns) seriously injured, some of these situations could have been life-changing and even catastrophic events. These incidents were always a potent reminder of how wrong things can go in a blink of an eye.

While these situations sometimes tested protocols we had in place and the competency and response of other support staff (mainly sports medicine), in my opinion, these situations best showed which coaches and administrators truly understood the seriousness of the situation and those who did not.

I unfortunately also know of many situations where serious bodily harm was a result, often from a combination of negligence on the person leading the session or simply lack of focus from the athletes themselves; both of which can be traced back to poor leadership and associated lack of action at some point higher up in the chain.

There is always a critical point where someone (coach or athlete) could put a stop to what is happening: from doing a "log" PT session downhill in the rain and having a piece of telephone pole give an athlete a serious head injury; to using plastic Jazzercise step-up boxes for barbell step-ups with 295 lbs. on the bar and having them break and paralyze the athlete I personally pulled the plug on dozens of sessions and a few times challenged sport coaches on continuing a session if I thought the opportunity for negligence or serious harm to the athletes was a real possibility.

Negligence on the part of the person leading the session is absolutely preventable and honestly should never happen. It's too easy to control against. Don't get me wrong, I pushed my athletes—at times, farther than they thought they could go—but I always had a plan and purpose for doing so along with pre-planned adjustments if things ever truly became "too much."

The most egregious error I personally dealt with came in the form of athletes not paying attention. The one that sticks out in my mind the most is athletes removing weights from the rack unevenly and having the bar flip off. Two times in my career I had this happen and in one case someone was millimeters from getting hit and possibly killed. And when I say millimeters, I mean the space from the bar to their face being smaller than the hairs on their nose.

In one instance, a squat bar with 365 lbs. was unloaded unevenly due to the athlete on one side getting distracted talking to another teammate. The bar grazed the nose of a third athlete who was walking by as it flipped off the rack and came crashing to the floor. It not only missed the third athlete's face by millimeters, literally touching the tip of their nose, but missed their foot by inches as well—the toe of their shoe hitting the plates still attached to the bar as it settled on the floor.

The second instance, similar to the first, had the bar flying off the J-hooks of a Power Lift half rack directly lined-up for a teammates head when fortunately, the bar hit one of the adjustable, rotating pull-up handles at the top of the rack, moving it in such a way that the bar got wedged momentarily and lost its velocity.

The noise and the split-second of delay before the bar started to slide down towards the ground, gave the athlete (whose brain matter was about to be spilled onto the floor) enough time to jump back and evade the oncoming heap of iron that slid toward them and threatened to pin them to the ground.

In both situations, I did not directly see what happened as I was working with other athletes in the session. After the noise caught my attention and I saw the athletes standing there, eyes bugging out of their heads, I lost my marbles. And man, do I mean I lost my marbles. It was not pretty.

In both instances, my anger and frustration ignited to the same degree upon speaking to the sport coaches after the incidences about why I kicked their athletes out. The sport coaches didn't really care or see it as a big deal. One of them even got into an argument with me as to why I kicked their athlete out of the weight room—for giving me attitude and pretending it wasn't a big deal that he almost killed his teammate.

Perhaps, like most things in life, "it's only an issue if there was an issue." And because no one's life was radically altered forever, the coaches just didn't seem to care. Maybe it was both coaches' inability to understand how the little things mattered and added up and the reason why they always had such discipline issues on their respective teams. They didn't seem to understand why it was a big deal or why I had lost my shit over something that could have killed someone and was totally preventable. Thankfully, a jury was never needed to render a verdict.

Rules, Rules, Rules

Additional rules that help define culture can be related to the attire the athletes have to wear while they're training and what they're allowed or not allowed to do when they're in the environment.

Do they have to wear certain types of clothing or certain colors on certain days? (*Heartbreak Ridge* anyone?)

Are they able to sit down if they are not actively participating in a drill or exercise?

Do they have to huddle up, take a knee, and have eyes on the coach every time instruction is given or can they stop where they are and simply listen freely, able to adjust their position at their own discretion to hear or see better?

The key as a coach when figuring out what rules to use for building specific cultural frameworks—compared to maintaining a safe environment—is to ask yourself why you're doing what you're doing and how it impacts the situation and the things you are trying to build and develop.

For every rule I have given so far, you could have a situation or context where they don't make sense. If you're not critically evaluating how and why what you're putting effort into is accomplishing what you want it to, then you're doing one of the worst things you can: implementing rules for the sake of having rules.

This directly works against building culture and instead creates needless redundancy, wastes individuals' time as well as your own, and adds unnecessary stress and complexity for everyone.

In Relation to the Weight Room Itself (Setting Up and Taking Ownership of Your Classroom)

If you're coaching, teaching and mentoring athletes during your training, then consider your facility a classroom just like any academic setting. It's the physical representation of you.

Interesting to think of it that way, right?

From the macro details to the micro details, it all reflects on you, the director of the department. While we'll cover a lot of ground here, let's start by posing two of the most obvious questions in relation to a training facility.

Looking at it with a macro lens, is it secure? Who has access to it?

And how do those people have access to it?

Thousands of pounds of equipment, worth hundreds of thousands of dollars—that can maim, kill, and magically grow legs and disappear—all need to be kept in check.

From the micro viewpoint (literally microbiological), is the facility hygienic and uncontaminated? There are going to be all kinds of bodily fluids and harmful organisms floating around in there; you don't want your facility to be the place that infects anyone who enters.

Those two issues, while distantly impacting your decisions on how to train athletes, have a massive impact on the training of athletes.

The Body Language of the Facility

Now go up to a 10,000-foot view.

You naturally expect every classroom you walk into to have a certain vibe and style. A kindergarten classroom will not only look different than a college lecture hall but the layout and resources in the classrooms will be different too.

What is the body language of the classroom, or how does it present itself when you walk in? What preconceived notions end up in your head when you walk in? Does it perhaps look the part of having every shiny bell and whistle you'd expect but viewed from a knowledgeable eye have obvious limitations of use? Did you only buy full-size bumper plates and can't put more than 405 lbs. on a bar?

Would you judge the kindergarten teacher if the room was a mess or would you expect it to be messy and be surprised if it was spotless? What subconscious or verbalized notions do you think your coaches, athletes, and administrators have about the facility, and how does that change their thinking of you?

What view would your future boss have if they walked into your facility at three in the morning when no one was there? What if a sport coach doesn't tell you about a new recruit who is coming and the first impression they get of the facility is that it's a dirty, unkempt disaster?

What if any of those people walked into your office or had to sit at your desk? Regardless of what goes on, what does the body language of the space say to them about you?

The body language of the facility is also represented by papers, posted materials, or anything you use to present information. Are they organized, visible, and coherent or do you need a PhD and magnifying glass to decipher what is there? Where do you store these materials—in a binder, a cabinet—or are they just laying around scattered on equipment? Are posted signs laminated to keep them from getting ripped or is everything worn and tattered?

You should constantly ask yourself if you're presenting your classroom the way you want to; it's the only way to make sure it's telling the narrative that you want. It gives others a frame of reference from which to judge you if they don't know you. Perception is reality after all.

This also serves a second purpose—the true purpose to some degrees; it helps indoctrinate the athletes to the expectations and the culture you seek to create. I know of one particular S&C coach in the college world who, with masterful purpose, has crafted an indoctrination process at every level. To the untrained eye it comes off as just another S&C facility, but there is purpose in every placement and detail: from the Captains of Crush grippers on his desk, down to the weight class of the athletes in weight lifting videos shown on the TVs in the facility.

When I first started at one of my jobs, I walked around the weight room and noticed that there was nutritional information posted on the walls near the entrances and exits.

One of the first things I noticed about it however, was not the content or the great positioning near the door (it was the first and last thing seen when walking into the facility). What I first noticed was it looked terrible: it was crookedly taped to the wall, it was ripping in some places, and its visual design was cluttered and sophomoric.

As I reviewed it further, I also noticed that there were many errors in both its grammar as well as in the information itself. I took them down and threw them away—there was nothing to discuss about it. They lacked the proper representation of what I wanted to convey and seemed as if they were just thrown on the wall to take up space and check the "hey, look we did nutrition stuff" box.

Anything that was on the walls that needed to stay, such as training percentages, max charts, etc., I removed, reprinted, and laminated with our logo on them to make sure there was visual uniformity and they conveyed the right information as well.

At first, my staff thought I was nuts since they didn't see why it was a big deal. Most of the changes I had made were very subtle in the bigger scheme of things. But once I explained the purpose of it and gave some context, everyone was more receptive to the change—even if they still held some skepticism.

Clean and Organized

I could wax poetic about organization of equipment, both in placement for flow and safety as well as the aforementioned visual aspect, but I will leave that low hanging fruit. In whatever way you can accomplish it—have an organized facility. Even if that means having a picture at each station with what the equipment should look like at the end of a session to help make putting things in the right place as idiot-proof as possible.

In terms of being cleaned, there are a few considerations you need to think about. Do you have daily, weekly, and monthly cleaning and equipment maintenance schedules? Do you need to have individuals go through Occupational Safety and Health Administration (OSHA) related certifications on campus in order to use some of the cleaning supplies? Do you have appropriate gloves, masks, and storage for said materials?

Some of you may be laughing at these questions, but when you get sued and/or fired for not having a documented process in place—to prevent contagious diseases, mitigate risk from equipment failure, or deal with an intern who runs to HR about getting sick from huffing cleaning chemicals or burning their hands because they should have had a mask and gloves on—it won't be so funny.

Week of ________

Monday	Initials / Time
Clean Vinyl Surfaces	
Sweep Floor	
Drop-off/Pick-up towels to/from cage	
Replace displaced equipment	

Tuesday	Initials / Time
Clean Vinyl Surfaces	
Wipe Down Cardio Room	
Sweep Floor	
Re-stock Supplements to Refrigerator	
Replace displaced equipment	

Wednesday	Initials / Time
Clean Benches	
Sweep Floor	
Clean Foam Rollers, Medballs, Bosu, SB, Dynadiscs	
Replace displaced equipment	

Thursday	Initials / Time
Clean Vinyl Surfaces	
Sweep Floor	
Re-stock Supplements in Refrigerator	
Replace displaced equipment	

Friday	Initials / Time
Clean Vinyl Surfaces	
Wipe Down Cardio Room	
Sweep Floor	
Drop-off/Pick-up towels to/from cage	
Replace displaced equipment	

MONTHLY CLEANING RESPONSIBILITIES

Month of ________

RACKS	Initials / Date
Dust/Wipe Down	
WD-40 Plate Holders	
Check/tighten all parts	
WD-40 Center Ring of all Plates (Bi-Monthly)	

BENCHES & MACHINES	
Check/tighten all parts	
Check upholstery for damage	
Check/tighten all parts	
Lube guide rods/bar ends	
Check upholstery for damage	

DUMBBELLS & BARBELLS	
Wipe down racks	
Grease bar ends w/ WD-40	
Clean knurling w/ steel brush	

MISC	
Jump Stretch Bands - Clean/Check for damages	
Ankle Bands – Clean	
Plyo Boxes - Check for damages	
Chalk Bins – Refill	
Get more cleaning solution if necessary	

YEARLY CLEANING RESPONSIBILITIES Month of ________

	Initials / Date
Full clean of entire facility, move everything, clean every nook and cranny. Fix, repair, replace	

Use the previous examples as the basic outline for the most obvious things to be done at the facility every week, month and year.

Scheduling

Another one of the more obvious requirements regarding S&C: there needs to be policy and procedure supported by administrators with standard operating procedures (SOPs) for scheduling the use of the training facilities (weight room, indoor facilities, turf, etc.).

Just as there needs to be rules for coaches and staff to maintain a positive training environment and uphold the highest training standard, there needs to be outlined manners in which a team can access facilities and the weight room.

The same goes for open hours or free time for coaches and staff. They inherently should understand—and if not, have it explained to them—that their access time can be taken away at any time because the number one priority is for the development and betterment of athletes and not the coaches and staff.

I ran into issues around this with coaches and staff in too many cases for my liking and know many other S&C coaches who ran into the same issues.

Coaches, staff, and even administrators felt that they had the right, not the privilege, of being able to use the facility and get in the way of the athletes training. Their egos got in the way.

I once saw an administrator, who was trying to work out on their own when they shouldn't have been, almost get hit with a missed clean attempt by an athlete and came very close to clipping them on the foot. The administrator had no idea how to operate in the flow of an S&C session and put themselves into a dangerous situation. They told me, "I've been here for ten years and plan on working out when I want."

This brought back a very scary memory for me; I once saw someone have a life-changing tibia and fibula injury when I was at a commercial gym. One person was Olympic lifting, while another person was standing too close—with their back turned, headphones on, not paying attention. The guy lifting dropped the clean, the bar bounced, and the bar end hit the guy not paying attention mid-shin in the back of the leg. With his foot only connected by skin and muscle since his tibia-fibula was broken and sticking out of the skin, that guy's life was changed in an instant.

Is it wrong to say I, for a brief moment, wished that administrator got the same treatment? It's sad to say, but that person was so bullheaded and stubborn about what they thought was their privilege, it would have taken that kind of situation to get them to see the reason I made such a big deal about it.

There must be obvious policy and procedure in place for facility access: who has access, when do they have access, why do they have access, and who are they letting in?

Additionally, issues like equipment finding legs and disappearing need to have a remedy upfront. At one school I worked at, we were in a significant budget-deficit crisis with purchases as low as $100 being denied. And I had to go to my supervisor and explain to him that over $500 worth of equipment had magically disappeared from the facility over the summer. Too many people had access and couldn't be trusted to be responsible enough to maintain a secure environment.

There's a pretty good story in the "Hilarious Stories" chapter at the end of the book related to who can access the facility and the required attire when working out.

Don't Get Stuck on Other People's Time, Create Value to Your Time

Before I even start this section, if you're a S&C coach for one team and part of your job description includes being at practice and being on-call, this does not apply to you. Often, if you're in that situation, you have your own facility or access to a facility shared with a minimal number of others and are paid a higher amount to be on-call. Those circumstances negate some of what I'm going to say but there are a few things that could apply depending on the situation.

One of the most important things you must do in an S&C environment is mitigate bullshit time and increase the value of your time (actually, that's in all aspects of life).

What I mean is, as a support staff member, you're often stuck on another person's schedule. And since you have multiple people that need your time, you must have a formal structure for when a person or a group is late, cancels or in some way isn't respectful of your time.

Generally, this lack of professional respect will bleed out into issues across the board, because you're trying to serve multiple teams and therefore multiple personalities. Plus, you have limited resources (facilities, equipment, etc.) to help those you are trying to help.

If no one values you or what you do, there is no value to your time.

This is also an amazing opportunity to discover if you have a boss who values you. Because if you don't get support on this issue, you most likely need to find a new job because no one cares about the quality of what you do. You're most likely just a checkbox on the list of "things to do in athletics."

A great precedent to set after confirming a session—albeit difficult in application without administrative support—is to move on to the next appointment in your day if the team is more than twenty minutes late without communication.

While the athletes may suffer in the short term because they don't get to train that day, you set a better precedent that can be maintained for the long term. This helps shift the paradigm from someone whose time is not valuable to someone who add tremendous value and is in high demand for a reason.

If you make yourself available 24-7 with no boundaries, don't be mad when no one gives a shit about your time. You set the precedent. It's your fault.

I have two specific examples that reinforced this for me.

The first was when I was a GA at UConn. it was Labor Day weekend and I had a preseason team who had requested a Sunday afternoon training session. Training on Sundays for this group was nothing out of the ordinary. However, there was no competition coming up and with much of the team being local as well as it being a long weekend, many of the athletes were trying to go home before school kicked into high gear.

I made sure to double-check with the sport coach in our scheduling meeting a few weeks before that they wanted to train Sunday afternoon on Labor Day weekend.

The coach reiterated to me that they were certainly going to practice on that Sunday and that they would need me for both a forty-minute workout and a twenty-minute foam roll/cool-down stretch after practice. I said okay and I lost my Labor Day weekend; but I was being paid to do the job and that was the job I needed to do—par for the course.

A few weeks later on that Labor Day Sunday, thirty minutes had passed from when the group was supposed to be with me. And having not seen or heard from anyone, I called the coach to see what was going on. As soon as they picked up the phone, I could tell by the tone of their voice that something was wrong. "Hey Joe . . ." they stuttered and then after a long pause said, "I gave the kids today off because a lot of them wanted to go home to see their families over Labor Day before the season starts. You don't mind, right?"

As much as I wanted to scream, pull my hair out, or have any other type of visceral reaction, the coach did have a point. How could I mind when I so willingly and unquestionably committed to just being there? I had confirmed weeks prior, I didn't follow up in the days leading into the weekend, and I always was there. To my own detriment I was always available and always went out of my way to help "make it happen" for my teams.

I had set the precedent that my time had no value, and clearly, they showed me it had none to them.

Wanting to never let something like that happen again, I always looked to clearly define my time having value and overcommunicate about the schedule (especially around the holidays or other important dates).

The second situation that helped reinforce my need to constantly be an advocate for my own time happened a couple of years later. A sport coach had told me that he was going to have his group come into train with me that Saturday at 9:00 a.m. Again, it was not anything out of the ordinary for this group.

I double-checked mid-week with the coach to confirm and was all set for Saturday. By 9:45 a.m. without having any communication (no responses to my calls and texts at 8:50 a.m., 9:10 a.m. and 9:20 a.m.) and not knowing what was going on, I started to pack up to leave.

My time was valuable and I had other things to do.

Having already locked the doors from the inside as I got my things ready, I was about three steps away from the doors when—to my surprise—there was a furious pounding on the doors to the facility. My name was being screamed, "Joe! Open the doors! Joe!"

As I opened the door, I found the coach—very upset to say the least. And with as much calm restraint as I could muster (which if you know me, isn't exactly my forte), I said, "Hi, Coach. I hadn't heard from you. And I wasn't sure if you had canceled or changed the session without letting me know, which has happened before, so I'm going to leave for the day."

It was at that point his classic Napoleon complex kicked into hyperdrive; with his veins popping out of his forehead, he began yelling at me—most of which made little to no sense. And then he said something to me I will never forget.

"Joe, you're support staff. I don't have to communicate everything I plan to you. If I tell you to be here to train my kids, you sit here with a smile on your face and wait until my kids show up, because that's your job."

At that point I recognized that I had absolutely no value to this individual and nothing that I did was ever going to change his perception that I was nothing more than a lackey for him. In his mind, I didn't work with him, I worked for him, and I was of the lower caste.

While my gut instinct was to eviscerate him with a verbal onslaught of logic and facts on his ineffective communication, and my deep, primal, reptile brain wanted to make physical contact with my hand to his face, I smiled knowing that it would have been a pointless slaughter both ways.

Instead, I stepped slightly forward and off to the side not wanting to make the mistake of becoming physical (physically, I was significantly bigger). And as dramatically and in as big of an asshole fashion as I could, gingerly closed and locked the door while saying, "Please, don't bang on the doors. They're new and expensive." And I proceeded to walk out to my car.

As I was walking out, a large group of his athletes had been standing in the outer foyer and heard the interaction.

One of the leaders on the team said to me as I walked by, "Don't worry, Coach Joe. We understand. It's not your fault. Just Coach being Coach."

In a funny turn of events, this coach further shot himself in the foot by calling the sport admin and complaining (lying about what happened). I then got a call from said sport admin, and after explaining what happened and what was said, sending text screenshots with timestamps, throwing out the idea of me talking with HR about it,

I also recommended that the sport admin ask a bunch of the athletes who had been standing in the foyer and heard the whole exchange.

It was at that point—realizing that the athletes had witnessed the encounter and could weigh-in—the sport admin abruptly changed tone and said they would take care of it. They also said to make sure I let them know if anything like that happened again, especially around the athletes. Funny thing, nothing like that ever happened again—at least when the athletes were within earshot.

Do Not Become the Punishment Police

A dogma that you must break immediately is that you as the S&C coach are the one who "punishes" the athletes.

This doctrine from sport coaches (and many other staff) that you're the "enforcer" is not only antiquated, but in this current day and age, an extremely risky proposition for your career. It opens the door not only for legal liability but gross negligence.

There is a very fine line in using any kind of "punishment" for an athlete, especially physical punishment.

If an athlete needs to be "inspired" to achieve their full potential because they're not adequately meeting the standards set forth for their success, then the person who set the standard should "inspire" the athlete. (See what I did there? Semantics matters, thanks Beach.)

If it's due to an issue with you during S&C training, you need to deal with it.

If an athlete needs to be "inspired" due to an issue with the sport coach, academic support, sports medicine staff, or anyone else that they relate to as an athlete, then it's that person's or department's job to manage the manner in which "inspiration" takes place, as well as any of the possible repercussions.

I would often tell sport coaches to recruit better athletes or build better character in them; it wasn't my fault that their athletes skipped class, showed up late to practice, didn't listen to them, were disrespectful during tutoring, were not on time for rehab or whatever issue would come up.

You also need to make sure that the "inspiration" is consistent across the board for all athletes you work with and that everyone is equally and fairly held accountable.

You also must have SOPs in place as it relates to how to "inspire" someone who is injured, someone who recently competed, or someone who has a competition upcoming.

One of the worst things you can do to destroy your credibility with your athletes and your coaches, and risk your job, is trying to "inspire" an athlete the day before or the day after a competition.

"Inspiration" should never cause injury and can take many forms, from physical to menial to trivial.

Feel free to get creative with how you choose to "inspire" but remember, the key to inspiration is that it should be lasting and inspire other people to not need to be "inspired" by following all rules and regulations.

SIDE NOTE—Cleaning is one "inspiration" you need to be careful with doling out, especially if using chemicals that require OHSA certification. At some point, someone is going to get sued and/or fired for making an athlete clean using hazardous chemicals without proper equipment, etc.

Customizing the Classroom

One important but often overlooked action you need to be doing as a

S&C Coach in the collegiate environment is fundraising, both in the traditional sense (actively and passively) as well as in the role of an advocate.

How do you get the money required to have the needed equipment if you're not getting the budget you requested?

Let's be frank here, most S&C departments budgets wouldn't buy enough small items like bands, med balls, etc., never mind buy expensive equipment (outside of a capital project anyway). That has to change, and the person in charge of the department is the one to make the change.

In the voice of Smokey Bear, "Only you can advocate for your department."

Fundraising as an Advocate

As mentioned, as a director you have to be an advocate for your department. You not only have to put forth what you need but you need to support it with facts and purpose.

I purposefully set up my budget in two ways. First, there was the yearly cost of maintaining our current level of operation: from buying and replacing low-cost equipment and equipment that would "find legs," to recertification and conference attendance. This was the barebones, non-negotiable amount of money I needed to simply continue at the level we operated at—maybe a 1% growth approach per year. This was the core of what we needed to execute and what our philosophy was built on.

The second manner was the large-scale strategic plan that fell into a two-pronged approach of innovation and research and development. This was where the two, three, four, and five-year strategic plan was put into context and the cost versus development was shown. We had to have money allocated to the integration of innovations that would become part of our day-to-day; things that we wanted to evolve our core with. We also needed money allocated to experiment with—to test and check if it was something we wanted to continue to pursue—and it didn't matter if it worked or not since we still had our core intact. The purpose of this was to help show that the requested $50,000 for technology wasn't just for a shiny new toy: it was a vetted process integrated into our core that allowed for improved monitoring of athletes and their performance; it helped better integrate all associated staff within the domain of athlete performance; and it acted as a recruiting tool to "keep up with the Joneses."

See the section called "Plans of an Advocate" for examples of how I personally started to do this for the context I was in. To be honest, I never got to fully realize this personally as a coach—I left before I could. Although, I *have* helped others create this particular paradigm as a consultant with favorable results.

Passive Fundraising

From the passive side, make sure there are ways for people to put money in the S&C account. If you don't have a "booster" account, or "club" account or whatever your school calls it, *get one made immediately*.

You want to not only take donations and raise money, but you also want to sit on the money and not have to use it in the budget year.

Far too often, I see S&C coaches getting small donations and having to use the money or lose it. You find that $500 doesn't go far in training equipment. You need to take that $500 and put it in a savings account so that one day when you grow it to $7,500, you can buy multiple doodads or a single thingamabob.

You need to meet with your marketing and development people and make sure that the S&C name and logo (yes, you need a logo) are on the branded merchandise your school sells in the bookstore, online, etc.

You also need to make sure that on all the emails and paper materials your school spams out to request donations, S&C has a donation checkbox to receive donations too.

You'd be amazed at how many athletes don't want to donate to the sport they played but would donate to S&C if the option was presented to them. Let's be honest, not every athlete has a great experience in their sport or with their sport coach, but they might have had one working with S&C.

This is especially true if you as the S&C coach have been at a school for a long time, and the sport coach has changed or the athlete had a bad experience with the sport coach and that coach is still there. You can be that amazing person who gets athletes who never gave a dime to donate to

S&C. It will give you a lot of clout on the bean counter side of the athletics business. And it never hurts being able to add "money generator" to the résumé

Have you ever thought of becoming an AD? If you have no track record for development on the money side of things—good luck.

Here's another passive idea that can help you kick-start a fund: sell equipment and create donation opportunities.

Do you have one of something and never use it because you only have one? Sell it.

Do you have five hundred of something and only need ten? Sell four hundred and fifty of them.

Don't horde things without reason; but don't throw things away without reason either. Even selling metal for scrap is better than nothing. You must create value to what you do and what you have.

Tell your AD, "I'm selling two of *these* because two of them aren't functional to train groups of thirty athletes. I'm going to use that money to subsidize the purchase of five more of *those,* which will give us ten, and makes them functional to use and helps me better train our athletes."

Get in the office of your development people and advocate for large-scale donation opportunities such as naming rights to the facility and small-scale sponsorship opportunities like equipment purchases or having nameplates for artwork placed throughout the facility or on equipment.

I once worked at a school that had customizable, magnetic nameplates on each of the lifting racks in the facility. Each nameplate was a fixed amount of money for a multiyear-year commitment. On each nameplate, the individual or group who donated was able to put whatever one-hundred-character blurb they wanted: some were inspirational, some were dedications to family members, and all of them generated money to finance improvements. The money went into a fund and was able to grow and be used for bigger purchases outside of the regular budget when needed.

An additional idea is customizable quotes on the platform of each lifting rack or on the wall behind a rack (if the rack was against a wall or had a platform). By using a three-foot-by-five-foot space, donors could choose from multiple approved logos or graphic designs and include a quote or message to fill that space. The donor customizes what they want within the framework you give them: you get money coming in and something to show off during game days to donors and boosters. Yes, that's right, you should be actively touring donors and boosters around when you can. As a director you are as much a CEO as head coaches, and you have a political role to play in some senses.

SIDE NOTE—Make sure you throw away broken equipment, or not let athletes use things that are on their way to breaking. A band that snaps and hits someone in the eye is a bad enough when you could have just thrown it away. A bar that breaks when someone is using it because it's twenty years old, bent from improper use, and "costs too much to fix" is a multimillion-dollar lawsuit and potential paralysis for the athlete.

Using keywords like "liability" and "negligent" when discussing "in your professional opinion" or "as the subject matter expert" to your administrators (via email or text, because conversations didn't always happen), seems to magically make dollars grow on trees to buy what you need.

"I would rather risk injury to an athlete, lawsuits, bad press, and get fired than spending $5,000 on new equipment," said no college AD ever.

But be careful. Don't throw up that defense too often, or you risk creating some bigger problems for yourself with your administrators and you most likely won't have a job for long. See "Good" from Jocko for a deeper explanation as to how best to leverage this.

Active Fundraising

In regard to active fundraisers, you can host events, offer gifts as part of other athletics fundraisers, and meet with and tour important people on game days.

You can offer your department's services as a gift or prize at athletic fundraising events. Make a prize of three sixty-minute training sessions, a twelve-week training program, and workout gear. Don't you think someone is going to buy that for themselves to relive their glory days or give as a gift for their kids/grandkids? (Clearly, check with your compliance department before doing this.)

With private sport performance training sessions topping $150 a session in some cases, $500 donation for that prize pack is an easy ask. Imagine that being a prize at a silent auction? With the right marketing push behind it, you could pull in an easy $1,000 for something like that.

Bring the winning donor in, do a basic assessment and teach them some stuff. Boom, session one done. Session two and three can be spread out every four weeks. And you can find sixty minutes once a month to train them with a basic program (doubtful anyone will need more than that): adapt it to the equipment they have, make them sign a waiver and you're good to go.

You can bring in money to the program with little to no effort.

Hell, if you have more free time and they have the money, train them on the side, get paid more, and build the relationships that can help you in the big picture—not only in the job you have but in the one you might need later on.

Something Tangible for Their Money

In one situation I was in, a coworker was training a very significant athletics program donor.

One day a piece of equipment they had previously used and were supposed to use was broken. The benefactor asked my colleague why they weren't going to use it and he off-handedly said it had been broken due to use because almost all the athletes used it. He went on to say we were waiting to buy a new one but budget issues and purchasing-paperwork lag time had slowed things down—but they would have it soon.

The benefactor asked curiously why we were waiting if it was important to train the athletes. My buddy made a generic comment about how it was nothing out of the ordinary—just typical paper processing stuff that usually took a couple weeks.

To which the benefactor replied, in a more serious tone, "If you run into any trouble about not having money or getting things fast enough, let me know. I donate plenty of money here, so I know that is not the problem. And if paperwork is the issue, I'll just buy one and have it shipped to you to cut down on the time delays. If you say this is critical to helping the athletes here get better, then we should never not have one."

Low and beyond, a couple of days later, "paperwork and money issues" that had slowed things down for a few weeks magically didn't exist anymore. The business office had moved the order to the top of the queue and the new equipment was received the following week.

It came back to us a couple days later that someone in development had told the finance side that a donor had called and specifically asked why their funds allocated to S&C related needs had not yet been used to purchase requested equipment. Basically, they had come to the facility and not been able to see the tangible use of their money and they were not pleased.

Create Tangibility for Them

In a similar vein, and something that is for some reason massively overlooked, is meeting and touring donors through your facilities when they're on campus, during pregame or other athletics events. While I see this as an obvious tactic, it must be said: seek out as many ways to touch base with important people in your sphere as you can. Donors and boosters are one piece of the important-people pie but there are plenty of other people who directly or indirectly impact your world. If they don't know about you from you, then they only know you from someone else—if at all.

Help create tangibility with these people so they can see and understand or literally touch and feel how their money is directly impacting athletes with the equipment in the facility.

If they have their kids with them, let them throw around med balls, let them jump on force plates, and let them see the cool factor and the tangible impact their money has.

If your development people don't understand how and why this can be a massive help for them, then they probably aren't getting much money coming in.

Email forms, call marathons, and all that other basic marketing stuff is great but you need much more than transaction relationships—you need to make transformational relationships. Administrators and others who are trying to build strong ties with donors/boosters and supporters often fail to recognize critical opportunities to engage front-line staff they work with to help build more transformative relationships with those whose pockets they are trying to shake empty.

Everyone knows the S&C coach does more hands-on, direct work with the athletes than the development schmoozer. So, get that S&C coach to relate and define the athlete's experiences and what they do to help the athletes be successful to the benefactor. Granted, you as an S&C coach need to be able to present yourself and the program effectively to these people.

Events are another easy fundraiser to host: conferences, seminars, educational opportunities. Get people to come learn from you and build the brand or bring someone in and get a percentage of the money. Get others in the community to recognize that your place is the place to go to learn.

Juniata College, anyone? At first glance, it's a small, random school. With a second glance, it has one of the best S&C conferences and networking opportunities year after year—a place to learn and get better.

Communitas and Collaborations

By using community-based fitness as a driver for strength-related or fitness-related events, you can tie in with local gyms and partners to help facilitate community involvement.

Have you ever thought of having a summer-stadium run or (insert your place's special thing) training day for former athletes?

Get them back on campus to relive the glory days by working out, running stairs, or doing a team competition. Give them a T-shirt, do a bar night before or after, and/or partner with a charity.

Don't you think highly competitive people who have transitioned into the normal world would love to come back, get yelled at by an S&C coach, and workout? For all of the alternative, effort-based, high-intensity training (HIT) guys in football, make the "St. Valentine's Day Massacre workout" an S&C alumni day in the summer.

A small dose of the communitas they once had.

Take that beyond just using alumni—imagine if you did general workout circuits on the turf or in a gym open to the community—five dollars a person for seventy-five-minutes. Have them sign a waiver, sign up online—whatever—five dollars gets them basic community fitness and a handout after.

Partner with the public health department and make it a community health event. Hell, charge twenty dollars and give them access to a wider variety of free services (invite other professionals such as local gyms, chiropractors, massage therapists, etc., to be vendors), and give them a T-shirt too.

Yes, your job is "sport performance," but if you build strong ties to the community, use your skillset and experience to give back, and be helpful to others, you'll be amazed at how many doors and opportunities start to open for your program and thus, you.

S&C coaches often say they don't have the time or desire to do these kinds of things. And I laugh because it's comical when people think that. You don't do it on your own as a one-person show; you're at a college where almost everyone on the campus is looking for work experience.

Collaborative partnerships make these things happens.

Work with faculty, staff, and students with majors such as marketing, event planning, allied health sciences, and community promotions to gain the workforce and resources to synergistically accomplish these ideas.

Think about this and let these buzzwords sink in: cross-departmental collaboration, for-credit internships, professional experience and alumni relations.

Do you not want to be an S&C coach in the trenches forever? Here's a way to evolve.

Again, no AD at any college has ever said, "I don't want to positively engage the people we have on campus and in our community, to build synergies and tap into their resources in addition to ours, and to help us better promote and develop the school, athletics, athletes and alumni while also generating money."

SIDE NOTE—Okay, so before some of the bitching and moaning from S&C coaches starts: yes, you have time for this and no, you most likely aren't organized enough yet to realize it.

You need to do this but you most likely don't understand the value of it beyond just your program. So, let's make it pretty simple.

You most likely are not going to be an S&C Coach forever. Eventually, for one reason or another, you're going to need a new job—most likely in a new industry. Perhaps, you know people who can help you do that fast. People who like you, believe in you and value you, and who also have large networks and financial resources.

But here's a thought you might not have considered: it's not just the current donors and boosters you need to know—it's the athletes you work with too. How many athletes over your career have you coached? How many have gone on to work in different industries and climb the ladder? How many in five, ten, and fifteen years from now could you call for help or advice?

There are hundreds—if not thousands—of athletes if you've coached long enough. How many of them would love to have someone like you on their team now? Find time to add value where you can with people now because you never know when you're going to need help later on.

PART IV

BUILDING THE BUILDING

The frequent employment of one's will power masters all organs of movement and trains them to perform feats which otherwise would have been difficult, painful, and even impossible. The man becomes independent and self-reliant; he will never be a coward, and, when real danger threatens, he is the one who is looked up to by others. The knowledge of one's strength entails a real mastery over oneself; it breeds energy and courage, helps one over the most difficult tasks of life, and procures contentment and true enjoyment of living.

—George "The Russian Lion" Hackenschmidt

13

TRAINING PHILOSOPHIES

If I had to put my training philosophy into the shortest possible explanation, it would simply be this: using the physical act of training to address the process of generating and tying inner belief into outward action.

To expand on that though, I employ the two following maxims: training is evidence-driven not simply evidence-based and not every athlete is athletic.

While this section will mainly talk about the concepts and methodology I apply, as well as the conceptual framework I use to train athletes, the key idea I mentioned in my shortest possible explanation is *generating and tying inner belief into outward action*.

Why is this important? Because it should be obvious that confidence developed through the rigors of training not only allows an athlete to see the progress they have made, but it also helps generate belief from the athlete to buy into you as a coach.

And when an athlete sees the extra benefit of working with you from a physical training standpoint, they're going to start pushing a little harder and give a little more effort because they're starting to see that the benefit is furthering their outcomes in sport (or whichever aspect you are trying to develop).

It is this facilitation of outward action and results that creates the momentum of the coach-athlete dynamic. It allows you to influence and build inner confidence and ultimately the outward physical capabilities of an athlete. It allows you the opportunity to learn how to draw out and capitalize on that "little bit of extra," in order to help push the athlete in training, so that the athlete can draw it out in competition when it matters.

One of the ideas I often talk about with athletes I work with is to achieve the improbable; and you have to *believe* you can do the impossible.

Thus, the skill of building confidence through being a teacher, coach, and mentor is what matters here because you're getting someone to do something they have never done before, don't believe they can do, or don't want to do.

In the context of athletics and S&C, the physical action and associated dynamics of training is used to develop tools and skills to manage anxiety, build confidence, and create the outputs when needed/required to be successful in sport. And while it's often at a level of output that has never been achieved before, just because you have the physical capacity doesn't mean the output will manifest itself when you need it.

Not Every Athlete Is Athletic

"Not every athlete is athletic."

The first time I said it out loud I thought I sounded crazy. But the more I thought about and due to a combination of sociological factors related to youth and adolescent development both in a purely physical sense and specialized sporting context, I recognized that many people who were considered athletes because they participated in some version of organized sport actually *weren't* athletic.

Because of this—as well as other factors beyond the scope of this book related to global trends in nutrition, sleep, activity, exposure to activity, and in a lot of cases lack of exposure to activity—I needed to understand how to best train athletes who weren't athletic and often lacked fundamental skills and capacities.

Granted, I was working in collegiate athletics and those I trained had been selected to be here, thus requiring some level of sport-specific ability. Therefore, I framed a question to myself to help guide me in this process in the following way:

"Because not every athlete is athletic, how do I best develop their abilities to allow to them to succeed within their sport and not dampen or minimize what currently makes them special in their sport?"

I guess it begged the question of what it meant to be athletic versus an athlete. Being an athlete, operationally defined in this context, simply means being a participant in a sporting activity.

Being athletic, however, represented a combination of the innate physical abilities of a person, their ability to learn new physical abilities in any context of physical action or performance (i.e. hand-eye coordination, endurance, strength), as well as modulate the ability to perform those tasks in a controlled manner, in the sporting context they chose, and at the velocity required.

While there are many other ways to describe athletic individuals, the largest and most obvious divide is between an athlete and someone who is athletic. I provide this one further explanation for context: the athlete is good at the sport-specific physical outcome that they're trying to compete in, either by means of technical and/or tactical superiority to make up for the lack of overwhelming physical abilities. Someone who is athletic has the ability to draw on multiple, different physical skill sets to achieve outcomes across a multitude of competitive arenas that require physical output regardless of their technical or tactical skill in that specific competitive arena.

Building Better Athletes

I was having a conversation with a fellow S&C coach a few years ago via text. At one point, I texted him: "Not every athlete is athletic, our goal as professionals should be to build more athletic athletes, without sacrificing what makes them great at their sport now so they can maximize their ability to use the skills they develop in their sport when it counts."

After a bit of back and forth, he then responded with, "Well, what does it take to build a better athlete?" I took a few minutes to write it down in a note and took a screenshot of my response:

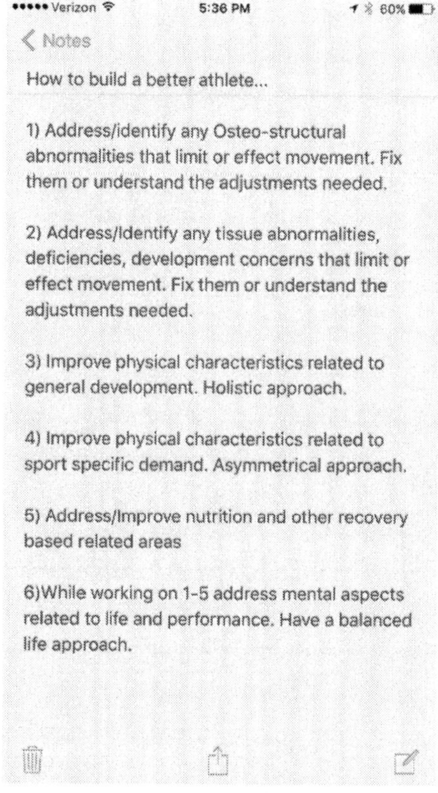

It's a rather simple six-step process to reach your optimal potential. It gets rather difficult, however, if you as the S&C coach don't know how to identify the right person with the specialized expertise needed at each step. You need that person to teach you the manner in which each step needs to be integrated and built on the other steps or have them help you in the process.

Also, you need the right perspective of how the process itself is both a linear progressive sequence at any singular moment and a longitudinal continuum over time.

It's not simply about lifting weights, cross-training, or throwing in some recovery work after a hard training cycle. It's about understanding how to address, approach, integrate, and at times innovate around a massive and complex array of factors (biomechanical, physiological, psychological, etc.) with a living, breathing, feeling organism called a human.

Evidence-Driven, Not Necessarily Evidence-Based

No one is 100% right, and no one is 100% wrong. Don't learn the tricks of the trade; learn the trade. It's no longer about just working out. Coaching effort coupled with concentration and focus isn't going to help get people better anymore. Just telling them to go :do it" isn't enough.

On the flip side, just using assessments and evaluative mechanisms and making everything a function of objective data isn't going to do anything either.

It's blending the art of coaching with the science of objective measurement; to put together the ability to know when and where to develop and refine technical skills and also when and where to step back and simply provide confidence and support for the athlete to go do what they need to do on their own.

I read a lot of research; I read even more books. I try to cover as far-ranging topics as I can in order to build a wider and deeper base of knowledge. Like Musashi said, "If you know the way broadly, you will see it in everything."

That's why I take the objective and the rational and mix it with the unknown, the potential, and sometimes the emotionally irrational.

Often the greatest performance of an individual is such an outlier to their ability that it seems crazy to have happened—yet it did. An outlier of performance like that can't always be objective and quantifiable—it's an example of the art of belief and why you cannot create concrete frameworks based only on scientific, peer-reviewed evidence. In the right moment, at the right time, in the right state, any individual can do something that can only be described as transcendent.

You need to understand how to guide your decision-making: take concrete concepts based on evidence with artistic liberty and apply them appropriately for your situation.

One of the most obvious things in being evidence-driven but not necessarily evidence-based is understanding how imitation is the greatest form of flattery. Sometimes you have to break away from the traditional or accepted dogmas of how things are done in order to generate a higher level of outcome.

This is especially true when looking at developing new levels of performance, which is a "tip of the spear" activity. You have to be willing to do what many may consider unorthodox, incorrect, or just plain silly and "risk it to get the biscuit" as they say.

However, you should only take those positions and attempt such things if you have a valid argument based on legitimate, rational logic. I certainly don't advocate "throwing shit on the wall" by trying random and unpredictable methodologies to see if you get the result you want "stick."

I do advocate, however, having an intelligent, defendable position based on a combination of scientific and anecdotal evidence, mixed in with a small pinch of gut instinct and faith.

Too Much Textbook, Not Enough Common Sense

I was at a national conference in a special interest group for track & field (T&F). I was invited due to the recent success the T&F team I was working with had at the time (championships, records, etc.).

A prominent S&C coach (by school logo association, salary and thus perceived competency) stood up and talked about how dealing with such a wide range of needs in T&F was tough.

He began by saying, "You know, I open the textbook, and all the things that we learn from there say, this is how you develop strength, this way for power, and this is how you develop that and this."

Then he pointed out that it didn't always line up with what he saw his T&F coaches asking to be done; that the coaches wanted things that differed from what "the research" says, and he struggled to go with it compared to doing "what the body of knowledge says."

I literally took down those quotes word for word in my notebook so I could refer back to them, because the fundamental problem had nothing to do with the textbooks or the track coaches (although I will say, track coaches often are their own worst enemies and self-impose many of the "problems" they face. And that's coming from track guy, go figure).

With the group pausing to reflect on his comment, I raised my hand to speak. And after the moderator gave me a quick introduction, I proceeded in the most sincere and innocuous way I could (remember, while successful, I was one of the youngest people in the room considered an "expert" and this was a "master").

I said, "While I agree on some of the stuff that you say, generally speaking, everything I do doesn't come from the textbook and some of what I do, I would never do with athletes that weren't trying to win at the highest level."

That got a few funny looks, but I pressed on.

"The book doesn't tell you the beliefs of the coach and how to connect with the athletes either. You have to take that knowledge, what was learned from research, what was learned from previous experience and you have to apply it in the correct manner for your given situation and context.

"You can't create concrete frameworks to operate from based on what a study says or based on what worked for someone else.

"You have to think of your philosophy and your style as scaffolding — and flexible scaffolding at that. Bamboo, for example—it allows you to climb up and down, left and right, and side to side around the project that you're doing. But you yourself can't be cement. Your scaffolding and your framework can't be so fixed and rigid that you're not able to be flexible for certain situations: the athletes you have, the resources you have , etc."

At that point, I had a captivated audience, and I was asked by the moderator to continue, so I took a breath and went meta (Surprised? Seriously, by now I figured you'd have known it was coming).

"The research is critical. The textbook is critical. But the written word and spoken word are just as important. You need to have a combination of websites and periodicals outside of scholarly research: websites such as T Nation, EliteFTS, Breaking Muscle, etc., as well as podcasts and videos of the spoken word that hasn't been written down yet.

"The file drawer effect is a real thing; more knowledge is not published than published. How many athletes or their coaches give away their secrets? Most of that stuff is hidden—not obvious, especially in track and field at the Olympic level. By listening now to the spoken word via media —video, podcast, and even videos of conferences—the ability to access unwritten or unrecorded knowledge is possible."

I continued, "You have to glean insights from tidbits of conversations, especially now with so many lifelong 'under the bar' practitioners coming around to sharing secrets as they approach the end of their careers and their lives."

As I closed on that final point, I saw that while I had lost quite a few people, I had also given a few of them something to chew on. I ended my moment with a clear and definitive statement to prove a point: "Nothing I've ever done hasn't been done before, but there's no research on much of it. Sure, I used fundamental concepts based on proven science and empirical evidence of generations of athletes. Don't get me wrong, nothing I did was special—nor in a sense was it new; it has all been done at some point. It's just never been done with the people I worked with and in the specific situational context we operated under at that moment in time. That's why it was novel."

Digging for Diamonds

This is one of my favorite analogies I use to discuss the concept of development to an athlete or parent. In this example, I will be referencing a collegiate athlete context, but it's easily appropriate to adjust to all settings.

In the offseason, you must consider yourself a miner digging for diamonds. You're trying to dig and find the biggest diamond possible: building your physical and athletic skill set.

That's the key to the offseason: develop the plan and do the work to build the technical, tactical, and strategic abilities in your sport in addition to the physical aspects.

Since we're talking about physical performance, you're trying to dig to find the biggest, nicest diamond you possibly can that gives you the widest and deepest range of skills and abilities to maximize everything you're trying to maximize.

Now, is everyone digging for diamonds? No. Some people may be digging for emeralds, or rubies, or sapphires. I'm using diamonds as an example to highlight that we're just trying to find something specific. Our goal is diamonds. Next year, it might be emeralds or gold.

We're trying to find the maximization of our abilities—that's the biggest diamond possible (be open to the conceptual understanding of the analogy and don't substantiate the thought or get stuck on the nuances . . . use your imagination muscle).

So, in this critical training period, you're digging. You're digging for the biggest diamond you can possibly find and then you hit the first transition point where you go from preparation to needing to have that diamond become ready to be used.

In this first transition point, the goal is no longer to dig and find a bigger diamond. The goal is to polish the diamond. Because at some point, you'll be limited in time and you'll only be able to polish what you have. Therefore, it will no longer be worth it to dig for another diamond—or develop new skills, athletically speaking (many bad sport coaches and S&C coaches fail their athletes at this first transition point by staying on the dig).

As you start to refine and enhance whatever you've developed, you shine that diamond up as nice as possible to sell it. You hope that by selling that diamond, you can get the greatest amount of return—or wins, because let's be honest, wins are money—literally and figuratively (in college athletics, however, the athletes just don't see the money for winning—a topic for another day).

Now, as an athlete, during that first phase where you're digging and you hit the transition point, there's also the need to change from the digging mindset to the refinement mindset of polishing.

So, here's where the performance side changes, and this is the shift in mindset you must have after you sell your diamond: whatever you fetched for your diamond is whatever it got you. You must go home, you must put the memory of that diamond on your mantle, and you must forget about it; it can no longer help you because its value has passed.

You must now go back to the mine and find a new diamond or instead, look for a different stone because maybe you no longer seek diamonds. That's the cyclical nature of trying to enhance your performance: put effort into improving, see where that takes you, refine your strategies, and seek to improve again. Once you've achieved a level of success, and once your diamond has gotten you to a certain point, the diamond from one season can't help you in future seasons.

You can acknowledge the diamond you once found and keep a picture of it up on your mantle as a reminder of how you got it and what it allowed you to accomplish. But you still must go back to being a miner if you're looking to continue to improve.

Much like Bill Belichick of the New England Patriots says, "We're on to the next," referring to the next opponent on their schedule. He uses his now trademark colloquialisms and analogies to set the stage for the process of digging for diamonds. At one point, you're digging; at another point, you're refining; and at some point, you've got to put it down, learn from the process, and move forward to achieve something new.

The Human Optimization Continuum

The human optimization continuum was designed to give specific, tangible visual representation to the differences in scope and demand placed upon performance roles relative to an athlete's lifecycle of performance development.

Understanding that this is a continuum is critical because knowledge from any one area can and often does carry over in some respects to the others. However, when you understand the specific purpose each role plays relative to the outcome of what the athlete is trying to achieve at that point in the continuum, you can start to understand why there are so many issues with people stepping outside of their specific role, believing that they can accomplish multiple aspects on the continuum when they in fact are not the correct person to be helping at that point.

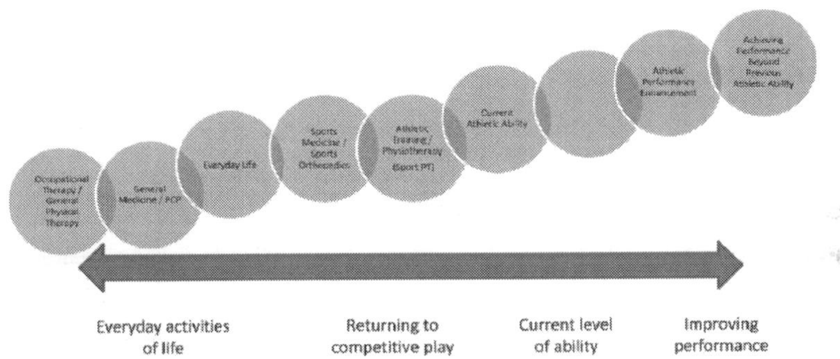

For almost everyone, this continuum starts slightly left of middle with your ability to physically function in everyday life.

But let's start at the far left of the continuum where returning to everyday life activities occur. There the goal is to get you back to a level of "everyday life." Quality of life and not the quality of performance is the driver here.

Generally, this is dictated by insurance companies seeking profit for service, limiting the practitioners in both their abilities to help and need to learn more than what they can charge to do.

The knowledge and expertise of the practitioners at this point is not typically performance-based and even if it is, given the population constraints, few if any true "performance" paradigms are implemented and instead remain concepts.

It's critical that if you have some level of athletic ability or wish to develop yourself beyond any level of ability previously achieved, don't limit yourself to being helped by this part of the continuum. They don't have the knowledge, experience, and lessons learned on the far right of the continuum to help you get to where you want to go.

These are the people that help normal people achieve normal things, which is fine for being normal.

However, performance means not being normal.

Thus, you cannot do normal things and expect supranormal results. It just doesn't work like that or most corporate, chain gyms would field the majority of athletes on Olympic teams.

As you shift out of everyday life and possess a "current" level of athletic ability, you get to a dichotomy of what you can do with that ability.

On the left side, you have a return to competitive play and regaining a level of previous athletic ability and the right-side entails achieving performance beyond "current" ability.

From everyday life to the "current" level of ability there's a very interesting space between sports medicine/orthopedics and athletic training or what other countries call physiotherapy. This is one of the largest areas where you can have people who have the "everyday life" mindset, and they will limit you because they fall to the left of the continuum in either their knowledge and experiences or mindset.

They don't truly know how and/or don't have the intensity needed to bring you back to "current" ability with a goal of achieving performance beyond that. They just happen to sit within this space.

Remember, getting back to a level of performance is never the goal for an athlete. The goal is constantly and consistently doing better than they previously did; this is both a difference in practical application as well as difference in mindset.

While "current athletic ability" defines the current manifestations of physical output, there is a void between achieving higher levels of output and staying where you are. When reaching to achieve this apex of development, you run the risk and have to walk a thin line of creating maladaptation in an acute sense or in a permanent one.

Being the foremost "tip of the spear" requires a willingness to be irreplaceably broken.

Training for Performance is Not Healthy

If you think reaching your maximum athletic potential is healthy, think again. It's one of the worst things you could ever do to yourself if the goal is to maximize your overall health.

When you train to achieve the apex of your physical abilities in whatever aspect you seek, understand and bear the consequences that this quest will be a damaging and life-altering one.

Your overall long-term health and wellness will suffer. Your mental and physical tolerances will be altered due to the asymmetric, time-intensive nature of the training you'll have to do. I'm talking about changes at the biochemical level affecting your DNA due to the constant, imposed demands on your system.

Training for longevity and optimal health has nothing to do with achieving optimal performance. From bodybuilding, to strongman/strongwoman competitions, to powerlifting, to athletics—to truly be the best of the best, you must be willing to take years off your physical life and bear a mental strain that could lead to diagnosable disorder.

This far end of the continuum can lead to many great rewards, but it has left more individuals broken and empty in more numerous ways than it has enriched.

Watch the documentary *Price of Gold* featuring Swedish athletes around their prep for the Olympics to gain better insight into this concept if it's something you don't understand.

Not everyone has the capacity to understand the mentality needed here. I explain it to people who don't have a clear idea about the cost of performance in the following way.

An athlete first has to have the underlying natural talent to get to the highest level. Most don't and never will no matter what they do.

Second, the individual has to be tolerant of the training. Durability is just as important as potential. They could have the talent but if they aren't able to handle the work that needs to be done, it's a moot point. Many with the talent break too easily.

Third, they have to be willing to do the work and be mentally engaged in the training. The mental side is just as important as the physical side. Untold numbers of athletes have had the gifts and the durability but not the mental strength to walk the path.

Last and most importantly, they have to be willing to do whatever is necessary—legal or illegal—to get themselves to that level. In certain sports that means performance-enhancing drugs, in others it means cheating in other ways. Many have had the first three but are unwilling to take the risks to separate themselves compared to their competitors. When winning comes down to single moments in time of millimeters and milliseconds, this fourth facet can mean the difference between a first-place victory to a last-place finish.

The Stereotypical Sports Medicine Mindset

In the same way, most S&C coaches are perceived to be nothing more than former-athlete meatheads who count reps wearing sweats, most athletic trainers are perceived to be nothing more than out of shape wannabes who weren't able to be athletes themselves (clearly huge generalizations here with big-time stereotyping, but that's the point).

The first time I met an athletic trainer, physical therapist, or MD in the sports medicine space, the two things I wanted to know were what the most significant injury they personally ever had was, and what they did at the time for their own physical training and why.

Answers to these two questions were the groundwork of their knowledge base (outside of the dogmas of their academic learning), their understanding of what optimizing performance entails, as well as their personal relatability to people in the pursuit of accomplishing physical outcomes they never have before achieved.

Much like in coaching, one doesn't have to be the inventor of a protocol or therapy aid to be a great sports medicine practitioner, but the person does have to have context. While absolute outcomes are important, the relative experience and ability to understand the context physically and mentally here is critical. "Hard" is perception and "heavy" is relative; the same as "soreness" and "pain" are.

I have had sports medicine professionals from all backgrounds not have the slightest clue what it takes to "get after it," misapply their knowledge, and create caustic environments as many times as I've had S&C professionals do the same. The difference is that sports medicine actually have the legal power to adjust training and what the athlete experiences regardless of their understanding. To use a fitting quote, "With great power, comes great responsibility."

Beyond that, in regard to department relations, you have to understand how information is transferred between staffs. How, when, and why are injury restrictions implemented and what is the philosophy and style of returning an athlete from injury?

Does the sport medicine professional have skills outside of their base certifications? Are they actively finding ways to not only get athletes back but better during and after the rehabilitation process? Are you still doing isotonic strengthening and "ice and stim" therapy or can you have the conversation about laser therapy or tool-assisted manual therapies?

Or are they doing one or all the following: going through the motions with their athletes, being overwhelmed and not able to handle the people and politics, or hiding behind professionals with greater scopes of practice to not take ownership of anything? HIPPA serves a purpose but it also acts as a great wall to hide behind for sports medicine professionals to not integrate into a performance team with the other relevant domains.

Optimized Performance

Optimized performance is a function of the minimum effective dose (MED) of training needed to accomplish a specific outcome over the ratio of the maximum trainable volume per session (MTVPS) to the maximum recoverable volume (MRV).

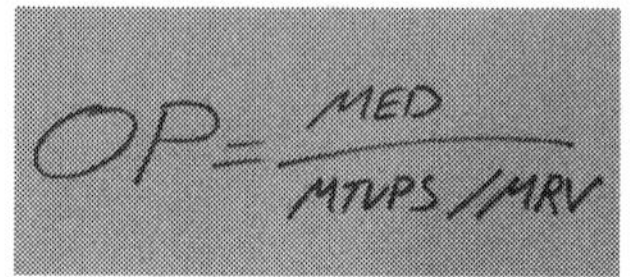

I'll expand on each of these below but before you read it, try to work out the formula for yourself and what you think it means.

Please note, that there is no scalar quantity to this formula. It's simply an anchor concept to understand optimizing physical development based on the manner in which the human state can create new physical (and mental) capabilities and express those capabilities outwardly.

Minimum Effective Dose (MED)

The idea of the minimum effective dose comes from pharmacology. It has to do with the effective drug dose needed for a given condition: how much of that drug is needed to effectively achieve the necessary outcome, in the shortest time, and with the least amount of the drug possible.

For example, if you get an infection and need to take antibiotics, the minimum effective dose to combat the infection might be four days. And while taking antibiotics for five or six days will also cure the infection, four days is the minimum effective dose needed to do the job.

Any less than four days and you risk not curing the infection; any more than four days and you risk other complications from taking the drug longer than you need to without the infection present.

How much of the drug is enough to fix the problem? And how much of the drug is too much and will cause problems if continuously taken?

This is basically the key underlying concept of physical training to optimize performance too. When you apply the concept to training, it creates an obvious paradigm: you can under do it, and you can overdo it. And most people fall into these two categories.

It's rare that people hone in on either the minimum required or optimum dose of training to achieve their goal because it varies widely for any individual. For whatever reason, people often do too much, and they think that the minimum effective dose is just doing a little bit less.

The MED concept (yes, it's a concept and not a concrete plan) is simply a way to look at how much of something you're doing and if it's too little or too much to get the response you desire. It has nothing to do with high-intensity training, high-intensity interval training, or fitness minimalism.

The MED concept is not a program. And while similar for certain goals, it's different for everyone. It requires time and effort to understand exactly what it is for you in your own training.

For example, the minimum effective dose for an average athlete trying to improve their sprint speed might be a much different minimum effective dose compared to that of a professional sprinter trying to shave one-one-hundredth of a second off their time.

It's a relative concept.

Additionally, there are some general frameworks within the systems of the human body that help create some boundaries for the acquisition, maintenance, and degradation of certain qualities.

For example, muscular strength is preserved significantly longer and with much less training than the body's ability to buffer increases in blood lactate due to intense exercise. If you don't understand that last sentence or don't agree with it, you need to go do some textbook learning. Much of what I'm going to discuss is beyond you at this moment.

One last note and two major points of understanding when talking about MED in relation to training.

First, the MED for a given response may be a supramaximal dosage compared to what the system can handle in its current state. Some of this is semantics and wordplay but let the idea sit for a moment.

There will be times when trying to achieve apex physical performance that the minimum you need to do is beyond what you're capable of doing. This is the boundary of risk in training and why training for performance can carry such a high cost.

Second, because the MED is a relative concept, time also becomes relative in the application of the MED.

The MED of training to achieve an absolute increase of 100 lbs. in your squat max is radically different for two different time periods (assuming the initial starting point is the same). If I said you had 60 days to add 100-lb. squats to a novice athlete's max—and then in a duplicate universe with the same athlete I said you had 600 days to do the same thing—would you go about it the same way? I know I wouldn't.

The MED of training needed to achieve the desired result is time-dependent, and the quality of that outcome also changes based on the time allowed. That's the single greatest challenge for college athletics' S&C programs in a nutshell.

Chew on that for a bit and digest as much as you can.

Progressive Minimalism Within the MED

Another thing that I think a lot of people struggle with understanding is the need for progressive minimalism. I don't mean minimalist equipment or any specific methodology that uses natural objects, etc.

What I mean by progressive minimalism is being in alignment to achieving the minimum effective dose of training, using the minimal or most basic skillsets for development for the desired adaptation, and actively not progressing those skills.

Too many times, people overly complicate what they do in training by adding unnecessary layers of methodology/equipment to their programs in order to drive adaptation and performance increases. However, the issue with this is the stimulus-response due to the varying and oftentimes overly complex stimulus. It doesn't allow the body to optimally adapt in the most effective way to the initial stress, leaving large development potential untapped.

This can also limit potential stimulus to develop pathways in the future that haven't yet been reached. Since exposure stress is cumulative, you lose some of the novelty effects down the road.

An example of this would be minimizing the complexity and depth of exercise selection and exercise order until true mastery and development has occurred. You can then progress into newer and more complicated exercise selections/order schemes that will help further drive adaptation and stimulus. Don't overload someone before they're ready; have them first be able to adequately draw from or maximize the stimulus they're currently using.

For those of you familiar with it, I'm not saying Louie Simmons and the

Conjugate Method are wrong. I believe he's actually right in the big picture and I consider him to be one of the true masters of the strength game. The difference is that he uses variation to drive an outcome in a progressive, structured manner based on the individual's ability and not variation for the sake of variation because it's a new training cycle. He has a purpose to his variation, and he's not just varying things for the sake of confusing the fibers.

You often see this with Olympic lifting and Olympic-lift style training for sports performance.

People bastardized the Olympic lifts and massively complicated the training stress and training demand on their athletes, in order to teach them what they believed to be the most efficient means for developing force and power through the explosive, triple-extension of the hips. However, many coaches—including one of the all-time greats in sport performance—don't even use Olympic lifting because the time it takes and the risk-reward in training compared to using plyometrics and another non-Olympic, explosive, lifting exercises is not worth it.

Using non-Olympic lifting methods can create the same, if not greater, development of power and rate of force without the learning curve and technical development needed to maximize the Olympic lifts.

There is nothing funnier to watch when I travel around than an athlete, who cannot properly move their own body in space, hammer away on sub 100-lb. hang cleans at moderate to low velocity and low to zero technical savvy and believe they're developing power.

I have, over the years, spoken on this topic as well as others and if you would like a copy of any of the presentations, send me an email. I'm happy to share.

SIDE NOTE—If you aren't strong enough to control your body in order to do basic plyometrics correctly, you probably haven't learned how to create, mitigate, and dissipate force through the system well enough yet to be trying to develop power and rate of force development (RFD) using Olympic lifts . . . just an opinion . . . would love to discuss it with you if you disagree, just bring the margaritas.

Maximum Trainable Volume Per Session (MTVPS)

This shouldn't need too much explanation.

There is only a certain amount of training you can do at a single time. The minimum effective dose (MED) is the total needed cumulative stimulus in a set time period to achieve the desired outcome, whereas the MTVPS is the amount you can acutely impose on someone at a single time.

This imposition, however, has nothing to do with the athlete's ability to recover from the stress in order to perform the same level of volume in the next session. That's where maximum recoverable volume (MRV) comes in.

MTVPS is an ever-changing "value" based on the performance profile of the athlete. It's dynamic that can be increased or decreased acutely and chronically. Things get interesting when you have a large MED requirement in a short time period to achieve a goal and the volume needed per session also exceeds the athlete's ability to perform it, never mind recover from it.

In that case, you're asking the body to tolerate supramaximal training volumes to get it where you need it to go in a certain timeframe and it can't handle the total body of work that needs to be done in any given instance. It's a recipe for disaster or a useful case for PEDs, depending on how you look at it.

Remember, it's all a function of time.

In truth, this is the simplified formula for optimal performance. There is a much more complicated form that I have purposely left out of this book to keep things simple and introduce the general concept.

Maximum Recoverable Volume (MRV)

Maximum recoverable volume is a concept I stole from Mike Israetel (so props to you, sir!) Granted, I stole the semantics and tweaked the context but nonetheless he inspired the idea. The MRV in my context is the capacity of the athlete to recover from an imposed stress: this can be both acute and chronic depending on where in time you are looking at it from.

Unlike the amount of training volume you can put on an athlete, which can be limitless regardless of what they can tolerate, MRV is a restricted quantity. It can increase with proper development, and it can decrease with improper development and with changes in chronological age, hormones, etc. In a sense, MRV is another way of looking at Hans Seyle's general adaptation syndrome (GAS) principle.

However, that begs a question: is the period of time long enough for you to recover from the required doses of stimulus and acute enough to develop a chronic adaptation given your biological state related to your chronological age?

MRV, in a sense, is the buffering mechanism. It buffers out the MTVPS allowing you to chip away at the MED to achieve the desired goal based around the time construct.

The Physical Performance Enhancement (PPE) Paradigm

The physical performance enhancement (PPE) paradigm gives a framework to the interrelated parts that comprise an individual's level of physical performance at any moment in their development. These "snapshots" can be taken longitudinally and help define and describe the process of optimization for physical output. Because the PPE paradigm encompasses all the components of physical output beyond just physical ability, it helps better define who's just an athlete in their sport and who's athletic.

Please note, the paradigm doesn't tell you what specific methodology to use or how to go about evaluating each of the related components against each other. It's merely a gross simplification in a global perspective of what goes into an individual's ability to generate physical skill. And it demonstrates the interaction of these pieces to the whole physical performance itself.

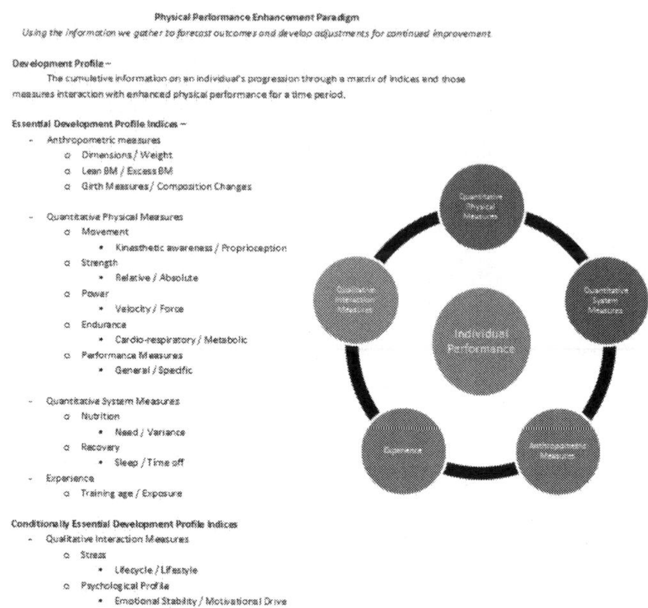

Physical Performance Enhancement Paradigm

Using the information we gather to forecast outcomes and develop adjustments for continued improvement

Development Profile ~

The cumulative information on an individual's progression through a matrix of indices and those measures interaction with enhanced physical performance for a time period.

Essential Development Profile Indices ~

- Anthropometric measures
  - Dimensions / Weight
  - Lean BM / Excess BM
  - Girth Measures / Composition Changes
- Quantitative Physical Measures
  - Movement
    - Kinasthetic awareness / Proprioception
  - Strength
    - Relative / Absolute
  - Power
    - Velocity / Force
  - Endurance
    - Cardio-respiratory / Metabolic
  - Performance Measures
    - General / Specific
- Quantitative System Measures
  - Nutrition
    - Need / Variance
  - Recovery
    - Sleep / Time off
- Experience
  - Training age / Exposure

Conditionally Essential Development Profile Indices

- Qualitative Interaction Measures
  - Stress
    - Lifecycle / Lifestyle
  - Psychological Profile
    - Emotional Stability / Motivational Drive

Also of note is the difference between the essential versus conditionally essential indices. In this context, we are looking at the essential indices as the hard, tangible metrics we can evaluate and monitor directly over time with regular consistency and accuracy, allowing us to show a trend, correlation, and possible causality. These are the essential blocks we base the training on in the development process as they show us the previous and current manifestation of actual physical output in the setting.

On the other hand, the conditionally essential indices, while able to be monitored (depending on your methodology and said belief in the methodology), are influenced and changed so regularly that their impact can be massive or negligible. Thus, it leaves their impact at times uncertain and at other times they are the root cause of change to physical output for any similar level of essential indices.

Anthropometric Measures

First, you must consider anthropometric measures such as lean mass and body weight and lean mass versus excess body mass.

Structure and composition are two major anthropometric measures that dictate performance.

You have to look at this both globally and acutely. (This section will be relatively short. I don't feel the need to dive too far down into this point because it seems self-evident and honestly, a common-sense consideration.)

If you're five-foot-five, you'll never be a center in the NBA. You don't have the correct anthropometrics to play in that certain position, regardless of any other ability (besides a superhuman vertical). However, on the flip side, just because you're five-foot-five it doesn't mean you don't have the ability to be a point guard or shooting guard—although the average for those positions in the NBA is probably somewhere around six-foot-two.

Anthropometrics aren't necessarily an excluder in the ability to perform athletic outcomes, but they're often limiting in certain sports, positions, or certain styles of play—and possibly even overall performance.

While there are always outliers and exceptions to the rule, a general rule of thumb is to look at the current, top 100 athletes for any given sport/position, normalize the anthropometric information for those 100 individuals, and you will have a loose framework for what is generally needed to be currently successful. In this writer's opinion, doing this cumulatively over decades and generations skews the results because of changes in training—never mind gear, nutrition, and many other factors of influence. It's only relative in contemporaries and not in predecessors.

In an acute sense, anthropometrics also allows you to determine or place value upon what has happened over time in training. For example, if a six-month training window is specifically geared to put on body mass for an offensive tackle in American football, the measure of body composition and body mass is an easy way to determine the level of success of that goal in context to whatever methodology was implemented to achieve it.

Bear in mind though, the methodology itself isn't the absolute reason for the change in anthropometric and morphological characteristics as there is a litany of other factors not discussed that impact this beyond cumulative physical training; it's purely an objective marker of surface-level success compared to the goal.

Experience

When we look at experience here, we're looking at far more than how much time someone has spent training.

Often, we simplify the idea of training age and experience into the same framework; how many chronological years someone has been developing their sports skills.

This view lacks the consideration of training age as a multifactor construct far beyond simply chronological years and does not include exposure stress or the history of positive and negative adaptations on future development and ability.

Training Age

Training age for any athlete looks at how long and how much development of the task they're being asked to complete versus the demand placed upon them given their current ability and their potential for growth.

Having context for the position on the continuum of natural underlying ability/potential compared to the technical/tactical knowledge and skill is critical here.

Someone with a low training age may not have the development of ability necessary to handle the demands placed upon them, even though they can perform a level of output that would—on the surface—suggest they, in fact, can (when compared to others with similar output ability).

An example of this is a sprinter I worked with in the collegiate setting. She was extremely talented and extremely fast with innate talent.

She had massive demands placed upon: she had to run multiple events every meet and she was expected to be the linchpin of success for the team —in everything from the 100 meters to the 4x4 relay.

She had the ability to perform at that level and dominate.

The issue was that her training age from a development standpoint was extremely limited—to the point that she couldn't handle the training stresses placed on her with any consistency. She was successful due to her natural underlying potential and that caused her to have significant up and down periods of performance and training. And unfortunately, she was marred by chronic, nagging injuries that would heal up enough to train, only to come back and limit training again.

Basically, her training age and development didn't match up with the training demand placed upon her.

It wasn't that the specific training she was doing was bad or wrong. In theory, and on the surface, she should have been able to handle it given her times on the track. But since she lacked the foundational development to manage those stressors without negative consequence, she responded poorly—even with such a high level of natural talent.

In the weight room, I often had to limit the total volume of work as well as the load, to try to better manage the stressors I was placing on her, in conjunction with the overwhelming stressors from practice.

Needless to say, the coach and I didn't see eye to eye—me, with a focus on basics and proper development and the coach, on what the clock on the track was saying and what other athletes who ran similar times could do.

The coach was asking the athlete to perform at a level high and above her training age because she was capable of performances at the highest level. They didn't understand why I was having her work on "basic lifting" when she needed to do things "like Olympians do—not high schoolers."

I've often been told it's unsexy and not cool just to do the basics. But what I found through all my years of training, especially working with the most elite of the elite athletes, is that the key to their success is a foundation built on being able to do the basics—repeatedly, without fail, under any conditions, and with savage intensity and focus (yes, I stole that from someone and bastardized it as my own, so credit to whoever said the general concept of that originally).

This sprinter did not have a well-developed foundation for her training age, and the training demand placed upon her was crushing and ultimately ruined her potential professional career.

Exposure Stress

In addition to training age, experience is the collection of exposure stresses placed upon the athlete.

Every single thing that you have ever done to develop your physical ability, good and bad, accumulate over time to build the level of exposure stress you have.

Acute changes, either positive or negative, cause adjustments to outcomes/outputs. The key is understanding how the exposure stresses of every day before today created, built, diminished, and prepared your body —and most importantly your mind—for what you will do today (and how that matters for tomorrow and down the road).

This is especially important when we get into how form fits function as it relates to building long-term adaptation. Because what you're exposed to in the short-term and long-term develops your ability and maximizes your potential or limits your ability and stifles you from reaching your potential.

Every exposure creates an adaptation—and that's just it, it's only an adaptation—neither good or bad. It's simply the manner in which the system created change based upon the stressors placed on it.

A bad adaptation is simply one that inhibits you from being able to output the desired outcome, which is based upon the perception of desiring a certain outcome originally. A bad adaptation for you might be a good adaptation for someone else.

However, negative exposure stress, often called maladaptation, is a different animal. Negative exposure stresses create maladaptations that can damage the system permanently and can limit or totally remove the functional capability of the system (either physical or mental).

Injuries, for example, are maladaptations from negative exposure stresses that must be accounted for and modulated against in future training to achieve desired outputs (if still possible).

Using the sprinter I previously talked about as an example—her training age was low from the standpoint of development and the length of her time training, but her performance level was high.

Because her ability was high, the demand that was placed upon her was high. And her potential was even higher, so she possibly could've gone on to be one of the top athletes in the US if not the world, had she been given a chance to appropriately develop in the way she needed to.

But because her output of abilities didn't match the exposure stresses and development of her training age, she was hampered by chronic, negative exposure stresses across her system. Like most collegiate track and field athletes, she was over-trained, under-recovered and over-raced; and it destroyed her ability for a future career in track and field before she even had a chance to have one. Ultimately, her injuries took away her ability to have outcomes at a level that would allow for a career in track and field, and she never ran after college with any success.

Physiological Adaptation and Exposure Stress

One of the key factors people don't take into consideration when looking at longitudinal development, is that every exposure stress and every previous developmental adaptation or maladaptation affects the plasticity of the body to respond and develop moving forward.

It seems fairly obvious to say that depending on the history of and previous demand on an individual, their training demand should change —but that isn't always the case.

Often times we plug training methodologies into situations for individuals regardless of their history of exposure and relative plasticity; we try to force these paradigms to be "correct" based around the sport or the physical demand we believe to be placed upon the individual.

Instead of looking at the needed longitudinal development cycle, we focus on the acute program for progression and/or reconditioning aspects only in the moment.

It's a viewpoint of, *What specifically is going to be done today?* compared to, *How does what's done today matter for what has been done in all previous days and is going to be done or needs to be done in all future days to achieve the goals I have?*

One of the biggest examples of this is in American football where there have been numerous highly successful NFL players who no longer lift or train in the manner that is customary in the high school, college and even entry-level NFL manner due to a combination of skill, experience, and injury.

They have had to adjust their training to be both individually specific to their own demands as well as globally specific to the demands placed on them in the sport.

There's a specific example of a quarterback who, after having multiple shoulder surgeries due to injury, was told he would never achieve the same level of performance he had been at. He used what many in the football world at the time considered "fluffy training"—using a body weight based training system as a means to rehabilitate and develop himself. He has gone on to not only thrive but become one of the all-time elite quarterbacks in the NFL and you'd be hard pressed to go into most any sport performance gym, rehab clinic, and even Globo Gym in the country and not see the tool he used hanging somewhere.

In terms of not understanding this concept, I can think of a no more obvious example than a college football coach taking an NFL job a few years ago. The coach made his team run a college-type conditioning test (that became a reported story on major sports outlets for the rift it was causing).

The problem there was obvious. Everyone on the team already played college football and experienced some sort of training exposure similar to it —regardless if their college S&C coach/training program was competent or not.

They had already been selected beyond that level of training and had no reason to accumulate significantly more "wear on the tires" doing it again. Regardless what the conditioning test was and if it was sport relative to their training demands (it was not) or a cultural differentiator (it was supposed to be), it lacked awareness of the population's situational context at the time.

This is exactly the same fundamental problem that happened in the military sector when human performance programs were first started there (I'm looking at you THOR3).

People perceived to be competent in their jobs (pro experience, long careers, and lots of certifications) were hired. Ego and lack of context to situational factors had allowed military professionals to hire them.

These "experts" (some with no actual understanding of the profession, just résumés with noteworthy logos) tried to tell highly specialized, rigorously selected military professionals that how they trained was wrong.

Regardless of how "textbook" or not the training was, you don't get through advanced military selection for the Navy SEALs, Green Berets and other more advanced units without doing something right in your training. Going in that space and telling those guys what they had done to get there wasn't right, good enough, or anything similar set the entire human performance movement back a solid decade.

Sure, the underlying theory behind THOR3 and other similar programs, of prolonging operational longevity through enhanced training methods and performance monitoring, made a ton of sense and should have created a significant return on the government's investment in those individuals. It has taken nearly a decade, mainly from private training entities outside of the actual government-funded programs, to make performance training "cool" for those looking to get into that type of work. It has only been recently that many of the contractors in those roles are actually qualified and competent to help that population.

Quantitative System Measures

Here we look at the two most important system-wide measures for enhancing performance, nutrition, and recovery.

To play devil's advocate, nutrition could be placed within recovery because the utilization of substrate via nutrition is in fact a recovery process. I differentiate the two on the grounds that nutrition has to both fuel output in the daily micro sense as well as fuel the system in all functions and adaptations in the macro sense.

Nutrition

Nutrition is the most adjustable, trackable, and easy to manipulate aspect of individual performance. You have to eat for both recovery and to fuel performance. And it's often the most undervalued aspect because most view it to have nothing to do with the efforts exerted in a physical sense (technically speaking).

Obviously, the athlete has to apply effort to gather, prepare and then eat food. But universally speaking which is the key perspective of this paradigm, it's fully controllable, can be adjusted in large and small scales across any time frame, and can be analyzed in micro and macro to understand what the needs and variance are for any given individual.

The boom of "sports nutrition" to both "keep up with the Joneses" and provide a valuable resource has dramatically improved the emphasis on nutrition, especially in the athletic sector in the last 8–10 years. Yet, it still amazes me when major programs, collegiate or professional, have a part-time person in this role and give them little to no resources. It's literally the lowest hanging fruit (pun intended) to enhance performance.

It's outside the scope of this book to discuss nutritionists versus dietitians and all the additional hoopla related to having a "performance-nutrition" mindset versus using recommended daily/dietary allowances (RDAs). But let it be known the difference exists. Just like S&C and sports medicine, there are *a lot* of frauds in the sport nutrition world. And in a sense, it's even worse than S&C is (that is freaking scary to read now that I wrote it but it's the truth).

You need to be looking at what nutritional needs the person has and what variation (i.e. short-term, long-term, lifestyle) does to the optimization of performance? Those are the essential questions that must be asked.

Since this is something you can quantify, especially now with a lot of new nutrition tracking, monitoring technology, and knowledge out there (including clinical testing like bloodwork—an often-overlooked aspect of dialing in nutrition and one I consider mandatory if you are doing it for real).

It's not about any specific methodology, food, supplement or approach, as again that's beyond the scope of this book.

Rather, it's the undertaking of relevant and purposeful incorporation of nutrition strategies: to optimally fuel the system, to meet the training demands placed upon it, and to best maximize outputs to drive outcomes.

Recovery

Recovery (currently bastardized as a pre/post-workout activity) encompasses the general concept of the body's restorative, repair processes when faced with stress; the means to return the body to optimal functionality given the exposure stress that created the need for adaptation.

Along with nutrition, sleep is the other most important—if not the most important—of all factors related to developing and driving performance.

Looking at sleep patterns in an acute sense, the rate of repair to light exposure stresses, napping, circadian rhythm, etc., all matter. While they can be difficult to gauge, a methodology for quantitative measure must be had (and can be had). It's a question of what system you believe best does so because there are a few.

Heart rate variability (HRV), for example, is great but it doesn't give you the ability to predict your soulmate. So, be careful of companies that solely use heart-rate-related data to tell you everything about your recovery. There are even elements beyond just the physical that play into recovery, some of which cannot be tracked or calculated. And not to get too "woo-woo" on you but the mind can do things to the body we do not fully understand just the same as "matters of the heart" can. If you aren't at least considering those as variables that influence things, I've got nothing for you (pretend I put three large emoji-shrug symbols here).

In the macro sense, recovery is also time off or periods of limited stress and minimalized exposure. What is the recovery as it relates to periodization training, from the micro cycle to the macro cycle to the long-term athlete development (LTAD) model for training age development?

What are you doing daily, weekly, monthly and yearly to address the need to recover from the daily, weekly, monthly, and yearly exposure stress you are placed under?

Obviously, there is also massive interplay here from the standpoint of mental and spiritual health. Psychological willingness and motivational drive are impacted as much physically as emotionally and spiritually. Time off and the ability to decompress in these areas is just as important in recovery as a good night of sleep.

Qualitative Interaction Measures

Don't get me wrong, there's a quantitative aspect to these areas now, depending on who/what you believe. We've come a long way in the last couple of years, and I'm sure that we will soon go even further in our ability to quantify these interactions. But the reason I keep them as qualitative—and this is where the art of coaching, self-belief, and the metaphysical comes in—is because this is the one area that acts as a chokepoint for the ability to maximize performance.

Sure, you can quantify all kinds of psychological traits and try to make a composite of people based on assessments of personality and personal history (and I agree with doing so). But how do you truly and objectively understand the depth to how every individual is different and include all of those variables into the training plan? I don't think a human truly can. Maybe one day a machine could with enough data, but no human could in my opinion.

It's what makes each person their own person. Nothing short of a unique paradigm for each individual person at a level unimaginable would be required; a paradigm encompassing literally everything they have ever done, felt, thought, and experienced all from their own perspective.

While how we grow and adapt physically is different from how we do so mentally, there are some similarities. That rabbit hole is one we won't jump down here, but let's just say that while we're closer than ever to understanding what makes people "tick" from an objective science-driven standpoint, we're further away than ever from allowing ourselves to accept certain things. Sometimes things will happen that just can't be explained or understood beyond the person who is living them. To me that is the beauty of the human condition.

Stress

What's the athlete's stress? How do you define stress?

What's their life-cycle stress? Or where are they biologically and chronologically in their physical maturation and in their development as an organism?

Where does their lifestyle stress come from?

What are they doing in their lifestyle that positively or negatively impacts their lifecycle stress?

How does that then interplay with their nutritional/recovery demands and change their psychological profile?

If you are not seeking answers to these questions, can you say you understand how your athlete is responding to the exposure stresses of training you are placing on them?

Far more things affect athletes than what they do in training and competition; to not attempt to incorporate them into their overall development is foolish.

You may train for four hours a day but there are still twenty more hours that matter.

Psychological Profile

The second qualitative interaction measure is the psychological profile. Yes, there are things you can do to measure this, many of which are well beyond the scope of this book and the scope of practice of many readers.

It's highly recommended to use a professional in this area to best design, implement, and assess this part of the PPE paradigm.

There are ways you can separate different groups of people based on personality types, cognitive development, and characteristics. An easy place to start is to learn the difference between mental toughness, resiliency, and hardiness.

Beyond that, there are general questions that should be asked.

Is the athlete emotionally stabile? Are they on medications for the function of their brain?

Are they able to manage the life-cycle and lifestyle stress associated with the different stages of their training age and exposure?

Are they able to manage the emotional stress of success and failure?

We've all met people who have had all the physical tools but just weren't motivated or were extremely motivated and didn't have all physical tools.

Helping better define what drives any individual and better understand their personal nature-nurture story is the emphasis here.

As mentioned, in my opinion, the picture will never be truly complete from an outside perspective. But the attention to it from the outside can help the athlete themselves understand the portrait being painted from the inside.

Quantitative Physical Measures

Last to be discussed, and what most people only look at—which I think is one of the major problems that limit development—are the quantitative physical measures.

I purposely put this after all the other parts of the PPE paradigm so you'd have to read about those things to get to *these* things. You need to have all that "other stuff" floating around in your head in order to understand how best to maximize this stuff.

Movement

When looking at physical measures, you first have to look at an athlete's movement skills: kinesthetic awareness and control, proprioceptive ability, and neuromuscular dexterity.

How you define movement is just as important as how you evaluate it. That is not something you hear often in this industry. So re-read it and think about it before moving on.

(Space to give you time and make you think . . .)

Does the athlete have the appropriate movement skills and abilities to perform the physical actions required?

Do they have enough range in motion in their joints and tissues or do they even need to have as much as they do? Is having too much actually a problem?

Can they control their body enough to output the fundamental movement skills they need to?

How do you test and monitor movement relative to what the demand is?

Are you considering how anthropometrics can limit movement as well as change movement so that it may be a requirement to change anthropometrics?

The key word here is "requirement." Contrary to what most of the gurus tell you, improving movement does not always guarantee an improvement in athletic output.

And here's one to kick around in your head for a while: sometimes being asymmetric is a positive developmental demand to achieve mastery in a specific output.

Symmetry has a place but asymmetry does as well.

Allowing asymmetry to exist without it compromising the entire system is the key. But even then, as discussed, if the goal is maximal performance, comprising the entire system for a single result is exactly what you are after.

Where Did the Forces Go?

There is also an interesting note to make here for people who like doing "correctives." Now before some of you climb up my ass about this, hear me out. I'm all for creating adaptations and "correctives" are simply forms of perceived, positive adaptions.

The question you have to ask yourself when you start down the path of trying to "correct" movement is, *Where are the forces going now*?

As soon as you deform, manipulate, fatigue, or otherwise affect a given area to create a change in another area, (regardless if it's neurological, musculoskeletal, biomechanical, etc.), the forces created and dissipated into and around that area also change.

If you do not know where the forces are going, you might be causing more injury risk than improvement. How much change and force an area can handle and how much change and force the new area has to take on to accommodate that change is something you should know or at the very least be considering.

Physics is physics: Power will always equal force times velocity ($P = F \times v$) and force will always equal mass times acceleration ($F = m \times a$).

Force will need to be generated, transferred, and dissipated for every physical action. Make sure you know where the force is going to go before you let it go somewhere it shouldn't, especially if it's at high velocities and the structures being used don't have the right development to handle the force at that speed.

Strength

Movement sets the stage to have the coordination and freedom to create action.

Once you have the ability to do the specific physical actions and outputs (moving your body and limbs in a coordinated functional manner) you have to be able to generate, control, and disperse the relative and absolute levels of force necessary for whatever you're trying to do.

It begs the question: what is strength and how much of it do you need?

Do you understand the difference between relative and absolute strength?

How does positional strength play into things for any given position you are in?

Where do you need to be relative to body mass and relative to internal force production for movement control versus external absolute force production, to generate force on outside objects, whether they are moving or static?

How are you determining and assessing strength beyond cross-sectional area of tissue and absolute weight being lifted?

Power

Power ($P = F \times v$) is a very interesting trait that people have bastardized recently with velocity-based training (yes, I know there are equations for strength—the whole point of not using them in the above section and making a point about having one for power down here is coming).

When you look at power, you have to ask yourself, *Am I trying to output something at a greater velocity* or *Am I trying to increase the force I'm generating at a given velocity*?

They are two different things that create different adaptations.

Often the rate-limiting factor of power (in the context of imposing force on an external object to accelerate it) isn't necessarily the force component as that can be easily modulated because it's an external load—it's the velocity part.

There is a spectrum of applying velocity on external objects: that which you can control and that which is truly ballistic (you have no control).

Controllable velocity is a concept that I think a lot of people lose sight of because, generally speaking, you *are* purposely trying to have some relative control over what you're doing.

Power thus becomes a question of at what velocity can you still control (mitigate or disperse safely) any given force output, while either trying to increase the overall velocity of the action or the force generated at the velocity you seek.

Maximal ballistic power or acceleration to a velocity beyond the ability to mitigate or disperse the created actions with control has a place. You just have to know when to train at that end of the velocity spectrum and take on the risks of not being in control at high velocities and high rates of force.

Endurance

From an endurance standpoint, this is kind of obvious if you're looking at energy system development and the ability to handle duration of activity from a cardiorespiratory and metabolic manner (task repeatability and duration).

One of my favorite things to throw out in this area is to ask people two questions (and if you don't instantly have an answer for both, you need to go learn bioenergetics and take a deep dive down into respiratory physiology):

1. When do you create lactate?
2. When are you truly only using the anaerobic energy systems?

The thing you have to remember, when we look at the fundamental continuum next, is that all of these things are interrelated.

When you look at qualitative physical measures, you have to understand that developing them—any one of them—affects all the others in different ways (based on underlying genetics, understood functions of the human systems and the unknown ones, as well as accumulated exposure).

You need all of them in different ways to improve the others but they also are self-limiting to the others if improved too much.

The fundamental continuum is an interesting concept and one that I had to personally grasp as a decathlete in my own training and then apply across all the athletes I ever worked with. Sometimes, to get better at something, you need to work on something that doesn't seem specific to the goal in order to get better at something that is specific to the goal. Let that float around in the brain for a bit. Does it sound familiar from somewhere else in here?

And without further ado, the answer to those two aforementioned questions:

1. You're always creating lactate. It's a natural part of the process of living. It's a question of can you buffer it or is the energy demand too high that you can't clear it fast enough in relation to the efficiency of your system and demand of the task you are undertaking.
2. You are only truly using anaerobic metabolism once you are in rigor mortis. Yes, you need to be dead; after you have died and all of the oxygen in your system has been used up and you are truly only turning over energy via the locally available substrate. After that gets used up, you go into rigor. So, if you're breathing, even minimally, say through one of those stupid altitude masks (shots fired, watch out), you're using some level of aerobic metabolism. It's simply a matter of whether it's efficient enough

to handle the task demand you're asking of it (duration and/or intensity) based on your current physiological state.

Performance Measures

What are you trying to look at relative to the person's performance? Is what you're looking at sport-specific or sport-relevant?

We've talked about measuring and testing movement, strength, power, and endurance relative to what you need to be successful in sport. But what are you looking at to consider if the individual is ready/competent to actually perform in their sport?

Why are general and specific measures needed? Are there positional differences or unique characteristics that one athlete needs and another doesn't? Or can all athletes be categorized within the same type of measurement strategy?

Are you trying to be sport-specific or sport-relevant in your performance measures?

Do you even know what the hell I 'm asking here? Should you even be evaluating a detailed level of sport-specific ability or should the sport coach be?

Sport-Specific or Sport-Relevant

Josh Bonhotal is the first person I heard explain this concept so he gets the credit.

Are you sport-specific? Do you develop a specific characteristic needed for the sport, like doing technically specific triple-jumping plyometrics?

Or are you sport-relevant? Do you help enhance the general properties it takes to be good at the sport, like using plyometrics to improve your reactive strength and better facilitate your ability to do the technically specific drills of triple jumping?

In both contexts, you're using plyos, but in the latter you're using them as a tool to do specific technically focused plyos that serve a different purpose given their technical nature.

I certainly could have used another example here, like one related to basketball regarding grip strength and holding a med ball with someone else trying to knock it out of your hands so during the games you can hold onto the ball better. But I wanted you to have to think about the triple jumping example a bit and mull over exactly what I'm referencing here.

The Physical Skill Mastery Model

I look at the pursuit of physical-skill mastery in four specific stages: the developmental stage that is prescribed by a coach; the limited experience stage that is also prescribed by a coach; the intermediate experience stage that is co-discussed and partly self-developed; and finally, the advanced stage that is self-developed and advised on.

You have to think of these stages—not as periods of training, or four lengths of time with start and end points—but instead, the athlete's placement among them as constantly in flux. Mastery "here" may not mean mastery over "there"; no athlete will ever achieve absolute mastery across all functional areas they need. It's just not possible.

It's a paradigm that, as one goes through it in their longitudinal development process in experiential sequence, helps give separation to the cognitive and physical requirements needed for advancement relative to the manner in which training is accomplished.

Developmental Stage (Prescribed)

In this first stage, the entire process is prescribed by a coach.

The initial exposure is of low demand to allow the athlete the ability to progress to a kinesthetic strengthening and self-learning process. This helps the athlete to internalize and refine, through the low demand exposure, the ability to execute the task.

From there a second exposure or high demand is imposed where there is some level of competitive external stress placed upon the athlete, relative to the first exposure, making it more challenging and taxing and allowing for weaknesses and limitations to come to the surface.

This is most easily conceptualized in the idea of a youth athlete first being exposed to a sport by a coach and having a majority of their exposure be low-demand, practice/skill development through the basic kinesthetic strengthening and self-learning processes of simply participating.

There's a learning effect in the overall sense.

From this low-demand exposure, the athlete is then able to face a second, higher exposure such as a scrimmage in order to "test" their readiness.

These first three blocks allow the proprioceptive strengthening of self-awareness for the athlete to determine if they have the physical ability and the cognitive willingness to develop and reach the third exposure, to develop proficiency in the tasks, and to do whatever it is they're trying to do with a baseline level of competence.

Often people cycle through this stage multiple times to manage and develop the technical/tactical demands required as they advance in skill and competitive level.

Imagine the difference between learning how to play soccer without previous experience starting at five years old compared to being a sixteen-year-old.

Each cycle allows for the exposures to be of greater intensity and duration externally to build an experiential model to self-learn and create self-awareness internally.

Limited Experience Stage (Prescribed)

After cycling out of the developmental stage, the athlete enters into the limited experience stage.

Their experiences are limited, relative to the number of times they have gone through the developmental cycle and there being no predetermined number that it must be gone through in order to make it to this stage.

At this point, the training process is still prescribed by an external individual because the person going through the process doesn't yet have the level of mastery of self to technically and tactically self-direct (although they may be starting to have insight into that being an option).

This stage starts out with a general level of strengthening—that's an additional exposure—to facilitate kinesthetic strengthening or help refine the self-learning methodology employed. It also removes bad habits or maladaptation that previously occurred.

Due to having an underlying level of experience—limited, task-specific exposure stresses of high demand are needed to facilitate the proprioceptive strengthening and refining of self-awareness.

This allows for combined strengthening of additional efficiency at a high level to optimize output relative to the specific tasks imposed.

Intermediate Experience Stage
(Co-Discussed and Partly Self-Developed)

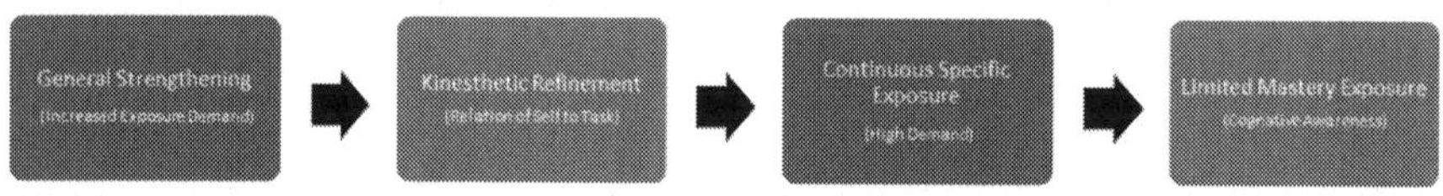

If athletes develop too great a dependence on the external guidance of a coach, they risk becoming stuck in the limited experience stage almost indefinitely.

This greatly hinders their ability to improve because they do not have the insight to their own internal influence on the mastery of task demands.

Shifts into the intermediate experience stage correspond with co-discussed and self-developed insights to development outside of just the external insights (generally from a coach) due to the internalization of self to the task.

It's at this point a coach can also hold development back by not being able to let the athlete self-direct. Generally speaking, if the coach the athlete has worked with up to this point doesn't have the capacity themselves to facilitate growth in this stage, the dynamic between the two breaks down and leads the athlete to find a new coaches (who may or may not actually have the skillset needed for the athlete to self-develop).

General strengthening in this stage is at its highest level, leading to optimized effort for anything outside of specific exposure demands. Given the history of training up to this point, many fundamental, developed characteristics are normalized into the system and no longer require intensive development. These qualities can simply be "touched on" to keep them at the required state of ability while the specific exposure demands reach their apex.

These specific exposures can enhance and develop the highest levels of physical output and technical/tactical refinement by creating limited mastery exposures and realizing true cognitive awareness during the outputs.

Advanced Experience Stage (Self-Directed and Advised On)

The final stage is a self-directed level of development that is merely advised on and not dictated by external entities (notice the plural).

This leads to the mastery loop where there is only the need for refinement and strengthening, adjusted by whether the general or specific exposures are needed to facilitate the refinement of whatever skill or ability is needed to achieve the outcome goal.

14

TRAINING PRINCIPLES

WHILE THIS SECTION MAY SEEM REDUNDANT AFTER HAVING JUST GONE OVER training philosophy, my goal here is to specifically give context to some of the basic principles of training that are often overlooked, misunderstood, and / or misapplied (at least from my perspective).

If You Don't Know the Basics, I Can't Help You

If you don't know the basics of exercise science (size principle, specific adaptation to imposed demands (SAID) principle, law of diminishing returns, etc.) this section isn't for you. There are basics of chemistry, physics, and biology that you need to have a grasp of long before much of this will be helpful.

Take time to relearn the basics, reinvestigate areas you aren't strong in, and constantly challenge your own "why." Don't be held back by the dogmas you learned in certain areas by certain people who were strong or weak in said areas.

Everyone who peddles certifications promotes their method as superior to others. Understand what is objectively fundamental and what is subjectively perceptible: heavy is relative and hard is a perception. Everything works and nothing works.

The Four Days You Can Have Training

I always liked this idea. I have no idea where I came up with it or if I stole parts of it from someone else over time (which I'm sure I did to some degree).

When it comes to outputting effort and work, there are only four types of days you can have.

The trick is recognizing what kind of day you are having: knowing when it's really the second day, knowing when it's time to stop having the first day over and over again, and knowing to have a fourth day because everything is easy when it's the third day (but those don't come that often).

The fourth day, however, is when you separate yourself from everyone else. Although, if you have too many of these days over and over you risk a similar issue to having too many second days. Stew on that for a moment.

The first day is the one where you fight for it and may or may not find it. Those are the grind it out kind of days; the days when you're just putting in work and effort and you're just constantly slogging through the mud per se—and it either clicks or it doesn't—but either way, you got after it.

The second day is when you don't have it and you shouldn't look for it. These days, while rare, do happen. These are the days you need to pump the brakes and stop. Recover. Take a break, relax, and catch your breath. Go home, detach and wait for tomorrow.

The third day and the one people chase—sometimes to their detriment—are the days where you have it and nothing and no one can stop you. It's being in the zone—your flow state: where everything just goes right, where you can't miss, and with everything you do you have the Midas touch. These days are fleeting and are never guaranteed.

The fourth day—the truly most important kind of day—is the day where you don't have it, but you need to fight to find it, and cannot stop until you do. These are the "looking off the cliff days" if you will. How far are you willing to stand at the precipice of the cliff and lean forward? How far are you willing to look out and dangle yourself off the ledge? How close to that line of catastrophe are you willing to go? If you're not willing to risk total failure, how are you ever going to know what you're capable of? If you cannot push yourself to that point, you'll never actually know and you'll never be able to be as good as you could be.

Training Strategies

Some of the best training strategies are the simplest.

I don't who said it so please give the appropriate credit to that person. But I unequivocally believe in the idea that being exceptionally focused on and savagely attacking the basics will do far better for your development than any complex or over-technical program could. Especially if you're using S&C as a mechanism for improving your ability to compete in a sport.

The end goal is success in the sport competition you partake in. Thus, training in whatever form or with whatever methodology you use or have is just a means to that end.

If training isn't positively impacting your ability to achieve better results in competition, then you are just training for training sake.

The Most Advanced Training

I always get asked what I think the most advanced training is.

We could certainly debate the merits of any methodology and philosophically dissect what works and doesn't given whatever context and situational factors we could conceive of being in.

However, I would argue there is no "most advanced" training strategy.

The entire process of training, for any given individual at any given moment, is relative not absolute. Thus, the most advanced training someone can do is anything that forces them to create an adaptive response to the imposed demand, and accumulate exposure stresses in a way they never previously have before. Thus, changing their system in a way it's never been orientated before is the most "advanced" training it has ever undertaken.

Relative Intensity

I'm going to preface this section by saying I've spent my entire career, from when I was an intern to now, as a has-been thinking about this concept.

I literally wrote papers on it in school and studied hundreds of hours—learning, reading, and discussing—about how people applied the concept of relative intensity in their training of athletes. This chart is the culmination of that work.

Let it wow you with all its glory! (Was that sarcasm I smell?)

Staub - % Based Relative Intensity

	# of REP Percentage	1	2	3	4	5	6	8	10
		100.0%	95.0%	92.5%	90.0%	87.5%	85.0%	80.0%	75.0%
Maximal Effort	100.0%	100%	95%	93%	90%	88%	85%	80%	75%
Maximal Effort	97.5%	98%	93%	90%	88%	85%	83%	78%	73%
Heavy	95.0%	95%	90%	88%	86%	83%	81%	76%	71%
Heavy	92.5%	93%	88%	86%	83%	81%	79%	74%	69%
Medium Heavy	90.0%	89%	86%	83%	81%	79%	77%	72%	68%
Medium Heavy	87.5%	88%	83%	81%	79%	77%	74%	70%	66%
Medium	85.0%	85%	81%	79%	77%	74%	72%	68%	64%
Medium	82.5%	83%	78%	76%	74%	72%	70%	66%	62%
Medium	80.0%	80%	76%	74%	72%	70%	68%	64%	60%
Light	77.5%	77%	74%	72%	70%	68%	66%	62%	58%
Light	75.0%	75%	71%	69%	68%	66%	64%	60%	56%
Light	72.5%	73%	69%	67%	65%	63%	62%	58%	54%
Very Light	70.0%	70%	67%	65%	63%	61%	60%	56%	53%
Very Light	67.5%	68%	64%	62%	61%	59%	57%	54%	51%
Very Light	65.0%	65%	62%	60%	59%	57%	55%	52%	49%
Recovery	60.0%	60%	57%	56%	54%	53%	51%	48%	45%
Recovery	55.0%	55%	52%	51%	50%	48%	47%	44%	41%
Recovery	50.0%	50%	48%	46%	45%	44%	43%	40%	38%

RX	% Ab Max	Sets per	Reps p Set	Total Reps
Recovery	20-50	1-3	6-12	20-35
Moderate VOL	30-55	2-4	8-12	30-45
High VOL	30-65	3-6	8-12	40-65
Extreme VOL	50-70	5-8	8-12	60-90
Speed STR (V)	35-60	2-6	1-3	5-20
STR Speed (F)	80-90	2-5	1-3	5-15
PWR Endurance	40-65	2-6	4-8	20-35
Peak STR	90+	2-5	1-4	2-10
STR PWR	65-85	3-5	1-5	10-20
General STR	65-85	3-6	3-8	20-35
STR Endurance	50-75	3-6	5-10	25-40
Advanced STR	65-90	3-10	1-8	30-45

FIRST NOTE—This does not work for Olympic lifters. It works for Olympic lifting bastardization as a training methodology for athletes in other sports. If you're an Olympic lifter, you need a different chart, one that I never completed because I never worked with that population with enough depth to finish it. In the US right now, I'd go talk to Travis Mash if you want to know more about Olympic lifts for competing in weightlifting.

SECOND NOTE—I do not include velocity or tempo as a prescriptive factor because I don't see them that way. I view them as objective evaluative metrics of proper training focus, not the specific metric of focus (more on this later and something for a much larger discussion outside of this book).

THIRD NOTE—If you were looking for an in-depth discussion explaining the whole thing, you won't find it here. It would take way too long to type, so don't email me either. Just call me and we can talk about it. Seriously.

The Fundamental Continuum

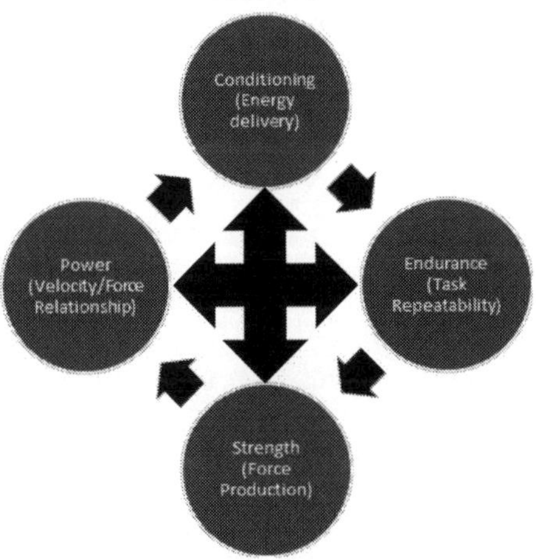

This concept came about from a conversation I had in the office one day during a chalk talk. Mind you, this is nothing new—just a way of putting things into context. We basically discussed how general conditioning or general physical preparedness (GPP) is the basis of having the appropriate energy delivery mechanisms within the body to layer on endurance, strength or power—and how you need a baseline level of any one aspect to do any of the others.

The concept is as follows: you have to have the basic level of conditioning or energy delivery to then be able to go do any type of endurance or task repeatability.

That task repeatability is what allows you to build strength or to produce higher levels of force by being able to output the effort with enough frequency to build cross-sectional area and neurological adaptation under the imposed demand.

Strength, in turn, allows you to generate greater levels of power by modulating how you approach generating power via the velocity-force relationship.

In this context, conditioning is the combination of the energy systems of the body being able to appropriately deliver the required kind of "power" needed.

It's not the person themselves who's considered "conditioned"; it's the pathways and processes of the body for the given demand that are.

Therefore, endurance is not a function of an activity's length of time but of the energy demand imposed by task repeatability.

This repeatability allows for the repetition necessary to learn (in many contexts) to develop strength in whatever context you need. By being able to generate more force, you can then manage the power output or the rate of force development in the force/velocity relationship to maximize the output at any given velocity or load.

This is a circular but also an integrated continuum because no one facet is capable of being achieved without relying on the development of another to some degree.

This may seem counterintuitive at first, mainly because of ingrained, semantic dogma and the shift of how to operationally define terms. But think of it this way—if you want to build the force-velocity relationship, you have to have the endurance to manage the training, task repeatability to develop the requested skills, and the strength needed to create, control, and dissipate the needed forces at the required velocities.

SIDE NOTE—You also see this dogmatic problem when discussing which muscles are used to do movements. It's the argument of teaching an isolated, mechanical, concept model compared to a holistic, integrated-system theory model.

Let's go back to track and field; it's the basis of all physical development and at its highest level is generally ten years ahead in training methodology than everyone else (partly why track coaches create so many of their own problems).

If you're a shot-putter, the "endurance" for task repeatability might be managing a long duration break between throws because that's the nature of your sport.

You throw. You wait a lot. You throw. You wait a lot. You throw. You wait even longer. And then, if you make the finals you throw, wait, throw, wait, throw, and wait. Now, if you're the first thrower out of three flights and make the final, you could have hours between your first three throws and your last three throws. Or if you're in a major competition, you could have a day or more between qualifying rounds and the final rounds. You must develop the appropriate endurance to have the correct task repeatability relative to the way you need to generate power.

Doing a lot of high-intensity circuits or taking dozens of throws in a small-time window—as task repeatability drills to develop power in throwing shot put—is a waste of time. You're not "building a base"; you're training the body to do the wrong thing in all four aspects of the continuum.

A shot-put competition might last three hours, depending on how many people are in it. Any individual will maximally take six, sub-two-second throws. However, most shot-put training sessions are 60–90 minutes and in that time, you throw maybe 3–5 times as many throws as you would in a competition.

Your endurance for task repeatability doesn't align with the rate of force development you need for power relative to the task. If you're fatiguing from the volume of throws and not able to generate maximal power with each throw, you're reinforcing sub-optimal throws as correct and helping the body get better at something it doesn't need to be good at.

You're better off managing and timing your power outputs relative to the task repeatability and endurance you need given the specific nature of the task, which in this case will be throwing shot put in competition with long breaks.

Don't get me wrong, training will never be a perfect 1–1 ratio with competition; it's not realistic and there are times when you need to have a higher density of work in training than you do in competition for any given period. The idea of the maximum effective dose (MED) at times being supramaximal.

The key is understanding when you need to mimic the demands of competition to fine-tune the body accordingly and when you need to increase the density of training to achieve a desired adaptation.

If you're struggling to understand this concept, sit with a stopwatch and time how things evolve in your competition. Use a wearable device to track whatever variables are relevant. Understand the demand and understand how and why your training reflects improvement to handle that demand. Because if it doesn't, your training might be pointless.

Remember, conditioning is relative to power output both ways: up and down. Strength is relative to endurance. Strength is relative to conditioning. You need these things all in a cross-integrated, circular continuum to manage and develop each other. And while each can enhance each other, they can always take away from each other too if focused beyond a needed level.

That isn't something that a lot of people learn, unfortunately, and that's kind of sad. So much wasted training time and so many underachieving results. To quote a good friend, "Don't tell me you did a hypertrophy cycle and no one physically got bigger or changed body comp."

Standard Model

Now, here's the fun part of the book. Things start to interrelate and build on each other in coherent and structured ways—sort of.

To create a training plan, you first need to have a standard model for everything you do.

Anything you consider important should have its own standard model. This standard model will act as a baseline and point of reference for what should be happening: to understand any deviations that are happening; to create uniformity across whatever it is you're looking at; and to accurately assess change in.

Whatever you set as the standard model should be the framework in which you base all deviations off. So, whatever your standard model is for whatever movement—drill, action, or outcome—that must then be the baseline you always adjust from. It can change however you want initially but once it's set it must stay set for the duration of the training cycle. You cannot flip-flop your standard models. It's that whole proper foundation thing and not building on sinkholes.

For example, let's consider what I view as the standard model of a squat: standing erect, feet shoulder-width apart, and toes slightly turned a few degrees off-center; as the descent of the movement happens, the body remains symmetric in its movement across all joints and in all planes as it passes through the actions of movement; the torso and head maintain an erect position relative to the axis of rotation, while the hip-knee-ankle complex are active; and gross body position is in balance and under control at every moment in all parts during the entirety of movement.

Now, think about that. It has nothing to do with what kind of squat I did. Hell, I didn't even mention what the arms are doing because I'm not even worried about them. I'm looking at what should be happening in the standard sense of doing a "squat."

Ask yourself what a squat is. What should you see across any variation and why would that change depending on what the goal and type of squat you are doing? That is the basis of your standard model.

What if I want to squat for a powerlifting meet? In my standard model, it becomes a question of adjusting the standard model to maximize mechanical advantage because the goal is to lift the largest possible weight given the parameters of the federation for what an acceptable squat is. The International Powerlifting (IPF) standard model is not the same as the CrossFit standard model because they are for two different purposes.

Thus, you must be careful not to fall into the dogmas of others' perceived standard model based on their specific context. Create your own from the largest most global point you can and not a specific version. And then, adjust off that standard based on what you're trying to do. By managing and developing your standard model, you can then baseline and adjust everything relative to it because you always know what you originally started with.

Form Fits Function

Taking the standard model idea one step further, you must remember that form fits function. To maximize function for performance, training should incorporate the exercises and movements that develop the whole system as well as specific parts. What an exercise and movement does and develops is relative to how it's performed.

A squat is not for strength, it's not for power, and it's not for mobility. It's for all those things and other "things" depending on how you go about doing it and why.

How you do things is the ultimate reason for their outputs and thus, the adaptations they cause (both good and bad).

Certain movements, exercises, and activities only do what they're relatively performed to do; everything can be anything. To partially quote Bruce Lee, ". . . be like water."

Additionally, movement found in sport rarely, if ever, contains movement in a single plane or in a single joint in isolation. There are very few actions across all sports that are truly in isolation. Most components work synergistically. Additionally, even if the movement seems to be in isolation, the system at large is still working synergistically to allow that isolation to happen.

At no point in time is only one single muscle doing one single thing to create an outcome. There's always some type of action, synergy, inhibition, agonist, and antagonist across the system, relative to some type of change in the length-tension of tissue, due to the activation of the nervous system and the biochemical and psychological induced changes caused by the process of "doing."

To really throw you for a tangent, ask yourself what role connective tissue and non-contractile protein structures have to do with how you adapt to training as well as their "trainability"? Stiffness, pliability, and rigidity are words currently used by many but few actually understand what they actually are referencing or how to measure/train those qualities.

Or how an issue in any part of the body relative to the specific bodies arthrokinematics can cause up and downstream problems related or unrelated to the issue. How can inefficient arm cadence in distance runners cause hamstring problems? Pretty freaking easily if you're reinforcing something over millions of steps that's creating the improper creation, mitigation, and dispersion of force across your specific system and causing alterations to the length tension relationship of tissues and thus structures.

If you feel like chasing the white rabbit: what impact does the mind have on the physical? Ever hear of the "yips"? What about rate of perceived exertion (RPE)? How can a subjective scalar perception marker influence training plan creation from both the coach side and the athlete side when used as the boundaries for objective markers of development?

Testing and Tracking

Now, comes the *evaluative* mechanism. By assessing throughout the training cycle, there's a greater level of ability to individualize by considering specific needs and changes of the athlete—while they are adapting—not after they have adapted.

Think about playing "connect the dots." Imagine the dots (your training plan to achieve your goals) makes a trophy (the goal). If you have four dots that makeup the trophy, sure it might resemble a trophy in a macro sense but it doesn't come into being until most all of the dots are connected. Now on the other hand, imagine the exact same size trophy with three hundred sixty-five dots. With that much more detail and refinement it's easier to understand what you are making and exactly where you are in the process of making it.

Of course, there is coaching paralysis by over-testing (the five hundred thousand dot trophy) and under-testing (the five-dot trophy) as well as the issue of using the wrong assessment tool / test. Additionally, you must look at what your general tests are and why and how they're different than others.

For the specific things or culturally traditional things—such as the beep test in soccer or the forty-yard dash in football—you need to use as an *evaluative* mechanism. Think back to the context in which I talked about golfers running the mile; globally irrelevant but extremely important in the specific context.

What is the validity of what you're doing in both context and construct validity? Do you truly know what the technology you're using is telling you? Do you have the time to break down the data after you collect it to make valid and purposeful adjustments or are you collecting data to collect it without the know-how or ability to apply it? Is the person who has the data and understands it not the person who makes decisions on training? If that is the case, how does the person who makes the decisions get the data shown and explained to them?

From a short-term and long-term development standpoint, much like what we talked about in the athlete enhancement paradigm, individual performance is a combination of a multitude of factors. Different training methodologies must be used over the course of an athlete's total career development to improve total physical ability as well as drive development.

Notice how I said total career—not college career, or professional career —*total* career.

Not all senior athletes are at senior-level training, while some new athletes are way beyond entry-level training. It goes back to the example of the sprinter and the mastery model I discussed previously.

The key issues here are coaches who do the wrong tests or try to get too specific and are not relevant in testing.

Coaches will do every test in the book. And initially, they analyze too many things and become either paralyzed by their analysis or blinded by what they're trying to achieve by tracking things that they think are valuable. Both are massive fallacies of the sports-performance, athletic-enhancement, human-performance paradigm, or whatever you want to call it. It's only useful if you use it. It's only applicable if it is repeatable, reliable, and measured consistently.

Just like the discussion on budgeting, you need to have your core principles that are your foundation. You need to have innovations in the pipeline to help evolve, adjust, and enhance those core principles when it makes sense too. You also need R&D effort to safely take in, test, and look for other cutting-edge innovations to possibly integrate into the core.

Gut-Check Tests

The first type of test that is the most common and often most useless is the gut check. Well, I shouldn't say it's entirely useless because it does have a purpose. Using some type of evaluative mechanism—its purpose being a mental challenge as much as it's a physical one—helps create an exclusive environment.

As mentioned previously Branden Marcello wrote a great piece related to this specifically using the context of the one-off, Navy-SEAL-style training that has become popular in the athletic world in the last few years. Worth the read for sure.

These mentally demanding and physically exhausting types of tests, while not always providing any type of true physiologic, developmental-based, evaluative mechanism, do provide a very good mechanism to weed out those not ready, willing, or prepared.

Because in any competitive arena, as discussed previously with the nature of exclusive versus inclusive environments, it's critical to have people who are physically capable, mentally strong enough, and emotionally willing enough to put themselves through things that may seem unnecessary or useless in order to demand of themselves a level of output many others are unwilling to give.

I believe David Goggin's 40% rule best puts this concept into words. The question always is do you need that mindset? And the answer, like it is to most things, is it depends.

Now, while these gut checks often do create a certain level of camaraderie and a certain level of acute, focal-point shifting—critical to help build and develop the team setting and group dynamic—they are not single entity fixes for culture or for evaluation of physical development.

These acute focal points are specific points in time you can use to build and create a certain type of team chemistry and act as an anchor for those who experienced them together. They are just a piece to a larger pie and not the pie itself. Much more is required outside of these moments on the journey.

General and Specific Tests

The second kind of testing is that which is relevant to the performance goals sought. This would be, for example, looking at acceleration and foot strike in a short sprinter: very easy relevant metrics to track over time to see progress, adaptation and how changes affect performance given the training imposed during the period of time looked at.

Most people, however, look at very standard general metrics and anthropometrics—body weight and body mass. And while these things are important, they also don't provide a full view of what's happening.

Just because you're leaner, it doesn't mean you're going to perform better.

I would argue that changes in strength to mass or power output to mass (whichever way you want to look at them) are significantly more important than changes in lean mass alone. Remember, nothing happens in isolation. No single marker will ever tell the whole story—stop trying to make it do so.

Developing human physical potential is the most advanced form of multivariate calculus you can try to do. Yes, there are ways to simplify it but it will never be single-variable algebra. When you look at it, you need to have a baseline level of assessment to build the general athletic profile.

What is the general athletic profile?

That general athletic profile consists of basic morphology and anthropometrics: height, weight, lean body mass, as well as basic gross physical output measures. These measures are physiologically dependent not sports specific. You're looking at the three levels of energy system development and you're looking at the ability to produce force, the rate of force production, and the task repeatability of force production.

So, what do I mean by gross output?

Since we're looking at generalizing big-picture, nonspecific baselines of ability, I'm more concerned with very standard, simplified, repeatable tests of gross coordination and ability.

Much can be said, both positive and negative, in relation to the US military's physical performance process, but they do have one of the best general, gross-level fitness testing processes that helps standardize the evaluation of baseline physical fitness. The ability to do push-ups, sit-ups, and pull-ups are great measures of general strength, strength endurance, and relative strength to body mass in the upper extremity and torso. The ability to go on mid-distance to long runs is a measurement of endurance of the lower extremity and cardiovascular system. Clearly, there are changes happening and depending on what branch or selection process you're going through there are additional tests. I'm not ignoring those—I'm just saying from the entry into the service, baseline-level standard tests.

Once you have built this general athletic profile, it allows for comparative value over time to assess development trends, or in situations like pre-and-post-injury, a baseline of whether the athlete is ready to return to play in the macro.

Specific testing should only be undertaken once general competency and a baseline of ability has been achieved. The reason for this is that the adaptation of skills, both neurological and physiological, need to develop and testing them too early makes their results worthless due to improvement strictly from the learning effect of doing the activity or a high-level state change (such as losing 20 lbs. due to being out of shape before training commenced).

Far too often, people try and test high output, high threshold, high-velocity movements without having built the appropriate rigidities into the system. Nothing is worse than watching an athlete try to test with cleans, plyos, or high-level fitness tests when they lack the ability to do basic components of those tests at a moderate to advanced level, with or without resistance.

I've seen plenty of S&C coaches use all kinds of crazy conditioning tests or max lifts when their athletes couldn't run one mile under eight minutes or get into the appropriate positions correctly with their own bodyweight, much less with added resistance.

Bastardizing a Test

The beep test is a tremendous test when performed correctly. In far too many instances, especially in the soccer setting, coaches bastardize the test to make it easier for the athletes and it allows mistakes to be made: false starts, not having to go around the markers, or not truly touching the line before the beep.

Manipulating and corrupting a test defeats its purpose and loses the original intent to create some type of physiological evaluation. While this is true for any test you're looking to repeat, it's especially true for tests that have been validated as reliable determiners of some characteristic, like the Beep Test to VO2. When corrupted, it tells you nothing since there is no way to compare two tests. To try to take any insight from it is pointless.

You must also look at differences in surface, weather, footwear etc., when comparing tests. While this is obvious to most people, I always had to spend time educating sport coaches, athletic trainers, and athletes to the fact that just because we did *X* test doesn't mean we will get the same results if we do *X* test again under different conditions, regardless of how much we want to have the "overcome the external" mindset.

One of my personal favorite examples was a coach who wanted their athletes to run a mile for "fitness." In the fall, the athletes ran the test on a track, in running shoes, on a perfect weather day, and with adequate recovery beforehand. They had the previous day off and the day before was a very light and short-duration practice.

In the winter, the athletes ran the mile again—but indoors, in a cold, poorly heated gym, on a hardwood surface, and over a fifty-yard linear distance with hard 180-degree turns, not rounded corners. So, the athletes ran having to cut back and forth compared to running in an oval and, unsurprising to me, times were significantly slower compared to running on the track. But when adjusted, some kids did better. This was a revelation to the sport coach because they couldn't understand how or why having to turn made any difference at all. "A mile is a mile" after all and they couldn't believe me saying a slower time on the clock from test two to test one actually meant there was an improvement. If you could run a 6:44 with turns and had run a 6:35 on the track months before, that was a significant improvement!

Unnecessary Assessment Syndrome

Unnecessary assessment syndrome is a process in which sport and S&C coaches do unnecessary assessments to those they work with based on belief or dogma. They think the assessment will provide them with a competitive advantage when, in fact, all it does is waste time and provide no benefit.

This is often seen in coaches trying to replicate assessments that their sport's national program or a highly successful contemporary does, a historical team in their sport once did, or worst yet, something that they themselves specially created.

Testing in this manner either lacks the physiological context appropriate for the situation and level of ability (like doing a national team test with half walk-ons—yes it happens) and/or lacks a valid and purposeful evaluative mechanism to define some type of quantifiable metric for performance development (all three aforementioned situations).

Many tests, especially conditioning tests, given the "creativity" people can come up with making them, often fall into the "gut check" category.

You see this in the weight room with S&C coaches using all kinds of technology-based systems—sometimes even multiple ones at the same time—including clinical equipment like a metabolic cart. This often leads to doing a lot of data collection but not having the know-how or ability/time to disseminate that data and make actionable decisions from it. More on this problem elsewhere.

Even testing lifting, jumping, or numerous other non-conditioning aspects to physical ability can fall into the "gut check" category given a context were taking the time to test whatever it is you are testing serves no purpose other than seeing how hard an athlete can push themselves. Max strength testing isn't always purposeful given certain contexts and in most cases, poses more risk than benefit.

Like most things and for the however many times I've said it—it all depends. Context matters.

Do You Need the S&C Coach There?

When it comes to testing, especially from the sport coaches' side, this question always must be asked: does the S&C coach need to be there?

While there are points about liability and subject-matter expertise that can be raised here, the argument would be if it's something the sport coach wants as a part of sport practice, on a whim, or for something that has no valid context other than the sport coach wanting to do it, then they can do it at practice or on their own time.

Of course, there's some need to have situational context in this as it relates to *The Game of Thrones* element (politics) you need to work within. But overall, this question should be asked: Is this worth my time as an S&C coach to facilitate if it has no purpose to the higher training goals and outcomes sought by the athletes? You always, always, always have to ask, *why?*

15

BUILDING A TRAINING PLAN

AT THIS POINT, I'M GOING TO DIVE INTO BOTH THE SPECIFIC, TECHNICAL-BASED concepts of physical development in order to build training plans as well as the global philosophical approach to do so. It's here that I want to stop and make two important points.

First, I never had an original idea in all of the human performance/strength and conditioning things I've ever done.

I may have developed some original approaches and processes, but I can guarantee that everything I ever did to help someone get better had been done—in some way, at some point, and by someone else before I ever did. All I did was adapt things to fit my situation and the moment I was in with the people and constraints I had.

Don't ever fool yourself into thinking that you were the first to do something in a training plan. You are not and never will be. That time has passed—about forty years ago to be honest.

Second, you need to be upfront and tell (at regular intervals) the sport coach (and anyone else above you that is involved with those athletes) that you are there to help the athletes get better; that you want their athletes and program to be successful; and that the better the athletes are, the more effective they can be (in whatever role they have), and the better it looks for all of you.

Their job is contingent on their athlete's success (make them understand that) and while you may not always agree on how to go about things, you're never actively trying to make their athletes worse, get hurt, or otherwise not be successful.

Consider it the S&C coach version of the Hippocratic oath but you have to constantly say it out loud to make it tangible to those you work with.

There have been countless times, for whatever reason, when a sport coach and I weren't seeing eye to eye and I always made it a point to reference the above and establish that we were both trying to go in the same direction at the end of the day.

We could disagree on approach but the goal was always the same. It often helped soften things to a conversational nature and help maintain professionalism before things got out of hand from either party—which I was certainly guilty of on more than one occasion (yes, there were times where I acted like the perception I wanted to avoid.) I had a tendency to favor the sledgehammer for all-sized nails when I was not as experienced or well-versed as I find myself today. I'm not ashamed to admit it because I learned from it.

Head Coach Analysis

Much of what you're about to read is obvious and common sense but so often overlooked—it's scary.

As an S&C coach you must understand who you're working with and what they need, especially if you're a support staff member in the collegiate setting—or any setting for that matter.

You need few things first. What's the philosophy of the program in terms of S&C? What are the head coaches' beliefs? Why do they believe that? What experiences do they have that makes them believe that or have had to shape their beliefs relative to S&C like that?

Do they operate with the mentality of the S&C coach being someone who works with them or for them? (That one is massive.)

If you can find out who has been the previous S&C coach and what kind of things they have done, you will be a long way ahead of understanding some of the background information: both from an injury and development standpoint of athletes and the cultural development of the S&C department relative to the head coach's perceptions of what S&C is and what it does for their team. Is training people "like football players" a good thing or is it the Grand Canyon you will have to cross because that's all the perception is?

Here are the "second layer of the onion" questions to ask: What traditions and customs does the program have in S&C? What do they have that falls under "strength and conditioning" but are governed by the coaches? Do you as an S&C coach need to continue to do these things or is it better the coaches themselves take ownership of them?

These are important questions to answer because although some of the training traditions may not make the most sense from a scientific, evidence-based, training-development theory, they're important to the program and thus can be leveraged by you in relationship building. Yet again, the "game of thrones" comes into play.

For example, I once worked with a golf coach who was formerly in the army. He liked doing the mile-run test to assess the fitness of his guys.

Now, is the mile-run test relative to golf performance? I would say no (although I could argue it both ways). But his logic was that if the guys on his team as college-age males couldn't run under eight minutes for a mile, how could they be in enough physical shape to carry their bag (which they have to in college golf) on the final thirty-six-hole day of a multi-day tournament, without it affecting their swing and their ability to play the game? Especially if they were in an extreme weather environment or dealing with any other kind of external impediment (rough course, etc.).

Looking at it through that lens you can at least see the reasoning and logic from the coach's perspective. So, we ran the mile because it made sense from his point of view and it was an easy eight minutes of my time 2–3 times per year to do it.

The path of least resistance sometimes yields the greatest results.

I was able to get a general barometer on what kind of general fitness we had, the coach was happy, and I was able to use this common ground to develop one of the best S&C-coach relationships I ever had—to the point where I went to his house for holidays and I even watched his three kids for a few days when he and his wife went on a vacation. If he ever moved from coaching to be an administrator, I'd go to work for him in a heartbeat.

Understanding that some traditions and customs may be outside the bounds of the most optimal training but have a significant role in the beliefs of the head coach and culture of the team (and get others related to the program to see that you are there to help them), you have to ask more questions: What additional needs does the team have for S&C? How else can you help? Is it with something you can do? Something you can't do but needs to be done? Or something you should draw a boundary for?

For example, often in collegiate S&C, the collegiate S&C coach must wear the hat of a nutritionist. This is often a hat worn that is bastardized by the "know-it-all" S&C coaches and illegal relative to scope of practice. So, you must be very careful as to what you do and why you do it.

I once had a coach tell me that they knew another S&C coach in our conference who did a lot of nutrition-related things for their team. "The problem is," I said, "I'm not licensed to able to do that stuff and the laws in our state are different than the laws in her state as it relates to being able to store, prepare and give food products."

"I'm not educated, certified, and licensed to do it, and our state doesn't allow it, unless you are," I told him. While he didn't like that as an answer, I proposed a few possible solutions to the "nutrition issue." I showed the coach that I both wanted to and was willing to help but within the boundaries of what was allowable and feasible for our context. We couldn't just do what someone else did, for a variety of reasons, but we could do the best we could (which was in fact more than current) and tried to.

You must understand and be able to manage and answer these questions related to the needs of the program, while also maintaining professional and personal boundaries.

Often, a head coach is always in a "draw-in" manner as it relates to the resources and efforts of those around them. They want all of the extra resources and all of the extra things available to them and constantly try to draw in more and more, regardless of optimization, effectiveness, or purpose. In a sense, it's how people take advantage of a zero-based budgeting system: if you don't use it and/or can't justify it, you lose it; so you try to use every possible dime you can get your hands on and make everything seem critical.

You must draw a line in the sand and put things in the appropriate box to not let a coach become a black hole, sucking the life out of your ability to provide resource to their athletes. There must always be boundaries—different for every circumstance.

What level of service you can provide—outside of just training—is important to clearly define for both new superiors and subordinates to understand. It makes sure there isn't future conflict due to improper or misapplied demands relative to resources and time-effort-energy (TEE).

Head coaches are always going to want you to skirt the rules and "do more" You have to set the right precedent to make sure you don't end up doing something that could kill your career, or worse, have something someone can hold over your head moving forward (yes, that happens).

Head Coach Types

The first and most important aspect of training any athlete in S&C is that the sport coaches who oversee that athlete not only believes in S&C but believes in you as their S&C coach. There are four general types of sport coaches that you can run into:

1. Those that had great experiences in S&C and allow you to use your expertise at full operational capacity. They make you part of their staff, and they're the best to work for. They "get it."
2. Those who have not had great experience in S&C but over time will be open to you and your method when you get them to buy in, show them results, and build the relationship. They're the wounded children who need to learn to trust. They're tough to work with initially but with time and effort can become your greatest advocate.
3. Those who have had bad experiences and will never be open to you because they refuse to accept that anyone who is in your

role will ever be good again. They're so jaded that they're a lost cause and will simply be tough to deal with regardless of what you do. These ones you must keep at a distance: CYA with a lot of record-keeping, look to keep and maintain a position where you each will be able to tolerate each other, and do the best you can for the athletes.

4. Those who don't care what you know or how you can help. And regardless if you're competent or not they will just want to do things the way they want because they think that they know best. These are the ones so full of ego, they lack the perspective that someone may know more than them or that change can be positive. When you find these ones, *run*. Hell, when you find anyone like that in life, *run*.

The National Team Does It

One unfortunately common issue is dealing with situations where what needs to be done or attempted is so far beyond the level that the athletes are capable of that it's actually a detriment to their development.

Often in Olympic sports, you'll deal with sport coaches who want to do what their respective sport's national team or the "XYZ" team does. In this situation, you must both explain and educate the sport coach that the level of output needed has to be developed over a long period of time or the athletes have to have the innate abilities to even achieve those efforts and is far beyond the situation you're in (unless of course your group is actually at that level in which case it might actually be totally appropriate).

In one job, I dealt with one sport coach (specific word choices there) who was still so far beyond the physical ability of their athletes. Even years after being retired from national-level, competitive play, this sport coach was so physically developed and genetically gifted as an athlete that they could easily outperform and outmaneuver—tactically, technically, and physically—every athlete on their team (a few even being at all-American level themselves.) But they lacked the awareness to see how difficult what they were doing was for their athletes when they attempted it.

This coach couldn't wrap their mind around the discrepancy in talent and mindset between the athletes and themselves at a comparable time in their own lives. And unfortunately, it led to ineffective training, underperforming, and significant cultural issues—often revolving around the team's failure of being unable to do the USA national team's conditioning test for their respective sport.

Stand Your Ground, but with Purpose

One of the toughest things to deal with is when ego gets in the way and we make snap judgments or snap decisions based on something we don't have appropriate context for.

The easiest examples of this are situations where sport coaches or other S&C coaches ask for the opinions of outside individuals. And those individuals, who don't have the context of what's going on, make recommendations that—while making sense on the surface—only create more problems.

One of the starkest examples of this is when I first started a new job and met with a sport coach who had certain ideas of what they wanted done in the weight room.

I agreed with them and liked what they said. About a week later, I sent the plan I had come up with to the coach to talk about before implementing.

A couple of days later I met with the coach and they were mad. The conversation started with lots of questions: "Why do you have this? Why don't you have this? Why aren't you doing this?"

I answered, "Well, okay. Well, we are. We are doing it this way and this way."

Finally, within a couple of minutes of conversation, it came out that the coach had sent my program to another S&C coach: "They said you should be doing stuff with cable columns, cable chops, and all these other things."

"No. I agree." I said, "I 100% agree. I think that's a great idea."

Then I got asked "Well, why didn't you do it?"

I said, "Well, our weight room doesn't have cable columns."

I would have liked to have done another type of exercise selection and exercise progression than what I did, but I didn't have the equipment available. Cable columns, being a couple of thousand dollars each, were well beyond the means of the situation I was in.

The S&C coach the sport coach had called, while having the appropriate knowledge and having the best intentions, had the lack of context and situational awareness to know what was truly going on. All they had was a snapshot.

Had this sport coach said, *Hey, I really like how this other strength coach trains. I think that you should talk to them because they're really successful and I've worked with them and I like their approach.* That's one thing. They could've done that. Within a couple of seconds of conversing we could've said, *Oh, yeah. Hey, I would've loved it if you would have done this or this, but you know I don't have this. I don't have this. I'm doing it this way. I'm doing it that way.* I would imagine we both would've been on the same page and that would've made a lot of sense.

Support Your Position

When you're going to take a stand and deflect some of what is being thrown at you, the key is to have the facts behind you. Do away with your emotional considerations to the situation and build your case on hard objective evidence and from multiple sources if possible.

I had a friend who had recently taken a job for which he spent over an hour of his interview talking with the head sport coach about the conditioning test the team needed to pass. This group of athletes was not yet mature or physically developed enough to handle the load at that output and weren't ready to even put the effort in to train for the test, let alone pass the test.

Given he had just started in early July, needed to get them ready by preseason in September, and had the coach putting such an emphasis on the test, he understood his only way of showing progress was their success at the test. As mentioned, the athletes were immature physically and mentally, one of the ways my friend protected himself was by videotaping each conditioning session. Because instead of just having a number on paper for the conversation—so-and-so did well, so-and-so didn't do well—he had hard video evidence of who put forth the effort in conjunction with how the athletes did.

What was the body language? What was the intensity? Who was stepping up? Who was making mistakes? Who simply got tired and stopped, walking out of the session halfway through? (Shocker that person didn't pass the test . . .)

It became an objective evaluation metric of the physical outputs compared to an objective measurement with subjective feedback. By being able to not only show the coaches who was and who wasn't doing the right things physically, mentally, and from an output standpoint, he was also able to show progress in the actual numerical metrics from a physical output standpoint.

It shifted the paradigm on its head, allowed him to put context to the time it would take to get the results the coach wanted, and showed the character and maturity of the group in question.

Go to Practice and Train Yourself

It should now be obvious that you must ask yourself this question: how do we as human-performance professionals fit into the philosophy, traditions, and needs of the program and head coach—based on all the expertise, resources, and abilities we bring to the table as coaches?

Like I said, that's obvious. The second layer of the onion in this situation has the following questions. Have you ever lived the life of the athlete? Can you relate on some level to their sport and to their daily demands? Do you know the difference between their biological-life stress and their social-life stress?

I once had a type of team that I never worked with previously— crew. I had never rowed. I knew nothing about the sport. And I had no expertise. Now, I knew all about the training of the body, energy systems, biomechanics, blah, blah, blah.

But I had no idea what rowing was all about: the feel, the tension, the effort, and the fatigue; the context of being at a regatta all day / weekend; warming up in a parking lot or grass patch and rowing multiple times;

syncing my efforts with a boat; and creating a group-flow state in a way I never had.

We know that sport naturally selects people based on physical traits, but it also naturally selects people based on personality and mental traits. Physical skill aside, you need a certain mental makeup to wrestle, to swim, or to do archery at a competitive level. I'm not talking rec league or JV in high school; I'm talking trying to win and crush the competition at the highest levels of the respective sport.

To get better and to know enough to truly help my athletes, I needed to practice, I needed to learn, and I needed to have context. I rowed in the water and on the erg (rowing machine). I got absolutely crushed doing a 2K and repeat 500s. I did a sixty-minute row for distance and I went to the C.R.A.S.H.-B. World Indoor Rowing Championships to see the culture and dynamics in action. I also went to a few regattas to experience the logistical flow of the weekend as well as the timeline of events from the competitors' and coaches' point of view.

I picked up as much as I could by hanging around practice and listening to coaches and athletes talk rowing. I went to staff meetings just to get a better sense of how everything I knew could be implemented into the demands of what was being asked of me to better these athletes.

While you don't have to be a master at a sport to train it from a sport-performance standpoint, you sure as hell better have tried the sport yourself and worked on figuring out what it means to do it.

The first time I ever rowed a hard 2K on an erg, I was in relatively good physical conditioning, having just finished my career as a decathlete—you know, the supposed group of "best all-around athletes on the planet." But I didn't know what it meant to feel the last sixty meters of a 400-meter track for a time of around seven minutes.

As I rolled off the erg in near blackout, I realized that I needed to reevaluate everything. Because in that moment, with only the faintest idea and experience of what it took physically and mentally to competitively row and the mindset needed to do that daily, I needed to adjust the training plans.

Trying to wrap my head around the chronic acidosis rowing involved and the changes to the system that kind of training caused led me down a wild rabbit hole of learning and touched on a gamut of things: from wrestling (the most demanding energy-system sport similar to rowing there is) to looking at muscle slides— a mosaic of muscle fiber—that profile elite rowers exhibit.

No matter how much you learn, there are some things you can only understand by firsthand experience. That experience then guides future learning with more purpose and a higher degree of clarity.

Finite Resources

From a resources and ability standpoint, you must remember the resources you have are finite.

No one has unlimited resources as a person. No one has all the knowledge. No one has all the time.

No one has all the equipment to train with or the ability to manage and disseminate information. And even if they did, you can't use it all at once. There is always a trade-off somewhere, or as I have said in other parts of the book, there is always a cost.

Especially now in the technology-driven age we live in, coaches are being inundated to have to spend time analyzing metrics and performance/training data that isn't being used correctly or at all in decision making at the head-coach level.

They're spending all this time collecting, monitoring, and tracking—taking hours and hours to refine and create useful information of that data (or think they're creating useful information from it)—and it's not being used. So why spend your time and resources collecting it if decisions aren't being accurately made from them? And that is just in the context of technology related to training.

The same can be said for making all kinds of special accommodations: scheduling training or attending practice for no purpose other than standing there.

Your time is valuable; it's the most valuable thing a performance coach has. People who work outside of full-time roles at schools or teams bill people hourly for their services and expertise.

Do not waste your time on purposeless endeavors. Track your time, see where it lacks effectiveness, and reorganize your day. Maximize your time and you automatically improve your resource allocation and usage, thus, improving your impact on your athletes.

There will be further commentary on this idea throughout many aspects of this book but I will summate the overarching idea here: time is valuable, do not waste it on bullshit things or stupid people. Assign a dollar value to your time and calculate the amount of money you are spending, wasting, and saving throughout the week. If it doesn't make obvious sense from a business standpoint, you need to fix it.

Once spent, you can never get back your TEE.

Understand Who You Connect With

As a coach, knowing who and how you connect with people is critical.

I know that I connect better with female athletes and male coaches. Not to say I didn't enjoy working with male athletes and female coaches, but upon reflection on the whole of my career, I realized it was easier and quicker for me to get the women's teams I worked with to buy-in and the same for male coaches. The only exception to this being the military/tactical-based individuals I worked with, although I will say I have only ever worked with males in that space.

Understanding your own ability—how you connect and how you relate and what does and doesn't work for you—allows you to best fit to who you work with.

There's a reason I never tried to chase football as an S&C coach, just like there was a reason I always wanted to work with more than one team and never wanted to work for a head coach directly. While all those opportunities presented themselves during my career, I knew how I operated and what made the most sense for me, so I actively chose not to pursue them. And it allowed me to best maximize myself as a coach and the athletes I trained.

Why would I want to knowingly put myself in a sub-optimal situation? That's just setting myself up to fail.

Needs Analysis of the Sport

You must understand demands placed upon the athlete and the sport. This goes back into the most basic of basic ideas as it relates to creating training programs. It's so obvious that it gets overlooked. As there is a massive wealth of knowledge on this subject, I'll leave it more global and reference questions you should be asking yourself while you create the specific parts of your training programs.

Goals

What is your goal? A simple question but not always simple to answer.

When I look at program design—program design is simple. It's just a science experiment.

The more controls you have, the easier it is to dictate and understand what's happening. The first and most important thing when we look at program design is what's the goal? Is that goal realistic? Is it attainable given the constraints you have imposed on yourself (i.e. time, equipment, talent, etc.)?

From there you must ask what is this year's/season's purpose? Why is that the purpose? How do we break things down to get to accomplish that purpose? Why are we breaking things down that way? You must give consideration to what must be learned, in order to do what you need to do, to achieve the goal.

You might have to accomplish ten other goals across a gamut of other areas before you're actually ready to achieve the original goal.

Pick a goal, define it appropriately, and work backwards to build the processes needed to achieve the result you seek. The key to achieving goals beyond having them be viable (realistic goals or stretch goals) is making sure that everything you're doing now helps build upon what you need to do tomorrow, and what you're doing tomorrow sets you up for what needs to be done the day after that and so on, and so on, and so on, and so on.

If you're doing something that isn't purposeful for future requirements to achieve the goal, then it's pointless. All too frequently, you see programs designed to create a massive level of improvement in an unrealistic timeframe. You can't cheat time, don't try to.

Time-Dependent

Something to bear in mind that often gets thrown out the window when designing training programs is that the goals of the training program are always time-dependent.

When you start to look at it from this vantage point, you realize that the length of time you have to achieve a certain goal/outcome automatically includes or precludes the possibility of achieving that goal/outcome.

Far too often, I see people who have the right end goal in mind built into the wrong timeline. Context and situation-specific variables can shorten or lengthen any given goal/outcome relative to the time frame someone else may have been able to achieve similar results in or you were able to achieve similar results in a previous instance.

Weight cutting in combat sports is one of the easiest examples of this. Sure, you can cut twenty pounds or more in twenty-four hours. It's not that hard when you know the tricks to pull it off. But there is a cost. You might be able to get away with it once or twice—extreme measures for an extreme situation. But wouldn't it make more sense to have a process-driven diet to get you to only need to cut seven pounds in twenty-four hours?

Far too many people aren't doing the right things weeks and months before they need to and then they crush, into a limited time boundary, an exposure stress that can be permanently damaging in the long term.

Put it this way:

I once had a fitness model who was coming back from a significant injury and badly out of shape by the standards she needed to be at. She asked me in December to help her tweak her training program to get ready for a big photoshoot in March.

I said to her, "Sure, I can help you get ready for next March. Fifteen months is plenty of time to accomplish the things you want to do."

She looked at me with a confused look. "No, Joe, I mean this March. Like twelve weeks from now!"

I could only shrug and say, "Sorry, can't help—outside of disordered eating and PEDs— what you're asking for is just not possible."

She ended up working with someone else and found a level of the success she wanted. She admitted to me afterwards when I checked in on her: "Yeah, I basically didn't eat for twelve weeks and did five hours of cardio every day and still wasn't the way I needed to be. I should have tried to move the shoot back or cancelled it all together. I never want to have to do that again!"

Physiological Demands

What are the energy systems and musculoskeletal demands placed upon the body to order to perform the sport, the position, or the actions needed for any single person or group of people?

For example, the physiological demand for a quarterback is different than a lineman but they're both playing football.

You must understand the differences and similarities because they're all playing the same sport but they're doing two different things. This basically applies across the micro and macro perspectives; from the individual positions to the overall sport respectively.

Biomechanical Demands

What are the movements and actions required of the sport, the position, etc. And why are those needed? What level of movement is needed versus what lack of movement can be got away with?

An example of this would be having some type of compensation of mobility in one part of the body by creating movement in a different part of the body. For instance, if your hips are tight, you must create more movement at the knee/ankle or through the lumbar spine to find the range of motion needed.

Is that an okay compensation (if one exists) or is it something you need to fix? Can you "fix" it or has the body created an unchangeable compensation due to permanent damage or ossification of a structure?

What happens when you "fix" it because then you must create, mitigate, and disperse force across new positions of movement through your body? Do you really understand the neurophysiology to "reprogram" someone's nervous system to change entrenched motor patterns?

What about the psychology involved in getting an athlete to sacrifice their current ability of performance now, for improved performance later?

Changing How the Body is Programmed

While I'm sure this could be its own section and is something that needs much more discussion—as most people believe the idea of acute, prescriptive, corrective exercise is a precursor to creating change long-term —I challenge that idea and put out the interesting concept of motor relearning.

We've established that the body adapts to the stimulus imposed upon it, regardless of what it is. And it adapts to down-regulate the amount of effort needed and create the maximum efficiency for the specific adaptation.

Thus, in order to try and change something that's been ingrained — over years, possibly decades in hundreds of thousands if not millions of repetitions—the best way to help "reprogram" is to bring the physical and neurological structures to a level of maximal fatigue before trying to reinforce a new order to the system.

We could take a riff on the neurophysiological or cognitive-behavioral perspective this and a few other disciplines that this idea comes from. But strictly speaking from the athletic-performance standpoint, you have to deplete the system of its capabilities to do what it knows how to do (especially it's "reflexive actions"), in order to impose a new stress adaptation response in order for it to learn how it should do something from then on.

Injury Risk and Epidemiology

You must know the risk factors for injury. You must know both the chronic trends of the sport as well as the finite trends of the individual.

This may blow some people's minds: you must know the injury risk factors, how to prevent them, and how to manage training around them when needed.

Don't leave it to just the athletic trainer or physical therapist. You should be able to have an educated position within the conversation related to rehabilitation and return to play.

The stronger your knowledge base in this area the better suited you will be to align all of sports medicine to the performance-growth mindset and not be limited by a "cleared to participate" approach many people take.

If you haven't read anything by William Prentice, you might want to hit Amazon and brush up on speaking the language most of sports medicine people learned when they were undergrads. It's like sports medicine all reading the *NSCA Essentials* book. You need to be able to speak a common language and understand the roots of where the taught dogma comes from.

Psychological Demands

Where are you? This is one of the things that we talked about before in the athlete enhancement paradigm.

These are questions to ask the athlete. Where are you in your training? Are you just training for fun? Are you training to train? Or are you training to win? Where are you in the competitive spectrum of intensity that you're putting on yourself or that's being put on you externally relative to what you're trying to compete in?

The easiest example of external pressure misaligned with the athlete's mindset is when you look at parents in youth sports. At a time when sport and training should be fun and a learning ground for the future, parents put massive external pressures on their children to win and be successful *now*.

This is one of many factors that can lead to burnout and all related things .

If the psychological demand is way out of whack relative to the physiological and biomechanical abilities for a given level or given individual, you're going to run into issues. How they will manifest is the question.

What you try to do to mitigate them and maintain a positive mindset and growth trajectory will determine the athlete's success in the long run.

Special Circumstance Analysis

Special circumstance analysis is situation and context relative.

Now, if we're talking about collegiate S&C, we're going to talk about NCAA rules such as time limitations (not just CARA) and dead periods.

If we're just talking from a global sense, we're talking about whatever the key limiting factor is for the situation. It could be a variety of things such as—but not limited to—facility size, equipment type, equipment quantity, availability of athlete, and scheduling of the facility.

The special circumstances that dictate your needs analysis are relative to your situation just like everything we've talked about. It's all context. There is no set answer. It's all framework that you must work within and adjust to.

I've only worked in NCAA Division I institutions but the difference between them might as well be as wide as the cognitive capabilities of Neanderthals to Mensa members.

One place I worked at had unlimited resources to develop the facility and equipment needs, whereas another one barely had enough financial resources to keep the lights on, never mind trying to catch up to the current trends. But they were both Division I.

You must look at the special circumstances that affect your ability to do your job. This plays right into the story of the cable columns I mentioned while addressing a different topic. If you don't have cable columns in your facility, it's hard to program using them regardless of what program you're trying to do.

Variation and Progression

I just want to take a minute and outline a very important concept. Variation is important and progression is important, but they're both macro and micro concepts that apply to every aspect of the variables of training programs.

They mainly relate to exercise selection and order but conceptually can be applied to volume, frequency, etc. Don't get lost in trying to use variation and progression in every variable of training.

If you're not a chef, don't try to be one without learning the skills and gaining the experience first. The simpler you keep things the easier it is to understand what adaptations you're causing.

Exercise progression has recently been taken far too literally in my opinion. Not everything needs progression (or regression for that matter).

Progression can be simply gaining efficiency and mastery of a given movement not just changing grip, stance, posture or action of that movement.

Progression and variation are a function of selection and order when it really boils down. This is a nuance lost on many.

Exercise Selection and Order

When we look at actual exercise selection and/or order, what type of exercises and movements are we capable of and what do we need to do to achieve the goals we have planned? What are we trying to learn and why are we trying to learn things?

People go back and forth with Olympic lifts or all of these different methodologies of training, but the question is, what are you doing and what are you using them for?

How are you developing a progressive system to take Skill *A* and develop it into Skill *F*? Because if you need Skill *F* but you only have Skill *A*, how do you get to *F* by making sure you get to hit *B*, *C*, *D*, and *E* in the appropriate manners and long enough to have the needed ability to move on to the next. And then why? You always must ask yourself, why?

Exercise selection and order is always a question of why. If you don't have a good why for exercise selection and order, then don't stray from the basics. More can be done with the basics with purposeful effort than with all kinds of variations.

Grip, Stance, Posture and Action (GSPA)

For any given exercise, instead of thinking of progression as a series of more complex tasks (bodyweight squat to goblet squat to barbell squat for example), consider this framework to create adaptive response from your standard model by manipulating grip, stance, posture and action.

By changing any onc or more of those four variables off of the standard model you have for any given movement, you have inherently changed the angles of movement (at some or many parts of the body), thus, inherently changing the muscle fibers being activated (in a relative ratio not as an absolute light switch).

The adage "change the angle, change the exercise" is one many people have not heard but need to spend time getting to know (both relative and absolute contexts of said expression).

No single exercise does anything but it can do everything.

Volume

You must calculate volume per exercise, per session, per day, per cycle, and per the "big picture" of longitudinal cycle you're trying to achieve a goal in.

Volume in its most universal sense is the combination of applied load and intensity of effort. How you choose to differentiate and calculate the two is up to you, but it needs to be done.

Considerations also need to be in place to understand the volume of training in all other physical demands. While this may seem obvious, many sport coaches and S&C coaches have no answer for the following question: How do you calculate the volume of conditioning you do compared to the volume of lower-body training (lifts, plyos, etc.) you do?

Or worse yet, in the collegiate realm when all you hear is silence when the following is asked: "How do you adjust your training for academic testing periods or other known periods of high stress, especially if you are in season?"

Tempo of movement also has a very big impact on volume. If you are looking at tempo, you must understand that there is average and peak velocity of movements and know when and why tempos are important to increase or decrease volume. Tempo is big right now—brought to the forefront for many by Cal Dietz's triphasic training approach

The concept that we all have a unique and individual underlying tempo we all move at is also critical to understand. Not everyone naturally moves at the same "frequency." I personally only used assigned tempos if I was specifically trying to achieve an adaptation for a specific developmental purpose.

I almost always let athletes move at their natural cadence and let the purpose of what I was trying to accomplish autoregulate the tempo.

If you think that a five-second, eccentric squat is the same as a fifteen-second isometric pause squat below parallel in the hole, and is the same as an autoregulated tempo squat—even if they're at the same absolute load for the same amount of repetitions—then you don't understand how adjusting the tempo of any phase of the movement modulates the impact of that movement on the adaptive mechanisms of the body (and causes different degrees of mechanical trauma relative to the phase of movement it happens in).

Applied Load

Applied load is the concept that considers the forces and relative external forces you're applying to the athlete for a given task.

This is most commonly thought of as a percentage of max in lifting, ground contacts in plyometrics, or number/type of changes of direction in agility.

There are dozens if not hundreds of ways coaches have tried to quantify applied load. The goal isn't to have the perfect mechanism to calculate it (although the technology is rapidly improving to have one); the goal is to have a consistent way to do so.

Constantly ask yourself why you're doing it in that way and how you can be more specific/accurate in doing so. You'll make significant progress in your athletes' development.

Here's a thought and one some might find interesting: why are you not measuring "system effort" or some other form of internal measurement of the body to give context to and better understand how the body itself is accomplishing the externally imposed demands?

Intensity of Effort

When I look at intensity of effort, I'm looking at the relative or absolute applied load of the session, day, and cycle and its perceived/calculated intensity of effort by the athlete.

When you start to manage and monitor your intensity and quantify your intensity of effort, the key is understanding the perceptive effort of the individual athlete compared to the actual effort taken to achieve the prescribed load of the training intensity you thought you were achieving.

This is especially important to consider over time as the exposure stress of training is not only physical but psychological—and changes.

There is a whole conversation within this framework: for progressing athletes and groups over time, for using previous "data" to guide future decisions, and for how you adjust that "data" given changes in situational context. I see far too many coaches and S&C coaches using previous years' information or results to plan future years training with no thought to the adjustments needed for the new context (and new people involved).

Frequency

Questions to ask your athletes: How often do you train? Have often do you train per day, per cycle, etc.?

Also, frequency inherently brings rest into the equation. How much rest do you have? And that is per set, per exercise, per session, per day, and per cycle.

You must think of frequency both in the macro and in the micro senses as it is a function of time. The manipulation of time against the stress imposed is one of the key determinants of what kind of adaptation response you will get.

Hans Selye's general adaptation principle is one of the easiest things to look at, from the largest macro to the most finite micro, when you look at program design—but it's often the most misunderstood.

If you can truly understand Hans Selye's general adaptation syndrome in the macro and micro scale, you'll then be able to apply things such as size principle, SAID principle, and some of the other principles that dictate physiological adaptation. Frequency is the undercurrent to all of this, as the MED, MTVPS and MRV are all time-dependent.

Periodization/Annual Plan

This is going to be one of the most obvious statements you'll ever read but sadly not everyone follows it.

You must have a strategic, systematic, goal-orientated approach that acts as a framework to outline the purpose for each moment of a training cycle in the entire training duration.

The emphasis must be on improving the fundamental continuum while limiting the potential for injury; improving the skills and techniques required for sport and required by the individual's ability—current as well as their potential—personally and for the sport which they play. A person's potential and their potential in a sport are not the same. Not every athlete is athletic.

Now to unpack that, the first big thing you must remember is it's a framework. You cannot "get stuck in concrete."

What I mean by that is just because you come up with a periodic plan and you have a systematic approach, you must be willing to change, adapt, and adjust that plan and approach every second, of every minute, of every hour, of every day, week, month, and year you have planned for.

Only by having a thought-out plan relative to the A/B goal objective with some relevant and purposeful evaluation mechanism can you see what has been accomplished and then what needs to be done. Think back to the connect-the-dots concept and then think *Goldilocks and the Three Bears*: not too hot, not too cold, just right.

This allows modification in the acute phases, via adaptation and monitoring through the evaluative mechanism you chose to use, to make sure you are reaching the goal you set at the beginning.

Specifically, in College S&C

One of the most obvious but overlooked things in planning is using the natural break periods in the given context you have as periods of transition or recovery.

This allows for easy modulation of training and planning. The most obvious example of this I have is collegiate sport and sport coaches and S&C coaches trying to fit in key parts of training during break periods.

"My athletes are never ready for testing after Thanksgiving."

"My athletes always fail spring conditioning when we get back from break."

"They just never do the work!"

Those are all common things I hear when discussing training plans.

Well, why are you asking them to do that if it doesn't work? Don't fit a square peg into a round hole.

With that being said, you often don't even need to plan a deload in the college-setting.

Between the natural breaks in the calendar and the natural decrease in intensity that happens when implementing a new program/exercise selection (learning effect), you inherently make things easier.

I would not only look at how much people improve from a technical or load standpoint but how much time it takes to do the same amount of work.

Not everyone looks at the relationship of work done to time— density of training, if you will—and how efficiency there can be an expression of positive adaptation beyond the value of the weight lifted or time on the stopwatch.

That is a huge factor in college-athletic development since time is the number one constraint on development. You're, in a sense, cramming a decade of training into multi-week segments with numerous planned and unplanned breaks over four years. You have to skip a lot of steps or only touch things in the briefest of manners because of the time boundaries you have. Funny how it all comes back to time and context.

Additional Thoughts on Training Principles

While I certainly could put some of these in multiple sections of this book, I'm specifically putting them here as additional thoughts and principles to consider when developing training plans. To the untrained eye, they may seem far afield of what is needed for developing human performance, but in my mind, they're critical in order to do so at the highest level.

The only thought not included here but one that needs to be learned is the the observe, orient, decide, act (OODA) loops (a four-step decision-making process). This is such a well-defined and explained concept, so t I will not attempt to do it justice here. Go forth and learn.

The Law of the Instrument and Applying Information, Not Relying on It

As Abraham Maslow said and many others have echoed in similar but different ways, "I suppose it is tempting, if the only tool you have is a hammer, to treat everything as if it were a nail."

If you become entrenched in your dogma of training, then that will be the only training you use. This carries over to all aspects of the Performance continuum and all aspects of life. If you have never heard of this idea, consider this your call to action. Other things you should also look into are the idea of the law of the instrument, *Cognitive Entrenchment* by Erik Dane, the "Carter Racing Case Study," and (another Abraham) Abraham Wald and his insights on armoring planes during World War II.

Seriously, you need to learn all that stuff.

Allostasis vs. Homeostasis

A big issue that I find when I deal with all levels of performance coaches is that they do not have a very good understanding of the difference between allostasis and homeostasis.

You must be able to understand and juggle the physiological and biochemical processes that regulate adaptive change across all aspects of the system. And you must know how that then affects the cognitive functions consciously and unconsciously.

If you're not monitoring and adjusting to allostatic load and allostatic overload, you'll be missing the boat on true adaptive physiology development.

Poverty of the Stimulus

Drawing on the field of linguistics, you must take the time to understand and grasp the poverty of the stimulus concept (related to language learning); how it can be conceptually integrated to the development of physiological capability and managing training program development, depending on the training age versus the ability to output demand.

False Consensus Bias

This one is a must for anyone coaching another person. It shouldn't be inherently obvious; but if you don't have the words and ability to explain it, understand it, and maneuver around it, then you aren't going to get far getting others to buy-in.

Take the Training Wheels Off and Go

While teaching, I was fortunate to have Derek Poundstone come in person to speak. He lived in somewhat close proximity to the place that I was working at the time.

Derek, for those who don't know, is a full-time police officer in addition to being a former, elite-level strongman. The day he came to speak he happened to have worked a shift and then drove a couple of hours to come to speak.

Within an hour of arriving, wearing khakis, a polo shirt, and dress shoes, he proceeded to pull a 545-lb. dead lift—cold. No warm-up —nothing.

We were literally talking shop and the only physically active thing he did beforehand was walk up to the bar.

He was talking to us as he did it and his view was, that at some point, you just have to be able to do it. You can't have all the warm-ups, fluff, and all the "perfect situation" stuff.

The act of doing is sometimes the most important thing. And people get paralyzed by trying to do all the other things around what they're supposed to be doing versus doing it. He discussed how warm-ups, cooldowns, and all the other parts of training have their place but not to get lost in them or have them take away from the ability to *go. To do.*

I used this point to articulate the key concept that sometimes you have to take the training wheels off and *go.*

While Derek was highly experienced and that weight for him trivial (having done over 900 lbs. in the deadlift before), in far too many instances coaches and athletes don't know how to "go" when things aren't perfectly lined up for them.

At times, you have to put yourself in abnormal situations to make yourself do something you otherwise wouldn't do. You can't train in perfect conditions and expect to be okay when the shit storm gets thrown at you in real life.

You sometimes have to take the training wheels off and let yourself risk falling in order to know you can push yourself to a level where falling is possible and not actually fall.

Slow Cooking Development

There is not always a reason to have progression. Sometimes progress is achieved by simply getting better at the same thing versus doing something else.

When dealing with someone who doesn't have the training age or exposure to the training stresses being placed upon them, the best bet is slow cooking their development and minimizing the additional training stresses placed upon them outside of practice and competition.

This is because the accumulation of training stresses and new exposures can be so overwhelming that they can create maladaptation's and reinforce negative adaptations quickly. In a sense, it's like being indefinitely in a state of overreaching, therefore, leading to an even longer duration of decreased performance and recovery and opening the risk of overtraining.

My personal favorite "slow cook" is an athlete I trained who played basketball. He was just under seven-feet tall and had never done any type of physical training other than basketball. He lacked basic movement competencies but was physically big enough to do things at a level smaller teammate couldn't. It looked like he was strong but for his size and ability he was extremely weak and moved poorly.

With his limited development came potential for extreme growth. But instead of rushing into things, his entire first year I "slow-cooked" him, focusing on quality over quantity and never sacrificing a strong foundation for a number. Hell, I never let him squat more than 95 lbs. his first year—not that he could correctly at first anyway—so there was no point in loading him.

He didn't have the required mobility, coordination, nor the cognitive focus to safely lift more weight even though he had the physical ability to manifest the force to do so.

In about eighteen months we began to unleash his new-found abilities and at about seven-feet tall and 245 lbs. he increased every physical variable in a positive direction. He was able to squat to parallel, deadlift from the floor, and do everything that was asked of him he previously couldn't do. Over those eighteen months, there was a direct correlation between his performance tests and physical skillset on the court all moving in a positive direction and the weight on the bar never changing.

Unfortunately for him, the muscle between the ears did not develop at the same rate and his career never took off because of self-inflicted wounds.

16

CRACKS AND SHARDS

THIS SECTION IS EXACTLY WHAT ITS TITLE MEANS. IT'S ALL THE REMAINING things I wanted to add but didn't want to put into the main framework of the book. It's truly an amalgamation of cracks and shards. So, let's start with some of the wackiest and funniest things I experienced as an S&C coach and we can just hop around from there.

Hilarious Stories

Okay, so the rumors are true. I do have a folder labelled "Hilarious Shit." I saved notes on some of the most bizarre and wacky things that have happened to me during my time as a coach. They have been funny, sad, insightful, maddening, simply bizarre, or a combination of all of the above. But they made the folder for a reason. The following are obviously some cherry-picked highlights that run the gamut. Enjoy!

A Tale of Social Media No-No's

So, one night during the school year, a Frenchman and a fisherman walk into a bar. They get wasted—and not just a little drunk—I'm talking *Hangover* meets *Animal House* kind of plastered. For whatever reason they think it's a good idea to post—what they believe—is a private message to their team. They rant about their new head coach, about the rules he has that they don't like, and a few choice words about being on the team.

Unfortunately, instead of posting it to a private group chat, they publicly post it. The saying goes "nothing good happens after 2:00 a.m." and drinking with social media proves it might as well be gospel to live by.

A couple of hours later, the head coach got a copy of their post from someone who saw it. A day or so later, the Frenchman is off to his third team in his college career and the fisherman off to his second—both having lost their scholarships and removed from the team.

You can't make up that level of stupidity.

Performance T-Shirts Preventing Athletes from Training at Their Best

One of my favorite stories happened in a meeting with none other than track and field coaches.

During a meeting that included senior administrators, one of the event coaches told me that because the weight room temperature wasn't properly regulated in the winter, the facility was cold. And it was an issue because the athletes couldn't properly keep warm due to having to wear moisture-wicking, performance-style T-shirts from the apparel company the school had a contract with, instead of standard, cotton T-shirts like he wore back when he was an athlete (cotton T-shirts, mind you, that became such gross, heavy messes at times you could ring the sweat out of them, but I digress).

He said that after the athletes sweated in the moisture-wicking, super-fabric designed specifically for athletes, it cooled them and kept them from training at their best. And I needed to make the facility warmer *and* I needed to find better training attire since S&C was requiring athletes to wear school-issued clothing.

I sat there in stunned into silence, and I searched the faces in the room to see if I was being messed with. When I realized the other sport coaches were actually waiting for my response to such a "pressing issue" and the senior administrators were looking at me, curious as to what I was going to say, my response was, "I'll check with facilities to see if we can change the temp of the room to anything warmer than the sixty-seven degree's the entire building is set to. Also, I'll send an email to the apparel company rep to see if this has been an issue anywhere else with the performance shirts compared to cotton."

I barely got it out with a straight face, trying my best to pretend to take it all seriously. For a brief moment, the most senior of the administrators—generally a stoic, blank slate—had the best shit-eating grin on their face I had ever seen, before giving me a wink and turning back to a stone face.

Blind Rage: Wait There are Cameras in Here?

One day, out of nowhere, a sport coach walked into my office hot under the collar. And I mean fire-out-of-their-eyes, white-knuckle, fist-clenched anger, looking to steamroll whatever was in their path. It was the kind of rage and hatred I can only imagine being reserved for someone who committed an atrocity against humankind.

Curses started flying toward me, ear-rattling decibels of maximum volume hitting my face. I was shocked, confused, and frozen like a deer in headlights. I had never seen that side of this person before. I didn't know if I was impressed or scared. I felt like Ron Burgundy after seeing Baxter had eaten the cheese.

As I put up my hands up in self-defense from both the volume and a possible physical threat from this enraged human, I eked out, "What are you talking about? Slow down. I can't understand you."

The coach stopped and said—in what I can only describe as a Nagini-like hiss in parseltongue—said something that included the words "someone stole," "unacceptable," and "your fault."

As calmly as I could (which was not that calm looking back on it as every other word was the f-word), I said something to the effect of, "What are you yelling at me for? If someone stole it from the weight room we can just go watch the security cameras."

As the last of that statement sank into this coach's brain, a deep realization came to them that they uttered out loud. "Wait, there are cameras in here?" I will omit my twenty-word response, but let's say it included no less than ten words that rhymed with "duck," "plucked" and "mother-clucker."

I rose from my seat and walked past the diffused bomb. I proceeded to the other office which housed the security system and pulled up the tape for the time period in question. We watched an athlete who was on the coach's team take the weight belt in question off the counter and throw it in the trash.

Ah yes, a weight belt was the item in question. A "sweet," thirty-dollar, run-of-the mill, ordered-out-of-an-equipment-magazine weight belt.

The coach cooled down and began to notice me being not so cool. I rose from the chair to go back to my office, turned, looked them in the face, and said something like, "Go pick it out of the trash can and don't ever come into my office like that again. Or blame me for something one of your athletes did, you disrespectful lout." Albeit, with a bit more color added in there in places.

That coach never raised their voice at me again, and I actually had little to no issues with them afterwards about anything.

Shirtless Treadmill Runs and Talking to Recruits

It was 10:30 a.m. on a Saturday during basketball season. I was walking the coaching staff and a recruit with their family to the weight room while giving my recruiting talk.

We walked through the doors of the weight room to find the lights on, ESPN on TVs full blare, and Development guy running on the treadmill shirtless and wearing way too short shorts. Drops of sweat shot off the back of the treadmill and were visible as they splashed on the floor behind him like a tsunami. It was a real sight to see as this was at least five years before dad bods became a thing. He was a man ahead of his time, I guess.

Everyone paused, eyes locked onto the train wreck in front of us, no one knowing what to do. I had abruptly stopped my diatribe, walked over, and grabbed the remote for the TV, turning the volume down from EDM-rave loud to reasonable.

As the TV began to quiet down, our shirtless wonder proceeded to give me a, "Hey, what's up Joe," before realizing who else was in the room. He looked over, gave a wave, and a, "Hey, guys." He hopped off the treadmill, walked over, and introduced himself to everyone. And without missing a beat, he walked away, back to the treadmill, and continued running—turning the volume up to almost where it was previously.

As I watched the visible horror on the coaching staff's faces and the extremely uncomfortable interaction between the recruit and the parents, I could only help but laugh in my mind thinking, *This guy doesn't get it. He thinks this is totally okay.*

Unsurprisingly, when I followed up with him later on about why that was not acceptable, both in the weight room or professionally, he said he saw nothing wrong and didn't understand why I took issue with it. I'll leave it at we agreed to disagree.

Can't Come Because My Mom is Here for My Birthday

A team had moved their training session from the afternoon to the morning because they were in their off-season. So, the intern emailed a coworker the following at 4:30 p.m. the day before he was scheduled to be at a 6:00 a.m. session (and 6:00 a.m. sessions the remainder of the week).

"Coach, sorry I can't come in tomorrow. My mom is here for my birthday and we're going out tonight."

He then proceeded to miss all 6:00 a.m. sessions that week and was never seen from again. That's a hell of a birthday if you ask me.

SIDE NOTE—I actually ran into this person in 2019 at a conference. I recognized them immediately (very distinctive physical appearance and visible tattoos) and even talked to them. I confirmed it as the person in question and that in their own words, "Yeah, I just hated being an intern so I needed an excuse to not come anymore." Legend, for all the wrong reasons.

You Owe Me a Recommendation Because I Showed Up Early Every Morning

I once had an intern who only came to a single session of mine per week because they worked with other coaches / teams during the rest of the week. This person showed up every Tuesday morning at 5:45 a.m., as asked, for a 6:00 a.m. session. After putting their stuff down in the office, they would ask what needed to be setup, go about setting it up, and then stand in the corner.

And when I say, stand in the corner, I mean literally stand in the same corner and in the same spot for sixty minutes.

After about 4–5 weeks of this, and asking them numerous times before and after the session to engage, ask questions, and do more—but to no avail —there was a change of schedule with football. They were no longer able to make my session as they had to be over in football.

Going forward six months, we were in the middle of summer training and I got an email with the subject: "Recommendation Request (name of this intern)." Not really recognizing the name, I opened the email and saw the following:

Dear Coach Joe,

I need a recommendation for a job I am applying to and since I helped you, I wanted to ask you for a recommendation.

Not really sure who it was, I replied with the following:

Hi, to be honest, I don't remember working with you as I don't recognize your name. Could you please refresh my memory?

The response, which came back to my inbox literally in thirty seconds left me laughing out loud for almost ten minutes.

I helped you with tennis. You owe me a recommendation because I showed up early every morning to setup.

It took me a while to find my bearings and draft an appropriate response:

Unfortunately, I do not owe you a recommendation. To be honest, you came a handful of times, setup in the morning and then stood in the corner the entire time. And at no time did you ever coach or, from what I remember, even engage with an athlete. I asked you multiple times to do so and you never did.

As a personal rule for interns, I don't give recommendations to anyone who hasn't completed an entire semester of interning with me and shown the ability to take on progressive responsibility. This allows me to make sure I have a complete picture of the person as a coach and their development over the semester before attaching my name to them.

Since you worked with football more than you did me, you should ask (the football coach) as he may be more willing to help given you spent more time with him.

Best of luck in your future endeavors"

Yet again, within thirty seconds I got a reply:

Thanks.

Later that day when I was over at football, I asked the football S&C coach about this person.

And their response was, "Who?"

I tried my best to describe the person and said that for me all they did was stand in the corner and not do anything. At this the football S&C coach said he knew exactly who I was talking about. He had let the person go as an intern halfway through the semester (a few weeks after they stopped coming to my session) because all they did was stand there and not do a damn thing.

I had a good laugh at that one.

Gronking A Cup of Coffee

There is no finer place to watch unchecked egos and textbook workplace harassment than collegiate athletic departments. Many of these departments are insulated environments with a lack of professional accountability and a sole focus on money instead of character (yes, that is harsh, but prove me wrong). These attributes allow things to happen that in any other work place would be an HR director's nightmare and a good lawyer's fantasy come true.

There is a lot lacking in places where the "leaders" push an agenda of buzzwords to sound good to parents, athletes and the public but often fall short in holding themselves to those standards. (For the record, I specifically say "college" not "professional" for a reason. Professional sports are about the money: different rules, still a lot of HR nightmares, but no one's pretending it isn't about the money like in college.)

Okay, okay, okay. Some places aren't like that but *a lot* are. I would say that 50% of sport coaches and administrators would be fired if they were audited by a legitimate third party and held to a realistic professional conduct standard found in most other industries. The shit that people get away with in athletics is straight up "crazy town."

Other times, it's just plain funny.

Enter women's basketball coach stage left. Well, technically, left courtside near the bleachers. I was sitting at the scorer's table mid-gym and in direct line of sight to this coach on my left and the men's team straight ahead on the court.

It's 11:54 a.m. and the men's team is on the court for a pregame walk-through as they were scheduled to play at 4:00 p.m. that night. The timer on the scoreboard read five minutes and twenty-one seconds and was counting down because the walk-through ended at noon. The men's team meal was at 12:30 p.m. and the women's practice started at 12:05 p.m.

As the time ticked down and 12:00 p.m. got closer and closer, the women's coach began pacing frantically, sort of in a manic state, murmuring loud enough to be heard from where I was about "the men never being on time," "fucking up my schedule," and all sorts of similar things. It made little to no sense as her practice wasn't until 12:05 p.m. and it was 11:56 a.m. And she was notorious for running over time herself often having to deal with compliance on CARA issues.

Out of the corner of my eye I saw the AD for facilities and another member of the facilities crew walk out near the coach. Given it's a game day they are deep into the logistics of setup.

I heard the coach yell, "We have a game tomorrow!" And as I looked over to see the exchange, *boom*!

The coach spiked a nearly-full cup of coffee onto the court as if she was doing her best Gronk TD celebration impression. Coffee spewed in all directions and the coach stormed off.

I sat there stunned not sure if I just saw what I just saw.

So, naturally I did the obvious thing. I got up, walked over and went to see what happened. I looked at the facilities people, who still had equal looks of shock, frustration, and growing anger on their faces (since they had to clean the mess up). I asked, "What the fuck was that?" as I tried not to step in coffee to make more of a mess.

I could do nothing but laugh out loud at the response I received: "Well, we heard Coach complaining the men weren't done yet and it was going to ruin her practice. So, we suggested she use the basketball practice facility instead of waiting for the main court, and she screamed she had a game tomorrow and stormed off."

Suddenly, the men's team was upon us as they left the court. And while still laughing, I helped direct them to not step on the spilled coffee. For the sake of argument, I checked my watch: 11:58 a.m.

While still having my funny bone tickled, I lingered around the gym waiting to see what was going to happen. Would the women's coach move practice to the brand new multi-million-dollar practice facility that isn't being used by anyone else at all today and is 150 feet away from the main court? I just had to know.

12:02 p.m. Athletes from the women's team start rolling in, putting up shots, and bullshitting with each other.

12:05 p.m. Not a single coach in the gym.

12:10 p.m. Tick-tock.

12:15 p.m. Assistant coaches show up and tell everyone to hold tight for the head coach.

12:20 p.m. The entire team hanging around, not sure what to do.

12:23 p.m. Head coach rolls back into gym with a new coffee cup in hand.

12:25 p.m. Coach comes over to me to chat while athletes go through pre-practice warmup.

Before she got too close, I deadpanned to her, "If you're going to Gronk that one, do it away from me. I don't want coffee stains on my new shoes." Coach made some snarky comment about me being a sarcastic ass and the men's coach being a dick purposefully running late to mess with her.

I accepted said comment and replied, "Well, he can be a dick, that's true. But they were done today at 11:58 a.m." And I thought to myself but didn't say, *Funny coming from the person who threw a temper tantrum, spiked a cup of coffee off the floor for someone else to clean up, then showed up almost twenty minutes late to practice, to go to the fancy coffee shop across the street for a refill.*

Bikini Pics and Dick Pics

As I mentioned earlier, there was one time when an assistant coach, who was hanging around the weight room during a session, was sitting on a hammer row machine using his phone. He got caught by one of the athletes actually looking at a Barstool Sports Smokeshow picture of the day.

The athlete, wanting to use the row machine, saw the coach was posted up on his phone not paying attention. The athlete walked over—and before the coach noticed to put his phone away—caught a glimpse of what was on the screen. Being a pretty witty kid, the athlete yelled out to everyone in the room, "Yo, coach over here looking at Barstool Smokeshow getting ready to send that dick pic on the 'gram."

It was at that point the entire room came to a screeching halt and all eyes went to the assistant coach and the kid standing beside him.

The athlete then looked right at the coach and said, "I peeped that girl earlier today Coach. She fine as hell." And the entire room erupted both laughing at and with the assistant coach, who tried to play it off before quickly exiting the facility.

If I didn't make this point clear enough already, if you're "watching" your athletes train and you're on your phone looking at Barstool or something of a similar vein, you might need to rethink your time management skills.

The Ship

"Welcome everyone. Congratulations on being here." This was how the head coach would start every season. He'd have a meeting with the entire team, and run down how his program was like a pirate ship.

"Now, I want you to understand how we do things here. Think of this team like a ship going to an island that has treasure on it. As the head coach, I'm the captain of the ship. The other coaches are my first mate and dock bosses. To keep your place on ship, do what is asked of you, the way it is asked of you, and be respectful of all those on the ship. We all contribute something in different ways—some more than others—but we all contribute. I'll do my job, which is to guide us to the island as safe and as fast as possible. Once we get there you can have as much treasure as you can handle. If at any point you do not want to do what is asked of you or the treasure on the island isn't what you want, you're free to jump off the ship and swim anywhere you like to go on your own. You will never change the direction of the ship—don't try."

We Aren't Ready for That

I had an assistant director (AD) at a mid-major school call me recently and ask if I was interested in an assistant AD for sport performance role.

I said, "Sure, I would be interested in a senior associate AD for athlete performance, innovation, and wellness; a position that would be third from the top after yourself and the SWA/deputy director who sit lateral to one another in the second position. That way, the systems and processes as well as the capital projects I would champion would have more pull at the table. I don't want to be getting into a pissing contest with a facilities person when I say the turf needs to be replaced because it's a hazard and they say it isn't in the capital improvement timeline for five more years. The entire purpose of a collegiate athletics department is to serve the athletes, not the coach's, the other departments or anyone else's ego."

He laughed and said, "Okay, Joe what other demands do you have. Out with them now before we go any further."

I replied, "Outside of a monthly bottle of tequila for the headache it would be, it would have to pay just under what the SWA and deputy make —public school, public records, and all. It would have to have not only the title and org-chart empowerment for external credibility but the salary to match it. That's important for everyone perception-wise and helps justify the empowerment you would give directly to me both publicly and behind the scenes.

Then I would need, after a six-month review period, the ability to promote, terminate, reorganize, reassign and give raises too anyone under my purview. If you want me to build it so it works, I need a team that is competent, capable, and most importantly empowered. I would also need three budgets: an operating budget for standard yearly based "stuff"; both an innovation and R&D budget for small and large-scale projects across internal and external entities to test out ideas, products, etc., so we truly knew where to invest and divest our resources. And a thirty-month capital improvement budget, so every thirty months I could do the major upgrades required to stay at the "tip of the spear"

After a brief pause he replied "We aren't ready for that. I hear you and that's why I want you here. I think we can get there. It's just going to take a handful of years to get to the point where we could position everything in that manner to start that kind of vision."

I cut him off and said, "So in 3–5 years we might possibly be at the starting point I just outlined. To be honest, don't even bother hiring a person for the job if it's just a token title and you're putting them in the trenches. You're better off giving the people you have a raise instead of adding a fake position and creating more headaches for everyone."

His response to that even caught me off guard both in his candor and insight. "That's exactly what I wanted to do in the first place but the president of the university wants us to have an administrator overseeing performance, after all the national attention at other schools, to cover our ass in case something goes wrong. He told me he'd sign off on creating a $70,000 full-time role for the job with HR and I told him we wouldn't get the right person for less than $115,000. He said he didn't care if it was the right person, just that he wanted *a* person. That's why I want you to come here and help me grow this into what it should be."

I politely passed on the role, leaving the door open for the future and also to help if needed. As of writing this, the role was hired and has already turned over. The first person left after a semester for what they told the AD was "a similar role with better pay and actually empowered to do the job". Go figure.

Empowering the Role

Here's the most basic job description that these positions would need. It empowers the role in title, salary, and function within the domain areas.

Senior Associate Athletic Director, Athlete Performance and Wellness

Summary of Role:

As the third-highest paid administrator of the department after the AD and deputy/SWA, provide supervision, mentoring and administrative oversight to the performance and wellness areas and staff. In conjunction with federal, state and NCAA policies, practices, and guidelines relating to athlete health and safety, develop and implement institutional specific processes, policies, and procedures to help athletes achieve their individual and team athletic goals in conjunction with success in their individual respective academic pursuits.

Role Description and Essential Functions:

- Report directly to athletics director and/or president of institution providing strategic guidance and counsel on all matters related to athlete performance, health and safety and innovation
- Develop a vision, mission and strategy for growth, integration and utilization for each area within the SAP-W team (sports medicine, athletic training, strength and conditioning, sports

psychology (including mental health counseling), sports nutrition and SAP-W education) including scheduling, assignment of responsibilities and functions, reviewing performance, recommending salary actions, promotions and terminations
- Identify, create and execute partnerships/synergies institution and outside institution resources to accomplish SAP-W objectives
- Oversee and manage budget for SAP-W entities working directly with CFO to allocate appropriate fiscal resources for SAP-W functions and needs

Preferred Competencies:

- Six years working in collegiate or professional sport with relevant experience, specifically four years of hands on experience with athletes in a frontline role and at least two in an administrative or management role
- Master's degree in performance-related field and MBA or additional business/management/leadership-related graduate degree
- All the obvious stuff: communicate, collaborate, and don't break the law

---

The Realizing Optimal Athlete Readiness (ROAR) Framework

If you get hired into an empowered role, you need a framework to start from. Here you go.

Realizing Optimal Athlete Readiness (ROAR)

Purpose:

Survey, gather, and define the needed personnel, processes, and structures to create and implement a cross-functional, athlete-centric performance-enhancement service, comprised of the functional areas related to sport performance and sports medicine.

Mission:

Provide athletes with optimized performance enhancement and sports medicine services to maximize their athletic abilities during their career in athletics as well as give them the tools, resources, and education necessary to have a healthy and balanced lifestyle after their playing career is over.

SIDE NOTE—If you're not leveraging ways to take care of them after they're done at school, you will never get the needed traction from the appropriate parties due to the shifting landscape.

Vision:

The ROAR initiative is the foundation stone that will help build and develop a highly specialized, cross-functional team of experts in their areas to service and assist with athlete development related to performing at the highest level of athletic competition and living a healthy life post-competition. This includes hiring staff, building facilities, leveraging resources, cultivating new partnerships, and continuing to develop synergistic efforts within athletics and the university, and with external entities.

SIDE NOTE—You have a purpose to do this; you need a mission for what that purpose is; and then you have to have a vision for what it can become

Tentative Action Plan:

Phase 1-A: 0–6 Months

- Survey internally all levels of staff and any other necessary

parties to determine needs, gaps, and potential improvements related to critical functional areas encompassing the athletic performance team
- Seek outside best practices for related areas from the NCAA, conference, national contemporaries, and non-collegiate entities to determine the best structure and scope of each role within the associated paradigm

Phase 1-B: 3 Months–1 Year (Simultaneous Development)

- Build and develop the appropriate specialist positions, job description, duties and responsibilities, salary demands, chain of command/organizational charting, policy and procedure per department, etc.
- Optimize current internal structure hierarchy/chain of command budget, etc.
- Standardize general forms, technology systems, and other initializing processes to streamline communication and access for necessary parties

Phase 2: 1–2 Years

- Hire and begin to integrate the lacking personnel to fill the paradigm
- Update, monitor, and manage all policies and structure related to functional areas for implementing actionable progress to align structure appropriately

Critical Launch Pad Questions:

- What do you need?
- Why do you need it?
- How do you know that is what you need?
- Who did you ask? Why them?
- How will it look when operating at its best?

- What happens when things go wrong?
- Who has authority?
- How do you deal with subverted authority?
- What would be the expectations for each role?
- What would be the expectations for collaboration for each role be?
- What policies would define those interactions?

Plans of an Advocate

These were all sample reports submitted up the chain to help spur on progress. Their form and style was based on preference of the individual administrator they were being created for.

S&C Review 2014–2015

Facilities: (March 2014–May 2015)

Overview:

Starting with the actual facility spaces themselves, there are only a few areas that need attention. They are mostly cosmetic/functional enhancements mentioned below, such as fixing leaks and rewiring the sound system.

Of the current areas, the biggest renovation would be the cardio room. This room would need a full renovation if we were going to replace the cardio equipment as the room itself has been worn significantly (ceiling tiles broken, walls scuffed/damaged, and floor damaged).

Also, the offices in both facilities are in need of upgrades but for the cost (compared to other S&C needs) they are a tertiary project. In July of 2014, we had the renovations quoted out at a cost of approximately $14,000 total: $9,500 and $3,500 respectively.

Big picture, the cost of large-scale, equipment upgrades in our current spaces plus the cost of facility improvements must be weighed against a new facility. Significant investment in our current spaces, while improving how we train, does not address the limitations of facility size that plays a larger role in the training dynamics due to scheduling, availability, and capacity.

With no current plan to improve facilities in size or large-scale upgrades to current generation equipment, S&C will be on the outside looking in within 3–5 years compared to our conference, our region, and Division-I athletics in general. With a large-scale project generally taking years to realize from initial planning to completion, we would only be getting on track and not ahead of the curve, in regard to S&C facilities and equipment, limiting the current student-athlete experience and impacting the recruiting process of future student-athletes.

In order to stay competitive and relevant in the current climate and not risk upgrades being obsolete by the time they are implemented, we would need to significantly expedite the process to within the next two years so we could then be able to address additional sports performance domains (nutrition, sport psychology) outside of the training facilities.

Future Facility Development:

The creation of a new facility that can cater to the growing usage demands of S&C and better facilitate the team training environment would be ideal. Such a facility could also become the linchpin in creating the sport performance department as it would be able to encompass all of Sports Medicine and S&C under one roof centrally located on campus.

An ideal locale for this would be at the extra field between the soccer stadium and parking lot. The current weight room, athletic training room, and alternate athletic training room would act as satellite locations to this central hub while the second weight room and second training room would be removed and used for other needs.

As a part of a larger sport performance complex, the weight room portion would need to be 10,000–12,000 square feet with space for approximately fifty athletes at a time.

Outside of building a new facility, additional options to improve facility size to an adequate level within existing buildings would be encasing the pavilion (approximately 6,000 square feet), expanding the second weight room out towards the field (adding approximately 1,500–2,000 square feet) and expanding the first weight room when they fix the water damaged wall by expanding it out towards the Softball field (adding approximately 1,500–2,500 square feet).

Accomplishments at Both Facilities:

- Inventoried equipment and estimated total worth for each facility
- Removed broken/damaged equipment
- Reorganized layout for safety (equipment spacing) and efficiency (path of travel)
- Improved quality of small-scale equipment (less than $300 per item) for this year (approximately $2,000 per facility)
- Created a list of equipment to sell to generate additional fiscal resources (potentially $10,000–$15,000)
- Sold approximately $2,500 so far with additional sales currently pending
- Worked with custodial/equipment-room staff to better clean facilities and gathered needed items for daily maintenance
- Established weekly and monthly cleaning responsibilities sheet for interns/staff to monitor cleaning
- Developed relationships with equipment reps, nutrition companies, etc.
- Received two Gatorade-brand fridges to put shakes in for free from Gatorade (estimated $2,000 value)
- Received sample nutrition products from numerous companies to test
- Cleaned and reorganized the office spaces
- Removed unneeded office materials (storage, chairs, etc.)
- Improved professional appearance of professional spaces

Accomplishments at First Weight Room:

- Worked with wrestling to swap out unused equipment from their facility with equipment from first weight room
- Added additional storage for stability balls near white board
- Removed unneeded equipment and organized in-storage container outside near, loading ramp
- Reported missing equipment from storage container to staff member on December 3rd. Staff member said they would file a report with public safety.

Further Considerations for Both Facilities:

- Temperature control/humidity control throughout the year: summer condensation causes rust on equipment and creates unsafe environment (slippery floors); winter (alternate weight room specifically) heat is inconsistent in weight room area
- Graphics on the wall (to tie in to donor opportunities)
- Recognition board for college records/achievements
- Sound-system controls in the weight room itself and out of the offices
- Update office spaces/office furniture
- Update cardio equipment (consider renting versus buying)
- Major equipment needs: cable columns, bars, plyo boxes, testing systems, etc.

Equipment

Major Equipment:

While the vast majority of major equipment is in good condition and functional, there are multiple pieces of equipment that must be replaced or updated to maintain safety. This does not consider the minor equipment (less than $500 per item) such as bands, medicine balls, plyo hurdles, etc., which we update annually (approximately $1,500–2,000 per facility, per year).

Major equipment needs have been broken up into three categories: critical, necessary, and wish-list.

Critical equipment upgrades are those that should be taken care of within the next six months and have liability implications for allowing their continued use long term.

Necessary equipment upgrades are where there are currently not enough items, items are in need of upgrades due to age/use, or items are needed to effectively train and without them limit the effectiveness of the S&C department.

Wish-list items are those that, while eventually needed, are tertiary and can be looked at being acquired in the years to come.

Critical ($12,000)	Necessary ($37,000 + Cardio)	Wish-list ($42,000)
7ft Bars for Arena Est. $5,000 (5 Olympic Style)	7ft Bars for Arena Est. $3,000 (5 Strength Style)	Timing Gates for Testing Est $3,000 (2 sets – 1 Arena 1 Marg)
Plyo Boxes for Arena Est. $3,500 (3 sets)	Trap Bars Est $2,500 (9 total – 7 Marg - 2Arena)	EZ-Curl Bars for Arena Est $500 (5 total)
Plyo Boxes for Marg Est $3,500 (3 sets)	Safety Squat Bars for Arena Est $2,500 (5 total)	Cable Columns for Marg Est $17,000 (4 total)
	Cable Columns for Arena Est $13,000 (3 total)	Pit Shark Est $20,000 (4 total – 2 Arena 2 Marg)
	Cardio Upgrades for Arena Est $800per month lease / $20,000 Buy	Rouge Kettle Bell Set Est $1,500 (1 set split between Arena & Marg)
	Cardio Upgrade for Marg Est $1,000 per month lease / $35,000 Buy	20# Iron Mind Weight Vests Est $16,000 (60 total)

Minor Equipment:

As per usual, there are multiple pieces of minor equipment that need to be replaced annually.

Due to the heavy use and limited life span of such items across two weight room facilities (even with regular maintenance and proper use), the annual cost of upkeep of these items is $3,500–$4,000 or $1,500–$2,000 per weight room.

** SAMPLE LIST OF EQUIPMENT THAT NEEDS ANNUAL REPLACEMENT - ACTUAL NEEDS & QUANTITY MAY VARY **					
Annual Equipment Purchases	**Margiotta**	**Arena**	**Total #**	**Est. Cost**	**Total Cost**
10' Jump Ropes	5	10	15	$ 10.00	$ 150.00
9' Jump Ropes	20	20	40	$ 10.00	$ 400.00
8' Jump Ropes	10	5	15	$ 10.00	$ 150.00
Dynamax Medballs-10lb	1	1	2	$ 36.95	$ 73.90
Dynamax Medballs-12lb	1	1	2	$ 42.95	$ 85.90
Foam Rollers	2	2	4	$ 15.95	$ 63.80
Gym Chalk 1lb box	6	6	12	$ 10.95	$ 131.40
Hurdles 12"	5	15	20	$ 10.95	$ 219.00
Hurdles 18"	5	15	20	$ 15.95	$ 313.00
Hurdles 24"	5	10	15	$ 18.95	$ 284.25
Hurdles 6"	5	15	20	$ 6.99	$ 139.80
Muscle and Driver Slammer Med balls 10lb	1	1	2	$ 34.99	$ 69.98
Muscle and Driver Slammer Med balls 15lb	1	1	2	$ 44.99	$ 89.98
Muscle and Driver Slammer Med balls 20lb	1	1	2	$ 54.99	$ 109.98
Perform Better - Purple Super band 1 1/8" Wide	7	5	12	$ 19.00	$ 228.00
Perform Better - Red Super band 1/2" Wide	7	5	12	$ 8.00	$ 96.00
Perform Better - Yellow Super band 3/4" Wide	7	5	12	$ 14.00	$ 168.00
Perform Better Monster Bands 10pack	1	1	2	$ 20.00	$ 40.00
Saucer Cones set of 50	1	0	1	$ 22.99	$ 22.99
Stop watches	2	2	4	$ 18.95	$ 75.80
				Subtotal	$ 2,917.78

Department and Staff

Department Overview:

We have significantly improved intra-staff dynamics and are well into forming a solid unit with a singular vision to help improve the physical abilities of our athletes. Previously, the primary limiting factor to this development was the physical separation of the two weight rooms that caused S&C staff to not be able to "be around" due to schedule demands.

Because of this, two significantly separate training cultures have evolved. The second weight room has a better developed training culture and environment compared to the first and this is in large part due to the efforts of the weight room staff, the consistency of them being here for six years, and the sport coaches who use the second weight room having a high priority on S&C as part of their overall program.

The first weight room, on the other hand for many sports historically it has been a type of environment where "we use it because we have too, not because we believe in it," causing inconsistency in training and a laissez-faire culture. While this isn't the case for all sports, for a large majority them it was or still is, and these sports hinder the development of themselves and others due to this approach.

The reason for this had been due to a litany of factors such as sport coaches not having S&C as an emphasis in their program, sport coaches and athletes not getting along with the S&C coaches, and high turnover of S&C staff who train these teams causing inconsistency in training.

Having improved S&C staff dynamics and particularly focusing on getting sport coaches and athletes to buy into S&C is a vital part of the development process. Along with recent head coach changes there has been a significant improvement in S&C department integration in most if not all sports that train in the arena.

There is significant upside in the years to come with this continued trend. However, the ability to provide a greater level of service will eventually be hampered by personnel resources because there will be more activities going on than the current number of S&C staff can handle and maintain and exceeds current quality.

Future Staff Development:

As we look to build the department from a personnel standpoint, consideration must be given to the need for a fourth full-time employee versus a graduate assistant/part-time, position to fill the required role of the fourth staff member. Compared to other schools in our conference we are tied for second-to-last for both the number of S&C staff as well as athletic training staff.

Name	# of S&C Positions	# FT / PT	# of AT Positions	# FT / PT	# of Sports	Football	Separate S&C For Football
	6	6 / 0	15	10 / 5	17	Yes	Yes
	5	3 / 2	13	6 / 7	21	Yes	No
	5	4 / 1	12	9 / 3	19	Yes	Yes
	5	5 / 0	11	11 / 0	16	No	N/A
	5	1 / 4	8	4 / 4	16	No	N/A
	4	4 / 0	10	3 / 7	22	No	N/A
	3	3 / 0	8	8 / 0	21	Yes	No
	3	3 / 0	7	7 / 0	17	No	N/A
	3	1 / 2	6	6 / 0	18	No	N/A
	2	2 / 0	9	9 / 0	17	No	N/A

Ideally, this role would be an entry-level, full-time employee and have a turnover cycle in the range of 2–3 years. Having this individual as full time would help provide the perception of competency and consistency to the sport coaches compared to a graduate assistant/part-time position. If a full-time position is not possible, a graduate assistant or part-time individual with a turnover cycle of 1–2 years would be extremely useful, although their work load should be adjusted to best fit the demands placed upon them.

Overall Total Training Session History Fall 2014

Only in WR time. Does not include prep or meetings

	Total # of Sessions	Total Time in Hours	# Of Required Sessions Per Semester	# of Required Hours Per Semester	# of Voluntary Sessions Per Semester	# Of Voluntary Hours Per Semester	Avg # of Athletes at Voluntary
MLax	106	106	92	92	14	14	1
Baseball	105	105	92	92	13	13	1
Softball	81	92.5	48	59.5	33	33	3
MBBall	81	80.5	51	50.5	30	30	1.7
WLax	65	65	31	31	34	34	N/A
WSoccer	62	62	8	8	54	54	3.7
WBBall	56	56	54	54	2	2	5
Tennis (M/W)	56	56	50	50	6	6	2
MSoccer	48	54	6	7	42	47	4.9
Volleyball	44	44	35	35	9	9	1
WGolf	37	37	33	33	4	4	1
Field Hockey	32	33.5	26	27.5	6	6	7.5
Wrestling	31	31	31	31	0	0	
XCountry (M/W)	27	25	26	24	1	1	1
MGolf	10	10	7	7	3	3	0.6
TOTALS	841	858	590	602	251	256	8

Proposal for Fueling Station—Spring 2016

SIDE NOTE—Keep in mind this was for a situation that did not have a full-time nutritionist on staff; if you have one, this is their world—help them or stay out of their way.

Objective:

Create a fueling station to provide appropriate supplemental food goods for improving athletic development and helping maintain competitive position within the NCAA landscape.

- Use as a recruiting tool for all teams
- Improve access to food goods due to the limited meal plan system the college offers
- Create and use an online survey of student-athletes to determine most interested food items and times of use

Requirements:

Create a secure environment for food goods to be stored and distributed from.

- Breezeway between the concourse and soccer fields or in the study hall building
- 1–2 full-size fridges and appropriate storage shelving
- Allocate necessary funds to the S&C department for purchase of such food items (i.e. fruit, yogurt, string cheese, ready-to-drink (RTD) nutrition shakes, trail mix, granola bars)
- Initial weekly food estimates of $300–$500 per week with true cost being determined by analysis of use trends over initial eight-week period and method of purchase

Have 2–3 work-study students under the direction of the S&C department to "work" the fueling station.

- Do not want athletes working the station due to conflict of interest

System of Distribution:

- Every athlete would be able to receive three items per day (no more than one of any singular kind), in order to control costs and prevent waste/overuse, while providing an adequate resource
- Items do not roll over to another day and cannot be used a day in advance
- When a station is open, an athlete would be able to come with their student ID and choose what items they want from what is available
- The student worker would then check their name off a computerized list (updated weekly) along with the number and type of items taken that day, ensuring consistent and accurate records
- Lists of eligible athletes would be based off of compliance department clearance rosters and sport coaches have no say in limiting or denying anyone access

Additional Thoughts:

- By tracking and monitoring who, what, and when, we can better adjust purchases to maintain costs within a realistic range and provide better hours of access
- Items are purchased in the most cost-effective method (weekly, monthly, etc.); if stock of an item runs out before the next purchase, that item will be out of stock until next purchase
- Are staff allowed to get items? If so, is there a different limit?
- Athletics staff should be allowed one item per day and will also need to bring ID for tracking purposes
- Do we need to go through food services for products? If not and a better price can be found elsewhere, what are the purchasing limitations, if any?

Proposal to Rebrand Strength & Conditioning Department

Objective:

Change the department name from strength and conditioning (S&C) to athletic enhancement.

- Provide greater credibility to the staff by recognizing the knowledge base, overall contribution to athletic development, overall impact on athlete development due to time spent with athletes as well as more accurately describe the scope and depth of services made available to the athletes beyond just resistance training and conditioning.

Change Job Titles:

- Director of athletic enhancement (formerly head S&C coach)
- Associate director of athletic enhancement (formerly associate head S&C coach)
- Assistant director of athletic enhancement (formerly assistant director S&C coach)
- Volunteer assistant athletic enhancement coach (if applicable)

Rationale:

The S&C staff currently utilizes a wide range of training methodologies, cutting edge sport technologies and takes a multidisciplinary approach, wearing many hats outside of just resistance training and conditioning, with the primary goal of improving overall Athletic Enhancement and decreasing injuries not just "strength and conditioning." Some of these include but are not limited to the following:

- Sports psychology component: develop and encourage a foundation for discipline, accountability, intensity, goal setting and achievement, leadership, teamwork, altruism, and positive mental attitude
- Sports nutrition component: provide educational materials related to sport nutrition for optimal performance, order and distribute nutrition supplements/shakes, and help sport coaches with training table
- Physical training component: create scientifically based, sport-specific training programs that help improve the needed physiological, biomechanical, and morphological attributes individuals need to succeed in their respective sport; this can also help possibly minimize the occurrence and severity of sport injuries as well as assist in the recovery process, with the goal of reducing time lost from competition and training; areas include muscular strength, muscular power, energy system development, agility, and non-traditional training methods (strongman/strongwoman competitions, boxing, swimming, etc.)
- Recovery/prehab component: implement specific and focused modalities (flexibility, mobility, self-myofascial release, proprioceptive/kinesthetic awareness tasks, yoga, etc.) that can help in healing the body and refreshing the mind from intense physical activity and to possibility assist in minimizing the occurrence and severity of sport injuries, with the goal of

reducing time lost from competition, training, and improving performance

- Creating a more welcoming and less intimidating atmosphere for the athlete and an initial expectation that a multidisciplinary, inclusive, holistic approach to improving Athletic Enhancement is being undertaken; this can also help encourage and promote long term commitment to health and physical activity as it goes beyond "lifting in the weight room"

In the changing climate of student-athletes having personal trainers before coming to college (sometimes multiple coaches for different areas of their development), being labeled a "strength and conditioning (S&C) coach" automatically puts us at a disadvantage because the perception is all we do is "train hard and yell" and lack the knowledge and ability to improve all aspects of athletic enhancement (which is what we are asked to do).

Improving athletic enhancement includes much more than lifting weights and running and we as a staff are educated academically, carry multiple certifications, and are recognized amongst our peers as being at the forefront of the profession.

This will improve the perception of the athletic enhancement department as it relates to other athletics staff, specifically sport coaches. With high department turnover in the last decade and many head coaches never making a consistent long-term commitment to using the S&C department due to the turnover, there is a void in understanding how crucial an athletic enhancement coach can be to a program when they are empowered to bring their full skillset to bear in the development of a given team's athletes.

Former Athlete Hangers-On

Don't be a hanger-on, draining time and resources from those who should have them when your time is up. I'm not talking about the athletes who drop off from the team or graduate but still linger around—especially socially. I'm specifically referencing when former athletes are a direct drain on the resources that are technically not for them anymore.

All too often, I see a lack in protocol and structure at schools to deal with former athletes sucking up resources away from current athletes and most importantly burdening staff.

One of the easiest examples of this is in the training room. If you look at most track & field teams—in a sport that has a high propensity for former athletes to linger around the college setting given the nature of trying to make it professionally—the training room is where you often find them sucking up valuable time, effort, and energy from staff.

Now, one of the dichotomies in this situation is that these people have given their time, effort, and energy into the success of the program and deserve some type of giveback. I wholly agree with that. They deserve some type of ability and some type of way to use, be a part of, and create a bond with the system that they were part of and help build up the next generation of athletes. But it cannot be at the expense of the people currently working there—consuming their time effort and energy.

There must be some type of standardized, defined protocol and system to allow these hangers-on the ability to still to rely upon and be part of a program that they were a part of but not drain or take away the resources from the current athletes. The simplest solution is giving them a 75% discount on the services they use compared to what they would cost on the outside world.

Imagine athletic training and S&C coaches being able to bill former athletes for services and split it fifty-fifty with the school. A $100.00 rehab session would cost $25.00 and the athletic trainer would pocket $12.50 and the school $12.50. Imagine if an athletic trainer did eight of those sessions a week for forty weeks, they would make an extra $4,000 and the department just got $4,000 to buy stuff with. For many, that's something like a 5–15% increase in their current salary. See what we did there? We quantified the value of the time, effort, and energy—that's the key.

What I Would Buy Now

It's a curious question to ask because knowing that I'm, in a sense, a philosophical/methodological agnostic, I do believe everything can be helpful or harmful.

I would buy equipment that lends itself to a singular philosophy. Although the application might be outside of the "made for us" mindset that the piece came from (Reverse Hyper, for example), I nonetheless would make a few certain choices of things that may seem specific to a single methodology.

At this point, what I would buy would be based around safety, risk mitigation, and the main KPI of being ready for on-field performance. I would use whatever tool allowed me to get the best result with the least risk depending the situation.

Would I Olympic lift? Yes, but only after competency and time has been put into developing power via general strength, plyometrics, and med ball work. After that, and only if it makes sense to take on the Olympic lifts as a tool for development, would I implement them.

Would I deadlift? Hell, yeah. But 85% of the time not with a straight bar or from the floor.

Would I have kettle bells and center-mass bells over dumbbells? Yes. No need to have all three.

Would I buy metal plates? No. Outside of a bunch of pairs of fives and tens—not only for the bar but to be used for other purposes (warming up, prehab, etc.)—metal plates (even polys) are a waste of space and money. Bumpers only.

Would I have raised platforms? No. Flat floor with inlaid platforms or platforms designed into the flooring.

Would I have machines? Yes, a dozen or so different things for specific purposes.

I could go on and on. So, to get granular on specific things I would have that I consider non-negotiable for athletic performance development: inverse curl, Reverse Hyper, athletic development platform (okay Louie, you're a nut but a genius), some form of a trap bar, Duffalo bar, Tansformer bar, sleds (push and pull types), wheelbarrows, weight vests, sandbags,

VersaClimbers, Jacobs Ladders, a velocity-based training (VBT) measuring system, a data management system to track programs/training history, and a 365-day wearable-tech solution

That's more the big picture major stuff. I haven't even touched the small stuff like bands, med balls, plyo boxes, etc.

Of note, if I was building/designing a facility, things like making sure the room has high enough ceilings so you don't hit your head when you try to do a pull-up or jump on a box, or break something if you throw a med ball. As does making sure the sunlight from the windows isn't directly in peoples' faces when they are training, requiring you to buy damn near a hundred thousand dollars' worth of electronic powered shades to make the space functional (true story).

Brands I would buy:

Racks and Metal

Dynamic and Rogue then PowerLift and Sorinex

Bars and Specialty Bars / Tools

Kabuki Strength, Black Widow, Eleiko, and Dynamic

Cardio

Jacobs Ladders, Versa Climbers, and TrueForm

Technology

EliteForm, Strive, Vald, and DARI

SIDE NOTE—There is clearly some overt bias here given my experience with some of the companies. There are many good products but I don't want good—I want great—and these are the best. So, I'm biased—deal with it. It's my book; I get to be.

Nutrition

- Anything that has the combination of science to support it and taste for the athletes to use it
- Many great products fail the latter while being great at the

former and many shitty products hang around too long because of the latter without the former. Yes, that is a cop-out but I 'm not a registered dietician (RD), so go ask a really good one

---

Self-Improvement Extras

Order of Magnitude (In Brief)

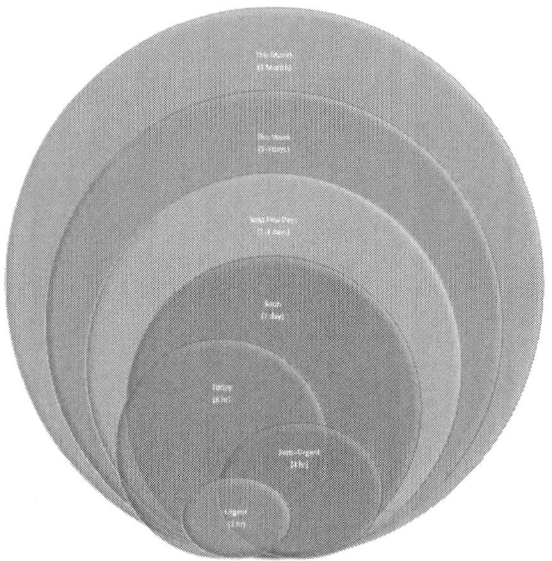

The order of magnitude is comprised of seven rings, each extending outward, further away from this current moment in time.

Often, we spend our time doing tasks or asking/seeking answers to things within the "urgent" ring, when in truth, what we are trying to accomplish is further outward on the order of magnitude. This confusion often leads us to feel overly stressed and attempt to accomplish too many non-urgent things urgently. This diminishes our efficiency, lowers our overall output quality, and puts us into a negative psychological state; we never feel we can do what we need to—how/when we need it—we are always playing catch-up.

Taking time each day to place our objectives and goals in the appropriate ring on the order of magnitude, and then re-evaluating their place every few days, is one skill to help better organize our own demands as well as the demands others place upon us. Be wary, however, of the risks involved in placing your demands in the further out rings. Such challenges include: transmission of information to others without the proper magnitude they are coming from; failure to initialize demands that have completion dates in outer rings; and deferment to outer rings due to laziness/lack of effort.

Single Task vs. Multitask

Understanding when to single task rather than multitask is key. Many people struggle with this, giving their bandwidth to multiple streams of thought or distractions that take them away from the single thing they need to be focused on.

Multitasking often leads to ineffective use of time.

Journaling

You need to be journaling in written form, audio recording, or whatever medium works for you. The asymmetrical development you'll initially need will require you to spend all of your time building and developing your professional and practitioner skill set and knowledge base.

Keep a record of your journey, write down your questions, write down your thoughts, and reflect on them over time. Build a history of the processes, experiences, and people that helped define your path.

For me personally, I have found great catharsis and value in keeping a journal. It's a combination of tracking progress, personal growth, etc., as well as collecting my thoughts and creating tangibility to my daily actions.

Below is my 2018 template (the left side of the page—and the right page is blank so I can fill them in). It has evolved significantly over the years and I feel I have honed-in on a pretty good setup for myself. Over time you can come up with whatever format works best for you. Every year I make tweaks and adjustments.

In 2018, I took this approach for myself:

- Did I do something for self-improvement?
- How much did I drink?
- Did I work-out? Did I stretch (outside of working out)?
- Was I up before 6:00 a.m. and did I travel or get home from work post 9:00 p.m.?
- What projects/goals do I need to keep track of and what deadlines/to-dos do I have to be aware of personally or professionally?

For me, those variables gave me a good picture of how I was doing in the big picture, kept me honest about aligning my actions to my values, and helped me achieve my goals.

Be mindful that, of course, I use online platforms for many functions such as my calendar, meeting notes, etc. This journal, for me, was to keep the big-picture/overview of things and have somewhere to scribble that wasn't electronic. It was the place for me to put what happened or comments on what happened—not the fine details of each event.

DATE:	Thought / Gratitude:

Self Improvement Task	Projects / Goals
Alcoholic Drink (#)	
Workout (L/C/P/M/R)	
Stretch (Min)	To Do's / Deadlines
Up Before 6am	
Travel Or Post 9pm	

SIDE NOTE—If you've never used Lulu.com, check it out. You can make custom journals/books and have them printed relatively cheap. There are plenty of places to do this online now but Lulu.com has been the place for me.

Read Like Mathis

In addition to journaling, you need to be a student of information. And the reference to General Mathis is not simply regarding reading military history but the act of reading itself. Be a student of information, the history of the industry or profession you are in, and all the different sectors and pieces of said profession.

From understanding Milo and his calf being the historical basis of progressive overload to the paper wasted for spiral-bound, summer-training packets—understand the history to best understand the future.

Also of note is that, at some point, you need to be able to learn and draw from things outside your profession in order to enhance your ability as a professional. To put it in a way some may have heard, once you are a foot wide and a mile deep, look to become a mile wide at the top funneling down to beyond a mile deep.

The List of Stuff You Need to Know and Suggested Readings

While this is not by any means an exhaustive list, it's at the very least a baseline set of resources that you should be familiar with and have some working knowledge around. Since I originally put this list together in 2014, it has grown, changed, and shifted—but fundamentally this is still a pretty solid list.

Things/People you should know, have seen, read etc.

Lifting Movies & Videos
Bigger Faster Stronger
CrossFit Videos (good and bad)
Generation Iron
Perfect
Polish weightlifting team
Pumping Iron
Pumping Iron 2
The Cost of Gold

Websites
www.strengthlegends.com
www.tnation.com
www.breakingmuscle.com
www.elitefts.com
www.danjohn.net
www.nsca.com

www.cscca.org

www.elathlete.com
www.irongamechalktalk.com
www.strengthcoach.com

People - Most People have Websites, google them.

Al Vermel
CT Fletcher
D Klokov
Hussan Rezazzedah
Jane Fonda
Louie Simmons

Mariusz Pudzianowski
Meg Stone
Ronnie Coleman
Werner Gunthor
Joe Defranco
Anatoliy Bondarchuk
Mike Boyle
Eric Cressey

Yuri Verkhoshansky
Charlie Francis
Grey Cook
Gary Grey
Dan John
Joe Kenn

Brandon Lilly
Tudor Bompa
Brian Mann
Mel Siff
Charles Poliquin
Kelly Starret
Mike Stone
William Kraemer

Jim Wendler
Chad Wesley Smith
Vladimir Zatsiorsky
Christian Thibideau
Mike Nitka
Loren Landow

Dave Tate
Alex Viada
Pat Davidson
Cal Dietz
Arnold
Ed Coan

The List Goes On....

Training Methodologies

Powerlifting
West Side
Juggernaut
5-3-1
"Puriest"
Raw vs Gear
Smolov

Bodybuilding
Training Density (Volume)
Training Intensity (Load)
Drug vs Drug Free

Olympic Style
American (USAW)
European (USSR)
Asian (Chinese)
Middle-East (Iranian)

Alternative
CrossFit
RKC
Strongman
Plyometrics
"Functional" Training
German Volume Training
Martial Arts (Contact)
Martial Arts (non-contact)

General
Metabolic Training
Strength Training
Power Training
Endurance Training
HIT Traditional Training
HIT Style Training

Non-Traditional
Yoga
Pilates
Gymnastics
Mobility / Movement Work

The suggested reading and listening list is exactly that— suggestions from someone who reads a lot and listens to a lot of things. Don't take it as gospel. I'm just someone who actively seeks out all sides and differences in opinion. I feel like the suggestions on this list present information in a manner that is coherent and understandable, regardless of your own personal views and opinions. Thing's in bold I consider priority.

General Books Covering a Variety of Topics (Bold are read first IMO) –	General Books Covering a Variety of Topics (cont) –
12 Rules For Life	Range
A passion for Leadership	**Sapiens**
A Whole New Mind	Sea Stories
Allostasis, Homeostasis, and the Costs of Physiological Adaptation	Stealing Fire
Anything by Patrick Lencioni	**Talk Like Ted**
Anything by Stephen Covey	**The 4-Hour Workweek**
Behave	The Obstacle is the Way
Braving the Wilderness	The Six Sigma Handbook:
Call Sign Choas	The Subtle Art of Not Giving a F*ck
Can't Hurt Me (buy the audio book)	Til Health Due Us Part
CEO Strength Coach	Tools of Titans
Concious Coaching	**Touching The Dragon**
Creating a Mentoring Culture: The Organization's Guide	Tribe: On Homecoming and Belonging
David And Goliath	
Deep Survival	**General Podcasts Covering a Variety of Topics –**
Dichotomy Of Leadership	HardCore History
Duty	Louie Simmons
Ego is the Enemy	Barbell Shrugged
Extreme Ownership: How U.S. Navy SEALs Lead and Win	Joe Rogan
Game Changers	Bruce Lee
Game theory and non-technical introduction	How Stuff Works
Gift of Injury	How I Built This
High Output Management	Froglogic
Homo Deus	MFCEO
Influence	Jocko Podcast
Inside of a Dog: What Dogs See, Smell, and Know	Tim Ferris Show
Labor Relations: Development, Structure, Process	
Leadership and Self-Deception: Getting Out of the Box	**Books That Cover What Some Consider Polarizing Issues –**
Leadership Conversations	About Face: The Odyssey of an American Warrior
Legacy	Blood Meridian: Or the Evening Redness in the West
Lexicon	Dirty Wars The World Is A Battlefield
Lincoln On Leadership for Today	Win Bigly
Man's search for meaning	
Marketing Management (14th Edition)	**Podcasts That Cover What Some Consider Polarizing Issues –**
Measure What Matters	Making Sense
Meditations	Scott Adams Blog
Multinational Management	
Never Split the Difference	**The key here is to gain perspective, hear opinions that may differ from my own*
Operations and Supply Chain Management	*and force myself to expand my critical thinking / awareness of things.*
Pre-Suasion	*Sometimes I agree, sometimes I disagree. Numerous others podcasts*
Principles	*and books with this approach I phase in / out. These are just well known.*
Principles And Practice Of Sport Management	

Micro Challenges to Test Your Own Willpower and Resolve

Challenge yourself in ways to confirm both the strength of your will and the consistency and dedication you have for yourself. Every year, for one month, I find a challenge for myself. Whether it's pushups or burpees or not drinking alcohol, I always have a goal to finish. It's very similar to the idea of Lent. And while I'm not very religious, part of the inspiration for doing this type of personal journey and process comes from the idea of sacrificing something to strengthen your own willpower, a common theme in religions.

There is a strong reason to do this: to develop confidence in yourself and know that you can stick to and be consistent with a goal you set.

Building these self-confidences through micro challenges allows you to parlay them into bigger and better things. When things get tough, you'll honestly know that you've been able to walk the walk as well as talk the talk.

Don't Be Self-limiting

Earlier today I was sent a message from a former colleague: *Did you ever come to your job every day and be so jaded towards it that you end up hating everyone involved in it and everything about it?*

My response to them: *I was pretty damn close a few times, but I never got there because I changed my circumstance instead of being trapped by it.* I went on to talk about how I pursued my MBA; how I made sure I took breaks to decompress and detach; how I hung out with family and friends, etc.

I realized it doesn't matter that I can't change other people; I can only change me. I did my part to impact who I was working with, I was never closed off to helping someone if they needed help or asked for it but I acknowledged that I couldn't change the world and not everyone wanted to be helped.

As the saying goes, you are the composite of those you spend the most time with. It's easy to fall into the trap of others and be pulled down. Unfortunately, a lot of the time (not just in athletics) all you hear is the negative and everyone complaining about their time, pay, or even family. Make sure you keep the appropriate perspective because at the moment when emotions run high, situations can get convoluted and clouded.

People get stuck in the cycle and are not able to detach and change their circumstance; like an addict, they simply fall back into the negative cycle of behavior because it's easy. Make sure you square yourself away first. Never get to a point where you're not spending time on yourself to improve yourself. Do that first and then go help others. And over time, like gravity, that mindset will attract certain people to you and will help push others away.

In the long haul, you may feel like you're drowning today but water tends to level out; what once felt like a tsunami is nothing but a ripple across a pond later on.

Imagination

Constantly create situations, scenarios, games or challenges that force you to stretch your own skills and be creative and inventive with things in your own mind. Force yourself to come up with new and different ways of doing things by limiting different factors in the planning process. Ask yourself how you would accomplish your goal if suddenly something that was a given was no longer? Keep your mind sharp by flexing the imagination muscle often.

This allows you to have fluidity and control in the environment when things go awry as you have already opened your mind to the possibility of having to adapt. For anything you assume to be a "guarantee" make sure you have a contingency plan for when it isn't.

Some Just Won't Get It.

To be blunt, some people just suck and don't get it.

What I mean by that is not every coach, not every administration, not every athlete is always going to come around.

Some people you will come across won't click with or you won't connect with. And no matter what you do it, doesn't matter.

You must allow yourself to detach.

Positively and effectively do your job as it relates to those people and not do anything in an unprofessional way.

You have to watch what you say and manage what you do to everyone else about that person, because that will allow you to maintain your credibility while also proving that you are still trying to do your best and that that other person is what's holding things up.

After Two Questions, You Generally Show Your Cards

For a very long-time, people have been told that there is no such thing as a dumb question.

That's a lie. There is such a thing as a dumb question.

You can tell within the first two questions someone asks you, on any topic, whether they're knowledgeable or not knowledgeable and whether they are making it up as they go or not.

The type, content, and depth of the question determines the level of conversation you can respond with and that the person asking the question is capable of understanding. Before you choose to answer a question, make sure you give thought to not only what the question was but who asked it and how best they can receive an answer.

Answering the Question

Often people can't scale up or scale down their ability to answer a question. One of the things you should practice with all levels of people you speak with is scaling your answer to the question based on who asked it and not the actual answer.

For example, why do you do *X* or what do you expect to happen by doing *Y* training method? Practice answering that in three ways with each one building on the other.

The one-minute elevator answer is a very short synopsis with limited technical or tactical knowledge and provides just the basic grasp of key information. This is the perfect answer for situations like the middle of training or in the brief social interactions with important people relative to the team, when you don't have the time to appropriately teach and develop the full train of thought. It just wouldn't make sense socially or in the length of engagement to go past this quick overview. It lends itself to being so simple that it prevents further questions and allows a polite but quick end to the question.

Past that one-minute framework, if you expand on the key points of emphasis, you suddenly have a small lesson. This small lesson should be 5–10 minutes of basic explanation with a little bit more advanced technical or tactical knowledge to describe or explain a more in-depth approach to what you're trying to do. This is what most people would consider a "conversation" on the topic. There will be some back and forth, most likely a few additional questions, and additional insight into what depth you can and cannot get into with whoever you are speaking to.

Lastly, the full explanation, which we will call the boardroom discussion, is the twenty to thirty minute (possibly longer) full-on explanation of anything related to the context. Often, it's easier to try and fully explain the boardroom presentation to yourself and put it on paper. And then simplify it to create your small lesson and elevator pitch explanations. This will not only allow you to have a firm grasp of the technical and tactical knowledge you're trying to explain, but by creating tangibility by putting it in words —whether written or orally presented—it also forces you to practice simplifying your explanation to those who don't have or don't care to have the knowledge that you have.

One of the key points you always must remember in explaining ideas to people is your technical/tactical knowledge is not their knowledge. If you're not speaking to someone who's at the same technical/tactical level, they generally don't care about it the way you do—like an athlete who cares more about their sport than their training for their sport. You must be able to discuss and rationalize what you're doing: to people who have never trained, have only been behind a desk, or are armchair quarterbacks; to sport coaches who may or may not have a wide range of physical, mental, and personal experiences; and to athletes who may or may not care to learn the reasons or rationales for what they are doing to get better at the sport they are trying to get better at.

Taking Notes to Gauge a Person

One of my favorite things to do to gauge both the person and their willingness to be truthful and held accountable is to take notes during a conversation. While this may seem trivial to some because it's common place in many workplaces, in the world of athletics—especially at the ground-floor level—it can be one of the most entertaining and enlightening things you can do.

I would often break eye contact for periods of time to take notes, even when the other person was done talking or I had yet to respond, letting the silence hang as I made my notes.

You will be surprised how quickly difficult and often deceitful people change their tune when you're taking notes during your conversation. Paired with a follow-up email after the meeting rehashing their points and yours, as well as action items, can quickly and effectively hold that person accountable for anything ridiculous that comes out of their mouth.

Training Programs

Ode to Jerry

The "ode to Jerry" is what happens when a protégé takes the thirty years of knowledge, science and hands on results of their mentor, adapts it with some new school understanding, and sets the bar for all others to match. The "ode to Jerry," simply put, is the most powerful program for strength and hypertrophy for the eighteen to twenty-two-year-old undertrained male athlete there is.

If you are looking to "clear the land to build a foundation," this is the program to do it. Coupled with adequate nutrition, rest, and sport-related energy-system development, expect to radically alter force production and power capabilities in seventeen weeks. This program will be available online at www.thezentagroup.com/book for purchase with a portion of the proceeds going to the NSCA Jerry Martin Scholarship fund.

Protocol Thirty-Five

It combines elements of and manipulates a variety of methods based around a system like auto-regulatory, progressive, resistance exercise (APRE). "Protocol thirty-five" is the best bang for your buck when you can only train 2–3 days per week for sixty minutes and overall strength is your goal in conjunction with sport-specific training. This program will be available online at www.thezentagroup.com/book for purchase with a portion of the proceeds going to the NSCA Jerry Martin Scholarship fund.

The success this program has had with soccer athletes is astounding. This program will be available online soon with a portion of the proceeds going to the NSCA Jerry Martin fund.

Massive Traumatic Acute Compensation (MTAC) Theory

MTAC theory is something that I came up with years and years ago after a personal experience of living in excess with a friend of mine for a couple of days. He had come to visit because he was getting ready to go on his first deployment overseas and for four days we "burned it down."

During the day, we would train as hard as I had in years, often pushing ourselves to total exhaustion due the competitiveness we shared with each other. At night, we would party like rock stars eating shit and drinking anything that was fermented. It was a massive departure from my customary physical training, alcohol and nutritional intake. The next day, we would get up and do the same thing all over again.

After three or four days of this, my body as well as my mind were pretty ravaged. But it was on the fifth day of doing another extremely strenuous and hard work out that I suddenly broke through and hit personal records in multiple lifts. Not just yearly bests or training program bests—but all-time bests—in things that I had been working at for a decade.

It came as a huge surprise to me that I was able to get to this level of performance given the traumatic experience I had put my body through the previous three days. Little did I know the cost of making my body compensate in such a massive degree; it would take me almost a month to recover in terms of my ability to physically exert effort and return to some type of baseline of ability/performance. Although, it also helped kick-start my body to gain weight and build size—something I always had an extreme difficulty doing, regardless of the training approach I took.

It was during this month of recovering that I started to create the concept of what would become the MTAC theory. Through a combination of eating and training in a very certain way for a long period of time in order to drive optimal improvement, most people actually plateau as the body adapts to this optimal adaption strategy. MTAC is thus based on the "George Costanza" decision model. I prefer to call it that than go into the actual science of what is happening. Technically speaking, this conceptually shares many characteristics of fasting, crash dieting, and other "shocks to the system."

I don't advocate taking three or four days eating like shit and drinking your face off while punishing yourself with extreme intense workouts or suddenly stopping heavy drinking and eating as clean as possible. But I do advocate the idea of making a plan of attack to disrupt cyclical, long-term patterns you have fallen into—in your nutrition, training, rest and recovery methodologies.

Take three or four days and do the opposite of everything you usually do—within reason (don't do anything illegal or unlawful to yourself or anyone else). Do a 180-degree U-turn in the most legally and safe but aggressive way possible to help drive a massive acute compensation curve.

Remember though, there is always a cost: rebound to a new baseline and positive growth is going to take time. And I would not suggest doing this more than once every couple of years because the stress and strain on the physiology and the psychology of the body are immense. It should be something that's supervised and organized into the development process as a means of shocking the system to adapt and not something to use as a "performance hack" only if absolutely necessary.

Clearly, this is a terrible idea if you have any underlying medical condition, psychiatric condition, or anything that could possibly be impacted by totally upending your lifestyle for 72–96 hours.

Why Do Athletes Seem to Get Hurt More Now Than Ever Before?

There's a very obvious reason why we're seeing a significant uptick in what used to be catastrophic injuries—but due to medical advances and rehabilitative methods are now just season-enders. The body hasn't developed the exposure-stress to create the rigidities necessary from the training stimulus to manage competition-effort.

Far too often, although people are competing more and training less, they are also not training the right way. They are not training to build their capacities and build their system development to handle and recover from the imposed stress.

What most people are doing is spending far more time doing recovery in lower-level modalities that they think are helping by fixing the problem; but they are not transferring and translating those lower-level, passive skillsets into the high-velocity, higher demand activity that they need to be competent in for competition.

Look at the mid-2000s, corrective-exercise boom. Everyone tried to correct or have a corrective for every possible asymmetric, dysmorphic, disproportionate "whatever" issue. What ended up happening? A lot of people got so far away from what was required in their training and they started getting hurt. This is an obvious problem that I argued a long time ago.

The body is so smart it's stupid. Anytime you take away a repeated training stress that has been adapted, and introduce a new training stress that hasn't been adapted, you're going to get weird shifts in how force is mitigated and dispersed. Because all of a sudden, things that were or were not transferring force appropriately are now transferring force. The length-tension relationships and the compensatory mechanisms of the body had change imposed upon them.

What was happening? There were increasing ranges in motion around joint spaces, increasing the pliability of tissues and the plastic deformation of the tissue without appropriately preparing it to handle and accept those changes in force creation, mitigation, and dispersion.

It's easy to see. For some reason though, people still don't get it. At some point, you must bring things to competition speed in a controlled simulated environment to see where the breakdown in the system occurs. This allows you to then develop the system in places where it needs to be developed during those breakdown moments in real-life action. Just like anything, if you are only addressing the issues that come up in a low-intensity environment, you will never refine the system in the manner needed to handle the high intensity of competition.

One of the simplest examples of this, in my mind, is the refinement of the technical model you need in any given lift changes depending on how much you lift. There is no one who can squat greater than three-and-a-half times their bodyweight for any duration of time, who has a massive asymmetry in one side versus the other. They might be able to get by at lower loads and intensities or a few times with such "heavy weights" but at that level the smallest errors compound into catastrophic potential.

Ask yourself this: how many times have you faked your warmup sets and been fine (poor form, being out of position, a lack of mental engagement, etc.)? How many times have you done that with your max? Now imagine only faking through your training which was never beyond an easy level of difficulty and being asked to max? The gap is too big to not be at risk.

Quotes

While not an all-encompassing list of my favorites, here are some select quotes that I just felt compelled to add here.

> "One of the greatest myths in America is that sports build character. That they can and they should. Indeed, sports may be a perfect venue in which to build character, but sports don't build character unless a coach possesses character and intentionally teaches it." —Joe Erman

> "The thinking is easy. Acting is difficult. And to put one's thoughts into action is the most difficult thing in the world." —Johann Wolfgang von Goethe

> "We face new challenges every day, but the question is not how we try to rationalize them to make up for inadequacies. But how we go about overcoming them with our strengths." —Me, I say this to myself all the time.

> "The leaders who work most effectively it seems to me never say I and that's not because they have trained themselves not to say I. They don't

think I. They think we. They think team. They understand their job to make the team more functional. They accept responsibility and don't sidestep it, but we get the credit. This is what creates trust. This is what enables you to get the task done." —Peter F. Drucker

"If you want nothing do what you want. If you want everything develop discipline." —Kostya Tszyu

"The best way to predict your future is to create it." —Unknown

"We become what we repeatedly do. Excellence then is not a single act but a habit." —Aristotle

"Just go out there and do what you've got to do. You see things and say why but I dream things that never were, and I say why not." —George Bernard Shaw

"Act as if it were impossible to fail." —Dorothea Brande

ACKNOWLEDGMENTS

I would like to take a moment and say thanks.

First to my wife: for without you I would be incomplete. Your love, patience, and willingness to understand me is far more than I deserve, and I am eternally grateful.

I will love you until the end of time.

To all of my friends and colleagues who helped knowingly or unknowingly in my effort to write and complete this book. Thank you for the long and often spirited conversations where I could battle test my ideas, formulate my words, and either feel emboldened in my position or realize I was wrong and go back to square one.

To all those I have worked with, learned from, taught, or had interaction with during my journey: may I have helped you on yours, you certainly have helped me on mine.

I would like to specifically thank the following people for their help bringing this book to life: Randee for designing the cover art (and the logos for The Zenta Group); Victoria and Terence for helping provide preliminary editing and guidance to me—without your initial efforts I would never have been able to shape things into something for someone else to read. Big thanks to Emily for helping make me believe this book could serve a purpose, providing feedback, and most importantly being a sounding board for all things the last six years.

And a special thanks to Deegy; for being willing to help put the finishing touches on things and formatting the book to be ready to publish. I truly do owe you a debt of gratitude for your time, effort, and energy.

ABOUT THE AUTHOR

Joe Staub is currently the executive director of The Zenta Group and lives in a small town in Connecticut with his wife, children, and dog.

As a life-long learner who is no stranger to wearing many hats, Joe seems to have found a way to take the expression "jack-of-all-trades, master of none" far too literally. From coaching numerous athletes who have achieved the pinnacle of success in their respective sport, to advising and mentoring individuals, entities, and organizations at all levels to achieve their goals, Joe, in his own words is, "Just an average joe, who does a little bit of this and a little bit of that."

He can be reached at Joe@TheZentaGroup.com, although he may be slow to respond so your patience is appreciated.

Made in the USA
Middletown, DE
02 February 2020